Frank Furness
The Complete Works

George E. Thomas
Michael J. Lewis
Jeffrey A. Cohen

Introduction by
Robert Venturi

Princeton Architectural Press
New York, New York

Princeton Architectural Press, Inc.
37 East Seventh Street
New York, New York 10003
212.995.9620
ISBN 1-878271-04-0 (cloth)
ISBN 1-878271-25-3 (paper)

Design: Kevin Lippert
Production editor: Clare Jacobson
Copy editors: Stefanie Lew, Ellen McGoldrick, and Andrea Kahn
Production: Samantha Hardingham and Scott Corbin
Special thanks to Sheila Cohen, Antje Fritsch, and Ann Urban.

Thomas, George E.
Frank Furness: the complete works / George E. Thomas, Michael J.
Lewis, Jeffrey A. Cohen; introduction by Robert Venturi.
386 pages   8 1/2 x 11 inches
ISBN 1-878271-04-0: $64.95   ISBN 1-878271-25-3 (pbk): $39.95
1. Furness, Frank, 1839–1912—Catalogs. 2. Architecture, Modern—
19th century—Pennsylvania—Philadelphia—Catalogs. 3. Architecture,
Modern—20th century—Pennsylvania—Philadelphia—Catalogs.
4. Philadelphia (Pa.)—Buildings, structures, etc.
I. Lewis, Michael J., 1957– . II. Cohen, Jeffrey A., 1952– . III. Title.
NA737.F84A4 1991   91–174
720'.92—dc20   CIP

Contents

Robert Venturi

Furness and Taste

I come to Furness as an architect and I write as a rather old architect. I signify the latter because most younger critics cannot comprehend how the work of Furness was hated before their time. (I refer to the period after his thriving practice; in his heyday, he *was* appreciated by a *lot* of people.) When I was young you hated Victorian architecture, especially the particularly perversely distorted forms and their gross juxtapositions in the work of *this* Victorian—and then also his work was sometimes banal, rather than repulsive, when his budget was low. Even Lou Kahn once told me the interior stair in the Pennsylvania Academy of the Fine Arts descended too closely to the main entrance—to him it was awkwardly big for the space it occupied in the lobby.

And I can remember loving to hate those squat columns as my father drove me past the Provident Life and Trust Company on Chestnut Street in the thirties, and I well remember hearing the serious debate in one of my first faculty meetings at the School of Fine Arts at the University of Pennsylvania in the early sixties on the subject of should the School come out and protest the demolition of the Furness Library on that campus. My future wife, Denise Scott Brown, spoke eloquently and courageously for saving the building; I sat there too shy to say I agreed.

All this to a great extent involves the matter of taste—your sensibility concerning what seems perceptually right—or rather the matter of cycles of taste. You usually hate what your father loved and like what your grandfather liked, as Donald D. Egbert pointed out, but, believe me, it was only we extreme sophisticates who could take Frank Furness even as late as the mid-sixties. Thank the Lord our great Furness Library did not feel the wrecker's ball as practically all the other major works of Furness did in the various goody-goody periods of architecture that succeeded his.

But I am leading up to something else that might relate to my limitations as an older person who is subject, despite his critical hyper-sophistication, if I may put it that way quasi-sarcastically, to an ingrained prejudice due to taste. My feeling for Furness is not hate-love; it is absolute unrestrained adoration and respect for his work; it elates me by its quality, spirit, diversity, wit, tragic dimension—but my love is a little perverse—I can't help feeling it a touch kinky, my love. And the impressive critiques I now read in this book on this subject don't have any touch of this quality in their admiration, which seems squeaky clean—an utterly wholesome affair.

But my admiration *is* OK—if I look at Furness as an American-Emersonian, individualist-reformist, naturalist-artist, as one who follows at the same time the sturdy, continental, functionalist Gothicism of Viollet-le-Duc in France and the exuberant Italianate Gothicism of Ruskin in Britain. And who is also a Mannerist. He is a Mannerist as the anguished artist described in these essays, evolving beyond the America of Manifest Destiny and Abolitionist idealism and toward the postwar realities of dynamic economic growth and unlimited political corruption. To me his Mannerist tensions are essential. They make my kind of love respectable, out of the closet, and profoundly valid. Furness does not use totally original forms, or vocabularies, or ornament, or organizations of these forms; he uses columns, colonettes, brackets, squinches, arches—pointed and otherwise—quoins, rustication, exposed steel, hammer beam trusses, etc. But of course he makes these conventional elements signally original and he composes them in crazy ways; his relative sizes and scales of elements and his juxtapositions are dissonant and ambiguous, complex and contradictory. But from these qualities that can be called Mannerist I have learned so much from Furness. Agreed he never heard of these terms or others that you might employ, empirical juxtapositions like ugly *and* beautiful, lyrical *and* gross. Above all, these forms are tense with a feeling of life and reality.

Anyhow, I think that's how I can love the work of Furness and respect it as much as that of any architect in the history of America, and why.

Introduction

Though the Furness office was still active in 1924, when Louis Sullivan proclaimed its merits, surviving even into 1931, when Lewis Mumford remarked on Furness's American vigor, no thought was ever given to gathering and preserving Furness's private papers, let alone the firm's voluminous records. By then the directions of American criticism and scholarship were turning towards European interpretations of the modern spirit. When the Depression finally put an end to the office, the drawings and records were abandoned, thrown out with the blueprint frames and the bentwood office furniture.

The destruction of the office records has been central to the problem of Furness studies ever since. Without the records to identify and locate work, Furness scholarship has been forced to work from visual attribution, based on known signature motifs, towards documentation. That has resulted in the skewing of the known *œuvre* towards the most extreme designs, which in turn is responsible for the romantic and irascible characterization of the Furness personality. Only with the recently rediscovered columns on building in the Philadelphia newspapers, and, for the years after 1886, with the weekly building magazine *The Philadelphia Real Estate Record and Builders' Guide*, can the full extent of the Furness career be gauged. Given a larger circle of potential clients and broadened visual definitions of Furness art, it has been possible to recapture still more commissions, and to enlarge our understanding of Furness's role in Philadelphia. It is now apparent that instead of being an isolated and misunderstood artist, Furness was one of the most successful architects of his era, working for the principal institutions and clients. In fact, if the pace of the Furness career during the period of extensive documentation is extrapolated back into the earlier years, it can be assumed that many more commissions remain to be discovered. Fortunately, the inherent originality and wit of most of the Furness designs make this roundabout and time consuming process worthwhile.

Our own work is based on the pioneering studies that began in the 1950s, when Furness's reputation was at its lowest ebb. In those years, the Federal government, the city of Philadelphia, and private developers were vying to clear out the commercial buildings around the landmarks of the American revolution—in the process destroying many of Furness's most astonishing creations. It was then that Charles Peterson and William Campbell of the National Park Service recognized the importance of the buildings which were being sacrificed to make Independence National Historic Park. They marshalled a force of young historians, architects and photographers who began the enormous task of resurrecting Furness's career. The local National Park Service offices contain record photographs by Penelope Hartshorne (now Bacheler). The Historic American Buildings Survey contains informative data sheets on buildings which James C. Massey identified as the work of Furness; handsome photographs by Cervin Robinson and Jack Boucher preserve the image of many of those structures. Articles by William Campbell and Massey's three pieces in *Charette* became the early benchmarks of Furness scholarship. With Robert Venturi's *Complexity and Contradiction in Architecture*, Frank Furness was returned to center stage as a resource for American designers.

In 1973 Furness's growing local cult led Evan Turner, director of the Philadelphia Museum of Art, to propose a major exhibition and exhibition catalogue of the architect's work. The catalogue's lead essay by James F. O'Gorman, a veteran of the HABS teams of the 1950s, and at that time teaching architectural history at the University of Pennsylvania, transformed the image of Furness from angry eccentric to successful Victorian architect, situating his work in the context of English, French and American theory; the splendid photography of Cervin Robinson established in ways that words never could the perverse yet deliberate structure of Furness's art; research by George E. Thomas and Hyman Myers added some three hundred buildings beyond the handful that had already been identified. The forty buildings in the exhibition, selected to span his career, demonstrated his versatility and the continuity and development of his ideas.

The publication of that catalogue transformed Furness into a respectable subject for study: since then numerous biographical sketches, and even two doctoral dissertations, have been written. Two of the principal Furness landmarks, the Pennsylvania Academy of the Fine Arts and the University of Pennsylvania Library, have been painstakingly restored, as have several of the more important houses. In 1990, April 26th was announced by the Philadelphia City Council as "Frank Furness Day," and a national television situation comedy even listed Frank Furness as an influence on the set design.

Still, despite the growing strength of the Furness reputation, the destruction of his work has continued. Nor have these been minor losses. The wrecker's ball was hammering at the western additions to the Northern Savings Fund Society when Federal agencies demanded its preservation; the Church of the Redeemer was destroyed by arson; Sedgwick Station on the Reading Railroad was replaced by a prosaic concrete platform. A dozen or more minor houses, offices and servant buildings listed in the 1973 checklist have been destroyed, as have an equal number of commissions since ascribed to Furness. At the moment the pace of new discoveries is outpacing demolition, though this state of affairs may not continue for long.

For those inclined to the hunt, numerous potentially fruitful areas exist. Philadelphia's suburbs, particularly those to the southwest in the vicinity of the family summer residences, are still understudied; the medium-sized railroad towns along the Philadelphia and Reading Railroad—particularly Reading, Norristown, Pottstown, and Lancaster, offer possibilities. In Pottstown, for instance, photographs of the 1880s building that replaced the original Hill School show the hallmark chimney, flaring shingle skirt over masonry, and free plan that mark Furness's institutional buildings of that decade. In Reading, Furness designed schools, houses and railroad buildings. Similar finds will probably be made along the route of the Baltimore and Ohio Railroad. Suburban newspapers offer another resource, as Ann Cook and Martha Wolf's research on Chester County commissions demonstrates.

As the discoveries of Earl Shettleworth of the Maine Historical Commission indicate, it is equally likely that other resort commissions remain to be discovered. In 1886, the *Philadelphia Real Estate Record and Builders' Guide* reported a new summer house at Point Pleasant, New Jersey, for Horace Howard Furness. If erected, it was presumably from his brother's design; likewise, Evans family papers indicate numerous cottages along the New England coast. Resorts from Cape May, New Jersey to Bar Harbor, Maine, as well as inland retreats west of Philadelphia, would bear extensive examination. Cemeteries are a resort of a different sort—but the Furness sketchbooks suggest that funeral monuments would be another likely source of commissions. Several markers for known Furness clients, and bearing the Furness touch, can be seen in the cemetery of St. Mary's Episcopal Church in Burlington, New Jersey; other monuments, with fellow warriors as likely clients, may yet be found in Philadelphia cemeteries.

Many of the entries in our catalogue are attributions (indicated by an "A" after the number), justified either by visual character, or family and business connections, and usually by a combination of both methods, supplementing written documentation. We have only occasionally erred on the side of liberal rather than strict interpretation to broaden the list, both in the hope that future research will provide documentation, and, in light of the ongoing pace of demolition, to encourage preservation or at the least, recording before demolition. Also, to be fair, we have paid more attention to the earlier work while attempting to provide the flavor of the later career. It might be said that as Furness showed up at his office less and less—so did we. It should also be noted that we as architectural historians have not paid sufficient attention to the decorative arts. Furness's reputation in the 1870s covered domestic and institutional furnishings, stencillings and leaded glass; we have reproduced several of the better known pieces, but have left that rewarding topic to others better qualified to analyze these treasures.

Some of the discoveries in the intervening seventeen years since the publication of the exhibition catalogue have not been of our doing. Interested historians, architects and cognoscenti have sent to the authors notes on houses, drawings, and photographs of pieces of furniture. A decade after the 1973 exhibit, encouraged by the renewed interest of Jeffrey Cohen and Michael Lewis, and the research stimulated by the *Drawing Toward Building* exhibit at the Pennsylvania Academy of the Fine Arts, the pursuit of Furness began again. In 1987 the original 1973 catalogue was augmented by fifty additional discoveries. Since then most of the hundreds of works that were known only from the documentation at the time of the 1973 publication have been visited. Another hundred documented or attributed commissions have been added in the present study. Hopefully, this publication will stimulate additional research — necessitating a future edition!

Numerous colleagues deserve thanks for their cooperation, comments and assistance. First and foremost we acknowledge James F. O'Gorman, who as teacher and friend encouraged our efforts even as he forwarded on to us the letters and notes sent by readers of the 1973 book. In a pleasurable dinner series over nearly two years, O'Gorman and our colleagues at the University of Pennsylvania, David Brownlee and David DeLong, shared ideas and offered their own perspectives on Furness's work.

The late George Wood Furness was unfailingly cooperative in making his materials available to us; we have continued to use them as he intended. Other family members have continued to support our research, notably Charles Savage and Maria Thompson. Maria Thompson has provided genealogical research which has served as the basis for the family trees in the Appendix; of greater importance have been her insights into the ideas and values of William Henry Furness. Our studies have been enriched by the family of Allen Evans III, who graciously opened the family records to us, enlarging our understanding of the contributions of Allen Evans as a significant designer in his own right. Those papers have been deposited at the Architectural Archives of the University of Pennsylvania.

Equally important has been the assistance of the staff persons of the major historical collections: Linda Stanley of the Manuscript Department of the Historical Society of Pennsylvania, who humored our search through all of the photographic collections; Kenneth Finkel, curator of prints of the Library Company of Philadelphia, whose knowledge of his collections materially reduced our research; Roger Moss and Bruce Laverty of the Athenaeum of Philadelphia who brought numerous drawings to our attention as they added to their own collection; Mark Frazier Lloyd and Hamilton Elliott of the University of Pennsylvania Archives aided our research on the Penn connection, and cheered our discoveries; Jefferson Moak of the City of Philadelphia Archives pointed out several important commissions and gave free access to the photographic files; Jeffrey Post of the Prints and Pictures Department of the Free Library of Philadelphia pushed us along when our interest flagged; Tony Wrenn of the American Institute of Architects archives in Washington, D. C. enabled us to find the critical records on Furness's brief professional association with the A.I.A.; David A. Hanks graciously sent us materials from his files on Furness's furniture. Finally, Julia Moore Converse of the Architectural Archives of the University of Pennsylvania gave freely of her time and has generously offered us a location for our research files. We are delighted to have the opportunity to make our negatives and notes available in Frank Furness's masterful University of Pennsylvania Library. Each of these collections has supported our effort by permitting the republication of their treasures; to them is owed a tremendous debt—one we hope can be at least partially repaid by this book.

Equally, we have benefitted from the amateurs and collectors of the Philadelphia region. Theodore Xaras opened his unsurpassed collection of railroadiana to us and provided links to other collectors whose files we searched. Frank Weer gave us access to his splendid collection as well. Numerous building owners took the time to let us see and photograph their buildings. We are grateful to all of them, as well as to the descendants of Furness clients and associates who took the time to search through family records for photographs, family diaries and records.

Students in several courses at the University of Pennsylvania have made remarkable contributions as well. Emily T. C. Jernigan pursued the Welsh family and found a previously unknown house on Wissahickon Avenue. Other students in Urban Studies 272 followed through on individual properties with intelligence and youthful vigor. Their contributions are noted in the various entries.

Our acknowledgement of indebtedness would be incomplete without recognition of Marianna M. Thomas, A.I.A., who since 1973 has measured and recorded many of Furness's buildings, and whose office has drafted many of those plans. They add immeasurably to our efforts. Other Philadelphia architects have aided and abetted our obsession. Hyman Myers, whose painstaking restoration of the Pennsylvania Academy of the Fine Arts played so important a role in the resurrection of the Furness legacy, provided plans, images and reviewed the manuscript. The work of David Marohn, project architect for Venturi, Scott Brown Associates, on the restoration of the University of Pennsylvania's library pushed us to fully develop our ideas. Our five year collaboration on the restoration of that landmark has been central to this publication. To the building committee at the University of Pennsylvania, which supported our research on the Library, and to the various departments whose records we used, we offer our gratitude.

Kevin Lippert and the Princeton Architectural Press are responsible for our seeing the light of day. We deeply appreciate the conscientious, careful, and creative editorial work of Clare Jacobson, Ellen McGoldrick, Andrea Kahn, and Stefanie Lew (who pushed the catalog to a higher level of completeness than we ever envisioned) as well as the attentive production work of Samantha Hardingham and Scott Corbin.

To Robert Venturi, who has guided us with his writing, inspired us with his inclusive perceptions of history, and delighted us with his own architecture, which bears the stamp of its origins in Frank Furness's Philadelphia, our debt is incalculable. It is made all the greater by the gift of his own time that produced the foreword to this book.

Finally, in that it explains our results, our collaborative and interactive process deserves comment. It has been a model of cooperation and mutual assistance, augmented by great food and appropriate libations calculated to stimulate conversation. Though we each wrote from our own perspectives and interests, we have each read, criticized and hopefully enhanced each other's texts. That was made immeasurably easier by our friendship and previous collaborations dating back more than a decade.

G. E. T.
M. J. L.
J. A. C.
Philadelphia, 1991

George E. Thomas

Frank Furness:
The Flowering of an American Architecture

On Tuesday the 12th of November 1889 Frank Furness turned fifty. If he had paused to look out from the windows of the nearly completed Provident Bank building at Fourth and Chestnut streets, he would have surveyed a Philadelphia transformed by his work as an architect. In the banking district within a block or two of the State House, a dozen or more commercial landmarks, each more dramatic than the last, declared their independence from the norms of commercial architecture; the largest of these buildings was the Provident bank tower, a commission won in a national competition. To the south were factories and institutional buildings serving the maritime community. To the north were hospital buildings for the Jewish community. To the west, in the vicinity of the rising bulk of the new City Hall, his office had designed the Pennsylvania Academy of the Fine Arts, and the Lutheran Church of the Holy Communion. Amidst the red brick rows of fashionable Rittenhouse Square were dozens of striking brick and sandstone town houses from designs by his office, including six superb mansions and a handsome club bordering on the Square itself. Finally, beyond the site where his Baltimore and Ohio Station would sit on the banks of the Schuylkill, rose the tower of the new library that the University of Pennsylvania was building from the plans he had prepared in consultation with the leading library experts of the day.

In the generation between 1867 and 1889 Furness had designed more than three hundred buildings; more than three hundred additional commissions would come his way before his death in 1912. Given the unbridled originality of the Furness designs, what is more remarkable than the torrent of his work is his ability to persuade the reputedly conservative Philadelphia gentry and their institutions to accept his metaphors and insights as their own. Furness found his niche in a culturally independent city, working for a clientele of confident, risk-taking businessmen who had fought in the Civil War, reformed the corrupt politics of Philadelphia, and reshaped the regional economy. Modifying methods learned in Richard Morris Hunt's atelier, and inspired by the values of his father's closest friend, Ralph Waldo Emerson, and the others who had prefigured the developing American culture, Furness culminated the nation's first century with a method of working that looked to the problem for the root of the solution. That approach led to making forms represent purpose, in turn opening up the possibility of functional expressionism as an alternative to Beaux-Arts formalism.

As manifestations of the forceful men who shaped post-Civil War Philadelphia, Furness's architectural designs are equalled only by Thomas Eakins's portraits in their tough-minded directness, and by Mark Twain's elaborate yarns in their ironic and engaging wit. Each of these artists shaped their art by turning from history towards the present, giving their efforts a visceral immediacy virtually unique. Furness's reality-based system became the basis for a flexible and adaptable architecture that spread into the Midwest through Louis Sullivan, and permeated the underlying values of Philadelphia architecture through Furness's local students, ultimately reaching the present so-called Philadelphia school centered around Louis Kahn and Robert Venturi (figs. 1.1, 1.2).

A century after Frank Furness completed the designs for his best known masterpieces, his career achievement is slowly being rediscovered. As a master of florid and original decoration, overlaid on complicated and expressive volumes that seem antithetical to modern conventions of simplicity and the expression of technics, Furness appeared to have reached an aesthetic dead end, one that dated quickly and was of little consequence to the directions of modern architecture. As early as the 1880s his work was being attacked on aesthetic grounds by out-of-town critics who did not understand that Furness was actually fighting a rear guard battle, overruling aesthetic formulas in favor of representing individualism. This was understood by his former pupil Louis Sullivan, who said that Furness's buildings had the effect of a person—an individual—speaking; indeed they did, and so long as they spoke to clients holding the same values, Furness remained the dominant architect of his region.

Furness is here presented merely as he was—an American architect active after the Civil War. By all accounts, Furness believed that he was doing no more and no less than developing a modern American architecture out of the elemental forces of the American experience. Unlike most of his contemporaries working in the English Modern Gothic and Queen Anne styles, whose work could have appeared in any American or British city, Furness's buildings are unmistakably the product of American culture, materials, and intentions.

1.1. Louis I. Kahn, Alfred Newton Richards Laboratories,
University of Pennsylvania, 1956–61

1.2. Venturi and Short, Guild House, 1960

1.3. 1700 block of Delancey Street, Philadelphia, c. 1868

1.4. Willis Hale, North Van Pelt Street, Philadelphia, 1888

Pre-Civil War Philadelphia

Frank Furness was a product of Philadelphia, the city of revolution and industry that provided the foil and the setting for his architecture.[1] In the first half of the nineteenth century, Philadelphia had diverged from the national culture, responding to its losses of the national capitol to Washington, and of supremacy in trade and commerce to New York, by turning inward. By the 1850s, national leadership in architecture had departed Philadelphia as well, casting its lot with New York, the center of the nation's communication and commerce, and Boston, which became the locus of the nation's intellectual establishment in education and literature. Philadelphia's loss of vigor could be seen across the city. Instead of revelling in the waves of styles and colors that gave identity to each decade of mid-century architecture in New York and Boston, the city remained plain and low, united in scale across its width and breadth and redolent of permanence. For three long generations, Philadelphia architecture was like a rural vernacular that changed only in the secondary features of cornices and door surrounds of its long row houses (figs. 1.3, 1.4).

Philadelphians were sustained in their contrary behavior by a value system shaped by their Quaker ancestors, who made a virtue of plain speech, plain garb, and plain architecture. These values were so deeply ingrained that even those who eventually joined other denominations were shaped to the pattern of the sect. It found a political voice in the Whig Party, whose anti-materialist values continued to govern elite Philadelphians long after the party had disappeared as a viable electoral force.[2] In the United States, individualism is preached as a virtue, but treated in reality as a vice. Those who don't go along have trouble getting along. Because they had avoided the new materialism that preoccupied the upwardly mobile society of industrial America, Philadelphians became a laughing stock nationally—and internationally. Dickens, for example, came to Philadelphia prepared to see drab Quakers in broad-brimmed hats, and quipped that the city was "handsome but distractingly regular" under "its quakerly influence." The nation was no kinder. As late as 1879, Martha Lamb, despite evidence to the contrary, attributed to the "tyranny of George Fox" (founder of the Society

1. General Philadelphia histories include the recent Russell Weigley, ed., *Philadelphia: A 300 Year History* (New York: W. W. Norton, 1982); J. Thomas Scharf and Thompson Westcott, *History of Philadelphia: 1609–1884* (Philadelphia: L. H. Everts, 1884) remains the most comprehensive and useful history; social history is addressed in Nathaniel Burt, *The Perennial Philadelphians: The Anatomy of an American Aristocracy* (Boston: Little Brown, 1963); and E. Digby Baltzell, *Philadelphia Gentlemen: The Making of a National Upper Class* (Glencoe, IL: Free Press, 1958); more recently Theodore Hershberg, ed., *Philadelphia: Work, Space, Family and Group Experience in the Nineteenth Century* (New York: Oxford University Press, 1981) has applied statistical analysis and the computer to the problem of the new social history of an entire population.

2. The values of the Society of Friends, as the Quakers are more properly known, are discussed by Burt and Baltzell, see note 1. Baltzell has compared the effects of Quaker values with those of their northern Puritan counterparts in *Puritan Boston and Quaker Philadelphia* (New York: Free Press, 1979).

of Friends) the shaping of the Quaker city.[3] By the 1880s, the city that in the eighteenth century had been universally viewed as metropolitan and sophisticated was being compared unfavorably to western cattle towns.

Elite Philadelphians survived the national enmity by being strongly "inner directed," to borrow a phrase from sociologist David Riesman; their culture was self-sustaining, valuing its own members for being a part of the noble past, and thereby maintaining the status quo.[4] But Philadelphia had another important characteristic: throughout the century it proudly proclaimed itself the "most American city," because it had the highest proportion of English stock and native born citizens. There can be no doubt that this character has proved hostile to the continental arts of opera, ballet and even theater—the art forms by which the cultured elite judge cities. Philadelphia's cultural taste ran, then as now, to Gilbert and Sullivan, cricket and golf matches, fox hunts and horse shows—art forms derived from the English squire gentry of Henry Fielding's *Tom Jones*. Here, save for the orchestra, the arts were not sustained for their own merits. A utilitarian high chest might be made to be beautiful, portraits of ancestors preserved a noble visage, a successful house was one whose rooms were the appropriate size and orientation—these were the modest goals of the regional artist. The ambitious artist left town for New York and Boston where the soil was richer and the opportunities greater.

The English tone of the society had the positive side effect of tolerating, even celebrating, eccentricity and personal expression. The same values that unleashed VanBrugh, Hawksmoor and Soane into British culture stimulated Frank Furness in Philadelphia. Like the English, Philadelphians relished individuality—as an outward expression of inner direction. Sustained by these values Philadelphians could weather, indeed relish, their own isolation. But to develop creative arts, more was required than a Quaker negativism, expressed in the rejection of display, that had shaped the regional identity. In this Furness was fortunate, for he had the additional resources of his family and the New England Unitarian positivism advocated by his father.[5] The Reverend William Henry Furness was the center of a one-family renaissance as each of his offspring expanded on his interests: daughter Annis Lee became a translator of

3. The numerous assaults on the Philadelphia Quakers by travelers are well known: Charles Dickens, *American Notes for General Circulation* (1842; reprint, London: J. Dent and Sons, 1908), 95–110; Martha Lamb, *The Homes of America* (New York: D. Appleton and Co., 1879), 219.

4. David Riesman, *The Lonely Crowd: A Study of the Changing American Character* (New Haven: Yale University Press, 1961). An argument based on Riesman is advanced by Baltzell in *Philadelphia Gentlemen* (58), but with the notable distinction that he presumes that upper class values are more conservative than those of the

remainder of society, and, thus, old Philadelphia was still in transition between the earlier state of "tradition-directed," a category that Riesman uses to describe folk or vernacular culture, and modern "inner and other-directed" societies. Though Philadelphians use tradition as an excuse, they have never been primitive.

5. Unitarians were products of the Enlightenment who were said to believe "in one God—at most." The history of the Philadelphia congregation is thoroughly presented by Elizabeth M. Geffen, *Philadelphia Unitarianism, 1796–1861* (Philadelphia: University of Pennsylvania Press, 1961).

German literature and the advisor to the city's premier novelist of the day, S. Weir Mitchell; oldest son William, though short-lived, became a gifted German-trained portraitist; Horace, whose law career was ended by deafness, became the Shakespearian scholar who restored the bard, emasculated by a century of bowdlerization, to manly vigor; the youngest son, Frank, would become an architect.

Philadelphia before the Civil War offered no training opportunities for the prospective architect. In this Philadelphia was not alone; no American college taught architecture until the Massachusetts Institute of Technology opened its course under William R. Ware in 1866. Though courses in drafting could be taken at the city's Franklin Institute, they offered little more than could be learned in any competent architectural office. When Frank Furness first warmed to the study of architecture, his father sought out professional training, as he had done for his older sons who had been sent to Harvard, but architecture would not be taught there until the 1890s. Years later, after the war had intervened, Frank's father recalled the family's ambitions in a letter to his abolitionist friend, Miller McKim:

> We meant to strain every nerve and live on potato skins if need be to get Frank off to study in Paris, but the war came and broke up his studies and when his three yrs. service was over he fell in love, was married and had to go to work. He sighs, however, over the loss of Paris advantages.[6]

The family correctly perceived that it was imperative that Frank study architecture in some other place than the anti-aesthetic environment of Philadelphia. Here the soil was too barren, the expectations too low. Ultimately, for those who returned with the objectivity created by distance, Philadelphia would offer much against which to rebel but also much on which to build.

In 1855, the Furness house at 1426 Pine Street was visited by Richard Morris Hunt, on his way back to New York from Washington where he had worked for a time for Thomas Ustick Walter (fig. 1.5). That visit was vividly remembered by Frank two generations later. He had been "learning the instruments" in the office of John Fraser while he was in high school, but it was Hunt who kindled his imagination.[7] If there was a Pine Street connection there also was a Harvard connection, for Frank's older brothers, William and Horace, knew the precocious group who would transform American architecture in the 1860s. It was the excited letters to the Furness family by Horace's classmates, Charles Gambrill and Henry Van Brunt, telling of their triumph in persuading Hunt to open an atelier, that resulted in Frank's joining Richard Morris Hunt's atelier in New York in 1858.[8]

6. William Henry Furness to Miller McKim (father of Charles Follen McKim of McKim, Mead & White), Spring 1867, McKim Collection, Library of Congress.
7. Frank Furness, "A Few Personal Reminiscences of His Old Teacher by One of His Old Pupils," edited TS with pencil alterations for Memorial to Richard Morris Hunt (1895), 28 pp., collection of George Wood Furness, 2.

8. There is some difference of opinion on when Furness arrived in Hunt's atelier. Furness himself remembered the first visit from Hunt when he was 16, therefore before the fall of 1856; Furness reported the letter from Gambrill and Van Brunt to his brother William as being sent in 1855, though in this he was probably mistaken. In Paul Baker, *Richard Morris Hunt* (Cambridge,

1.5. William Henry Furness residence, c. 1840

1.6. Company I, Sixth Pennsylvania Cavalry (Rush's Lancers), Falmouth, Virginia, June 1863
Lieutenant Frank Furness, with officer's shoulder straps, reclines in profile (front right)

Hunt's Atelier

Furness departed for New York as a youth, several months after his eighteenth birthday. When he arrived, the atelier already had moved into a room in the Studio Building on Tenth Street.[9] Designed by Hunt, it was the most adventurous building in the nation, bringing to New York's Greenwich Village a full blown example of abstract French *néo grec* brick design. Rather than using the usual grab bag of cast-iron window heads and columns that characterized contemporary American commercial architecture, Hunt's design demonstrated that architecture could be developed from aesthetic principle and still make economic sense. Moreover, it was the only building in the nation that paid homage to the artist as a serious professional by providing comfortable living quarters and well-lighted studio spaces. Art had become a booming business in New York in the 1850s, with exhibits drawing vast crowds, making artists the celebrities of the day. The Studio Building became the center of New York's art world, later containing the studios of Winslow Homer and John LaFarge, and from the outset housing the reigning artistic lion of the day, Frederic Church. The showings of his paintings filled the street below. One of those in the crowd to see *The Heart of the Andes* was Samuel Clemens, in New York as a printer, who visited the Studio Building three times and reported that it left his "brain gasping and straining with futile efforts to take all the wonders in."[10]

It was into that stimulating environment that Frank Furness came, joining an atelier that was already established with Charles Gambrill (1832–1880), George B. Post (1837–1913) and Henry Van Brunt (1832–1903) in attendance; they were shortly joined by Edmund Quincy and William Robert Ware (1832–1915). (Like Furness, Van Brunt and Ware were the sons of Unitarian ministers.) His mates were as much as seven years older; several had attended college and all had some office training. As the junior member of the group, Furness curried favor as the class clown, seeking approval by caricaturing his colleagues, while modelling his personal manner on that of his teacher, adopting both Hunt's delicate touch in drawing and his colorful language.[11] Indeed, Furness's description of Hunt's dashing appearance and verbal assertiveness, written in the 1890s, prefigures almost exactly Louis Sullivan's account in

MA: M.I.T. Press, 1980) it is assumed that Furness arrived in 1859, which would not square at all with Frank's father's recollection that Hunt had provided six years of training. Baker dates the opening of the Studio Building to 1858, a date that would correspond to Dr. Furness's recollection if Hunt's six years of training included the two years after Furness returned from the war. Other evidence is provided by the dates of initiation of Furness's atelier-mates into the A.I.A. See note 19.

9. Joe Sherman, "In the halcyon days when pictures of the land came first," *Smithsonian* 20, no. 7 (October 1989): 88–102.

10. Ibid., 98.

11. Hunt's language is noted by other sources than his apparently apt pupil; cf. Baker, *Hunt*, 162. Furness reported that Hunt's "forcible manner of expressing himself was the only accomplishment I acquired during my 'apprenticeship' which proved of energetic efficacy in the army—especially to a cavalry officer and above all, proverbially to a dragoon." Furness, "Reminiscences," 27.

The Autobiography of an Idea of his own encounter (at the similar age of 17) with Furness.[12] Though modern historians may be less convinced of the accuracy of A. J. Bloor's claim before the American Institute of Architects (A.I.A.) in 1876 that Hunt had formed an American School of Architecture, there can be no doubt that he established the archetype for its most imitated architectural personality.[13]

Furness's admitted emulation of Hunt gives the course of study at the atelier special interest. In 1895, at the request of Ware (who was assembling materials to commemorate Hunt), Furness recalled an atelier system based on the French method. It began with the study of the orders as the basis for proportion, then was modified to accommodate the modern Gothic, which Hunt recognized was intellectually, culturally, and aesthetically allied with American tastes. As the course progressed, more involved projects were assigned and studied, with a liberal dose of criticism followed by judiciously awarded praise, which was all the more memorable for its rarity.[14] No contemporary accounts of the atelier survive, but, in 1876, A. J. Bloor, who had met Furness during his New York student days, recorded some impressions about the atelier. While visiting Philadelphia in preparation for his lecture to the A.I.A. convention, Bloor presumably renewed his acquaintance with Furness and discussed his lecture, which was intended as a tribute to Hunt. The week after his visit to Philadelphia, apparently to corroborate a conversation with Furness, he wrote to Hunt inquiring as to his method:

> I have heard theories on the subject from some of your pupils, but I should like your own recollection and impressions. Did you consciously, or—as you may on retrospection think— unconsciously lead them into a certain groove of expression—classic, gothic, renaissance, Neo-Greek or what not? Or did you consciously, or unconsciously simply ground them in the elements of historical architecture and leave them to find out their method of expression for themselves?[15]

The training must have been remarkable, for, with the exception of Edward Quincy, who after a short stint in Van Brunt's office became a minister, all of Hunt's students went on to notable careers that shaped the nation's architecture through the end of the century. Each

12. Louis H. Sullivan, *The Autobiography of an Idea* (1924; reprint, New York: Dover Publications, 1956), 190–96.
13. For a while the *American Architect and Building News* (hereafter *AABN*) published the A.I.A. convention minutes as supplements to the journal. The 1876 convention was published in 1877 with Bloor's lecture and references to Hunt. A. J. Bloor, "Annual Address to the A.I.A.," 12 October 1876, *AABN* 2 (24 March 1877): xi.
14. Furness, "Reminiscences," 11–12.
15. A. J. Bloor to Richard Morris Hunt, 18 September

1876, *Letterbook*, vol. 2 (November 1875–May 1882), 167, A.I.A. Archives, Washington, D.C. No response from Hunt has been preserved, but from Bloor's presentation at the Centennial, it must be concluded that Hunt was in general agreement with the thesis that no one method was taught. Bloor also wrote, "I know that Furniss [sic], Gambrel [sic], Post, Van Brunt and Ware, (I leave out Quincy for I believe he has never practiced) were inoculated by you because it was in your studio I came to know them."

depended on Hunt throughout his career—for detail, ideas, and professional values. Theory within the atelier can be deduced from a number of articles and lectures prepared by Van Brunt and his fellows during and immediately after their years with Hunt. In "Greek Lines" (1861), Van Brunt proposed monumentalizing functional expression according to the method of Labrouste, which Hunt had learned in his Paris study.[16] In other talks to the A.I.A., Van Brunt addressed the role of "Cast Iron in Decorative Architecture" (7 Dec. 1858) and, a month later, "the use of iron in architecture;" Gambrill discoursed on nature; in another session the topic of the architect as artist was raised. These themes preoccupied the entire generation.[17] When William Robert Ware initiated the School of Architecture at M.I.T., he based it on the atelier system derived from Hunt's studio.[18]

Though the focus of the atelier was on independent thinking, Hunt actively encouraged professional association. One by one, he proposed his students as "associates" in the New York based American Institute of Architects, beginning with Henry Van Brunt in December of 1857, and followed two weeks later by Charles Gambrill. Quincy was made an associate in February of 1858, and William Ware in April of the same year.[19] George Post was next to be admitted in 1860. Frank Furness had not been advanced to membership by the fall of 1861, perhaps because he lacked office training. At that time, the organization suspended meetings because the outbreak of the Civil War so depleted its members that its clubrooms had to be reduced. Not until March of 1866 was Furness proposed by Charles Gambrill and seconded for membership by his friend and fellow Philadelphian Emlen Littell; it was in the same meeting that Gambrill also proposed his future partner, Henry Hobson Richardson.[20] Whether Furness felt slighted by his delayed initiation, or simply was not the sort to engage in social groups that did not relate to his known passions for hunting and fishing, he alone

16. Henry Van Brunt, "Greek Lines," *Atlantic Monthly* 7, no. 44, Part 1 (June 1861): 654–67; Part 2 (July 1861): 76–88.

17. The various lectures by members of the atelier to the A.I.A. are listed in the "Proceedings of the A.I.A.," vol. 1 (23 February 1857ff.) in the A.I.A. Archives in Washington, D.C. These include Van Brunt on cast iron in decorative architecture (7 December 1858); Van Brunt on the use of iron in architecture (4 January 1858); and Charles Gambrill on architecture as a fine art (5 February 1861). The topic of architecture as an art was raised by Thomas U. Walter in his address to the Philadelphia A.I.A., 9 October 1871; cf. A. H. Moses, "History of the Philadelphia Chapter of the A.I.A.," A.I.A. Archives, Misc. box. 15–f–17.

18. Carole Shillaber, *Massachusetts Institute of Technology School of Architecture and Planning, 1861–1961* (Cam-bridge, MA: M.I.T. Press, 1963).

19. Memberships and secondings were listed in the "Proceedings of the A.I.A.," vol. 1: on 1 December 1857, Henry Van Brunt by Hunt and J. C. Wells of the office; on 15 December 1857, Charles Gambrill by Hunt and Richard Upjohn; on 7 February 1858, Edmund Quincy; on 19 April 1858, William Ware. This would seem to indicate that Ware had already been in the atelier for some time and thus that Furness was correct in remembering that he had arrived some time before, certainly by 1857. George Post was admitted along with Emlen Littell "of Philadelphia" on 3 April 1860.

20. Furness and Richardson were both nominated at the meeting of 6 March 1866, Furness being proposed by Gambrill and seconded by Littell, Richardson being proposed by Gambrill and seconded by Vaux. Their member-ships were confirmed at the meeting of 19 March 1866.

of his classmates was not particularly active within the A.I.A. Though Furness was a charter member of the Philadelphia chapter, and ornamented its club rooms in the Athenaeum, he had dropped out before the Centennial and had no further contact with the organization for the remainder of his career.

Hunt's atelier flourished for four years, but it was affected by the war as well; by the fall of 1861 the early members had departed for military service or architectural practice, while Hunt himself took a two year tour of Europe. In the meantime, Van Brunt and Ware joined the Navy; Post and Furness entered the Army. Each had distinguished service records, with Furness earning the Medal of Honor during three years in northern Virginia as a member of Rush's Lancers of the Sixth Pennsylvania Cavalry (fig. 1.6). One characteristic anecdote about Furness was reported in the regimental history. When General McClellan urged the regiment to adopt the lance as one of its weapons, Furness dashed off a cartoon to

illustrate the superiority of the lance to the sabre. A cavalryman with a sabre rode into a charge and pierced one foe and carried him off in triumph on his sword, but a lancer rode in by his side, and transfixed half a dozen foes, and bore them off on his lance gaily. That would have settled the question, perhaps, if any grave doubts surrounded it.[21]

Recalling the last vestiges of medieval romance, Furness and his cohort rode into battle the first time with pennants flying from poised lances; as the war turned to horror, the lances were quickly abandoned for sabres and carbines, reappearing again only as the ornament of the Gettysburg monument to the Lancers which Furness designed a quarter of a century later (cat. 353).

The bearded Furness who returned to Hunt's office was very different from the slender youth who had left it in the autumn of 1861. Even his name was modified from the Frank H. Furness of his youthful signature to the crisp and soldierly Frank Furness. Physically matured by three years in the field and used to command, he was promoted to chief assistant, managing the office when Hunt was out of town.[22] There he supervised jobs and handled small designs, returning to the subordinate role only when Hunt was in the office. That this may have been difficult was suggested by a bit of doggerel by his former studio-mate, Charles Gambrill, written to Ware on the letterhead of Gambrill and Post:

Frank Furness has come to resume his profession,

Full sick of the glory of fighting secession—

And yet sicker at heart, and blue as the devil,

21. Reverend S. L. Gracey, Chaplain of the Regiment, *Annals of the Sixth Pennsylvania Cavalry* (Philadelphia: E. H. Butler, 1868), 353–54. Published before Furness was nominated for the Medal of Honor, the book makes no mention of that event. The book is a remarkably archaizing publication appropriate to the Lancers, using the f for s, thus writing "Furneſs."

22. Furness reported his later time in the Hunt office, in "Reminiscences," recalling that he "kept shop" during the summer of 1861 and remained in the office in the fall. After returning from the war Furness recalled that there were times "when the responsibilities of the business were more or less committed to my charge" (24–27).

To descend from command to a subordinate level

Yet so fearful his whiskers and so martial his bearing—

The dragoon thro' and thro' in superfluous swearing,

That Dick Hunt will appear like a lamb in comparison,

With a disbanded soldier, who so fearfully carries on.[23]

Post-Civil War Philadelphia

After two more years in Hunt's office, Furness married a Philadelphian, Fannie Fassitt, and returned to his native city where a commission for a Unitarian Church in Germantown awaited him (cat. 1). He arrived in Philadelphia at a fortuitous moment, when the Civil War industrial boom and the pent-up demand of a decade of economic depression and war offered a remarkable opportunity for a well-connected young architect. Those circumstances resulted in the swelling of the professional ranks, the formation of a Philadelphia Chapter of the American Institute of Architects in 1869, and the establishment of an architectural program at the University of Pennsylvania—all within four years of the end of the war.

During the war decade, Philadelphia had been transformed. Whether at the urging of center-city landholders, or because the citizenry foresaw the need to provide for future growth, a referendum was approved moving City Hall from the State House to Penn Square, a dozen blocks to the west of the center of the city. A decade later, as finance moved west to join City Hall, the railroads gained permission to bring locomotives on elevated viaducts into the heart of the city, creating the modern downtown. This in turn caused other institutions to rethink their positions in the city. Important church congregations moved west to the new residential neighborhoods; new institutional buildings were constructed along Broad Street, giving the city for the first time a metropolitan appearance, as befit its doubled land area and population.

Nurtured by the industrial expansion and the endeavors of the new generation of industrialists, post-war Philadelphia's values paralleled those of the national culture and resulted in a generation of optimistic growth. Ironically, despite Philadelphia's transformation, the national press was slow to discover the change, a case in point being the comments of the editor of the *American Architect and Business News* (*AABN*) in 1877:

> The old Quaker prejudices of Philadelphia die hard. There is no lack of liberality towards public institutions and educational movements, but when it comes to any thing in the nature of local art, it is very often quietly smothered.[24]

---

23. Charles Gambrill to William R. Ware, dated 16 November 1864, on Gambrill and Post letterhead, Ware papers, M.I.T. Archives.

24. "Correspondence," *AABN* 2, no. 60 (17 February 1877): 58.

Such comments were not always made by outsiders. The Philadelphia penchant for self-denigration was legendary. In 1877, a member of the University of Pennsylvania ascribed the backwardness of the city to "the indifference of our city to literature and to the higher education in any but its purely scientific form."[25] But despite the survival of these old stereotypes, Philadelphia's fundamental values had already been under assault for a decade by forces marshalled by the University of Pennsylvania's new provost, Charles Stille.[26]

If Stille was the Moses of Penn's westward move, the University's new literary publication, *The Penn Monthly*, was its ark of the covenant. Its editorial purpose was the stimulation of an intellectual dialogue across the city. Between 1870 and 1881 it published essays by leading scholars, book reviews, the texts of lectures of note given in the city, and essays on subjects of general interest, especially in the arts—an area in which the editors felt Philadelphia to be particularly deficient. The advent of the Centennial decade found Philadelphians, like their contemporaries, prepared for the fruition of an American culture that would certify the maturity of the nation. Though published in drab covers, the editorial stance was one of red, white, and blue Americanism that advocated the development of American schools of architecture and the arts. [27] Early essays analyzed the new American humor coming out of the west, noting in particular Mark Twain and his contemporaries; travelogs of the west reported the uniquely American character of the land and its people.[28] The theme of American progress in the arts was raised in the transcription of Christopher Dresser's lectures on industrial design, given in 1876 to the Pennsylvania Museum School.[29] In 1877 a Baltimore writer, Alfred Bierbower, wrote an essay calling for "American Architecture."[30] None was more astonishing, however, than the text of an address entitled "The Architect an Artist," which the Reverend William Henry Furness gave to the American Institute of Architects in

25. "M" "The University of Pennsylvania, Its needs and its Future," *The Penn Monthly* 8, no. 10 (October 1877): 763. Such comments about Philadelphia, by Philadelphians, are typical.

26. It was Stille who led the move of the University west across the Schuylkill and used modern Victorian gothic architecture to announce the university's national ambitions. See Charles Stille, *Reminiscences of a Provost 1866–80* (N.p., n.d.), 11–12; 17–27.

27. The articles on the American character appear throughout *The Penn Monthly*, see for example, "The Backbone of America," vol. 1, no. 6 (June 1870): 226–40; P. F., Jr., vol. 1, no. 7 (July 1870): 251–56, and vol. 1, no. 8 (August 1870).

28. "A California Humorist," *The Penn Monthly* 1, no. 8 (August 1870): 297–301. Twain is referred to as "the head and foot of a whole tribe of exaggerators, graduated

in a newspaper office, as a court jester of a sovereign people."

29. The Dresser lectures were given at the request of the Pennsylvania School of Industrial Art in 1876. The first of three lectures was published as "Art Industries," *The Penn Monthly* 8, no. 1 (January 1877): 12–29; the second entitled "Art Museums," vol. 8, no. 2 (February 1877): 117–29; the third, "Art Schools," vol. 8, no. 3 (March 1877): 215–25. David Van Zanten reports that Furness was on the committee for a lecture by theorist and design educator Walter Smith that led to the founding of the Museum School. David Van Zanten, *Louis Sullivan, The Function of Ornament*, Wim de Wit, ed. (New York: W. W. Norton, 1986), 22.

30. Alfred Bierbower, "American Architecture," *The Penn Monthly* 8, no. 12 (December 1877): 936–44. He began, "America ought to have an architecture of its own."

their convention in Philadelphia in 1870, and which appeared in the *Penn Monthly* the following year.[31]

Though Dr. Furness's speech was written and delivered in Philadelphia, and manifested the doctrine of duty to personal integrity, in many ways it was only partially a product of its Quaker environment. Its other values were derived from the rocky soil of New England, the home of the Furness clan and the spring of renewal to which they returned every summer—a privilege important enough to have been a stipulation in Dr. Furness's contract with his congregation. Philadelphia Quakers affirmed the divinity within each individual, while Unitarianism professed personal responsibility affirmed by human ingenuity—a logical counterpart to American liberty. It was this rich mixture of values, manifested in his own strength of character, that Furness passed on to his children, enabling them to buck the tides of popular opinion until their views won out—as would happen with Horace—or until they were carried off on their shield, as would be the case with Frank.

Pre-War Roots—Political Expression and Aesthetic Representation

In 1825, William Henry Furness (1802–1896) left Boston, the New England center of Unitarianism, to accept a call to the struggling parish founded in Philadelphia a generation earlier by Joseph Priestley.[32] Dr. Furness became a powerful speaker and a distinguished scholar, whose research on the evidence of the historical Jesus presented not the effeminate Pre-Raphaelite image, but the manly carpenter of Nazareth. In his homilies, Dr. Furness sought vivid images from the natural world to exemplify, not the divine and therefore uncontrollable order, but the means by which truth is passed to every conscious individual. Those interests in natural phenomena led him to translate G. H. Schubert's *The Mirror of Nature* in the same year (1849) that his son William, Jr. acquired a copy of Ruskin's *The Seven Lamps of Architecture*.[33] In the course of an activist ministry, rooted not in Philadelphia Quaker negativism but in New England Unitarian positivism, Dr. Furness stood for those outside of genteel society, championing the divorced Fanny Kemble, as well as Jews and slaves, ultimately winning over the support of the majority of his congregation for his abolition work. That he would champion an American architecture that exalted individual liberty could have been expected from his own values, which complemented those of Ralph Waldo

31. William Henry Furness, "The Architect an Artist," address to the A.I.A., 9 November 1870, *The Penn Monthly* 2, no. 6 (June 1871): 295–308.

32. The history of Furness's move to Philadelphia, and his effects on the First Congregational Unitarian Church, are included in Elizabeth Geffen, *Philadelphia*

Unitarianism, passim.

33. William Henry Furness, Jr.'s copy of John Ruskin, *The Seven Lamps of Architecture* (New York: John Wiley, 1849) is in the collection of George E. Thomas; it is signed W. H. Furness, Jr. in the flyleaf and, in the same hand, dated 1849.

Emerson, his closest friend from nursery school through Harvard (fig. 1.7). After Furness moved to Philadelphia, a constant stream of communication between the two women exchanged ideas, celebrated family triumphs, and marked family visits.[34]

Though Emerson's ideas have generally been presumed to be the pivot on which modern American architecture turned, from Richardson to Sullivan to Wright, his teachings reached Furness directly through his father's Sunday homilies in the Unitarian Church. These were often illustrated by Emerson's poems and fragments of his essays; certainly, the Furness dining table was regularly the setting for discussions of Emerson's writings—often with the author himself present. Letters between the families prove that Emerson played the role of favorite uncle, bringing small presents for the children. He found for young Frank a stereopticon viewer, introducing him to the nature that Emerson celebrated. It was the one toy that his father reported held his attention.[35] When the Reverend William Henry Furness lectured at the A.I.A. Convention, he used Emerson's poetry to prove that architecture was an art, Emerson's argument that architecture was like nature to shape his call for originality, and Emerson's stereopticon to show a means by which the world's variety of architecture could be studied in any American village.

Emerson also served as a cultural antenna for the Furness family, reporting to them items that interested him; he touted within weeks of its publication "that wonderful book—with all its formlessness and faults, 'Leaves of Grass.' " He was equally supportive of *Walden* and Thoreau, "a great man in Concord, a man of original genius & character who knows Greek & knows Indian also."[36] Though Emerson, by William Furness's account, was not visually oriented, he advocated the expression of a native American culture. The train of his argument began with the essay, "The Young American," (1837) in which he stated a new premise:

> It is a remarkable thing that our people have their intellectual culture from one country and
> their duties from another. This false state of things is newly in a way to be corrected. America

---

34. The bulk of the correspondence between William Henry Furness and Ralph Waldo Emerson was edited and published by H[orace] H[oward] F[urness], *Records of a Lifelong Friendship, 1807–1882* (New York: Houghton Mifflin, 1910).

35. Ibid., WHF to RWE, 25 August 1854: "I never told you of Frank's great pleasure in the stereoscope. It was in his hand for days" (97); 18 October 1854: "Did I tell you how much Frank was pleased with the Stereoscope? It lasted an unusually long time with him" (101).

36. Ibid., RWE to WHF, 1 October 1855. Emerson had written to Whitman about his delight in receiving his

volume, 21 July 1855. "I find it the most extraordinary piece of wit and wisdom that America has yet contributed . . . I find incomparable things said incomparably well, as they must be." Whitman wrote back the following summer. Walt Whitman, *Leaves of Grass*, ed. Harold W. Blodgett and Scully Bradley (New York: New York University Press, 1965), 729 ff. Emerson wrote of Thoreau to WHF, 6 August 1847, *Records of a Lifelong Friendship*, 60; Thoreau and Furness met in 1854 when Thoreau was in Philadelphia to give a lecture at the Academy of Natural Sciences; though he missed the lecture, WHF sketched a profile.

1.7. Samuel Bradford, Ralph Waldo Emerson, and William Henry Furness, 1875

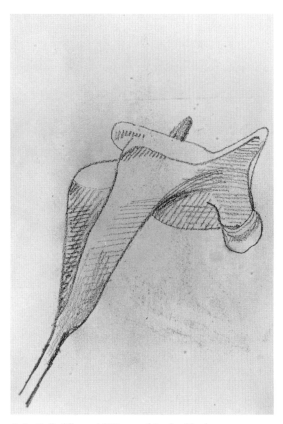

1.8. Calla lilly, c. 1875, pencil in sketchbook

1.9. Ornamental study, c. 1873, pencil in sketchbook

is beginning to assert herself to the senses and to the imagination of her children, and Europe is receding to the same degree.[37]

Though nationalism shaped European architectural revivals, Americans should chart a different course. Emerson asserted that American culture would not be attained by stylistic variations on continental ideas, but by incorporating into its arts the scale of the American continent, and the native idea of a "manifest destiny" to be advanced by American ingenuity and technology. Unlike his English predecessors and contemporaries, who had relied on the authority of the past, justifying architectural theory on Biblical precedent, and elevating the examples of Greeks, Romans, and Goths, Emerson was alive to the possibilities of the present, drawing his metaphors from railroads and commerce, dignifying the American experience:

> I hasten to speak of the utility of these improvements in creating an American sentiment. An unlooked for consequence of the railroad is the increased acquaintance it has given the American people with the boundless resources of their own soil. Railroad iron is a magician's rod in its power to evoke the sleeping energies of land and water.[38]

The railroad became the manifestation of American enterprise and the principle artistic symbol of the age, augmenting nature's Mississippi River with tributaries of steel that eddied at our great cities and flowed relentlessly across the continent. The modern genie unleashed by the railroad, the steamship, and the machine became the muse of the American artist.

> The task of surveying and planting and building upon this immense tract requires an education and a sentiment commensurate thereto. A consciousness of this fact is beginning to take the place of the purely trading spirit and education which sprang up whilst all the population lived on the fringe of seacoast. And even on the coast, prudent men have begun to see that every American should be educated with a view to the values of the land. The arts of engineering and of architecture are studied.[39]

The new imagery that infused American literature and arts came from the exhilarating scenery of America then being depicted in paintings and shortly in photographs:

> the nervous, rocky West is intruding a new and continental element into the national mind, and we shall yet have an American genius . . . I think we must regard the land as a commanding and increasing power on the citizen, the sanative American influence on the citizen which promises to disclose new virtues for ages to come.[40]

Living and timeless nature, not a dead past, inspired Americans.

> Let us live in America too thankful for our want of feudal institutions. Our houses and towns are like mosses and lichens, so slight and new; but youth is a fault of which we shall daily mend. This land is as old as the Flood, and wants no ornament or privilege which nature could bestow.

---

37. Ralph Waldo Emerson, "The Young American," *The Complete Writings* (1929; reprint, New York: William Wise, 1875), 111; all references are to this edition.

38. Ibid.
39. Ibid.
40. Ibid., 113.

Here stars, here woods, here hills, here animals, here men abound and the vast tendencies concur
of a new order.[41]

The "new order," presumably an intellectual and social system, and not Latrobe's corn or
tobacco Corinthian capitals at the Capitol, would transform art as well. From its origins as
the embellishment of class and authority it would become the natural accompaniment of free
men who would use it in their daily activities:

Beauty must come back to the useful arts, and the distinction between the fine and useful arts
be forgotten. In nature, all is useful, all is beautiful. It is therefore beautiful because it is alive,
moving, reproductive.[42]

The new order would be beautiful because it conformed to nature; in Whitman's word it
would be "organic." From such an interpretation it was no great step for Emerson to abstract,
from a conversation with sculptor Horatio Greenough (another Harvard classmate of
Emerson and Furness), the theory that natural process was the logical basis for aesthetic
expression, and thus that form and function would be related in design as they were thought
to be in the natural world. When Greenough was in Florence around 1843, he wrote a letter
to Emerson that expressed ideas anticipating Ruskin's *Seven Lamps of Architecture*, though
diverging from Ruskin in sources and outcome (Greenough was a grecophile and had no
patience with medieval art).

Here is my theory of structure: a scientific arrangement of spaces and forms to functions and to
site; an emphasis of features proportioned to their graduated importance in function; color and
ornament to be decided and arranged and varied by strictly organic laws having a distinct reason
for each decision; the entire and immediate banishment of all make-shift and make-believe.[43]

Emerson was in agreement with him, though he was probably put off by the sculptor's
dependence on the past, which, in Emerson's phrase,

made every man a borrower and a mimic. Life is theatrical and literature a quotation; and hence
the depression of spirits, that furrow of care, said to mark every American brow. Self trust is the
first secret of success.[44]

Literature was in the vanguard in determining the direction of the American arts, perhaps
because words can conjure place, action, and emotion without the capital costs of construction or even the literal detail of painting. (Frederic Church chartered schooners to sail among
icebergs and nearly drowned when he was researching *The Icebergs*).[45] American authors in
the 1830s and 40s found powerful images in contemporary situations and settings, which
became the impetus for the heroes of the novels of Emerson's contemporaries—Herman
Melville, James Fenimore Cooper, and Nathaniel Hawthorne. In such diverse settings as

41. Ibid., 121.
42. Ibid., 235.
43. Ibid., "Diary, First Visit to England," 418.
44. Ibid., "Success," 709.
45. Sherman, "In halcyon days . . . ," 96.

whaling ships, the woodlands, the crumbling city of Rome, and the utopian Blythedale, the immediate situation, not the predetermined and inescapable past of the old world novelist, confronted the American hero.

Allowing for such independent masterpieces as Jefferson's Monticello, architecture was first joined to the national culture through pattern books by A. J. Downing, Hudson Holly, Samuel Sloan, and others.[46] Most were no more than advertisements for their authors, offering little theory and less content; they served principally to fan the flames of nascent American materialism. By contrast, Downing's *The Architecture of Country Houses* (1850) advanced an independent theory of American architecture and was published in numerous editions until the end of the century. Downing represented informed opinion in the decade before the war, and was the only pre-war writer to be accorded merit by post-war critics.[47]

Before Downing, American architecture had been dominated by the borrowed political iconography of the early republic, which reflected the political focus of the nation. The social equality of the English row house, the recollection of democratic Greek and republican Roman temples for farmhouses, and the more exacting revival of those temple forms for public buildings had provided a measure of visual unity across the nation. When A. J. Downing proposed the substitution of picturesque cottages for the Greek temple facade, he assaulted the underlying political metaphor, but republican modesty remained central to his thesis that architecture should express the national political values. Whig and aristocratic in attitude, Downing feared that the competitive expression of great wealth was "contrary to the spirit of republican institutions" and damaging to the political myths that had been central to the nation since its founding.[48] Despite these concerns, he left an opening for the expression of an alternate theme—not the invidious celebration of wealth but the representation of the individual. Thus, Downing argued that the house should "above all things, manifest individuality. It should say something of the family within—as much as possible of their life and history, their tastes and associations, should mould and fashion themselves upon its walls."[49] Linking "truthfulness and significance," Downing drew on Ruskin and English sentiment as the core of aesthetic expression. However, by his call for political expression, his rejection of the European past, and his claim that the individual was the proper subject of the American artist, Downing echoed Emerson and anticipated the post-war generation.

46. Holly's long list of inappropriate English names to use for American estates is particularly amusing; see Henry Hudson Holly, Country Seats (New York: D. Appleton, 1863), 57.

47. Bloor, "Annual Address," iv. "The fifth decade of the century also saw A. J. Downing's contributions . . .

and in the direction of architecture no doubt helped to educate the masses towards a higher plane."

48. A. J. Downing, *The Architecture of Country Houses* (New York: D. Appleton, 1850), 267.

49. Ibid., 262.

While Downing directly connected Emersonian values to architectural practice, his choice of designs rooted in historic styles conflicted with his written message. There could be no doubt, however, about the intentions of Walt Whitman, who in three hundred pages of *Leaves of Grass* made not one reference to ancient sibyls, muses, or gods. It was Whitman who heard America singing its songs of work and celebrated its cultural uniqueness. In *Democratic Vistas* (1871) and *A Backward Glance o'er Travelled Roads* (1888), Whitman outlined a direction for the nation's artists—though few would take it.[50] Rather than finding formulas for beauty in classicism derived from the past, Whitman had deduced that "the greatest lessons of Nature through the universe are . . . the lessons of variety and freedom."[51] Instead of an unchanging past, or endlessly repeated classical models, he posited a dynamic and hopeful future, based on the political democracy that would prove itself only when "it grows its own forms of art, poems, schools, theology, displacing all that exists, or has been proved anywhere in the past, under opposite influences."[52] The old arts Whitman discarded:

> Painting, sculpture, and the dramatic theater, it would seem, no longer play an indispensable or even important part in the workings and mediumship of intellect, utility, or even high aesthetics.[53]

It was a measure of Whitman's imagination that he could envision that architecture, hitherto bound by tradition and taking its forms from its past, would ever be an original art. "Architecture remains, doubtless with capacities, and a real future." For a subject and a theme of America's arts, Whitman returned to the Democracy but reversed its meaning, seeing it not as a political means of giving power to the people, but as emblematic of the individual. To express that idea, he coined the word "Personalism" to represent the theme of individuality as the core of the American culture.[54]

Whitman's biographer, Scully Bradley, probed the poet's roots and discovered three sources that are surprisingly like those of Furness. Both had parents who were deeply mindful of the importance of the democratic values of the society (Whitman's three brothers were named for early political leaders—Washington, Jefferson, and Jackson); both held the Quaker belief in the value of each individual (which Whitman had learned from fellow Long Islander Elias Hicks, a family friend and the creator of the great Quaker schism); both were strongly influenced by Emerson's transcendentalism as it diverged from New England Unitarianism (here Whitman found the roots of his celebration of the land and its people).[55] These native sources provided the basis for Whitman's claim that "great poetry is always (like the Homeric or Biblical canticles) the result of a national spirit, and not the privilege of

50. Walt Whitman, "Democratic Vistas," *Leaves of Grass and Selected Prose*, ed. Scully Bradley (New York: W. W. Norton, 1949), 488.
51. Ibid.

52. Ibid., 490.
53. Ibid., 493.
54. Ibid., 520.
55. Ibid., "Introduction," x.

a polished and select few; Second, the strongest and sweetest songs yet remain to be sung."[56] Such native musings must have been attractive to any young American architect fortunate enough to encounter them.

Though it would be difficult to imagine such ideas being current in the households of most nineteenth-century American architects, it is more difficult to conceive that they would not have been known at the Furness family's Pine Street house.[57] The politics of the democracy, particularly the abolition of slavery, preoccupied Dr. Furness; the celebration of the land and the nation were directly absorbed through Emerson's transcendentalism. Finally, the Quaker City ingrained the cultural values of respect for the individual while the coming Centennial made urgent the search for national expression.

William Henry Furness's Ideas on Architecture

The currency of these ideas in the Furness family can be demonstrated in the address that Dr. Furness gave to the closing session of the American Institute of Architects at its meeting in Philadelphia in 1870.[58] The oratorical skills and advanced education of nineteenth century ministers made them sought-after speakers; both of the A.I.A. conventions held in Philadelphia in the 1870s ended with addresses by clergymen. Though nearing seventy, the Reverend William Furness was vigorous and entertaining, bringing a broad range of interests to his subject entitled, "The Architect an Artist."[59]

His talk began with the statement that he was the typical uneducated observer who would not presume to tell them how to run their craft, nor would he discredit their learning by attempting to "cram" an understanding of their craft in a week or two (as the Reverend E. I. Magoon would do in his address at the 1876 conference). Instead, Furness offered himself as a representative of the public needed by architects to fund and appreciate their work. As the public's taste for art grew, so would the opportunities of the designer; but the architect's problem was that in a new country, architecture was scarcely appreciated and in a democracy

56. Ibid., 487.

57. Something of the extensive family circle of the Furness family can be understood from Ernest Earnest, *Silas Weir Mitchell* (Philadelphia: University of Pennsylvania, 1950), passim. Earnest identifies the Furness family as the subject of S. Weir Mitchell's *Characteristics* (1891; reprint, New York: The Century Co., 1910).

58. For a sketch of the life of William Henry Furness, see "William Henry Furness," *Dictionary of American Biography*, vol. 7 (New York: Charles Scribner, 1929), 80.

59. Furness, "The Architect an Artist." Many of the themes in the lecture appear in his sermons. See William Henry Furness, *Discourses* (Philadelphia: G. Collins, 1855). In "Sources of False Doctrine," Furness attacks authority, "I pass to another great source of error: the undue fondness for authority. The generality of men are afraid to think each for himself. They love to cling to some outward support . . . the misfortune is that we crave external support long after we are . . . able to go alone. We are commanded to judge each for himself . . . but we are afraid to differ from others, and forsake the sympathy and countenance of the multitude" (199–200).

such as ours, every man presumed to have the judgement to criticize architecture. This Furness answered by claiming that architecture should be treated with the respect accorded to other arts; for proof of its status, Dr. Furness quoted his old friend Emerson, who had claimed a "blood relationship of architecture to nature" in the poem "The Problem":

> Know'st thou what wove yon woodbird's nest
>
> Of leaves, and feathers from her breast?
>
> Or how the fish outbuilds her shell
>
> Painting with morn each annual cell?
>
> Or how the sacred-pine tree adds
>
> To her old leaves new myriads?
>
> Such and so grew those holy piles
>
> While love and terror laid the tiles.
>
> Earth proudly wears the Parthenon,
>
> As the best gem upon her zone;
>
> And Morning opes with haste her lids
>
> To gaze upon the Pyramids;
>
> O'er England's abbeys bends the sky
>
> As on its friends with kindred eye;
>
> For out of thoughts' interior sphere
>
> These wonders rose to upper air
>
> And Nature gladly gave them place,
>
> Adopted them into her race,
>
> And granted them an equal date
>
> With Andes and with Ararat.[60]

Having given architects the weapons to defend their self-definition as artists, Dr. Furness shifted to the relationship between art and national character, which he phrased in the Whitmanesque term of "individual liberty." Though liberty might be presumed to free the architect, it in fact had the opposite effect, causing the client to take the safe course of following precedent, because, as Furness noted, the uneducated merely judge excellence by

> whether it is old or new. If we have never seen it before, either in buildings, or in prints and photographs, we pronounce it odd; and when we call a thing odd, we find it difficult to see how it can be called beautiful. With all our freedom, we do not tolerate oddness. We insist, in this country, upon everything's being cut to one pattern.

After noting the duration of Philadelphia's Quaker architecture with its red brick walls, marble steps, and wood shutters, he concluded:

---

60. Furness, "The Architect an Artist," 308.

It is an adventurous thing in this land to set before us anything which we cannot at once tell what to think. We resent it as a personal insult and take satisfaction—the law of taste—into our own hands, and condemn it.

A similar idea had been raised by Cooper, two generations and a Civil War earlier. However, Dr. Furness suggested, by changing the analogy and giving architecture the same suspension of judgement accorded music, familiarity might make the new acceptable. On the other hand, architecture, like music, has a social compact of giving pleasure while representing its purpose. Thus ornament was valued, even if it was not in the best style, because it expressed the ease and wealth of the people. He ended by contradicting Ruskin's resort to Biblical authority with a call for a new architecture, paraphrasing the demand made by an earlier member of the A.I.A. (perhaps Van Brunt) to design an architecture appropriate to new materials such as iron:

> Shall this homely, stolid substance have its rights, and will not Universal Liberty, now no longer a dream but a fact, a component of the heart's blood of forty millions of people, no longer a dead letter, but a spirit, a vital principle—will it not demand—will it not create new orders of Architecture? Answer us, gentlemen, please, in your works.

Furness and his fellow graduates of Hunt's atelier were uniquely qualified to meet that challenge in the first decade after the end of the Civil War.

The American Generation

Though slowed by the economic depression at the end of the 1850s and the Civil War, a new generation of artists quickly returned to the task that had preoccupied them before the war—the invention of a native approach to the arts. In this goal they were sustained by a Scot, James Fergusson, whose *History of the Modern Styles of Architecture* (1862) proposed that each nation would have its own architecture as an expression of its ethnic heritage and its regional environment. Though he criticized Americans for their lack of discipline, Fergusson expected that "in a new and free country" an original architecture might result—if Americans were willing to "abandon scissors as their principal drawing instrument."[61] With the added focus of the Centennial, it was widely anticipated that American civilization would mark its maturation with original creations in the fine arts, as had already been marked in the mechanical and constructive arts—from bridges to clipper ships and locomotives.[62]

61. James Fergusson, *History of the Modern Styles of Architecture* (London: John Murray, 1862), 437.
62. That theme dots American literature from James Jarves, *The Art-Idea* (New York, 1864), to Walt Whitman, "Democratic Vistas," to Lewis Mumford, *The Brown Decades* (1931; reprint, New York: Dover Publications, 1955). It is important to note that it was Mumford who established this American sequence of Whitman and Emerson to Sullivan and Wright and who here made the first favorable remarks on Furness in half

Within five years of the end of the war those predictions were fulfilled. The litany of those giants—Winslow Homer, John LaFarge, Augustus Saint-Gaudens, Frederick Law Olmsted, and Henry Hobson Richardson—was celebrated by Lewis Mumford in *The Brown Decades*; it remains central to our understanding of the nascent American culture. With few exceptions, these artists found metaphors for their roles in a generally artless society by transforming useful and honest work into art rather than making aesthetics their sole and ostensible goal. Samuel Clemens, who split his personality into editor and writer, produced an American literature out of journalism; Thomas Eakins, an instructor, produced an American pictorial art out of nearly scientific observation; Frank Furness, as is demonstrated below, produced an American architecture out of the expression of political and social reform.[63] Again, the constructive arts were preceded by literature, which announced its new direction in strong voices from the west, chiefly Bret Harte, Petroleum V. Nasby, and Mark Twain. They overturned the literary conventions of generations in a barrage of short stories, tall tales, and thinly veiled satires. Mark Twain fired the first salvo when he published an account of a tour of Europe in *The Innocents Abroad* (1869).[64] To the world of art that celebrated the authority of the past, Europe had been the repository of models for teaching young artists. In the hands of Twain it was the perfect foil to set against the relentless American pursuit of the new. Mercilessly skewering any who were not as aggressively innovative as his countrymen as "slow, poor, shiftless, sleepy and lazy," and dismissing most cultural objects as "Jesuit humbuggery," Twain sneered his way through Europe, reporting the journey in a regular newspaper column that attracted a wide readership across the country. Twain nurtured a readership by accepting the commercial processes of journalism and subscription publication, presenting his writing as a part of the work-a-day world of the nation rather than as an elitist frill. Using the tools of exaggeration and irony to pierce pomposity and convention, Twain gave the era its nickname, "the Gilded Age," as well as its enduring literary masterpieces.

The year after the publication of Twain's travelogue, Thomas Eakins returned to his native Philadelphia from four years of study at the École des Beaux-Arts. While teaching at the Academy of the Fine Arts, he began the meticulous pictorial study of the individual in his setting. "Max Schmitt in the Single Shell" dates from these years, as does his first masterpiece, "The Gross Clinic," which was completed in time to be rejected by the art committee of

a century, "the designer of a bold, unabashed, ugly and yet somehow healthily pregnant architecture" (144). However, Mumford does not make the connection between Furness and the foundation of modernism, which he saw in terms of mass politics.

63. The sleight of hand of nineteenth-century American artists to produce art while seeming to do something else was noted by Leo Steinberg, "Not Art but Work," *Other Criteria* (New York: Oxford University Press, 1972), 57.

64. *Innocents Abroad* began as one of the first "package tours," and was sold on the basis that numerous celebrities and ministers would accompany the trip; Twain arrived at the ticket agency pretending to be a drunken Baptist minister.

the Centennial Exhibition, who were daunted by its nearly documentary realism. Despite Eakins's later difficulties with the Academy of Fine Arts, in the 1870s he embarked on a career as a teacher and researcher at the Academy and at the University of Pennsylvania, two of the city's most important institutions.

Nearly simultaneous with Eakins's return to Philadelphia and one year after his father's address to the A.I.A., Frank Furness, with his partner George Hewitt, won the competition for the new building for the Pennsylvania Academy of the Fine Arts (cat. 27). There Furness met his father's challenge, expressing iron construction in its direct application on the sides of the building, while manifesting individual liberty in the overlay of classical forms and French themes with medieval motifs and English polychromy. By the Centennial year, mature works by Olmsted, Richardson, and Hunt and his pupils dotted the land, while native pictorial and literary landmarks graced the homes of cultured Americans. With these works in hand, it was all the more surprising that the Centennial Exhibition was not an affirmation of a bright and creative future but instead was the beginning of the end of the American generation, which would soon be overwhelmed by the display of Europe's treasures and the sophistication of Beaux-Arts training.[65]

Though the foundations of the new American architecture would shortly be eroded by the currents of imported taste, visitors to the Centennial Exposition could not help but find Furness's work stimulating. One writer for the *American Architect and Building News*, perhaps his old atelier-mate Ware, reported Furness's buildings as "by far the most important element in the recent building of Philadelphia," and praised them as "full of life."[66] Equally supportive was A. J. Bloor, who singled out Furness's work before the assembled A.I.A.:

> whereas the first experiments of Furness in design show the most timidity and least promise, his
> last achievements (how far modified by the influence of his partner, Hewitt, I have no means
> of judging) show the most audacity certainly, and perhaps the most individualism.[67]

Though he attributed the source of Furness's direction to Hunt, it was Furness's "unchastened spirit of exaggeration" that caught his eye and suggested that American architects had risen to Fergusson's challenge after the Civil War:

> Fergusson says that, 'if it were possible to conceive the Americans taking the time and trouble
> necessary to think out a common sense style, . . . they might really become the authors of a new

65. The 1893 Columbian Exposition in Chicago merely ratified a change of taste that had begun nearly twenty years earlier at the Philadelphia Centennial Exposition. The move towards historicism began with the popularity of the English Commissioner's Building, a Queen Anne design, and the Memorial Hall, based on German classicism. The histories of the Exposition made no mention of modern American design, cf. Joseph M. Wilson, *History, Mechanics, Science*, vol. 3 of *The Masterpieces of the Centennial International Exhibition* (Philadelphia: Gebbie and Barrie, 1877).

66. "Building in Philadelphia," *AABN* 1 (14 October 1876): 334–36.

67. Bloor, "Annual Address," xi–xii.

form of art.' But, I cannot help thinking that if Fergusson were to see some of the work done here in the last decade, he would at least modify his opinion, and own that there is a distinctive school of American architecture and that Hunt, more than anyone else, may be considered its father.[68]

Despite the widespread belief that a national art had been attained, the lack of recognition by professionals and the informed public at the Centennial Exhibition suggests the general failure to comprehend the real achievement of the 1870s. Instead of adapting old aesthetic principles and modifying the architectural orders, the Americans of the post-war generation had rejected the tradition-bound premises of the arts, substituting the present for the past and the particular for the ideal. An art that paralleled Whitman's infinite variety and freedom and was nurtured by Emerson had been attained by a new generation. This was an art appropriate to the remarkable men who had invented the telegraph, constructed the railroads, founded great industries, subdued the continent, and won the war. By the 1880s, however, these entrepreneurial, inner-directed and self-sufficient patrons and clients were being supplanted by the managers of the new corporations and trusts that were changing the economy from invention and production towards finance and monopoly. The new clients were members of Thorstein Veblen's "leisure class" who found honor not in their work, but in how they were perceived by others.[69] Taste and patronage of the arts became a badge of honor to be desired, not for itself, but because it elicited admiration; the houses of the period overflowed with European paintings, mass-produced plaster Rogers groups, and floral displays.[70] After the Centennial, members of this new generation rediscovered European-based historicism and transformed the culture towards its present mass materialism. That great sea-change in values was furthered by ever easier travel to the continent, the influence of New York journals that used Europe as a barometer of American achievement, and the underlying insecurity of nouveau-riche Americans.

68. Ibid., xii.

69. See Veblen on the concept of the "honorific" and the "pecuniary canons of taste," meaning if it looks expensive, it is good. Thorstein Veblen, *Theory of the Leisure Class* (1899; reprint, New York: Mentor, 1953).

70. For the overstuffed character of the post-Civil War American interior see *Artistic Houses*, 2 vols. (New York: D. Appleton and Co., 1883–84). The plates to this extraordinary publication have been beautifully republished in *The Opulent Interiors of the Gilded Age* (New York: Dover, 1987), but unaccountably without its original highly informative text, for which is substituted a scandalously inaccurate text. For example, see the entry for the Mrs. Bloomfield Moore house, here renamed the Clara Jessup Moore house, which lists Charles M. Burns as architect, though he only replaced its facade in 1900; it had been correctly identified as the work of Furness 14 years before in George E. Thomas and Hyman Myers "Checklist," in James F. O'Gorman, *The Architecture of Frank Furness* (Philadelphia: Philadelphia Museum of Art, 1973), 200. The Dover edition also prints the library photograph backwards. Similar errors appear in the text for the Rudolf Ellis house, which is somehow confused with the commission of 1889 for R. Winder Johnson, two doors away. Finally, Frank Furness's own smoking room, derived from his experiences in the northern Rocky Mountains, presumably either the Big Horn Mountains of Wyoming or the area near Yellowstone National Park, is for some reason transformed into a Colorado camp. In addition, the reprint misses numerous attributions to Furness including the Gibson house and the Clarence H. Clark library.

The transformation of the client caused a similar transformation in architecture. The seeds of those changes were already planted within the profession; with few exceptions, those with the capacity to initiate an American art had been trained in Europe. For those who were so trained, most did not see the necessity of an independent American art—any more than they believed in an American mathematics. Indeed, in three admirably thorough lectures at the 1876 A.I.A. Meeting in Philadelphia by French-trained Richard Morris Hunt, German-born Alfred Cluss, and English-born A. J. Bloor, the eminently appropriate topic of an American architecture appeared but once, and then by way of a graceful salute from Bloor to Hunt, who was presented as the titular head of the American School on the basis of the prominence of his students rather than for any peculiarly American characteristics in his method.[71] In fact, only Bloor raised the concept of national character, which he phrased in terms of a "vernacular" affected by climate and materials, implying that America represented one more regionalism—like those of the various shires of Britain—but united to the central authority of international art.[72] Without exception each of these men supported American architecture's becoming more European and not more independent, initiating the conservative direction of the A.I.A. towards academic training, historicism, and, ultimately, the rejection of architectural nationalism.

Indeed, in the same lecture in which he so extravagantly praised Furness, Bloor commented favorably on the arrival of examples of the English Queen Anne to America's shores.[73] He reported that the *New York Sketch Book* had published American versions and that the new style had already influenced Gambrill and Richardson's Watts Sherman house—drawings for which were on display at the Centennial. From the Queen Anne to historicism was but a small step. By the late 1870s the Hunt office had turned from the fusion of the Greek and the Gothic towards the adaptation of historic styles to contemporary use in mansions such as the Vanderbilt house in New York and Ogden Goelet's Ochre Court in Newport. Hunt, trained in France to look to the past for models, and as comfortable in Europe as New York, would have felt no overwhelming urge to remain true to a purely American direction. Richardson's course towards historicism in Boston was similarly rooted in French method and values, just as his clientele represented the new cultured elite who valued Richardson enough to pay a considerable premium for his services. Though Richardson would attain his own independent vision, his peers too often mimicked the historical sources but missed his ability to "vitalize building materials, to animate them with thought," as Sullivan put it. By the 1880s, the English journal *The Builder* was happy to report that Montgomery Schuyler had stated in *Harper's Magazine* that "American civilization is the same thing in the main as European

71. Bloor, "Annual Address," xi.
72. Ibid.

73. Ibid., x.

civilization. The civilized world is becoming what we may call, for want of a better word, Europeanized."[74] Historicism would sweep the nation.

In the decade after the Centennial, educated America would rediscover Europe: Mrs. Van Rensselaer would turn from Richardson to English and French cathedrals and Henry James would become an expatriate. In the early twentieth century, Harvard-educated Henry Adams would write *Mont St. Michel and Chartres* (1904), turning American aesthetes away from native imagery towards the genteel charm of the Norman countryside. Even Mark Twain lived in Germany for several years in the late seventies and eighties. By the 1880s, the comings and goings to Europe of Philadelphia architects were frequent events, as when *The Builder and Decorator* reported that Walter Cope had just returned from Europe and that Wilson Eyre and John Stewardson were off together for a tour of the continent, remarking: "It is pleasant to know that our architects can avail themselves of such a useful recreation. The public is reaping a substantial advantage from what they are able to bring back of value in their profession."[75] Frank Furness, ensconced in his Montana hunting lodge sitting room in the rear of his Philadelphia row house, was unaffected by such sentiments. So far as can be determined, though other members of his family visited Europe regularly, Furness never did, preferring instead the rigors of the American West where the rugged individualist could still be found.

Furness Intentions and Corroborations

Louis Sullivan affirmed that Furness intended to shape a distinctive American architecture—though not a school—in his account of his time in the Furness office. *The Autobiography of an Idea*, written in 1923 as part of his attempt to develop an American connection to developing European modernism, gained not a whit in the public estimation by praising the long dead and out-of-favor Furness. And yet, Sullivan reported that, like his own boyhood image of an architect, Furness "made buildings out of his head." Sullivan, who had just finished denouncing his M.I.T experience under Ware, praised Furness for the high quality of his expectations and the guild-like environment of his office, making it clear that Furness more than any other had shaped his ideas.[76]

Two parallel accounts confirm that Sullivan was not romanticizing his youthful experience in the Furness office. The first is an unpublished autobiographical sketch by Furness's student and long time partner, Allen Evans, who entered the Furness office shortly before Sullivan and was exposed to many of the same experiences.[77] The second is Albert Kelsey's published commentary on Sullivan's *Autobiography*, which draws similar conclusions to those of Sullivan.

74. *The Builder* (15 September 1883): 345.

75. *Builder and Decorator* 7, no. 2 (October 1888): 8.

76. Sullivan, *Autobiography of an Idea*, 194.

77. Mrs. Manlius Evans to Allen Evans, 2 January 1872, Evans MS.

The Evans manuscript records a letter to Furness from his aunt, Mrs. Manlius Evans, a close friend of Fannie Fassitt Furness, inquiring whether there might be a position for her nephew. Mrs. Evans describes Allen to Furness as "a gentleman, an honest, conscientious worker and thoroughly reliable," but indicates that she is not qualified to judge his capabilities though she believes that he is an "excellent draughtsman." In response to her inquiry, Furness offered a position, though it was not without its drawbacks:

> I would do anything in the world to oblige you in regard to your nephew. Mr. Sloan's way of working is so different from the way that Mr. Hewitt and I work that I fear Mr. Evans would have to unlearn all that he has been through with Mr. S. Should this be the case he would be of little or no use to us for some time, the length of which would of course depend on himself. We will take him therefore, paying him nothing while he is learning our ways and as soon as he becomes useful to us we should of course expect to pay him. I do not wish to seem conceited but I really think if Mr. Evans can spare the time it would be of benefit to him to work with Mr. Hewitt and myself.[78]

The following year, Sullivan's employment with Furness & Hewitt began on the same generous terms.

Just as Sullivan's account of the Furness gruff and self-assured manner was corroborated by Evans's experience, so too his recollections of Furness's intentions were corroborated by Albert Kelsey in an interview given to the *Philadelphia Bulletin*. The interview appeared in April 1924, the day after Sullivan's astonishing claims about Furness's importance were reported in the same newspaper. Kelsey had also trained in the Furness office, a generation after Sullivan, but for some reason—perhaps because he feared being tarred with the brush that had discredited Furness—he did not mention his own apprenticeship.[79] He recalled learning ideas while in the Furness office in 1894 that were surprisingly similar to those Sullivan remembered, proving that the Furness values remained central to the office method into the mid-1890s. Kelsey recalled Furness as "determined that America should create an architecture of its own and opposed to the copying of European styles whether of ancient or medieval design." Corroborating Sullivan's analysis, he concluded with a memorable claim:

> Eccentricities of design and treatment abound in them [his works], but Frank Furness was too good an architect not to know what he was doing and I sometimes think that some of the oddities he introduced were merely the rebellion of a freedom-loving soul who refused to be bound by the rules."[80]

78. Frank Furness to Mrs. Manlius Evans, 30 December 1871, Evans MS.

79. "Men and Things," *Philadelphia Evening Bulletin*, 18 April 1924, p. 8, col. 5.

80. Ibid.

Further along in his interview Kelsey recalled Furness's masculine field manner—born perhaps in the cavalry thirty years earlier:

> That he never hesitated a minute in striking out boldly along lines of his own making, was to his credit and in most of his works here and elsewhere—for he did much for the Pennsylvania Railroad at other points—he displayed masterful directness in achieving the objects he had in mind. What he did was entirely of his own making and, although it was sometimes hastily and roughly done, as when he would sit down beside a pile of lumber on a building job and sketch out, on wrapping paper, a new design for the workmen, it was always serviceable and to the point.[81]

Kelsey was not merely riding on the coattails of Sullivan's memories, as demonstrated by the Furness projects that he listed. Most were long gone or forgotten, including Graver's Lane Station, whose "sweep of structure was masterful," the bank building at Seventh and Market (the Penn National Bank), which he termed "admirable," Rodef Shalom Synagogue, and the Pennsylvania Railroad Station at 32nd and Market streets. He was even able to identify the house that had attracted Sullivan to Furness—the Bloomfield Moore mansion.[82] Kelsey's knowledge of Furness's early work, completed long before he joined the office, suggests that those Furness pupils who were attracted to his method learned the catechism of his work as a part of their office training. Calling him "the Whistler of his craft," Kelsey linked Furness to the origins of an American modernism long since buried by changing tastes and fashions.

Furness and Post-War Philadelphia

By the summer of 1867, Furness had formed a partnership with his old teacher, John Fraser, and with the successor to John Notman's ecclesiastical and socially elite practice, George Hewitt. Soon they were engaged in designing churches, houses, and places of business in the growing city. Their early designs were given both praise and analysis by his apprentices. As Jeffrey Cohen demonstrates in this book, the initial manner of the Furness office owed much to his training in the Hunt atelier and office, where he learned the current design methods of the day—French-influenced *néo grec* classicism and the English modern Gothic.

Instead of merely adapting historic styles, these represented new methods. No longer were salient historical features simply draped on boxes so that function might be represented by association (i.e., Gothic for churches and schools, Egyptian for prisons and cemeteries); in the modern French classical style, ornament established a system of expression and articulation, described the structural forces of the wall, and framed elements. Such a system, as Henri Labrouste and his students demonstrated, was capable of considerable variety and expression—though it remained wedded to the fundamental formal basis of classicism.[83]

81. Ibid.
82. Ibid.

83. The merits of the Beaux-Arts and modern French design are now well known, thanks to Arthur Drexler,

Paralleling this French *néo grec* was the English "modern Gothic," which found advocates because its flexibility was based not on form but on the requirements of the plan. By subdividing facades according to the structural bay, and placing ornament of a circumscribed type so as to accent the structure, a remarkably free style evolved. Moreover, because the modern Gothic laid no emphasis on specific prototypes but was the result of the application of principles, it could be adapted to any building type, adding more ornament to express higher purpose and reducing ornament for industrial and institutional design. As such it was the first truly "international" style, both in its ability to solve the myriad building types of the modern world and in its multinational loci, ranging from Germany and Holland to Britain and the United States.

Both the French and the English methods appealed to Americans because of their descriptive character and their decorative potential. Ornament, far from being inimicable to the values of industrial America, as post-Siegfried Giedion critics have argued, was desirable as an affirmation of American economic success. In Dr. Furness's phrase, ornament produced a "cheering effect . . . Be it ever so bad, it hints of plenty."[84] There was no desire for Shaker asceticism in the mainstream of nineteenth-century America. So long as Furness worked from the basis of his training in Hunt's atelier, and recalled the buildings that he had seen in New York, his work would remain within the American mainstream.[85]

The Hunt method dominated Furness's designs for the Pennsylvania Academy of the Fine Arts and the Northern Savings Fund Society, both designed in 1871. In each, Furness's personal sense of proportion and ironic juxtaposition of forms made them his own. This fusion had characterized Hunt's work in the 1860s and has been explained by Bloor as "Neo-Greek lines . . . infused with Gothic sentiment;" Furness, in typical reversal, infused Gothic lines with *néo grec* sentiment.[86] From Ware and Van Brunt's Memorial Hall at Harvard to the Pennsylvania Academy of the Fine Arts, the flexibility and expressive potential of the style was obvious—at least to Hunt's pupils. Within a few years, as Bloor had noted, the Furness course shifted, paralleling but no longer duplicating the work of his contemporaries. Those designs require an alternate explanation—for they are rooted in the Emersonian values and theories that he had absorbed before Hunt and that became the theme of his later approach to architecture.

ed., *The Architecture of the École des Beaux-Arts* (New York: Museum of Modern Art, 1977). See particularly, Neil Levine, "The Romantic Idea of Architectural Legibility: Henri Labrouste and the Neo-Grec," 325–416.

84. Furness, "The Architect an Artist," 304.

85. James F. O'Gorman's 1973 text admirably ties these strands together and needs little amplification. O'Gorman, *The Architecture of Frank Furness*, passim.

86. Bloor, "Annual Address," viii. He restates the equation several times, noting that other architects infuse the Renaissance revival with *néo grec* lines.

Industrial Symbolism and Botanical Realism

By the mid-1870s, around the time that his partnership with Hewitt ended, Furness abandoned the monochromatic stone facades, with their thinly articulated overlay of incised lines and floral ornament, of his early work. Never again would he be so close to the Hunt manner. In place of stylish cut stone, Furness returned to local pressed red brick for urban architecture and an equally traditional fieldstone for suburban projects. Massing and fenestration displayed the functions and activities within. Furness's formal literalism soon demanded its own ornament. To that end, Furness abandoned the flattened architectonic abstractions of nature derived from the publications of Owen Jones and Ruprich Robert which had appeared on the Pennsylvania Academy of the Fine Arts and the Ellis house. It was presumably this early work which had so pleased Christopher Dresser when he visited Philadelphia in 1876 and which Sullivan had taken with him to Chicago.[87] In place of the *néo grec* system and the Queen Anne style, Furness substituted a sort of ornamental literalism that only Quaker Philadelphia could approve. This literalism would form a constant in the Furness lexicon until the end of the century, taking the form of fiercely sculptural and botanically identifiable plants, perhaps intended as a tribute to Emerson's naturalism but also a reflection of Philadelphia's rich botanical tradition.

Ornament has another role, for it hints at the metaphors of creation central to every art. This becomes all the more important when conventional systems of design are abandoned. While Furness was formulating his art, he wrote little. Fortunately however, in 1878, he did publish an essay on ornament entitled "Hints to Designers." It is replete with the martial imagery that must have characterized his speech: "lead-pencils [are not] highly combustible and liable to explode and destroy the holder."[88] Undoubtedly recalling points of Hunt's instruction, particularly the importance of repetition, Furness emphasized an anti-academic dependence on nature and self (fig. 1.8).

> In all cases the student must go for knowledge to the fountain-head, Nature. If the author of
> the best book upon ornamentation gives original designs, he went to Nature for them: go and
> look for yourself, trust nobody's eyes but your own.[89]

The earliest surviving manifestation of this approach occurred on the handsome baptismal font of the Lutheran Church of the Holy Communion (cat. 22), which is adorned with sculpted bunches of lilies of the valley. But unlike the medievalizing character of Ruskin-influenced designs, these were neither medievalizing nor abstracted, but were simply the flowers themselves. Moreover, Furness found ornamental possibilities in more than just

87. Christopher Dresser, "Art Industries," *The Penn Monthly* 8, no. 1 (January 1877): 14.

88. Frank Furness, "Hints to Designers," *Lippincott's Magazine* 21 (May 1878): 612–14.

89. Ibid., 613.

flowers, claiming, "There is nothing in Nature—plant, bird, beast or fish—that cannot be brought into play as either the main feature or an accessory in a design." The lobsters, storks, frogs, and cattails of the Roosevelt dining room are evidence of his literal application of the principle (fig. 1.9; cat. 45). In a much later example, Furness justified a twin-tailed mermaid as the ornament of the stateroom of one of Griscom's Red Star Line steamships (cat. 444) as representing the fact that it was "a twin-screw steamer."[90] The search for similar descriptive metaphors would preoccupy Furness for much of the post-Centennial generation. Into the 1890s, naturalistic flowers were scattered across urban banks and houses, as well as on firebacks and mantels, ironically celebrating the nature displaced by man's handiwork.

A more remarkable source of ornamentation was derived from Emerson's potent symbol of America—the railroad as the "magician's rod" that transformed American culture. Furness found in railroading many effective forms: the flaring smoke stacks of early locomotives were remembered in his chimneys; their pistons anticipated his short columns; their particularized design of boiler, cab, and great wheels provided a model for functional design. Trenton Junction Station, for example, with its locomotive-headlamp-like clock and additive composition, was obviously rooted in the forms of the railroad industry (cat. 125). Furness went so far as to use railroad tracks to carry the second floor chimney of the Shipley house (cat. 264). The same industrial-modern character was celebrated in the bridge truss on the side of the Academy of the Fine Arts; a similar motif in wood appeared on the facade of the Shamokin Station later in the decade (cat. 133).

When Furness changed the character of his ornament, he also changed its compositional role. Initially, like his peers, Furness made ornament subservient to composition, denoting structure and filling voids. As Furness shifted away from formal composition towards functional expression, ornament was largely freed from its architectonic role and, as twentieth-century architects have demonstrated, could well have been abandoned. Though it was not required in Furness's new functional mode, ornament was still needed to express the forces of commerce and industry that were at the core of the American soul. His father had called for ornament as the representation of the wealth and happiness of the society which made the buildings; later he proposed that "It is a great service rendered to put and keep men, anxious men of business, in good spirits."[91] Can there be any other explanation for the English lions appearing to leap off the parapets of the Commercial Union Assurance Company (cat. 261) and the distressing uneasiness of the oversized *putti* in the dormers of the Jayne house (cat. 468)?

90. The twin screw steamer's maneuverability enabled it to enter harbors without the aid of tugboats, a major advance in marine transportation which Furness's mermaid advertised. For a discussion of the iconography of the smoking room on the same ship (cat. 444) see *Scientific American* 72, no. 24 (15 June 1895): 376.

91. Furness, "The Architect an Artist," 305.

Irony and Exaggeration and Reversal

Once Furness left the Hunt fold he never looked back; instead he essayed ever more independent approaches to design. If the evolution of the artistic personality could be expressed in the terminology of personality development, Furness's early work, a childlike imitation of Hunt's parental style, was succeeded by a phase of adolescent rebellion. In the late 1870s and early 1880s, Furness's designs became progressively more contrary, reversing every norm just for the shock value. This he could do because architecture in America, and more particularly in Philadelphia, was not like the state-sponsored architecture of France or even the estate architecture of Britain. Often having no deeper purpose than simply to call attention to itself in the commercial strip, its character depended more on attracting attention than on being attractive. In short, the more wrong it was, the better.[92]

This approach also suited Furness's self-reliant personality. Inspired by his father's independence, he went his own way long after contemporary journals had abandoned his work. Being something of a loner may have made that easier. By his own account in 1868 he was "not on terms of intimacy with any of the Architects of Phila."[93] Though he was admired by his students, there are no accounts by Sullivan or Kelsey of afternoons strolling the city, or trips to his seashore house in Cape May. In a club-oriented city, his social contacts were few, for apart from the Social Arts Club (later renamed the Rittenhouse Club), which included most of his clients, and the Civil War-related Military Order of the Loyal Legion, he held no memberships. Nor were there artistic soirees or recitals at his office in the manner of Richardson in Brookline. Though he appeared at family gatherings at his father's and brother's houses until the end of the 1870s, by the 1890s even those sessions ended, as Furness apparently withdrew even from his own family. The evidence of the Furness caricatures suggests that his wit was piercing and deflating (fig. 1.10), while the Montana room at his home confirmed the evidence of history—that he was his own man throughout his life (cat. 38). What Whitman saw in Eakins, a determination to resist "the temptation to see what [others] think ought to be rather than what is," probably described Furness as well.[94]

92. This idea was well known at the end of the nineteenth century and was attacked by high-minded critics as introducing the vulgarity of commerce into the art of architecture. See [Montgomery Schuyler?], "Architectural Aberrations, no. 7: The Fagin Building," *Architectural Record* 2, no. 4 (April–June 1893): 470–72. The author ended with a slam at Philadelphia, "As we have remarked, the commercial architecture of Philadelphia is upon the whole more western than anything in the West

. . . But it is significant, we fear, of the same lack of anything which can fairly be called a public from which Philadelphia suffers that such a defiance of common sense and common decency should be offered to the people of St. Louis as has been offered in the Fagin Building."

93. Frank Furness to A. J. Bloor, 10 July 1868, *Letterbook*, vol. 1, A.I.A. Archives, Washington, D.C.

94. Fairfield Porter, *Thomas Eakins* (New York: Braziller, 1959), 24.

Three banks show the possibilities of this approach. The first, the Provident of 1876–79, was derived from the conventional tripartite bank facade (cat. 86). But unlike the usual classical form, it grew larger as it rose above the street. Its cornice was supported by an immense, vaguely Gothic leaf, which seemed to grow out of an angled roof that capped the central motif.[95] Columns, which Furness knew from his training had a specific canon of proportion, were reduced to short piston-like cylinders far removed from their classical origins. (In other instances they were elongated into spindle-like delicacy.) Classical themes were similarly dismembered in the Penn National Bank (cat. 268). Built on the site where Jefferson wrote the Declaration of Independence, it could be interpreted as an emblem of American independence. Though Palladian windows graced the upper stories—and perhaps indicated that Furness was thinking of Independence Hall—the bank was profoundly nonclassical. Its lower walls were smooth; its upper walls were rusticated; ornamental carving disrupted the solidity of its cut stone gables, recalling in position the clutter and textures, but not the historicizing motifs, of the English Queen Anne. Finally, solids on the upper levels line up over voids on the lower level, disrupting the usual appearance of the mass and solidity of a bank.

The National Bank of the Republic (cat. 281) marked an even more remarkable assault on architectural custom. Though unified by an all-over red tone of stone, brick, terra-cotta, and wood trim, it was fractured in composition. The facade almost seemed to be halves of separate buildings: the entrance, in the projecting portion of the facade, was spanned by a half arch above the door; the other half appeared inside the vestibule. A curved transition to the recessed portion of the facade served as the base for a tower that nearly bisected the building; jarringly independent roofs and fenestration mark the adjacent portions. Though the asymmetry in fact described internal functions, the logic was not directly expressed, making this whimsically detailed bank both non-Gothic and nonclassical. Contemporary Philadelphia critics could only gasp that it was "Furnessque," implying that they were as bemused by his originality as later generations.[96] The interior was equally unconventional with half arches flanking, but flaring away from, a central fireplace, destabilizing the composition; even the oversized supports of the roof trusses were eroded away to emphasize their expressive rather than constructive role. Here sardonic wit, ironic misappropriation of form, and the reversal of expectation caught the eye and made for great commercial architecture.

Mature Work—the Expression of Function

Though Furness's contradictory crescendos made for profound urban drama, they used a reactive and fundamentally superficial method, suited only for creating facades. Eventually,

---

95. O'Gorman, *The Architecture of Frank Furness*, 44–45.   May 1885, 10.
96. "Buildings of Beauty," *The Press* (Philadelphia), 24

1.10. Frank Furness, cover to book of caricatures, c. 1895

1.11. Frank Price, Joseph Clarke House, c. 1884

1.12. Price and McLanahan, Blenheim Hotel, 1905

Furness evolved a third approach to design rooted in a more direct response to purpose and function, which served as the fundamental method of the office into the 1890s. Elements of this system had already appeared in the functional expressionism of the Academy facades, which differentiated between the student doorway on Cherry Street and the public portal on Broad Street, denoted galleries by the absence of windows, and represented studios by visible skylights on the north side. Instead of seeking the perverse, this direction merely sought to express the thing itself. It was here that Furness's work corresponded most directly to Emerson's idea that architecture ought to be the closest art to nature in its ability to visually convey purpose.

"Naturalism," as this method might be called, was initially explored in country houses that simply unfold in the order in which they are encountered. Entrances project, stairs are marked by diagonal lines of windows, living rooms have big windows that open onto porches, dining rooms provide more privacy. Each room has its own volume and is denoted on the outside by fenestration. Beginning in the late 1870s many of the suburban houses by the firm took this approach, beginning with the William Henszey (cat. 250) and the Clement Griscom (cat. 253) houses and culminating with the Latta Crabtree house (cat. 320) at Lake Hopatcong, New Jersey.

Equally remarkable are a group of institutional buildings that followed the same principles. Among the first were the Undine Barge Club (cat. 277) along the Schuylkill River, and the Veterinary Hospital of the University of Pennsylvania (cat. 283) in which the various functions took separate forms and materials. In the case of the boat house, the boat shed forms the principal volume, while the stair is attached on the side, leading up to the clubrooms on the river end, which open onto a porch. For the hospital, Furness announced the street entrance by a heraldic stone gable framing an archway that opened into the courtyard through a different lattice gable—perhaps derived from a Chinese structure in Fergusson. The contrast denotes the difference between street architecture and the interior court. The inorganically attached volumes were similarly expressive: low, utilitarian brick stable wings collided with the monumental stone amphitheater whose octagonal form mirrored the auditorium seating around a horseshoe-shaped operating table.

The next buildings of this series were the Pennsylvania Terminal of the Baltimore and Ohio (cat. 332) and the Library of the University of Pennsylvania (cat. 370), in which form expressed function to a degree unprecedented in American architecture. Complicated assemblages of volumes denoted purpose by fenestration, scale, and shape—leading to a blurring of building typologies even as they denoted the various activities within. Legends about the library reported that it was adapted from a railroad station. In fact it could only work as a library. However, the realization that it no longer looked back to historic forms, but instead to the most modern building type that then existed, denoted the nature of the Furness achievement. Sham had been banished, historicism was supplanted by realism, and one hundred years ago, an American architecture had been discovered—one which was then overturned by the simultaneous rediscovery of Europe, historicism, and taste.

Furness's office proceeded on its own course through the 1880s and 1890s, avoiding historicism and continuing to follow the Furness lead. In a country that celebrated liberty but tore down those who dared to be different, the results were predictable. The last time that an architectural journal published a Furness design as something other than an aesthetic curiosity probably occurred in 1878; popular taste being slower to catch the drift, several Furness designs were published in house books into the early 1880s. From that point on, American architectural journals, working from other criteria, ignored Furness or mentioned his work only to criticize its appearance. It would be well into the 1890s before the Furness office would of its own volition produce a historicizing design, long after that approach had dominated the national architectural scene.

Influence

For those who encountered Furness—particularly in the 1870s and 1880s—his achievement of an original American architecture was clear. Sullivan's admiration of Furness was reflected in his own initial approach to ornament and form; indeed it is probably fair to say that every project that Sullivan designed before he saw Richardson's Marshall Field Wholesale Store was derived in one way or another from the work that was in the Furness office during his tenure there. From the ornamental screens at the top and the angled piers at the base of the Borden block (1880), which were based on the Union Trust (cat. 43) of 1872–73, to the fleshy floral ornament, derived from Furness stencil patterns, on the front door of the Adler and Sullivan office (1883), the Philadelphia experience was remembered. Equally Furnessic was the polychromed Jeweler's Building (Dankmar Adler and Co., 1881–82), which was based on the same bank but included bits of *néo grec* from the Northern Savings Fund (cat. 28) and the chamfered lintels and incised ornament from the Philadelphia Warehouse Company (cat. 37). The heraldic floral ornament marking the structural bays of the Rothschild Store was taken from the Warehouse Company as well. Sullivan's domestic architecture shows similar influences but has largely been ignored by recent scholarship, perhaps because it is so embarrassingly close to the Furness original. Indeed, it would be tempting to try to reconstruct Furness's demolished Bloomfield Moore house from Sullivan houses that seem to reflect aspects of Furness's work for which there remains no direct source. Eventually, late in his career, Sullivan's small banks of the Midwest returned to the improbable combinations of functional expressionism and passionate ornament that Furness had used to enliven Philadelphia's bankers' row half a century earlier—and for similarly self-reliant and entrepreneurial men.[97]

97. The most recent study of Sullivan, *The Function of Ornament*, ignores all but the commercial buildings. De Wit's essay, "Banks and the Image of Progressive Banking" (159 ff.), is important in linking Sullivan to the issue of the values of the client.

That Sullivan passed on Furness's attitudes to Frank Lloyd Wright in both attitude and form is apparent. It is only a modest stretch to reach back from Wright's pinwheel design for the *Ladies Home Journal* house to an earlier Furness solution for Samuel Shipley's country house in West Chester (cat. 264) in which wings were added in all four directions to an existing stone farm house. When Wright visited Philadelphia in the 1950s, it was Frank Furness's work that he found of interest—proclaiming it the "work of an artist"—and it was tales about Frank Furness that he recalled having heard from Sullivan, which he in turn repeated to Albert Bendiner.[98] The one that appealed most to Wright was Furness's apparently oft stated desire to gather all of his clients at the Academy of Music, so that he could "tell them all to go to hell." As with Sullivan's praise of Furness in the 1920s, there could have been no reflected glory for Wright in his admiration of an architect long removed from public favor.

Furness was not without his local followers as well. The Philadelphia office shaped others, notably Frank Price and Albert Kelsey. Kelsey, in his role as President of the Architectural League, regularly linked Furness to Sullivan and Wright, and published Furness projects into the twentieth century. In certain projects, notably the Carson College for Orphan Girls, Kelsey was as original as any of his day. Frank Price's Clark house (fig. 1.11) in Bryn Mawr could have passed for Furness work; presumably he conveyed to his partner and brother, William Price, something of the Furness attitudes and method, which reappeared in Price and McLanahan's great seashore hotels (fig. 1.12). It was William Price, himself deeply aware of the anomaly of his Quaker roots and his design career, who made the final pronouncement on the relationship between historical sources and individualism that had preoccupied Philadelphia architects for two generations: "We have to consider a great many things; to look at history and experience. There is only one thing worse in my judgement than ignoring precedent and that is following it."[99] The Philadelphia transformed by Frank Furness justifies that statement.

98. Alfred Bendiner, "Life in A Martini Glass," *Journal of the American Institute of Architects*, 28 (July 1957): 207.
99. William L. Price, "A Philadelphia Architect's Views on Architecture," *American Architect* 82, no. 1452 (23 October 1903): 27.

George E. Thomas

Frank Furness's Red City: Patronage of Reform

In the summer of 1894 Charles Custis Harrison accepted the position of acting provost of the University of Pennsylvania, replacing William Pepper, who had made Frank Furness the unofficial architect of the University (fig. 2.1). Though Furness was not a graduate of the University's architectural program, he was the logical choice for Penn in the 1880s. All of his major constituencies were on Pepper's board: his brother Horace and Horace's brother-in-law, Fairman Rogers, represented the family and the Unitarian connections; engineer William Sellers and publisher Joshua Lippincott represented the new industrialism; the old Philadelphia bankers were present in John Ashhurst; and army ties were there in John Welsh, the father of fellow dragoon John Lowber Welsh.[1]

1. This has not been undertaken as a social-scientific study in the fashion of Leonard K. Eaton, *Two Chicago Architects and Their Clients, Frank Lloyd Wright and Howard Van Doren Shaw* (Cambridge, MA: M.I.T. Press 1969), but is instead an impressionistic overview based on studies of Philadelphia and its patronage patterns. Cf. George E. Thomas, "Architectural Patronage and Social Stratification in Philadelphia between 1840 and 1920," in William Cutler and Howard Gillette, eds., *The Divided Metropolis* (Westport, CT: Greenwood Press, 1980), 85–123. In 1883, the University board included Rev. Henry Morton (the governor of Pennsylvania); Frederick Fraley; Rev. Charles Scheaffer; John Welsh; Rev. William Bacon Stevens; John Ashhurst; William Sellers; Rev. Richard Newton; Eli K. Price; J. Vaughan Merrick; Fairman Rogers; Richard Wood; S. Weir Mitchell, M.D.; George Whitney; Joshua B. Lippincott, Charles C. Harrison; James Hutchinson, M.D.; Rev. George Dana Boardman; William Hunt, M.D.; Horace Howard Furness; Wharton Barker; and Samuel Dickson. *University of Pennsylvania Bulletin, 1883–84* (Philadelphia, 1884): 2.

2.1. Frank Furness, "The past and the future, 1898, Wm Pepper, Charles Harrison, Provosts of University of Penn," pencil on lined paper

2.2. Fairman Rogers, c. 1900

2.3. Frank Furness, "A Wistar Party," c. 1890

2.4. Allen and Rebecca Lewis, c. 1910

The new provost, though the partner of Furness's long-time friend and patron William West Frazier, nevertheless immediately fired Furness and hired the firm of Cope and Stewardson as campus architects. This move signalled the end of Penn's allegiance to the lively activists who had transformed Philadelphia in the previous generation. The anguish of Horace Howard Furness, addressed to Harrison, was noteworthy: "Why have you done this dreadful thing when you have a 'Poem in bricks' to look at every day in the new library?" Writing in his "Autobiography," Harrison replied that if he was "obliged to raise the money [for the new dormitories] I would like architects with whom I could work happily" and described Furness as "intensely interested in his own architectural views." A different perspective on the decision is provided by Lincoln Steffens, whose remark that Harrison was "the provost who declined to join the revolt [against the machine politics of Matthew Quay]" gives weight to Horace's comment as perhaps reflecting more than just familial relationship and aesthetics.[2]

The next year, 1895, brought the election of a political hack as mayor and the collapse of the political reform movement that had reshaped Philadelphia into a dynamic modern city. In 1896 Furness's father, who had been the focus of political and social reform in Philadelphia for half a century and whose values had fundamentally influenced his son's work, died at the age of 93. These events triggered several years of depression in Furness, at a time when, as an aging architect, he could ill afford to falter. Because his loss of the Penn work coincided with Philadelphia's gradual, albeit delayed, turn toward the national architectural mainstream, it has generally been assumed that Furness's career was affected by those broad cultural forces, rather than by local politics; age and evolving American architectural fashion had finally caught up with Furness's high-wire act. This account, however, does not explain how Furness

2. Two drafts of Charles Custis Harrison's autobiography exist at the University of Pennsylvania Archives: the apparently earlier and less polished "Autobiography," which includes the account of Furness's personality in the section "Flotsam and Jetsam," and the account of the "Poem in bricks," in the "Memoirs," finished between 1925–27 (40–42). That there were those outside of the Furness family with reservations about the University's use of historicizing design is clear from Albert Kelsey's editorial comment on "the outrage on history" and the "fact that Franklin and Thomas Penn were among the original founders of the University and that five out of six of the first graduates were either signers of the Declaration of Independence or conspicuous in Revolutionary history." Albert Kelsey, *Architectural Annual* (Philadelphia: Architectural Annual, 1901). Later Kelsey referred to Cope and Stewardson's dormitory quadrangle as "artful stage setting and a travesty on actual life. But what inspiration might they not impart if they reflected the poetry of the present as well as they suggest the romance of an alien past." Kelsey was in the Furness office in 1895, and may well have heard Horace term Furness's work "poetry." For the reference to Harrison see Lincoln Steffens, *The Shame of the Cities* (1904; reprint, New York: Hill and Wang, 1957), 148. Harrison's betrayal of his class is further described in the *roman à clef* by William C. Bullitt, *It's Not Done* (New York: Harcourt Brace, 1926): "Since Uncle Drayton has been President of the University he's had to spend his time going around hat in hand begging and of course his chief almoners are Leather [Widener], Roediger [Wanamaker] and Co. so that he's under their thumb too" (306). See note 34.

continued to capture and retain so many clients and persuade them to go along with his ever more unconventional aesthetic ideas. Furness retained his clients even beyond 1900, several years after the nation's architects had turned towards the historicism that received its first impetus with the Centennial Exhibition and was epitomized by the 1893 Columbian Exposition.

The fact of Furness's popularity had not escaped Harrison, who observed, "How he ever got the number of commissions which fell to his share, I do not know."[3] Contemporary critics in other cities, whose views on architecture were independent of local issues, pondered the same question; they responded with a variety of suppositions ranging from the supposed anti-aesthetic attitudes of the Quakers to Furness's force of character, implied in the phrase "the Furnessic reign of architectural terror." Harrison, in fact, knew perfectly well how Furness got his work. He himself had hired Furness to design his "Happy Creek Farm" in Devon (cat. 404), and at the very moment that he was firing Furness from Penn, his partner Frazier was hiring Furness to design their Franklin Sugar Company office building (cat. 463). In part, Furness dominated his profession through skill, contacts, and good fortune. Luck would have it that he opened his practice when the city's metropolitan character was being transformed by the decision to build a new City Hall at Broad and Market streets, an event that unleashed a generation of urban and suburban building. In addition, his professional training gave him stature at a time when better educated clients demanded higher professional services. Further, he shrewdly hired the well-connected sons of his clients and made use of an unequalled array of contacts and friends known to him largely because of the social standing of his family, whose circle included the educated industrialists, civic leaders, and clubmen who dominated Philadelphia after the Civil War.[4] Still, other architects such as Henry Sims, Canadian-trained and from a wealthy family, and Theophilus Parsons Chandler, École-trained architect from Boston (and soon to wed Sophie Dupont), had similar advantages, but their success pales against the astonishing record of Furness.[5]

Furness dominated both his peers and the city at large through a forceful personality that found expression in designs that most of his colleagues imitated. However, urban architecture is rarely based solely upon the whimsical manifestation of an architect's personality; rather it

3. Charles Custis Harrison, "Flotsam and Jetsam," included in "Autobiography," n.p., University of Pennsylvania Archives.

4. Many, though not all, of the connections between Furness and his clients can be found in the family trees (see pp. 365–67).

5. Sims has been the subject of a master's thesis by Leslie L. Beller, "The Diary of Henry Augustus Sims" (University of Pennsylvania, 1976). Had Sims not died in his early forties he might have been a formidable competitor

to Furness—though he persisted in viewing the field of battle as aesthetic and not political. Beller quotes him: "I am the only architect here making any pretensions to a knowledge of Gothic" (17). Chandler was limited in a different way by his marriage to Sophie Dupont, which, while providing entry to Philadelphia society, reduced his incentive to join the urban fray. See Thomas, "Architectural Patronage"; Thomas, "Theophilus Parsons Chandler, Jr. F.A.I.A.," in O'Gorman et al., *Drawing Toward Building*, 166–68.

is purposeful, directly expressing the client's aspirations and affiliations. To a certain extent, "proper" Philadelphians' choice of Furness ratified their position outside of the national mainstream, but it also coincided with the post-war political and social reform movement, which was rooted in Philadelphia's peculiar situation. Unlike most American cities, run by Democratic machines, Philadelphia was dominated by a populist-Republican machine. With their logical political party so controlled, the gentry continued to adhere to the outdated but still satisfying tenets of the defunct Whig party. Confronted by the ongoing evidence of Republican corruption in the rising hulk of City Hall, Philadelphia reformers sought a distinctive image to represent what they perceived as receding values of honesty and individual responsibility.

Frank Furness, under the influence of his father's Unitarianism and Emerson's advocacy of the present, provided the distinctive reform image in an original architecture whose red brick surfaces recalled the old landmarks of Revolutionary Philadelphia. A fortuitous combination of predilection and circumstance allowed for Furness's originality because his architecture had more than aesthetic value to his clients. Prepared by their anticipation of the Centennial, elite Philadelphians could accept an original American architecture as heralding the political and social achievements of the nation. Transcending fashion, Frank Furness's red buildings became the emblem of Whig Philadelphia's progressive cultural, social, and municipal reform.

The Whig Meritocracy—Reformers from the Outside

Reform was not unique to Philadelphia. With the end of the Civil War, Americans turned their attention from the abolition of slavery to municipal and political corruption. These issues were portrayed on the popular stage in Mark Twain and Charles Dudley Warner's *Gilded Age*, filled the pages of *Harper's* in Thomas Nast's cartoons of New York's scandal-ridden Tammany Hall machine, and headlined the front pages of the nation's newspapers in stories of corruption in Grant's administration as well as local government. Into the 1890s, the war remained the fulcrum of the era, shaping a generation of activists described in S. Weir Mitchell's autobiographical novel of post-war Philadelphia society, *Characteristics* (1891). Mitchell's words evoke the drawing rooms of post-Civil War Philadelphia and capture the dialogue and values of the Furness circle. In one scene, a rather amoral character—the artist St. Clair (who had avoided the war)—archly states that there ought to be a war every fifty years to "educate" a nation. Another character, whom literary historians believe was based on Horace Howard Furness, retorts, "I don't care myself to manufacture any more history, but certainly the generation which emerged from our great strife, North and

---

6. S. Weir Mitchell, *Characteristics* (1891; reprint, New York: The Century Co., 1910), 185. Mitchell was a close friend of Horace; his younger brother was in the Sixth Pennsylvania Cavalry with Frank and that brother's son married Frank's daughter, Annis.

South, was the better for it."[6] Philadelphia would certainly benefit from its generation of soldier-reformers; Frank Furness returned to Philadelphia as a military hero who adhered to and represented the positive values of the soldiers with whom he had served.

Philadelphia's soldiers came home to their native city to find a community whose educated elite had largely decamped to their country estates—a move with unforseen consequences.[7] The elite may have avoided the irritants of industrialization and immigration, but they also lost their political voice. The Whig party, to which they were drawn in the battle against Andrew Jackson's financial policies, had fallen apart over the issue of states' rights; the Republican party, which would have been their natural refuge, was taken over by the machine. The Democrats were remembered with hatred for dismantling Philadelphia's control over the Bank of the United States. The result was a single-party city largely run by an entrenched and corrupt Republican political organization; from 1860 until 1950 the few brief episodes of reform originated from outside the governing party structure.

Although the Whigs have been given less attention than they deserve, the importance of their nostalgic and romantic values can be clearly discerned in the diaries of Sidney George Fisher (1809–1871). Fisher recorded with displeasure the displacement of forests by factories, the unseemly expression of wealth, and the inclusion of vulgar and uneducated people in society merely because they were rich. His positions echoed those of fellow Whig A. J. Downing, who had landscaped Alverthorpe, the estate of Fisher's brother.[8] Looking backwards, Philadelphia gentry chose conservative architectural solutions to distinguish themselves from the nouveau-riche. In their neighborhood around Rittenhouse Square, they continued to build red brick, white stone-trimmed town houses into the 1870s; in their farms they developed a gray, local-stone style based on the Federal vernacular; and even as late as the 1890s, in their resorts such as Cape May, they hired aged architects like Stephen D. Button,

7. Philadelphia politics are discussed in Sam Bass Warner, *The Private City: Philadelphia in Three Periods of Growth* (Philadelphia: University of Pennsylvania Press, 1968), which unfortunately misses the major reform eras, concentrating instead on the city of the Revolution, the pre-Civil War industrial city, and the post-World War I city. However, many of the issues of the post-Civil War years can be inferred from chapters five ("The Specialization of Leadership") and six ("Municipal Institutions"). Nathaniel Burt and Wallace E. Davies made politics the focus of their chapter, "The Iron Age 1876–1905," in *Philadelphia, A Three Hundred Year History*, ed. Russell Weigley, et al. (New York: W. W. Norton, 1981). See also Philip Benjamin, "Gentlemen Reformers in the Quaker City," *Political Science Quarterly*,

85 (March 1970): 65. That the Whig and elite value systems were entwined is suggested by four Chestnut Hillers, who ran as anti-Jackson Democrats in 1828 and 1832, whose initials spelled Whig—Watmough, Harper, Ingersoll, and Gowen, father of Furness's client. Samuel F. Hotchkin, *Germantown, Mount Airy and Chestnut Hill* (Philadelphia: P. W. Ziegler, 1889), 388.

8. The most Whig portions of A. J. Downing's *The Architecture of Country Houses* (New York: D. Appleton, 1850) are the chapters on "What a Country House or Villa Should Be" and "Designs for Villa or Country Houses." Fisher's diaries have been edited. See Nicholas Wainwright, ed. *A Philadelphia Perspective: The Diary of Sidney George Fisher Covering the Years 1834–1871* (Philadelphia: Historical Society of Pennsylvania, 1967).

then in his eighties, to design old-fashioned Italianate cottages, thereby maintaining the image of the resort of their childhood.[9] When guided by the Whig gentry, reform would take on the cast of the past.

Their sons, most of whom were born around 1840 and were typically college-educated for one of the professions, became Furness's clients. With many he shared the bonds of common experiences—the patriotic zeal and subsequent horrific reality of the Civil War, the excitement of the new age of the railroad and the steamship, and the nationalistic fervor of the Centennial. Many of his clients even looked like Furness—lean activists turned bulky capitalists, always screened behind a beard 17or mustache (fig. 2.2). Those bearded faces, in deliberate contrast to the smooth faces of the pre-war era, masked the remaining traces of war-induced psychological trauma, and the stench of economic, governmental, and social corruption that soiled the reputation of the Quaker City.

Of the families important in the previous generation, only a few retained a significant presence in the city. These included philanthropist and statesman John Welsh, who shepherded the Centennial Exhibition to its triumphant conclusion; newspaper publisher George Childs, who provided the city with ethical journalism; and Furness's own father, the Reverend William Henry Furness, who was an important moral leader in a city that often took the low road. Each in one way or another became a Furness client.

Philadelphia: Public Corruption and Private Response

After the Civil War, Philadelphia appeared to be poised for a triumphant return to the national mainstream, as industry flourished and the unequalled success of the Centennial gave the nation a new and momentarily positive image of the Quaker City. The image was deceptive. Generations of neglect by its social and cultural leaders had left a city diseased by the cancer of influence-peddling and drugged by the opiate of municipal expenditure. Philadelphia was on the brink of financial collapse; the evidence of pervasive rot and decay was inescapable. In part the city's collapse was the result of evolution from its eighteenth-century roots as a sophisticated mercantile and financial community—the appropriate center of state and federal government—to a blackened and begrimed agglomeration of industrial villages around a small downtown. Urban only in political designation, little of Philadelphia's population shared the social, intellectual, and cultural benefits of city life. Factory wages and Philadelphia thrift institutions made physical comfort possible for the working classes in their row houses, but this constituency was particularly susceptible to the local ward-run machine politics that had

9. For the *retardataire* character of Cape May, see George E. Thomas and Carl E. Doebley, *Cape May: Queen of the Seaside Resorts* (Philadelphia: Art Alliance Press, 1975), 42–43.

no interest in altering the status quo. It was a dinosaur of a city, its large body and small brain prone to misadventures.

The tensions of urban growth were not new; a generation earlier they had produced the Know-Nothing riots of the 1840s. The forces at work were described with revulsion in Sidney George Fisher's private pre-war diaries, and discussed openly after the war in the learned texts of the *Penn Monthly*.[10] They also provided a popular theme for literary works set in Philadelphia. As early as 1844, George Lippard's extraordinarily popular *The Monks of Monk Hall* (1844–45), a serialized piece of anti-Catholic and anti-immigrant propaganda, began with the claim "Philadelphia is not so pure as it looks!" and proceeded to compare the new marble-fronted city—with Girard College its symbol—to the Biblical whited sepulcher, pure without and rotted within.[11] *The Monks of Monk Hall* was a tale of depravity set amidst the remaining red brick buildings of the old Revolutionary society. The contrast between the honest, red "Quaker City," (a phrase that Lippard popularized), and the modern corrupt immigrant city of industry pervaded the imagery of Philadelphia for half a century; Lippard's novel, reprinted in 1876, played a part in the city's post-war reform movement. Its publisher, Edward Stuart, was later victorious as the second and last reform candidate for mayor, even as the white City Hall rose to supplant red Independence Hall as the seat of government. Agnes Repplier's 1898 description of that still new City Hall, its cracked and spalling marble veneers, already pollution-blackened, "writhing, struggling, decaying," and her description of city government employees as "wretched inmates" characterized public opinion from the 1880s until the 1950s.[12]

Municipal decay and corruption were unfortunately not the inventions of a despondent Whig diarist or a moralizing novelist, but were real enough. In the 1870s streets were in disrepair and the city was proclaimed "the worst paved and worst cleaned city in the civilized world."[13] City water tasted terrible and was so polluted that even bathing in it was offensive; the sewer system endangered public health. In 1883, Governor Pattison reported that "this

10. Similar views about the masses were stated by Agnes Repplier, *Philadelphia, the Place and its People* (New York: MacMillan, 1898), 356–61.

11. George Lippard, *The Monks of Monk Hall* (1844–45; reprint, Philadelphia: Leary and Stuart, 1876), 2, 3, and passim. A biography of Lippard appears in Joseph Jackson, *Encyclopedia of Philadelphia*, vol. 3 (Harrisburg: The National Historical Association, 1932), 842–45.

12. Repplier, *Philadelphia, the Place and its People*, 375. Sidney George Fisher was even more pessimistic, noting in his diary: "I have long had an idea that the present civilization . . . is destined to be destroyed by the irrup-

tion [sic] of the dark masses of ignorance & brutality which lie beneath it, like the fires of a volcano" (169).

13. Edward Allinson and Bois Penrose, *Philadelphia 1681–1887: A History of Municipal Development* (Philadelphia: Allen, Lane and Scott, 1887), 268. Penrose, acknowledged to be one of the most brilliant Philadelphia politicians, with more than sufficient wealth to not be tempted by corruption, cynically joined the Quay forces after completing his history of Philadelphia government. He was described as playing "politics the way others played chess, not for personal profit, but for the pleasure of winning," in Burt and Davies, "The Iron Age," 498.

state of affairs was due to the failure of the people to elect good men to office," although separating cause and effect is difficult here.[14]

From the Civil War until the end of the century Philadelphia life was dominated by questions of governmental, social and cultural reform.Improving the city government and its institutions took the two decades from 1870 to 1890, and required the assistance of the state government in Harrisburg, which previously had manipulated Philadelphia for its own purposes. The first step toward change was the new State Constitution of 1874; this recognized Philadelphia as the only "first-class" city in the Pennsylvania Commonwealth, and gave it permission to reorganize its government in exchange for agreeing to a daunting pay-as-you-go requirement for city budgets. With Whig support, a reform Democrat, Robert Pattison, was elected city controller, thereby using the budget to control the Republican machine. Pattison eventually became governor, and during his last year in state office municipal reform efforts reached fruition with the passage of the new 1887 city charter. The so-called Bullitt Bill was hailed by Lincoln Steffens as a model for the nation, provided that good men could be persuaded to run for office.

With few exceptions, it was Furness's circle of clients who backed and rewrote the new city charter, introducing a decade of good government from the mid–1880s until 1895, transforming the city's institutions, and founding a network of clubs and associations to outwardly manifest the city's renewal. Their values fill the pages of Mitchell's *Characteristics*, which portrays the new urban meritocracy's concern with problems of urban poverty and municipal corruption. Working together at the University, the Union League, the Reform Club, and various churches, the reformers intended not merely economic expansion but the intellectual, visual, and spatial rebirth of the city of their forefathers. Drawing on the resources of a noble past, they displayed their commitment to reform by reviving aspects of their history in architecture, the visual arts, and literature. It was no surprise that Philadelphia gentry would typically look to the past when confronted with crises; loathing the industrial city of the present, their positive self-image was set in the red city of revolution and morality. This no doubt accounted for the ongoing practice of constructing red brick and light stone-trimmed buildings, and provokes the question of whether the Georgian and Federal styles had ever ended in Philadelphia. It is a measure of Furness's originality that he could express the reformist themes by adopting the elemental eighteenth-century material of brick, rather than by resorting to extensive stylistic quotations that soon would have become meaningless with the onslaught of late nineteenth-century colonial revival.

The immediate impact of the post-war activists could be seen in every quarter. New publications such as *Lippincott's Magazine* (1868) and *The Penn Monthly* (1870) provided vehicles for literary and intellectual discussion; institutional growth offered a promise for the

14. Allinson and Penrose, *Philadelphia 1681–1887*, 269.

future. The physical monuments to the activists were the Victorian banking district in the vicinity of Independence Hall and the residential neighborhood stretching south of Walnut Street from Seventh Street to 22nd Street. The latter region contained three decades of Frank Furness's and his contemporaries' houses, clubs, and churches, which, despite a century of grime, still recall the vitality and adventure of the rejuvenated city. In the end, the reform movement was short-lived, because it was the work of only a small cadre of individuals not rooted in Philadelphia's political structure. In 1887 Philadelphia elected the first of two reform mayors; by 1895 the machine had regained control, reinstalling the patronage hacks and spoils system that would dominate city government until a brief episode of good government in the 1950s, led by a similar outsider triumvirate of businesses, the University, and blue bloods. Frank Furness's direct and powerful architecture had a place as long as the reformers dominated the city; when his harsh but honest realism was supplanted by the suburban pastoral of Chestnut Hill and the charming historicism of the new University of Pennsylvania buildings, Philadelphia's brief day of reform ended.

Unitarian Liberalism and the Just Society

Furness did not immediately fall heir to the mantle of reform. Indeed in the 1860s, though Pugin and Ruskin had asserted that architecture gauged the moral worth of society, few in urban America conceived of architecture as a means to manifest social transformation. Rather, architecture too often became a device of social corruption, as politicians courted votes by commissioning buildings that would have to be paid for by future generations. But in his father's Unitarian Church, Frank Furness and the congregation were urged to reform; they heard the message that modern life required questioning assumptions, challenging established order, and relying on nature for an expression of truth.[15] This was neither Ruskin's backward-looking aspiration to medieval religious society nor William Morris's parallel Arts and Crafts movement, but Emerson's hope for the present and the future. Dr. Furness, whose abolition efforts had earned him national stature, spoke with moral authority when he claimed that each man's efforts might constitute a step towards truth, the logical goal of a society that professes individual liberty. As he claimed in his 1870 lecture to America's architects, even architecture had a role in the restructuring of society:

> You are by the ordination of Heaven, street-preachers, and whether you hold forth sound doctrine or false, we must listen to you, We cannot forbear. People may go to sleep inside the churches that you build, and hear nothing, unless indeed you make the interiors so much more

15. William Henry Furness, *Discourses* (Philadelphia: G. Collins, 1855), passim, esp. "Discourse VII, Sources of False Doctrine," 186–205.

eloquent than the preachers, that the people must needs keep awake and receive edification through their eyes.[16]

When Frank Furness returned to Philadelphia from New York in 1866, his first project was a Unitarian Church in Germantown (cat. 1), organized by Edward W. Clark, the son of a New England-born stalwart of Furness's father's First Congregational Unitarian Church. The link between progressivism and Unitarianism is already well established in architectural history, from H. H. Richardson's first ecclesiastical commission in Springfield through Frank Lloyd Wright's Unity Temple in Chicago. The values that caused Unitarianism to commission important architects made the Philadelphia Unitarian congregation a center of reform activity. Especially at the beginning of his career, members of his father's congregation provided Furness with many important commissions: among these clients were his father's childhood friend Samuel Bradford, treasurer and director of the Philadelphia and Reading Railroad from 1838 until 1884 and responsible for many Furness commissions (cat. 121-247);[17] fellow New Englander Henry Winsor; Henry Duhring; Fairman Rogers; and of course, members of the Furness family. Another significant Unitarian commission was the house for Bloomfield Moore (cat. 32). As the house rose at its South Broad Street site, it was clear that Frank had heeded his father's call to reject authority and honor nature instead. Half a century later the Moore house lived on in Louis Sullivan's memory as "a flower by the roadside."

No Unitarian was more supportive than Fairman Rogers. Furness's relationship with Rogers was based on age, experience, family (Rogers was Horace's brother-in-law), and a common interest in the arts and building.[18] Rogers attended the University of Pennsylvania, graduated with a Master's degree in mathematics, and taught civil engineering at the University and the Franklin Institute. At the outbreak of the war, he joined the First City Troop, serving with distinction as its captain, and returning to serve as an engineering officer on the general staff during summer vacations from teaching. Rogers's range of interests and talents were remarkable: in his youth, he helped prepare the United States coastal surveys from Maine to Florida; later, the government asked him to solve the problem of compass accuracy on iron ships. His private passion, coachmanship, led to the 1899 publication *A Manual of Coaching* in which he gravely instructed, "If a man has not hands enough to spare

16. William Henry Furness, "The Architect an Artist," address to the A.I.A., 9 November 1870, *The Penn Monthly* 2, no. 6 (June 1871): 304.

17. *The Reading Railroad, The History of a Great Trunk Line* (Philadelphia: Reading Railroad, c. 1892), 56. Written at the beginning of the McLeod era of management of the railroad, it profiles members of the railroad staff. In the biography on William Church, treasurer, it noted that he replaced Samuel Bradford in 1884, who retired after having held the position for forty-six years. With his departure, the railroad was turned over to monied New York interests, who asked Furness to justify his tenure; shortly thereafter, he lost his position.

18. For a biography of Rogers, see HHF [Horace Howard Furness], *F.R.* (Philadelphia, 1903), passim.

one to take off his hat to bow to a lady, he should continue to practice driving until he can find one." Rogers retired from teaching in 1871, undertaking a career as a civic activist. A founder of the Union League, he helped supervise construction of its building, and was credited with many of its admirable features. Rogers served on the Board of Directors of the Pennsylvania Academy of the Fine Arts (cat. 27), Jefferson Medical College Hospital (cat. 70), and the University of Pennsylvania (cat. 283, 305, 370, 403), guiding these institutions as they embarked on major architectural enterprises.

When the Academy decided to move from its old location on Chestnut Street, Rogers was made chairman of the Building Committee; then-director John Sartain recalled that "much that is admirable and best is owing to his careful and earnest thought."[19] Later, as a member of the instruction committee, Rogers permitted women to study art under the same conditions as men and advocated Thomas Eakins's method of teaching, reporting to the board on its merits:

> Mr. Eakins teaches that the great masses of the body are the first thing that should be put upon the canvas in preference to the outline . . . the students building up their figures from the inside rather than fill them up after having lined in the outside.[20]

Rogers was one of the few "proper" Philadelphians who commissioned an Eakins painting: "Fairman Rogers Four-in-hand Coach" (1879). The multiple studies required by Eakins may have been the impetus for Rogers, a skilled amateur photographer who had done theoretical work on the Zootrope, to assist Eakins and Muybridge with the photography of animals in motion.[21] A scientist, Rogers believed in Eakins's approach to teaching, which advanced from the cast to the nude model to the dissecting room, moving toward ever greater realism. Furness's own account of his similar method of working, not from nature but toward it, suggests one reason for the long and fruitful relationship between the two men.

Multi-member boards make it difficult to name one person as responsible for the choice of an architect, yet whenever Rogers sat on an important board that intended to build a new structure, Frank Furness was selected as its architect and usually given a free hand. After attending to the Academy, Rogers was involved with the planning for the new armory of the First City Troop (cat. 47); he was a board member during the construction of two handsome buildings for Jefferson Medical College as well as three buildings at the University of Pennsylvania. For Rogers, Furness designed the remarkable ocean house, "Fairlawn," at Newport (cat. 34), and remodelled 202 South Nineteenth Street (cat. 35A).

19. Ibid., 13.
20. Fairfield Porter, *Thomas Eakins* (New York: Braziller, 1959), 21–22.
21. HHF, *F.R.*, 16.

Clubmen and Municipal Reform

Rogers was a strong link to the urban reform movement through the city clubs, which were vital assets to the maturing city. In typical Philadelphia fashion, in lieu of forming a broad-based popular reform movement, private associations of businessmen and gentry attacked municipal corruption. The first such agent of change was the Saturday Club. This organization grew out of the Wistar Parties (fig. 2.3), gatherings of the old Whig elite at the Wistar home which were reinstituted after the Civil War. Horace Howard Furness, a member of the Club, recounted its role in municipal and institutional affairs:

> The indebtedness of our city in times past to the Saturday Club is noteworthy. Composed as it was of men of influence and wealth, it fairly represented the working force of the city, and gave to this force a unity which neither New York nor Boston possessed. It used to be jocularly said that half the affairs of The University were transacted at The Saturday Club. It was in these social gatherings that the design and scope of a Union League had its origin.[22]

Other clubs with wider membership included the Union League and the Reform Club. These advocated cooperation between business competitors, encouraged a perspective broader than the corporate balance sheet, and afforded a setting where businessmen and civic leaders could hammer out agreements on social and political policy. Establishment of the clubs coincided with a post-war generation who returned to the city rather than retreated to their paternal suburban estates.

In 1871, members of the old Saturday Club, including Fairman Rogers, purchased a mansion, with the intention of establishing a club dedicated to the municipal reform of Philadelphia. The Reform Club represented a broader circle than that of just the Unitarians and old Philadelphians: it numbered among its members historian Henry Charles Lea, publisher Joshua B. Lippincott, and merchant-turned-civic-leader John Welsh.[23] Welsh would later rescue the Centennial from default—the Federal Government refused to fund it—and from mismanagement by the city, which saw the event as an opportunity for corrupt dealings. For his efforts, Welsh was given a $50,000 gift from grateful citizens of Philadelphia, which he in turn donated to the University to establish the John Welsh Chair in History. With Welsh as its first president, the Reform Club soon had 1100 members, making it one of the largest clubs in the city and a potent force for urban change.

By 1878, the needs of the club's lady visitors led to construction of a two-story addition on the site of the old side garden; the newspapers described the building as "a highly original work by Frank Furness"(cat. 99).[24] The new clubrooms for women associates contained a

---

22. Ibid., 14.
23. The Reform Club is discussed in a paper by Cheryl Wilson, Urban Studies 272 (Autumn 1989), which is based on Thompson Westcott, comp., *Scrapbook: Build-ings, Public Places, Public Things* (Philadelphia: Historical Society of Pennsylvania, 1874–80), 1:68; 2:156, 159.
24. A description of the building is included in the checklist. See also Westcott, *Scrapbook* 2:164.

roof garden and a women's restaurant, the first in a major Philadelphia club. Unfortunately, reform was not so passionate a subject that its advocates could resist more mundane pursuits. The following year, as card-playing and drinking replaced debate and discussion, 200 members resigned "on account of differences with its management, by reason of the subversion of its political aims to mere social pleasure."[25] Ultimately, reform was too important to be left to a club, and in 1880 the most dedicated activists organized the Committee of 100, which directed reform into the 1900s.

The addition to the Reform Club was only one of Furness's urban club commissions. In 1873, Furness, his brother Horace, Henry C. Gibson, Fairman Rogers and others, formed the Social Arts Club to promote literary, artistic, and antiquarian inquiry as a corollary to the ongoing municipal reform. After renting a building across Chestnut Street from the Reform Club, they purchased a house on Rittenhouse Square, and in 1878 commissioned Furness to design interior alterations and a spotless white marble front that stood out from the brownstones on the Square (cat. 100).[26] Like the Reform Club, the Social Arts Club—later renamed the Rittenhouse Club—numbered among its members many Furness clients, and while it would later become little more than a daytime gentleman's club, its starched white front was an early symbol of the quest for change during the 1870s.

The Reform and Social Arts clubs were the most prominent examples of Furness's architecture for urban reformers, but numerous other commissions testified to his affiliations with progressive Philadelphians. He added to the Philadelphia Club, the chief rival of the Social Arts for social supremacy, and designed several of the athletic clubs that began to appear in the 1880s, the most notable being the Racquet Club (cat. 382). Whether through his Reform Club acquaintances or his army connection to Welsh's son, Furness was chosen to design several country houses for the Welsh family (cat. 108, 109A). At the end of the century, Furness altered a house for William C. Bullitt (cat. 561), John C. Bullitt's son and the state representative who pushed his father's "Bullitt Bill" for municipal charter reform through the legislature. Furness also designed houses for the Locust Street Real Estate Investment Company, a venture that used private capital to upgrade a festering slum located on Locust Street (cat. 392, 394, 432). After 1870, no Philadelphia architect could challenge Furness's monopoly on commissions from the reform community. Although his former partner, George Hewitt, was selected to design John C. Bullitt's house on 22nd Street, when the Hewitts subsequently sold out to the city machine in the early twentieth century the Furness office was selected to undertake Bullitt family work.

25. Westcott, *Scrapbook* 2:164.
26. Jerry McFadden has kindly made his manuscript on the Rittenhouse Club available to me.

Privatism and Public Spirit

Breaking the back of the political machine required an educated electorate with access to information. Thus, in the 1880s, William Pepper, provost of the University of Pennsylvania, helped found the Free Library system to supplement Philadelphia's private libraries. Because the Free Library was taken over by the city, its early buildings were designed by political appointees, but Furness received commissions for the city's privately funded libraries, culminating in 1888 with the University's own new library (cat. 370). The role of these buildings in transforming society was proclaimed by Horace Furness in his address at the cornerstone laying ceremony of the University Library. He described its construction, with "foundations deep so that they might bear the enlarging needs of the public; in the cornerstone, were interred truth, liberty, the love of mankind and the service of society which were to be the motives and aims of its existence." In closing, he evoked the cadences of Lincoln's Gettysburg Address and the Declaration of Independence, hoping that the building would be "a library for the people, erected under a covenant with the people, and by the liberality of the people."[27]

Charitable and educational institutions performed parallel functions in breaking the cycle of dependency of the working classes on the political machine. From the early 1870s through the mid-1890s Furness designed most of Philadelphia's privately funded hospital buildings, becoming the chief institutional architect of his day. A dozen buildings at the Jewish Hospital alone, and another dozen clinical structures at other institutions, formed a significant part of his practice. Most were erected to serve the immigrant community—the wealthy still received medical care at home. Furness's clients retained him to design a day care center (cat. 503), settlement house (cat. 525), public bath house (cat. 477), retirement homes for the aged (cat. 339, 443), and other facilities, each intended as a wedge between the corrupt political machine and the populace.

It is worth noting that Furness regularly benefitted from connections that would be viewed as conflicts of interest by current standards. The issue was seen differently by his contemporaries, who proclaimed nepotism as "a form of paternal pride in all successful institutions."[28] That Furness's brother was chairman of the University Library Building Committee, and that Fairman Rogers, his brother's brother-in-law, was Building Committee chairman of the Academy of the Fine Arts, would not have seemed inequitable according to the rules of the

27. Horace Howard Furness, "Cornerstone Address," pencil MS, University of Pennsylvania Archives.
28. On nepotism, see Ernest Earnest, *Silas Weir Mitchell* (Philadelphia: University of Pennsylvania Press, 1950), 113. A contemporary example occurred in the competition for the cathedral of St. John the Divine in New York: Bishop Potter called for a "blind" competition of unsigned, coded entries. A few known architects such as McKim, Hunt, and Bishop Potter's brother, William A. Potter, were invited and paid a premium of $500.00 to participate. One of the four finalists was William A. Potter, who was asked to withdraw—which he did over many objections. See *The New York Times*, 17 May 1889, p. 8, col. 2 and 24 June 1889, p. 1, col. 6.

day. In the case of the University Library, the committee was initially instructed to research design solutions, prepare a program, retain an architect to draw up their studies, and finally hold a competition for the design; early in the project the committee reported that it had retained Mr. Frank Furness to assist them in their work and nothing more was said on the subject.

Similarly, although it could be claimed that skill alone won the Jewish Hospital commission (cat. 29), since it came to Furness's firm after the office had successfully completed Rodef Shalom Synagogue (cat. 15), it is equally probable that the job resulted from a close friendship between Furness's father and Rebecca Gratz, long time member of Rodef Shalom and a fervent admirer of Dr. Furness.[29] Furness designed houses for many of the synagogue's directors; the Jewish orphanage (cat. 596) of which Rebecca Gratz had been secretary; and the Mount Sinai Cemetery chapel (cat. 421), another Rodef Shalom project. Only when Jewish architects began to graduate from the University of Pennsylvania's architecture program in this century did Furness lose the Rodef Shalom work. Furness was equally well connected to the donors and backers of Philadelphia's Main Line institutions. He designed houses of many of the Main Line matrons who organized the benefits that paid for the Rosemont Hospital (cat. 482) and the Bryn Mawr Hospital (cat. 429). Such consistent repeat business suggests that Furness's clientele were devoted as much to his reform values as to his aesthetics.

Patronage at the Public Trough

If Furness was patronized by reformers, then one might assume that he would not receive commissions connected to the political machine, and, in fact, this was the case. Research makes the patterns of Philadelphia city patronage clear: Furness corralled the vast majority of commissions from private institutions and such quasi-public corporations as railroads, but he received only one city project before the battle lines of reform were clearly drawn—a hospital at the House of Corrections (cat. 26), when Daniel Fox was mayor.[30]

The year after Furness received this lone public commission, with a new mayor in office, the city hired the discredited Samuel Sloan (a sympathizer with the South in the Civil War) for a dozen police stations. Sloan was succeeded by James H. Windrim, first as architect for the machine-controlled Board of City Trusts and then as Director of Public Works. The latter position gave him direct control of the city patronage, much of which was managed

29. Research on Furness and the Jewish community was undertaken by University of Pennsylvania Urban Studies 272 student, Rachel Rubin: she noted *Letters of Rebecca Gratz*, ed. Rabbi David Phillipson (Philadelphia, 1929), 250.

30. The most informative tool for studying the city's architecture is a data base, prepared by the Clio Group, Inc. in Philadelphia, which is accessed by address, architect, and owner. It is derived from *The Philadelphia Real Estate Record and Builders' Guide, The Philadelphia Inquirer,* and other published sources. See Thomas, "Architectural Patronage."

by his son, John T. Windrim.[31] The elder Windrim handled the Girard College work for forty years (having graduated from that city-run institution it may be said that he regarded the City Trusts with almost filial piety); during the 1870s and 1880s he designed numerous fire stations and public works. When Windrim moved to Washington, D.C. as the Supervising Architect of the Treasury in the 1880s, W. Bleddyn Powell, the assistant on City Hall, became the city architect. Powell and Windrim were associated with North Philadelphia developers Peter Widener, William Elkins, and William Kemble, who had systematically looted municipal coffers in the 1870s and 1880s, making the city pay for streets and utilities to their developments. These same architects had been commissioned to plan the immense mansions for the ostentatious rich; Windrim designed the home of William Kemble, Powell the William Elkins house.[32] These stone-faced, palatial piles contrasted with the modest houses of elite Rittenhouse, which remained red brick long after the Victorian and Queen Anne had been supplanted by limestone-clad classicism in New York, Boston, Chicago, and Washington.

The contrast between Furness and the city patronage of the architects of the well-connected developer was obvious. Not only did he not receive municipal commissions, but his buildings for old Philadelphia families were visually distinct from those built for the nouveau-riche, emphasizing the social split. By 1900, the city regularized the graft system by hiring its own architect, Philip Johnson, the brother-in-law of Israel Durham, the boss of the Seventh Ward. He designed the home of Boss Vare on South Broad Street and provided plans for alterations to various mayors' houses as well as for every major city project until 1930.[33]

The Style of Reform—Architecture without Grace Notes

Furness's charitable commissions, constructed over thirty years, uniformly expressed the established Philadelphia prejudice against ostentatious display and contrasted with the false municipal grandeur that characterized Girard College and the new City Hall. The "honorific" display, typical of other cities and pleasing to the general public, was despised by proper Philadelphians who tolerated—even preferred—Furness's approach, in part because it was incomprehensible to the nouveau-riche. Furness achieved architectural character through varied forms, combinations of materials, and striking proportions that expressed function. His signature motifs, such as the flaring tops and clustering of chimneys, were ornamental in

31. The Windrim city connections can be gauged in Sandra Tatman and Roger Moss, *Biographical Dictionary of Philadelphia Architects* (Boston: G. K. Hall, 1983), 871–77.
32. For Powell, see Tatman and Moss, *Biographical*

Dictionary, 621–22.
33. This is not the current Cambridge/New York Philip Johnson, but an architect active 1899–1933. See Tatman and Moss, *Biographical Dictionary*, 418–21.

character but were acceptable by virtue of their necessity; his banding of materials, ostensibly selected for reasons of economy, had decorative effect.

Local red pressed brick or fieldstone, atypical in the 1880s and 1890s, linked Furness's designs to the earlier regional Quaker architecture. Like these older buildings, Furness's architecture was of true load-bearing masonry, not the thin marble revetments of the scandal-plagued City Hall. Literary evidence suggests that Furness's choice of red brick was widely understood as linking his buildings to the virtues of the city's history, recalling Lippard's "Quaker City" as a metaphor for Philadelphia's past glory and its independence from the national taste. A generation later, when S. Weir Mitchell wrote a historical novel about Philadelphia's era of greatness, he set the story in the 1790s, in Washington's second presidential term, and called it *The Red City*.[34]

Philadelphia, more than any other American city in the 1880s and 1890s, remained a red brick city. The material was not limited to residential construction, as in Boston's Back Bay and Washington, D.C.'s Massachusetts Avenue district. Instead, red brick clad the Quaker City's churches, libraries, hospitals, and even its clubs and buildings devoted to the arts, which in other cities had from an early date taken on classical garb. W. W. Lockington, a foreign-born critic for William Singerly's machine-oriented *Record* in the 1880s, sharply criticized the city because of its dark red buildings, terming Philadelphia the "most conservatively unarchitectural of the large American cities." Its few modern classical buildings, built mainly in North Philadelphia for Singerly's circle, were praised as "specks of light in a dark red ocean." He went on to claim "in its redness no other city resembles Philadelphia except to some extent Baltimore."[35] This critical position was probably intended as a slap against the Whig aesthetic opposed by Singerly's paper; in 1892, the same paper refused "on personal grounds" to publish a Furness design for an elevated railroad.[36]

34. The most direct connection between Whig nostalgia and the "red city" occurs at the end of this novel when Mitchell proudly recounts the survival into his own time of people who could claim that their lips had touched lips that had touched Washington's. Burt and Davies record Mitchell as a part of the "Mitchell-Furness circle." He, like H. H. Furness, was described as a "friend of Whitman" (511). The Whitman-Mitchell-Furness connection is one of the episodes in another remarkable novel: William C. Bullitt, *It's Not Done* (1926). It asks of Chesterbridge [Philadelphia], "is there any other city of a million in which everyone who counts lives in an area three streets by eight surrounding a Sacred Square?" (7) and states the values of the old aristocracy: "If the United States is to amount to anything, it will be because we make people accept our standards" (21). Its theme

was based on the fear that "America is falling more and more into the hands of middle class politicians and crooked businessmen" (50). The heroes are clearly Eakins and Whitman. The aesthetic disgust that turned the city towards the suburbs was stated as hostility to the automobile, which made everyone mobile. "These damned automobiles [are] driving out horses. Everybody in Chesterbridge [is] getting richer everyday and the city [is] becoming noisier, uglier, and sootier and smellier" (197); it concludes that you "can't mix gentlemen and anyone."

35. W. W. Lockington, "Philadelphia's Architecture," *Builder, Decorator and Woodworker* 5, no. 2 (October 1887): 17.

36. In the Allen Evans papers, Architectural Archives, University of Pennsylvania, is a letter to a photo-plate

The corollary to Furness's choice of plain materials in his charitable and institutional projects was the gradual reduction of the ornament he had learned at Hunt's studio, leading him toward the direct expression of function as the basis of design. Beginning with the Jewish Hospital (cat. 29) and the Deaf and Dumb additions (cat. 57), his institutional commissions stressed a concern for massing and manipulation of material that would later characterize his mature work. Raw redness, functional expression, and powerful proportions became his buildings' salient features. Despite contemporary criticism from outside Philadelphia, which attacked this use of material as *retardataire*, it would continue to wear surprisingly well in Furness's hometown. As late as 1892 Furness used red brick, red terra-cotta, red stone, and red tile for the grand entrance to the very heart of the city—Broad Street Station (cat. 430). The same color scheme would reappear in 1901 for the Arcade Building (cat. 535) erected across Market Street. In Philadelphia, Furness's course represented the virtues of economy and honesty. When in 1913 George Howe entered the Furness office as an employee, he reported that it was an "ancient and honorable office more noted for its probity than its artistic gifts."[37] In a corrupt city, this was a noble epitaph.

Commercial Clients in Finance and Industry

The explicit frugality of Furness's institutional buildings may have contrasted with his florid and expansive designs for the financial community, but these two approaches were opposite sides of the same coin. The flamboyance of commerce underscored the spartan simplicity of those institutions; each expressed hope for the growing modern city. In the financial industry, every bank was a separate entity and relied on strong visual identity to attract customers. Such a requirement was like a bugle blowing "Charge!" to a dragoon. A century before Robert Venturi rediscovered the "Bill-ding Board" architecture of the commercial strip, Furness's banks offered advertising, attracting attention even while under construction, as newspaper columnists provided blow-by-blow accounts of their idiosyncrasies and speculated on their final appearance. Between 1870 and 1900, Furness's remarkable ability to manipulate period forms, motifs, and materials brought him a banker's dozen of major financial and trust company buildings in Philadelphia and at least three banks outside the city limits, spanning the state from First National Bank of Montrose (cat. 311) to Farmers Deposit National Bank in Pittsburgh (cat. 296). James Windrim was the sole Furness contemporary to design more than half a dozen banks.

business recounting the allocation of an order of plates of a Furness design for an elevated railroad. The office apparently sent this around as a part of the press release for publication on 8 December 1892. Every paper in the city published the piece except for *The Record*.
37. Robert A. M. Stern, *George Howe* (New Haven: Yale University Press, 1975), 24, quotes Howe's *Harvard University, Class of 1908: Secretary's Fourth Report*.

Furness was obviously stimulated by the naked commercial aggression of the banking industry to produce many of his most daring works. These commissions can again be linked to his regular circle of clients. Mayor Daniel Fox, who had retained Furness to design the hospital for the House of Corrections, was the chairman of the board of the Northern Savings Fund Society (cat. 28), whose bank at Sixth and Spring Garden streets stood in the midst of the German community. One of its other board members was Gilles Dallett, president of the Penn National Bank (cat. 268); when he commissioned Furness to design his bank's new building at Seventh and Market streets, he sent his grandson, E. J. Dallett, to work in Furness's office as a draftsman.[38] At least one other young architect took the same route into the Furness office. Frank Price, son of James Price, the treasurer of the Provident Bank (cat. 86), entered the office around 1876 and left in 1881 to form a partnership with his brother, William, who had trained in the office of an earlier Provident architect, Addison Hutton. For the Provident president, Quaker Samuel Shipley, Furness also designed numerous additions to the first bank, including a ten story tower at the corner of Fourth and Chestnut streets (cat. 369), and a summer house, "Windon" (cat. 264) in West Chester.

Connections again worked to Furness's advantage in his dealings with the Centennial National Bank (cat. 81). Its president, Clarence H. Clark, was the son of another Unitarian congregation stalwart and transplanted New Englander, Enoch W. Clark. When the younger Clark converted to the more fashionable Episcopal church, he kept his early architectural commissions in the old circle, hiring Furness for the bank in 1876, a speculative row of houses on Spruce Street in 1878 (cat. 91), and probably for alterations on his own house at 42nd and Spruce streets (cat. 75).

Partners and Draftsmen—the Hiring of Clients

Furness was not the only office member capable of soliciting work. Hewitt, having succeeded John Notman, brought ecclesiastical and secular clients to the office. (Presumably the early Episcopal church projects, as well as several notable client families, came to the office through Notman and left with him when he withdrew in 1875.) One of Hewitt's clients was Travis Cochran, an officer of the Guarantee Trust and Safe Deposit Company (cat. 44), which had hired Furness's firm in 1873. A decade later Cochran retained Hewitt to design a house on 22nd Street amidst the great mansions across from St. James Episcopal Church. The church's lofty spire was designed by Hewitt in honor of Henry Gibson, another early client who passed from Notman to Hewitt. Hewitt designed Gibson's Scotch castle in Wynnewood in 1881.

38. Susan Begelman unraveled the history of the Penn National Bank for University of Pennsylvania Urban Studies 272, and turned up Francis J. Dallett, *The Genealogy of the Dallett Family* (Philadelphia: Innes and Sons, 1946).

Hewitt retained the Henry Houston commission after designing St. Peter's Church in Germantown (cat. 40). The Hewitts would later design other houses for Houston's family, speculative rows and offices, and a second church, St. Martin-in-the-Fields, near the family compound.

Furness also acquired a circle of clients through his careful selection of draftsmen. Most important among these was his future partner, Allen Evans. Allen's father, Edmund Cadwalder Evans, M.D., graduated from the University of Pennsylvania Medical School and was a contrary-minded states' rightist who resigned his Union League membership immediately after having been reinstated by a court order that had barred the club from terminating his membership based on his political beliefs. Evans acquired a large tract of land on Montgomery Avenue and hired his son's office to design a family house in 1874 (cat. 51). Other portions of the property were sold off to titans of late nineteenth-century industry who coveted its proximity to the Haverford Station. The most prominent of these, Alexander J. Cassatt, hired the office to design his suburban residence (cat. 36), and later commissioned alterations to Fairman Rogers's Rittenhouse Square home (cat. 364), which he purchased in 1888. During Cassatt's tenure as president of the Pennsylvania Railroad, Furness designed the new 32th Street Station (cat. 544) (since demolished and replaced by Graham, Anderson, Probst and White's station), the Wilmington Station (cat. 630), and numerous small suburban stations west to Pittsburgh and beyond. Even though it must have rankled Furness to lose the Pennsylvania Railroad's urban plums—the Pittsburgh Terminal to Burnham and New York's Pennsylvania Station to McKim, Mead & White—he was still the only American architect who could lay claim to the title of chief designer for three of the nation's great railroads.

The Evans connection brought in other commissions. In 1873, Evans became engaged to Rebecca Lewis (fig. 2.4), daughter of John T. Lewis, manufacturer of paints and member of the vestry of St. Peter's Episcopal Church, Robert Smith's eighteenth-century landmark at Third and Pine streets (cat. 63).[39] While Evans was a draftsman there, Samuel Sloan's office received the commission for St. Peter's Choir School; shortly after Evans moved to the Furness office the church commissions moved with him. Furness & Hewitt was given the task of restoring the church and designing its missionary chapel, the Church of the Holy Comforter (cat. 54), which was paid for by another branch of the Lewis family. Domestic commissions for many of the Lewises were interspersed with designs for their churches and clubs.

A similar but less extensive series of projects entered the office by way of another early draftsman, William Masters Camac. Like Evans, Camac belonged to an established Philadelphia family, graduated from the University of Pennsylvania's fledgling school of architecture,

39. The St. Peter's Episcopal Church parish contains numerous records of the Lewis family connection to the Church; the interior of the Church is ornamented with numerous memorial plaques to the Lewis family.

and entered the Furness office shortly after the Centennial. His father was President of the Zoological Society (cat. 67–69), and a member of the First City Troop (cat. 47). Camac drifts in and out of office records, but in the 1880s was associated with a cluster of important houses on Mount Desert Island in Maine, where he vacationed.

Camac's contacts in Maine may have brought the James Blaine houses in Washington, D.C. (cat. 399–401) to the office after he had supervised Blaine's vast "Stanwood," which overlooked the north Atlantic (cat. 314). A considerable coup for Furness, Blaine was a transplanted Pennsylvanian who became a Maine Congressman, served as Speaker of the U.S. House of Representatives (1869–75), later was elected a Senator, and was a strong Republican presidential contender in three elections.[40]

Fellow Warriors

The image of the brash and manly dragoon, whom Albert Kelsey recalled marching "down the street, with his shoulder squared, head erect and with a free swinging soldierly stride and a devil-may-care attitude,"[41] defined another side of Furness and attracted yet another group of clients. At every turn throughout his career, the bonds forged in the war between Furness and his fellow veterans remained strong, carrying him past what must have been crushing blows—the death of his father, the collapse of the political reform movement, and the rejection of his architectural values by his own city in the final onslaught of historicism and then Beaux-Arts classicism.

In the 1880s, Furness designed a powerful, tapering, rough-hewn, granite shaft surrounded by eight bronze lances and capped by permanently fluttering bronze pennants. The monument (cat. 353) celebrated the twenty-fifth anniversary of those days in July 1863 when the Sixth Pennsylvania Cavalry had played its vital role at Gettysburg. In the next decade, when Furness was finally forced to try his hand at the white classicism that had swept the nation, the efforts of his fellow veterans afforded him one last brief moment to shine as the architect of the 1899 "Avenue of Fame" (cat. 516) for the Grand Army of the Republic Encampment in Philadelphia. Using the plaster "staff" of Chicago's Columbian Exposition, Furness

40. A history of Blaine from Thomas Nast's bias can be found in Albert B. Paine, *Thomas Nast, His Period and His Pictures* (New York: Harpers, 1904), 62; Blaine's autobiography, *Twenty years of Congress*, vol. 2 (Norwich, CT: Henry Bill Publishing Co., 1884–86), was widely read in the period. Blaine's national image was as a reformer, hence his sobriquet—"the plumed knight." He lost the Republican presidential nomination by the barest of margins in 1876 to Hayes and again in 1880

to Garfield, who appointed him Secretary of State. In 1884 Blaine finally won the nomination, but lost the Presidency to Grover Cleveland largely because of the hostility of Thomas Nast's cartoons, which depicted him as an agent of special interests. His ill-advised remarks that the Democrats were the party of "Rum, Romanism and Rebellion" also hurt him at the polls.
41. "Men and Things," *Philadelphia Evening Bulletin*, 18 April 1924, p. 8, col. 5.

demonstrated his ability to brutally transform conventional Beaux-Arts classicism into an effective foil for the heroic J. J. Boyle figures of soldiers and sailors of the great war. With this project, Furness's career was ironically framed between his heroism as a soldier in 1863 and his position, thirty years later, as a relic of the war.

The simultaneous waning of Philadelphia's reform movement and Furness's career was appropriate, since both were products of the war. When Furness's contemporaries returned to their native city, their war experiences led them to battle the ills of society. After Furness had left Hunt's atelier and returned to Philadelphia, he joined some of his boyhood playmates, Thomas Hockley, William West Frazier, Charles Churchman, and John Lowber Welsh, in forming the Landis Independent Battery, Pennsylvania Artillery.[42] Hockley and Welsh stayed with the Battery; Frazier and Furness, joined by Henry Winsor, Jr., ended up in Rush's Lancers. Each served his full term and was distinguished for his heroism. Later, while advancing in business in Philadelphia, each had the opportunity to commission buildings. Invariably they chose Furness: in 1875 Thomas Hockley, by then an established lawyer, hired Furness to design his city house (cat. 65); five years later John Lowber Welsh commissioned a country house looking out over the Whitemarsh Valley north of Philadelphia (cat. 108); and Welsh's father also commissioned Furness to design alterations to an existing house (cat. 111A), construct a new carriage house, and a house for his daughter (cat. 109). It was probably not coincidental that John L. Welsh sold his father's city house at 1034 Spruce Street to another important Furness client, Samuel Shipley (cat. 390). William Winsor (a member of the Unitarian congregation whose daughter would marry Frank's nephew, Horace Howard Furness, Jr.), commissioned a country house in Lower Merion (cat. 345).

Each of those men remained close associates of Furness, but none equalled the devotion of William West Frazier, Jr. Frazier married the daughter of his father's partner and made an immense fortune in sugar refining, which he then turned to good use by supporting institutions ranging from the Episcopal Church to the University of Pennsylvania. Like fellow veteran Fairman Rogers, Frazier used his power to secure work for Furness. The first of these projects appeared in 1881 when Furness designed a spectacular triple-width, red brick, brownstone-trimmed mansion on the southeast corner of Rittenhouse Square (cat. 256). This was followed by a double house for Frazier's two sons (cat. 386A), a summer house in Maine (cat. 475), the Sailors Home (cat. 395), the Episcopal Church in Jenkintown (cat. 422) near his country house, various other church commissions, a day nursery named for his brother-in-law (cat. 503), and eventually a Jenkintown club where his cronies could attend lectures and shoot billiards (cat. 510).

42. Kelsey, ever Furness's promoter and champion, published Furness's "Avenue of Fame," *Architectural Annual* (Philadelphia: Architectural Annual, 1900): 234–37.

The architecture of these commissions, generally red brick, strongly formed, and with great signature chimneys, continued with only sight modification into the twentieth century. There was, however, one noticeable difference. As the last decade of the century progressed, more and more of Furness's commissions were erected outside the city, in its seductive and pleasant suburbs. There, the old warriors rode horses, relived battles that had made them crusaders, and turned away from the city that they had transformed a generation earlier. The reforms that had preoccupied these men were gradually overturned; soon the purpose and meaning of Furness's designs were forgotten as well. One by one their children hired architects versed in classicism and historicism. Only after World War II did another generation of soldier-reformers revive the commitment of elite Philadelphia to the urban center. It was the ultimate irony that, out of touch with their own history and guided by the revolutionary values of the International Style, in so doing they demolished the surviving fragments of Furness's now meaningless Red City, replacing it with the white architecture of modernism.

George E. Thomas

Originality, Responsibility, and Authorship

At one point in the early 1880s, Frank Furness's staff of five or six people was producing a building a week. Allowing for the simpler documents of those days and simple enough specifications—often no more than, "for the beam ends, give me your best detail"—the workload was still prodigious. Moreover, despite a common approach that sought to represent function, use materials for their constructive rather than aesthetic character, and transform contemporary and historical motifs into forms unique to the office—the work produced evokes a variety of underlying attitudes and personalities. While it is tempting to try to make Furness the star, crediting him with every muscular robust triumph while blaming his assistants for the more pedestrian projects, the truth probably lies elsewhere—in a method that gave Furness, George Hewitt, and, later, several design associates, control of major decisions while delegating the production work to a well-trained and efficient staff.

The basic directions of office principles dating from 1871 can be traced back to Furness's training in Hunt's office and Hewitt's training with John Notman. However, between 1867 and 1871, while John Fraser was the first named partner, the situation was somewhat different. Though Fraser had already received numerous important commissions, including the Roman classical refacing of Robert Smith's Old Pine Presbyterian Church and the red brick and brownstone Second Empire Union League, it is hard to distinguish his work from pattern-book architecture of the day. There was a political side to Fraser: he was working for the city as a school architect immediately after the war, and he was visiting Washington seeking government commissions at the moment when he was unceremoniously dropped by his younger partners. Given the reform clientele of Furness's office in the 1870s and 1880s, Fraser's politics may have been a source of friction. In any event, he left no discernable mark on the office's early work. Apart from having taught Furness the use of the instruments, and his presumed acquaintance with Fairman Rogers (through the Union League), Fraser's connection with Furness & Hewitt was one of convenience, not of intellectual or artistic compatibility. It is presumably no coincidence that the office's mature style, which made it unique in American architecture, was only established after Fraser left.[1]

After 1871 the office began producing the work that is typically identified with the Furness personality. Early articles and even James O'Gorman's 1973 essay presume that most, if not all, original designs were by Furness, not his various partners. Few of the drawings are signed or initialled; still, a considerable body of information can be brought to bear on the question of authorship. This includes lists of projects in the Furness sketchbooks, as well as the evidence of the sketchbooks themselves, which presumably represent projects that Furness supervised. These materials are augmented by a list of buildings from the Hewitt office, various subsequent references to project architects in the *Builders' Guide*, correspondence from clients, and institutional histories. Although the evidence gleaned from these documents is often circumstantial, still it does provide insight into office methods and helps establish responsibility for particular designs, perhaps reflecting Sullivan's account of a guildlike manner of working—the assistants laying out designs, along established office principles, for criticism by the principals.

Sullivan's Account

The most illuminating document on the Furness & Hewitt practice is the well-known account written by Louis Sullivan (see text beginning on page 357). Of his six-month tenure in the office, Sullivan presents a clear dichotomy—George Hewitt described as doing "Victorian Gothic in its pantalettes, when a church building or something of that sort was on the boards," working from "English current magazines and other English sources" and Furness, on the other hand, described as a hero who "made buildings out of his head."[2] Scholars have had no difficulty disproving the second claim, citing numerous examples of sources that influenced Furness ranging from Viollet-le-Duc's designs in *Lectures on Architecture*

1. The Fraser bibliography includes Michael J. Lewis, "John Fraser, A.I.A.," in James F. O'Gorman et al., *Drawing Toward Building: Philadelphia Architectural Graphics 1732–1986* (Philadelphia: University of Pennsylvania Press, 1986), 128; Sandra Tatman and Roger Moss, *Biographical Dictionary of Philadelphia Architects* (Boston: G. K. Hall, 1983), 281–82; and an unpublished paper by Richard Derman, "John Fraser, 19th Century Architect" (Philadelphia: University of Pennsylvania, 1972). Fraser served as acting supervisory architect for the Treasury when he moved to Washington in 1871;

though he continued to maintain a residence at Riverton, NJ, he did not return to Philadelphia until the 1890s.

2. Louis H. Sullivan, *The Autobiography of an Idea* (1924; reprint, New York: Dover Publications, 1956), 193. For Hewitt's biography, see George E. Thomas, "G. W. and W. D. Hewitt," in O'Gorman et al., *Drawing Toward Building*, 155; "G. W. and W. D. Hewitt," *Philadelphia and Popular Philadelphians* (Philadelphia: North American, 1891), 223–24; Tatman and Moss, *Biographical Dictionary*, 367–75.

and Labrouste's *néo grec*, (presumably via Hunt), to the conventions of English Victorian Gothic.[3] It is generally overlooked, however, that Sullivan accorded both men roles as designers. This characterization is fundamentally accurate but worth some elaboration. Hewitt's work, skilled and handsome as it was, remained, with few exceptions, conventional. By contrast, Furness's work was invariably unconventional in proportion, color, and detail.

Attribution based on style is not, however, a cut and dried affair. It has been assumed that Furness authored the more Hunt- or French-influenced schemes while Hewitt designed the less interesting anglicizing buildings and the churches. Their post-partnership work seems to bear out this split, despite the fact that by the mid 1870s Furness had moved away from direct quotations of Hunt and French sources, and Hewitt had designed projects, such as the late 1870s Girard Bank on West Chestnut Street, that would fool historians like Vincent Scully.

In his ability to recall fine points regarding the office after half a century, Sullivan's memory may have been prompted by his long-standing friend, Albert Kelsey. Kelsey had studied in the Furness office during the 1890s and was, by his own admission, an admirer of Furness. As the president of the Architectural League, he also knew and admired Sullivan, and during a brief editorship of the *Architectural Annual* published Sullivan's designs, compared him to other architects of merit, and celebrated him as an American genius even before Sullivan had acquired this sense of himself.[4] Kelsey also included Furness in these publications, listing him as a creative American giant, second only to Sullivan and ahead of Stanford White, Frank Lloyd Wright, John Calvin Stevens, and Robert Spencer.[5] It was Kelsey who championed Furness the day after Sullivan's *Autobiography of an Idea* was reviewed in Philadelphia. Sullivan and Kelsey's friendship lasted thirty years, and Furness was probably a regular topic of conversation.

Contemporary Documents

The principal early document supporting Sullivan's recollections about the office is a page from Furness's sketchbook. His square vertical script lists eighteen or twenty names, most of which can be identified with a specific project executed before the partnership split in 1875

3. For the sources of Frank Furness, see James F. O'Gorman, *The Architecture of Frank Furness* (Philadelphia: Philadelphia Museum of Art, 1973); see also David Van Zanten et al., "Sullivan to 1890," *Louis Sullivan, The Function of Ornament*, ed. Wim de Wit (New York: W. W. Norton, 1986), 19–33.

4. Albert Kelsey, ed., *The Architectural Annual* (Philadelphia: The Architectural Annual, 1900; 1901). The 1900 journal published Sullivan's address to The Architectural League, "The Modern Phase of Architecture" (27), which calls for architects to be not artists, but poets; the frontispiece for 1901 is a portrait of Louis Sullivan, which is followed by two pieces on Sullivan.

5. The list of giants is included in an editorial by Kelsey, "The So-Called Architects," *Architectural Annual* (1901): 14. It lists as "talented and proficient architects . . . Messrs. Sullivan, Furnace [sic], Eyre, White, Wright, Codman, Stevens, and Spencer."

(fig. 3.1).[6] These names are followed by numbers, which probably represent fees, and then by an "H" or "F." The initials presumably denote responsibility, although whether they specify the designer or the link to the client is unclear. Hastily written, the names are often difficult to decipher, but the fee notations help clarify any confusion. (The numbers in parentheses refer to the catalogue listing in this volume.) The list reads: Deaf & Dumb 850 F (cat. 57); Titan Church 700 H (cat. 54); St. Luke 300 F (cat. 59); B & A Church 700 H (cat. 22); St. Peters 150 F (cat. 63); F. Rogers 300 [crossed out and 500 appears elsewhere] F (cat. 34); Hockley 300 F (cat. 65); Churchman 272 F (cat. 74); Judge Hair [Hare] 300 F (cat. 49); Elephant 412 F (cat. 69); Moore 900 F (cat. 32); Bache 75 F; H. Brooks 100 F; E. Brooks 200 F (cat. 72); Kingston 183 H (cat. 73); Organ Front 30 F; Catherwood 50 H (cat. 55); Restaurant 50 (cat. 68). Elsewhere on the same page, the name Clark 75, and Lxxx 50 appear. Noteworthy by their absence are the early commissions—the Holy Apostles Episcopal Church (cat. 13), the Pennsylvania Academy of the Fine Arts (cat. 27), the McKean houses (cat. 16 and 17), and so on—suggesting, and confirmed by research, that this list refers to office work dating from around 1874–75. Even if it does not answer the question of authorship of the Academy of the Fine Arts, the Guarantee Trust (cat. 44), the Union Bank (cat. 43) and other early works, the sketchbook account offers insight to the office immediately prior to the dissolution of the partnership.

The list seems to corroborate Sullivan's claim that Hewitt was designing Victorian Gothic Churches "in pantalettes"— an astute description of both the Holy Comforter Episcopal Church (cat. 54) at 19th and Titan streets, with its roof-skirted spires, and the Lutheran Church of the Holy Communion at Broad and Arch streets. It is therefore surprising to find Furness listed as the architect of St. Peter's, especially since the church history of another St. Peter's (cat. 40), in Germantown, lists Hewitt as the architect of record. More likely, the notation refers to a job of 1873–74, when the firm was working on repairs and a heating system for St. Peter's (cat. 63) at Third and Pine streets. In addition, the Furness list seems to indicate that the architects worked for clients acquired through family connections—Hewitt for the Catherwoods (cat. 55), linked to his Gibson circle, and Furness for his in-law, Fairman Rogers (cat. 34, 35A), his fellow veteran, Thomas Hockley (cat. 65), and the Unitarian, Bloomfield Moore (cat. 32). The latter connection supports Sullivan's contention that the Moore house was the work of one man.

Furness's sketchbooks provide additional clues in the little sketches executed for his projects. Sections and plans of the Elephant House at the Philadelphia Zoo confirm that the *F* next to the project designated the designer. By contrast, the similarity of the Catherwood

6. The list is included in a sketchbook that was in the possession of George Wood Furness in 1973, when it was photographed.

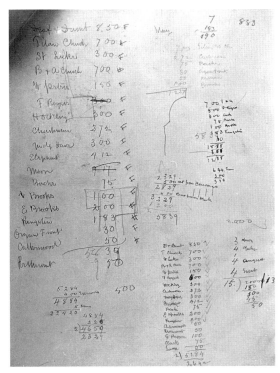

3.1. List of projects by Furness and Hewitt, 1875.

3.2. Frank Furness, study for interlocking rubber tiles, c. 1890, pencil in sketchbook

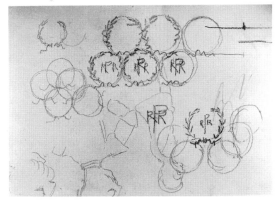

3.3. Frank Furness, studies for Pennsylvania Railroad insignia, c. 1892, pencil in sketchbook

facade to the Sibley house (cat. 60A) around the corner confirms Hewitt's role. The list was perhaps one-sided, more salt in the wounds of a hostile split. This page presumably marks Furness's attempt to prove that he had brought in and done more work and hence deserved a larger share of the office profits. Useful as they are, the sketchbooks record only projects dating from before 1875. Occasional detail studies, interlocking rubber floor tile patterns (fig. 3.2), an 1890s insignia for the Pennsylvania Railroad (fig. 3.3), and other fragmentary images from the eighties and nineties suggest that, in later years, Furness carried his notebooks only at odd moments. He either stopped using the sketchbook method as the office grew larger or his later books have not survived.

The Hewitt Evidence

No sketchbooks and few renderings by Hewitt have been found. However, a significant document survives from Hewitt, Granger and Paist, twentieth-century successors to George Hewitt's office. It is an undated list, arranged alphabetically according to building type, on Hewitt, Granger and Paist's stationery.[7] Surprisingly, it lists numerous projects from the era of the Furness & Hewitt partnership, including the Pennsylvania Academy of the Fine Arts, the Guarantee Trust, the Northern Savings Fund, the Centennial Bank (accurately listed as being in West Philadelphia) as well as names associated with residential commissions, including at least one (Catherwood) that overlaps with an "H" on the Furness document. The list also includes names such as Sibley, the name of an owner of an attributed house on Rittenhouse Square, and C. H. Clark of "W. Phila.," perhaps the Clark of the Furness sketchbook. Numbers after the names range from the 700s to the high 1200s, with most of the documented early commissions having lower figures. While the alphabetical ordering precludes accurate dating, those entries with last names alone and no address may signal early buildings, while entries including location, first names, and some details perhaps reflect later commissions within the memory of the list's compiler. The document may have been initially an inventory of architectural drawings in the office, with the numbering system referring to their location.

More puzzling is the inclusion on the list of the Academy, the Guarantee Trust, and the Northern Savings Fund, conventionally assumed as either shared projects between Furness & Hewitt or the work of Furness alone. As suggested in the previous chapter, Travis Cochran, for whom Hewitt designed a house on 22nd Street in 1882, may have been the contact for the Guarantee. If the commission did indeed come through Hewitt, he certainly would have

7. The list is included in the Hewitt work files at the Athenaeum of Philadelphia. Though it was published in Tatman and Moss's, *Biographical Dictionary*, the list's form—originally organized by building groups and with numbers—was ignored, thus losing most of its value as a historic document.

retained its drawings and documents. Similarly, perhaps Hewitt's client, Henry Gibson (the Gibson house is cat. 24A) was one of the prime movers on the Pennsylvania Academy of the Fine Arts; and Hewitt, listed by the Holy Communion congregation as its architect, may have been the connection to church board member Daniel Fox, who was on board of the Northern Savings Fund. If this was the case, then apparently work was not always parceled out to the staff member who brought in the project, but rather was divided by interest and inclination, with some percentage of the fee perhaps reserved for snaring the client. Still Furness's *F*s outnumbered *H*s fifteen to four, hinting that Hewitt's line of clients, based on Notman, was drying up, while Furness continued to receive work through the Unitarian-soldier-reform line. Alternatively, Hewitt may have kept copies of shared projects for later use. We know nothing of the Furness holdings because no similar list has ever appeared. Barring the discovery of a list by either architect of their specific works, or the testimony of the dissolution of their partnership, the historical evidence of Sullivan and the Furness list will have to suffice: it corroborates the character of both architects' later work and confirms their earlier course of study.

1876–1881: Furness's Own Practice and the Evolution of Allen Evans

Between 1876 and 1881, Furness's name was alone on the masthead, even though numerous young architects had begun passing through his office. These included Allen Evans (1872–1923), Louis Sullivan (1873), Paul Beck (c. 1873–75, later with McKim, Mead & White), William M. Camac (c. 1875–1895), Edward Hazelhurst (c. 1875–77), Lindley Johnson, and Frank Price (c. 1877–1880).[8] Apart from Camac's monogram on the Provident engraving and a few bits of correspondence, all evidence points to Furness as principal designer for every major project in this period, with the notable exception of a cluster of commissions by Allen Evans.

Evans's projects include his father's house (cat. 51), his brother's (cat. 116), and a rental house, "The Breezes" (cat. 98), which he and his brother jointly built. By the early 1880s, Evans was credited in various documents for the house of his wife's brother-in-law, Thomas DeWitt Cuyler (cat. 284), his father-in-law's country house (cat. 107), and a grammar school for Haverford College (cat. 301).[9] It is noteworthy that Evans initially designed primarily for

8. There is no one single list of the various members of the office. Several useful tools have appeared, the most important being the A.I.A. Archives in Washington, which contain the membership applications on which are listed prior work experience; much of this has been recorded in Tatman and Moss's, *Biographical Dictionary*. More arcane bits can be found in Charles J. Cohen, *Memoir of Reverend John Wiley Faires* (Philadelphia,

1926), which includes biographies of Paul Beck (59) and Edward Hazelhurst (365).

9. The most useful document is the family biography of the Evans family, in the possession of the family, (Evans MS, 62). It compiles diary notes, pieces of letters, and other material, making it a significant tool for studying Evans and his career. Parallel sources include the archives of Haverford College, particularly the Minutes of the

his family, or for family property in Haverford, and that his projects have a common palette of simple materials—typically, shingles above fieldstone. Those materials were shaped into an array of small volumes, with each piece defined by roof forms that were assembled into a larger whole. The stylistic evidence of those buildings suggests that Evans may have handled many of the country houses of this period, including the Griscom house near his family compound (cat. 253), the Hare country house (cat. 110), and the Shipley's "Windon" (cat. 264).

Evans's characteristic "anti-monumental" approach to the small-scaled country houses also appears in at least three urban projects—two houses on South 13th Street, one for his father-in-law (cat. 272) and the other for his wife's brother-in-law, Edward S. Beale (cat. 273), and his own house and row on South 21st Street (cat. 280). These are similar to the country houses in their assembled character, jerkinheads, and assertive dormers. Compositional parallels with the Seamen's Church (cat. 96) suggest that it was designed by the same hand. Whether the projects describe a variant of the Furness method or an independently developed functional expressionism is not clear; Evans's earlier training with Sloan may have provided a more discursive and fragmented approach than Furness's formal synthetic method. Perhaps Furness recognized that Evans's antiheroic counterpoint was appropriate for certain projects and assigned work accordingly. Nonetheless, Evans's work is closely related to, albeit less daring than, Furness's expressionism.

While Evans was establishing his own design personality, Furness was moving away from his early dependence on classical forms, as in the Kensington Bank (cat. 89), toward the more sculptural and abstract sensibility seen in projects such as the National Bank of the Republic (cat. 281) and the Kempton house on Walnut Street (cat. 282), the railroad terminals of the mid-1880s, and finally the University Library (cat. 370). Certainly from the 1870s into the mid-1880s, Furness would have designed most of the best commissions—great city houses like the Preston (cat. 257), Frazier (cat. 256) and Scott (cat. 343) mansions, and the First Unitarian Church (cat. 285), as well as the decorative scheme for St. Michael's Church in Birdsboro (cat. 323), whose history lists a "Frank Furniss" (the characteristic phonetic misspelling) of Philadelphia as the designer. It is likely that Furness also produced the initial designs for the numerous suburban railroad stations for the Philadelphia and Reading Railroads (cat. 121-247), leaving junior draftsmen to work out second and third variations.

The tendency for groups of projects to look alike probably reflected the working method of the office, which frequently adapted a previously studied building type to other settings. This is most clearly seen in the case of railroad stations, with their themes of square towers, half round towers, or no towers at all. The same thematic approach marks the suburban houses. The cubic mass of the Earl house, "Earlham" (cat. 113), was modified for the Physick

Board of Overseers in the 1880s, which report various phases of the Haverford Grammar School. See also

Tatman and Moss, *Biographical Dictionary*, 249.

house (cat. 104A) by slightly shifting side rooms back on the east and forward on the west; the center hall plan, flanked by stacks of rooms, was modified again for the Rhawn house of 1880 (cat. 114), where one single room on the parlor side was surrounded by the great U-shaped porch, which supported a great pyramidal roof. Similarly, the rough fieldstone wall capped by a brick cornice of the Veterinary Hospital (cat. 283) was adapted to the Reading High School (cat. 266), and was reused with modifications on the facade of the Consumptives Home (cat. 299). Motifs, from fireplaces and stair newels to overscaled belt courses and top-heavy chimneys, spanned decades as if they had a life of their own, that, genielike, could be called forth as required to enliven a design. The ability of the architectural office to reuse motifs made drawings some of Furness's most important tools, and made it worth his while to lash immense care on individual details.

The banks and major urban buildings, by contrast, only appeared once, perhaps because their advertising value would be diminished by repetition. As Michael Lewis demonstrates in his discussion of Furness's contemporaries in this book, although Furness was frequently paid the tribute of imitation, even his copyists avoided duplicating his work on the same block. Furness was proud of the "honor," as demonstrated in a letter he wrote to the president of the Reading stating that the Pennsylvania Railroad architects had copied his suburban station designs:

> Surely it is with pardonable pride that I refer to the economical way in which the stations, buildings, and cars, have been built and altered under my supervision, whereby the Reading Railroad Company stands confessedly second to none in those particulars.
>
> In proof of this I would cite the fact that the new stations on the Pennsylvania Railroad are close copies both in plan, constructition and detail, of those which have been erected by the Reading Railroad Company.[10]

The Enlarging Office, 1881–1886

The easy working relationship between Furness and Evans was tested by a flood of work beginning in the early 1880s. It was resolved by hiring the first group of academically trained draftsmen, despite Furness's expressed contempt for schooling. The most notable of these were Louis C. Baker and Elijah J. Dallett, who, after eight years of training and partnership, left to form their own office in 1889. Their presence soon shifted the office from its sole dependence on Furness for design toward a broader accommodation of contemporary style: it was then that the Queen Anne made its first inroads, perhaps because it shared the redness that had become the office's badge of honor. Houses such as that for J. Dundas Lippincott (cat. 269A), a Princeton schoolmate of Baker, reflected some of this change; but, in the main, a draftsman either accepted the Furness method or left.

Despite the consistency of his method, Furness's works varied in function, scale, and approach. Office projects ranged from tight, monumental, urban banks to the University of

Pennsylvania Veterinary Hospital and the University Library, with their descriptive forms. Very possibly some of these schemes represent the work of different hands, particularly the young architects who were made associates in the office in 1886: William M. Camac, James Fassitt, Louis C. Baker, and E. James Dallett. Certainly, however, these designers had little influence until they had been in the office for a few years. By the mid-1880s, projects by the assistants can often be spotted as heavy-handed variations of Furness's work, incorporating motifs from previous projects and overscaling elements to the point of parody. Several houses between West Chester and Wilmington, such as the Chalfont mansion in Kennett Square (cat. 292A) and the Trump house outside of Wilmington (cat. 293), show these tendencies. The latter was listed in an 1891 publication as the work of Baker and Dallett, but like several other buildings on the list, it was actually done during their tenure in the Furness office.[11] Generally those draftsmen who were most interested in design soon left to establish their own firms, as did Baker and Dallett in 1889, and Joseph Huston in 1895.

Cases of imitation within the office were not limited to junior members. Furness himself directed the reuse of the earlier motifs on dissimilar projects: the gap-toothed belt course of the Penn National Bank (cat. 268) reappeared on the Livingston house (cat. 352), and the half arch of the National Bank of the Republic (cat. 281) entrance resurfaced on the Kempton house (cat. 282). The office did not loot history, but, like other modern firms, it did develop a lasting vocabulary of its own forms.

The Large Office, 1886–1895

It becomes increasingly difficult to assign responsibility within the office after 1886, when a number of the staff were made associates. Even though *The Philadelphia Real Estate Record and Builders' Guide* frequently listed the individual in charge, it is unclear whether that citation represented design supervision or merely an office contact for bidding information. For example, L. C. Baker was listed as supervising the Breslin Hotel (cat. 319) and the Latta Crabtree house (cat. 320) in northern New Jersey, although they have little in common as designs, while William M. Camac was in charge of all of the Maine work, probably because he summered there and knew the clients and builders. The variations between the Flemish bond, colonial revival, octagonal plan library in New Castle (cat. 396), the austere Episcopal mission chapel of St. Michael and All the Angels (cat. 379), and the cacophonous

10. Frank Furness to John Wooten, 1884, collection of Historical Society of Pennsylvania.

11. "Baker and Dallett," *Philadelphia and Popular Philadelphians* (Philadelphia: The North American, 1891), 222–23. It is more than likely that other projects in their list were done during their Furness years or reflected contacts made while they were in the office. Two stables for the Fox family are perhaps two such projects.

composition of the Blaine house (cat. 314) in Maine, each listed as having Camac in charge, suggests he may have been merely the contact and not the designer. Without detailed office records the question is difficult, if not impossible, to resolve.

Two other draftsmen entered the Furness office in the mid-1880s, Cornell-trained George W. Casey and Herman Kleinfelder. They would remain for the next half century, continuing the practice first with Allen Evans under the original name and finally under Casey and Kleinfelder. Only rarely were they listed as being in charge of a project, and they never established an identity separate from Furness or Evans. Henry Muhlenberg was another in this category who remained in the office in the mid- to late 1880s; perhaps he arrived when the office was working in Reading, his home city, where he would later establish his own practice. Muhlenberg's family was the source of the photograph entitled "The Second Story Gang" (fig. 3.4), which apparently represented the junior draftsmen. Its title suggests that the office contained two levels, with the junior staff relegated to the attic. At the same time, a host of young socially connected architects, many from the University of Pennsylvania's school of architecture, used the office as a sort of finishing school: John Stewardson, Herman L. Duhring, Albert Kelsey, John I. Bright, Evans's nephew Edmund Evans, Charles Willing, Joseph Sims, James Talbutt and, in 1913, Harvard-trained George Howe.[12]

After 1905, talented young designers were quickly offered part-ownership in the firm; this practice was a means of perpetuating the office at a time when aging senior partners did little more than hold on to old clients. Charles Willing remained with the office under these terms, marking its transition toward the colonial revival that characterized Willing's later practice. Willing co-authored a handsome book on colonial revival architecture of Philadelphia with Sims, and the two left with several associates to form the office of Willing, Sims and Talbutt. Howe, hired in 1913, was offered a partnership at the Furness office at the end of his first year "with the avowed intention of infusing new life into its outworn Victorian traditions." He left three years later.

Decline and Transition, 1895–1912

Furness gradually reduced his workload as he lost interest in turn-of-the-century design, and as his community of reformers began to retire. With his income from the firm tied directly to his personal productivity, Furness was forced at one point to sue his partner Evans over the allocation of fees from the Girard Bank (cat. 590) commission. The project marked a low point. Furness's specific style was rejected by Effingham B. Morris, president of the bank,

12. Later architectural graduates are listed in *General Alumni Catalogue of the University of Pennsylvania* (Philadel-phia, 1917); for Howe see Robert A. M. Stern, *George Howe* (New Haven: Yale University Press, 1975), 24–30.

3.4. *"2nd Floor Gang," c. 1890*

3.5. *Frank Furness, c. 1900*

who wrote to Evans, stating bluntly, "My interest is in you and not in your firm, for while I have the highest respect and esteem for Mr. Furness we do not wish a building design on his well known lines." According to his deposition, Furness marched into Morris's office and poignantly stated his abilities in a manner that might have described a vaudeville act, but very different from his self-confident assertions of the previous decade. "I told him what I had heard. I stated to him that I was more or less of a variety artist and that my only aim in the practice of my profession had been to carry out, to the best of my ability the wishes of my clients."[13] The suit recounted how Furness laid out the plan and general scheme and then turned it over to Evans and McKim, Mead & White, who concealed Furness's role from the bank board. It was a disheartening end for an old reformer.

Through the last decade of his life, Furness's proportion of profit fell off sharply and by 1909 he was receiving a third of Evans's dividend and even less than the chief of the drafting room, George W. Casey.[14] In 1911, Herman Kleinfelder had taken over third place and Furness had nearly fallen behind draftsman Charles Willing; in 1912, with the fees of the Morris building pushing office receipts to $53,000, Furness received less than five percent of Evans's remuneration. Fortunately, he had developed another source of income; the sales of interlocking rubber tile patents were producing as much as a quarter of his annual income by the late 1890s.

Despite Furness's diminishing involvement in the office, the Girard Bank *parti*, with its low mass entered through a screen of columns, and opened through another column screen into a dazzling, skylit, sail-vaulted room that contrasted with the exterior hemispherical dome, recalled the old Furness inventiveness in a new classical garb. Some perverse variations on classicism dot the last generation of the office, including the calculated asymmetry of the Franklin Building (cat. 463), with atlantids by Karl Bitter, (the associated sculptor of the red Broad Street Station), holding up an off-center balcony. The Lippincott, Johnson Building (cat. 425), with its story-high voussoirs arrayed across the top of a six-story building, displayed a similar Furnessic wit about the conventions of classicism. Had Furness wished to adapt to changing taste as Hunt, Post, Van Brunt, and Ware each did several times, he certainly had the training and the daring to make turn-of-the-century architecture visually engaging and demanding. But, to Furness, architecture was not merely aesthetic play; rather it was a battleground where morality confronted indifference. When that battle ended for his generation around 1900, Furness retired to his dogs, his hunting, and his fishing, leaving the

13. Frank Furness, affidavit filed 17 June 1905 which recounts the letter of 16 June 1904 from Effingham B. Morris to Allen Evans. See George E. Thomas, "Masterpieces of Finance, the Banks of Frank Furness," promotional flyer for Mellon Bank exhibition (Phila-delphia, 1986).

14. Incomplete financial records of the office from 1907 until the mid-1920s survive with descendants of the Evans family, who kindly made them available to me.

office to assistants who bent to changing tastes (fig. 3.5). From that point on, the office lacked the clear internal direction that had typified it during the nearly forty years when it existed as the vehicle for Furness's individual expression. The time was past when each project manifested a viscerally powerful visual identity; never again would the work of the office be so visually identifiable, exhibiting the strength of the highly personal signature elements of a Frank Furness design.

Jeffrey A. Cohen

Styles and Motives in the Architecture of Frank Furness

In 1885 a now familiar image of the stylistic persona of Frank Furness was already afoot. A commentator in a local newspaper made note of the architect's recently completed National Bank of the Republic (cat. 281). "It was erected by Frank Furness," he wrote, "and as there is no particular period or class to which it can be said to belong, local architects call it 'Furnessque.' "[1]

Few who have encountered the architecture of Frank Furness since then have not entertained such a notion—received or perceived—of the individualism and vigor of his designs. In fact, for many less familiar with the works of Furness's contemporaries, there is a tendency to attribute to his prodigality much of the forcefulness of High Victorian design that many architects of the era shared. To those who have reflected upon buildings from the two decades after the Civil War by E. T. Potter, R. M. Hunt, Vaux & Withers, and even H. H. Richardson, however, it is clear that many of the forceful aspects of Furness's work are also found in the work of his American peers. Further, despite the local grounding and the Americanism that writers have attributed to Furness, there are clearly important characteristics that his work shares with that of Englishmen G. E. Street and William Butterfield, for example, or of Frenchmen E. E. Viollet-le-Duc and Henri Labrouste.

Furness was a Victorian architect. He was undoubtedly attuned to the architectural dialogue swirling around him in the late nineteenth century, and was responsive to some of the same spurs toward change felt by others. He held a great deal in common with his peers and with his era generally. Much of this commonality of thought and intent was expressed, affirmed, and embraced in Furness's recourse to known formal languages, to shared styles. If Furness has long appeared to have blazed his own path, that path branched off a better-traveled road.

Yet if at first Furness seems a quintessential High Victorian, in the leading part of the mainstream, on better acquaintance he seems an exception, someone set apart even from those among his contemporaries with whom he most closely shared elements of a formal language. This essay will explore the issue of the shared versus the exceptional in his work, and will seek some of the roots of each: it will examine the means he devised in his departure from his peers, describe patterns of evolution in his work, and speculate on his goals and intentions.

Knowing Furness

Apart from our intuitive appreciations, we have relatively little direct knowledge of Furness's intent in his designs. Our knowledge of him suffers from his having been rather tight-lipped toward posterity, despite his family's literary bent. He did write two pieces that allow us a glimpse of his experience and his orientation—a popular article giving "Hints to Designers" in 1878, and a recollection of his teacher Richard Morris Hunt apparently written in the mid-1890s[2]—but for the most part we are left to our own devices when trying to peer into the mind that created such visually provocative buildings. These buildings still provoke strong and immediate responses, often probably those anticipated by Furness, intent as he seems to have been on a kind of universal empathy. Our own modern responses might bring insight, but this insight is qualified by the degree to which we share with the architect's intended audience certain sensibilities that have not changed—or to which we have returned in this eclectic age. Our responses inform history to the extent that they depend on something connected with elemental human reactions and on a common cultural vocabulary that our time shares with his.

Beyond this and his few words, our best cues to Furness's understanding of his work probably lie in connections his biography draws between him and his more verbal peers. Good informants are rare, but two sources throw a special light on the subject. The first is a Philadelphia architect who was a near contemporary, Henry A. Sims. Sims described the architectural scene into which he and Furness stepped shortly after the Civil War. The second is Henry Van Brunt, one of Furness's fellow students in Richard Morris Hunt's studio. He recalled the lessons imparted there, and his words help account for some of the important, distinctive characteristics that certain works by Hunt and by his students share with early

1. "Buildings of Beauty," *The Press* (Philadelphia), 24 May 1885, 10.
2. Frank Furness, "Hints to Designers," *Lippincott's Magazine* 21 (May 1878): 612–14; Frank Furness, "A Few Personal Reminiscences of His Old Teacher by One of His Old Pupils," edited TS with pencil alterations for Memorial to Richard Morris Hunt (1895), 28pp., collection of George Wood Furness.

works by Furness. Van Brunt's words offer an approximation of, and a proxy for, some of Furness's ideas, just as Sims aptly portrays some of the stylistic alternatives that presented themselves to Furness.

Henry A. Sims and Styles in the 1870s

Henry Augustus Sims (1832–75) was seven years Furness's senior and came from quite a different professional and familial background, but he opened his architectural office in Philadelphia at about the same time Furness began his independent career in the mid-1860s. Sims is particularly helpful to us because he, almost alone among Philadelphia architects of this generation, left a written legacy about style.

Sims discussed his views on style with unusual clarity in an article titled "Architectural Fashions" that appeared posthumously in the *Penn Monthly* in September 1876. He pointed out two dominant stylistic languages—a modern classical one advanced by French architects and a modern Gothic one advanced by English architects. Of the first of these two styles, the *néo grec*, he remarked:

> it was not the production of one man, as nothing praiseworthy as a novelty ever was or ever will be, but was the result of the labors and studies of a whole generation of French architects and workmen laboring to the same end.[3]

Sims looked forward to the result of a search for an appropriate formal language for iron, but he expressed a certain disdain for most other work that looked outside these two European styles or that represented a more individualistic approach. "To be capable of producing what is really good," he wrote, the architect had to "confine himself to one school" and be "thoroughly imbued" with the fundamentals and spirit behind one of "two styles as essentially different as the Greek and Gothic as they now stand."

Sims's published words and his known works—most notably his Second Presbyterian Church in Philadelphia (1869–72; fig. 4.1)—attest to his own preference for the modern Gothic, particularly as practiced in England (he mentioned William Burges, G. E. Street, E. W. Godwin, and G. G. Scott, but he also included E. E. Viollet-le-Duc of France and Frederick Schmidt of Vienna in his list of six of the principal proponents of the style). He felt that the *néo grec*, by contrast, lacked "chiaro oscuro." It needed "the heavy vertical shadows of the thirteenth century" and other features "to interfere with the flatness of its mouldings on wall surfaces," and to add "more picturesqueness in its sky-lines than is usually seen." For Americans the attractions of the *néo grec* were too "intellectual, severe, and refined," too "Latin" to compete with the "Teutonic" attractions of the Gothic, a style whose virtues were "strikingly apparent to every beholder."[4]

In addition to setting the stage on which he and Furness walked, Sims stands as a convenient foil to Furness. He represents a decided pole among the broad range of architects of that era,

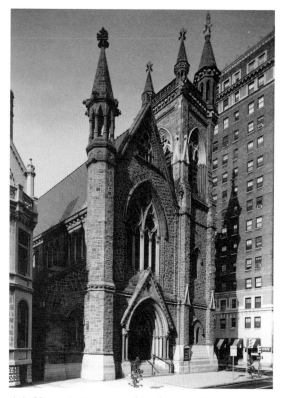

4.1. Henry A. Sims, Second Presbyterian Church

4.2. Arch Street Methodist Church, initial section

4.3. Richard Morris Hunt, Martin Brimmer houses

4.4. Richard Morris Hunt, "Details from Martin Brimmer's houses"

a pole distinguished by a marked attention to developments in the centers of the profession in London and Paris. He prided himself on the fullness of his understanding of the leading European styles. In early 1867 he claimed in his diary: "I am the only architect here making any pretensions to a knowledge of Gothic."[5]

Gothic Revival buildings had been rising in an unceasing stream since the beginning of the century. Then-recent examples like the first part of the Arch Street Methodist Church (1863–65; fig. 4.2) and Samuel Sloan's Emmanuel P. E. Church (1857–59) at Holmesburg effectively continued the kind of sculpturally applied Gothic seen in Sloan's design for a Gothic church from the second volume of his *Model Architect* (1853).[6] Architects for whose Gothic Sims would probably have had greater respect, John Notman and John E. Carver, had died in 1865 and 1859 respectively, while other Gothic designers active in Philadelphia, like Richard Upjohn and Emlen T. Littell (who was trained in Philadelphia but moved to New York City by 1860), were excluded from Sims's claim, being out-of-towners.[7] Furness himself had already begun his earliest independent commission, a Gothic church for the Unitarians of Germantown, but it was probably still incomplete when Sims wrote, and Sims's visit to it with Furness in August 1868 was probably his first. In 1867, then, Sims compared himself mainly to the group in which Sloan was prominent. His confidence among his peers was predicated on the modernity and correctness of his Gothic.

Sims came to this confidence as something of a self-made man. His training, between 1851 and 1858, was in the engineering and architectural offices of railroads in Canada and Georgia. He is not known to have traveled abroad, and he must have relied heavily on European journals for his knowledge of modern trends. An 1868 diary entry about binding English architectural journals—runs of *The Builder* and *Building News* for 1865–67—tends to affirm this dependence.[8] Sims seems to have staked much on his assiduous attention to the central

3. Henry A. Sims, "Architectural Fashions," *The Penn Monthly* 7, no. 9 (September 1876): 700–11.

4. Sims's personal taste had ranged somewhat more widely than his words might lead one to expect, and two projects from the early 1870s attest to a desire to emulate American colonial architecture some years before that source of inspiration found wider advocacy. Both of these projects, from the early 1870s, made clear reference to the external articulation of Philadelphia's Christ Church. See James F. O'Gorman et al., *Drawing Toward Building: Philadelphia Architectural Graphics 1732–1986* (Philadelphia: University of Pennsylvania Press, 1986), 131–32.

5. Sims diary, private collection, cited in Leslie L. Beller, "The Diary of Henry Augustus Sims" (M.A. thesis,

University of Pennsylvania, 1976), 8.

6. The 1869–70 extension of the Arch Street Methodist Church was by Addison Hutton, but the earlier part to the south may not have been. *Philadelphia Inquirer*, 23 May 1865, 8; Elizabeth B. Yarnall, *Addison Hutton, Quaker Architect, 1834–1916* (Philadelphia: Art Alliance Press, 1974), 34–36, 43; Harold N. Cooledge, *Samuel Sloan, Architect of Philadelphia, 1815–1884* (Philadelphia: University of Pennsylvania Press, 1986), 202–03.

7. Obituary, *Architecture and Building* 14 (7 March 1891): 121; Dennis S. Francis, comp., *Architects in Practice, New York City, 1840–1900* (New York: Committee for the Preservation of Architectural Records, 1979), 50.

8. Beller, "Sims," 80.

European currents, mistrusting innovation outside them, or at least expecting worthwhile innovations to be born of concentration within one stylistic current and mastery of its precepts. In this, Sims adopted the stance of generations of emigre architects, who served effectively as importing agents of European styles, except that in his case the knowledge was acquired secondhand, through publications and works of emulation by other American architects rather than from his own experience. He maintained an abiding faith in the sources and the substance of his professed distinction from other architects. His departures were measured, intended to connect with and participate in an international dialogue that would confer a certain benediction on vectors of change and would maintain some unity of impetus. In the mid-1870s Furness found himself in much the same stylistic setting described by Sims, but he developed a different attitude toward change and dialogue. This attitude was rooted in a different kind of training, and ultimately in a different attitude toward individualism in design.

The Experience of Hunt's Studio

During his time in Hunt's studio and office—some two or three years immediately before the Civil War and perhaps two more after his return—Frank Furness had been exposed to a much more catholic approach, one less bound to such orthodoxies as those Sims saw in the High Victorian Gothic and the *néo grec*. The evidence of Hunt's work and the recollections of him by his students present two seemingly divergent images of the man. One is of a progressive figure, encouraging originality and invention, who is best represented by his earlier buildings. The other, better known, is of Hunt the arch-cosmopolite, whose travels and intimate knowledge of historical styles were unmatched—as seen in his work of the late 1870s and after.

This better-known Hunt assessed American practice in comparison with his French experience and saw the underlying, fundamental shortcoming of American architecture as a lack of sympathy and knowledge among the American public. He found Americans unenthusiastic about (if not ignorant of or hostile toward) artistic aspects of architecture: "our profession does not hold in this country the elevated position it has always held in Europe." This made it difficult "to enlist the sympathies of the general public beyond the securing of the more material results." The "material results" included the appeals of "modern improvement" manifested in buildings of impressive size, new service systems like plumbing or heating, and evidence of the kind of intensified urbanization often viewed by Americans as a symbol of their community's maturation vis-à-vis older cities. In artistic terms such materialism was sometimes reflected in excessive decoration: "one is struck," Hunt noted, "with the ambitious pretension of our designs, overloaded as they too often are with meretricious ornament." Too frequently he encountered a conscious effort "to produce novelty of effect, often resulting in a want of harmony or repose, so essential to good work."

At times he found "a certain insane desire to carry up some portion of a building to an excessive height . . . Not until art-education has become more general," he concluded, "can we hope for that sympathy and appreciation which is born of knowledge."[9]

This cosmopolitanism that Hunt saw as crucial to higher standards in American architecture—founded on a more discriminating awareness and understanding of past and present architecture—was among Hunt's principal offerings to the aspiring architects who joined his atelier in the late 1850s. He intended to inculcate "the higher standard of taste, which naturally exists in the Old World" and a "thoroughness, both in architectural design and construction, which prevails abroad."[10] These values correlate with the image of Hunt as a champion of the Beaux-Arts public building and the monumental classicism that would reach a climax at the Columbian Exposition. In practice this was also the Hunt of château-styled magnificence, of compelling—if not always convincing—assemblies of time-honored motifs and grand ensembles.

This aspect of Hunt's persona, one casting him as the agent of cosmopolitanism and foreign standards, dominated Henry Van Brunt's memory of the man. He recalled the atelier as a setting where one was surrounded by "the spoils of foreign travel" and "Hunt's noble and inexhaustible library . . . of books on architecture and the other fine arts." There he and his fellow students found impressive illustrations of "the wealth of the old world but made living to us by the almost tempestuous zeal of the master."[11]

Hunt's zeal was directed not only to a knowledge of these riches, to a mastery of architectural precedent, but also to a constant insistence "upon the pre-eminent importance of academical discipline and order in design." Van Brunt remembered a "system of study and practice . . . based on that of the École des Beaux Arts," and Furness, in his memoir of the studio, recalled problems "first sketched and then worked up during the month."[12] According to Furness, Hunt also insisted upon a very thorough knowledge of the orders, and claimed that it would yield "a certain idea or instinct of proportion that will never leave you," one "essential to good designing in any of the different schools," even "if you never practice classical architecture."[13] Van Brunt recalled that:

> respect for authority and discipline was thus inculcated and we unlearned much of the romantic license which at that time tended to turn the practice of architecture into the hands of amateurs and virtuosos. But while he insisted on the preservation of the classic formulas for the sake of

9. R. M. Hunt, "Paper on the Architectural Exhibit of the Centennial Exhibition," *American Architect and Building News* 2 (24 February 1877): supplement, i–iii, 64ff. (hereafter AABN).

10. Hunt, "Architectural Exhibit," iii.

11. Henry Van Brunt, "Richard Morris Hunt," *Architecture and Society: Selected Essays of Henry Van Brunt*, ed. William A. Coles, (Cambridge, MA: Harvard University Press, Belknap Press, 1969), 332–33.

12. Van Brunt, "Hunt," 333; Furness, "Reminiscences," 11.

13. Ibid.

the training of mind and hand, he heartily encouraged the study of every style in which the thought of man had expressed itself in beauty or power.[14]

Van Brunt believed that Hunt and Richardson created buildings that "have been powerful agents in preventing the dangerous liberty of our art in America from degenerating into license." Hunt, he felt,

> did not pretend to be inventive, or desire to be original, and the impulsive individuality, so prompt to assert itself under all other conditions, nearly disappeared behind the historic types which he used in design. He respected them too much to use them consciously as a vehicle of his own temporary moods.[15]

The Lenox Library (1870–77) was reportedly the one exception to this discipline and respect for "historic types," an exception Van Brunt alluded to as a singular betrayal by Hunt's "natural vivacity of temperament."[16]

Certainly such restraint of vivacity, respect for history, and Beaux-Arts discipline of design method hardly seem like cardinal values absorbed by Furness. One should recall that Van Brunt wrote this homage to Hunt in 1895, by which time the radical shifts in taste since the 1880s and Van Brunt's own inclinations had perhaps colored his memory of Hunt's teachings. But if both students' recollections were weighted toward knowledge of historic models and approved methods of design, they also wrote of another, seemingly contradictory side of Hunt's influence. Both Van Brunt and Furness referred to Hunt's energetic encouragement of artistic expression and the inspiring force of his ebullient personality. Van Brunt admitted that on occasion Hunt, like Richardson, had expressed himself in practice "with a freedom from classical restraint and scholastic subserviency" that "would have been well-nigh impracticable in France."[17] This observation accords much better with Hunt's early work, which offered quite different lessons—suggesting that the respect he instilled for history and method was meant to provide instructive standards and a salutory awareness, but was not intended to close the catalogue of possibilities for modern design.

An 1876 account by New York architect A. J. Bloor confirms this ambivalence in Hunt's pedagogy:

> Hunt's training was conducted simply on the principle of grounding his students thoroughly in historical architecture, leaving each free to follow his inspirations in striking out a mode of expression for himself; or, if the pupil could not divest his mind of a certain bias toward his teacher's manner, he felt at least an eclectic influence.[18]

---

14. Van Brunt, "Hunt," 333.
15. Ibid., 338.
16. Ibid. The exception, merely alluded to by Van Brunt, was specified by William A. Coles.

17. Ibid.
18. A. J. Bloor, "Annual Address to the A.I.A.," 12 October 1876, *AABN* 2 (24 March 1877): xi, 96ff.

Set before the student were the architectural glories of ancient and modern, classical and medieval Europe. Some students, like Hunt in his later years, might follow these models in a rather literal manner; some might follow Hunt's early work; some might quickly discover their own light, departing from both Hunt and history except in subtle ways; and a few—Furness most notably—would tap into the eclectic breadth of this exposure, emulating the early Hunt while freely recombining from both historical models and modern schools in a way that Sims would have found contrary to his vision of progressive development.

Hunt's Fusion and a Difference in Furness

No architect exerted a stronger force on Furness's work than Hunt. If the cosmopolitan aspect in Hunt's tutelage and work presented a grounding, however, this more personal aspect of Hunt's style—syncretic, inventive, and responsive to temperament (or "betrayed" by it, in Van Brunt's eyes)—had a more decisive influence on Furness. Characteristic tendencies in Furness's work, tendencies somewhat independent of imported historic style, were anticipated in Hunt's early inclination to inflate certain elements, creating disjunctions of scale in single elevations—as in his 1865 Brooklyn Mercantile Library design, for example—or his willful manipulation of large volumetric pieces—as in the Coles (1869–70) and Marquand (1873) cottages at Newport, the New-York Historical Society Museum design (1865), and the Martin Brimmer houses in Boston (1869–70; figs. 4.3 and 4.4). But Hunt's most potent and abiding influence on Furness lies in another of his less historicizing inclinations, his work in a style that has been called "a fusion, in varying proportions, of the [High Victorian] Gothic and the *néo grec*."[19] Bloor praised this combination repeatedly in his 1876 address to the A.I.A. Speaking of the New York Tribune Building (1873–76), he noted "the current treatment which Hunt may be said to have introduced into this country, by which Neo-Grec lines are infused with Gothic sentiment." He cited Hunt's Brimmer houses, (and Ware & Van Brunt's F. J. Bumstead house in New York City), as examples of an emerging, "essentially eclectic," urban domestic vernacular "founded on the combination of so-called Neo-Grec lines with feeling expended on one or more of the numerous types of Gothicism."[20]

Three other buildings by Hunt from shortly after his 1867 trip to Paris—Presbyterian Hospital (fig. 4.5), Yale Divinity School, and the Stuyvesant Apartments, all begun in 1869—have also been pointed out as early exemplars of such fusion. In these buildings he melded two sets of motifs, two characteristic kinds of transformation of historic form, and

19. Sarah B. Landau, "Richard Morris Hunt: Architectural Innovator and Father of a 'Distinctive' American School," *The Architecture of Richard Morris Hunt*, ed. Susan R. Stein (Chicago and London: University of Chicago Press, 1986), 51.

20. Bloor, "Annual Address," viii, x.

ultimately two design philosophies, one rooted in what were seen as principles of classical architecture and the other in principles seen as Gothic. In addition to juxtaposing elements from the two separate traditions, Hunt introduced a breadth and emphatic malleability that transformed conventional High Victorian Gothic elements, and endowed *néo grec* forms with a degree of constructive anatomy.

Hunt's works that most expressly employed this language of fusion date from a relatively brief episode in his career, from the several years before and after 1870, a period that postdated Furness's close association with him. While the seeds were undoubtedly planted during his years in Hunt's studio and office, Furness must have remained attentive to Hunt's example after he left Hunt's office, and must have noted with a receptive interest these buildings of the late 1860s and early 1870s. Bloor felt that Furness's first works, like those of fellow-students Gambrill, Post, Van Brunt, and Ware, "closely resemble[d] that of . . . their preceptor." He thought these initial efforts by Furness showed "the most timidity and least promise." However, "his last achievements," Bloor wrote in 1876, "show the most audacity certainly, and perhaps the most individualism."[21]

If by the former Bloor meant early works on the order of the Thomas McKean house (c. 1869, cat. 16) and the 1867 Masonic Temple design (1867, cat. 4), there were indeed some striking similarities to Hunt's work. The McKean house (fig. 4.6) showed the progressive detachment of ornamental elements from a visibly thinned and less assertive wall, something present in Hunt's classical works from the Rossiter house (1855-57) to the Lenox Library. The dismissed pilaster between the third and fourth bays of the McKean facade showed the kind of unexpected asymmetry of Hunt's Osborn and Sturges houses (1869-70) on New York's Park Avenue, where nearly identical dormer assemblies appeared to project to different planes or rise to different heights. Furness's stonework showed the Brimmer houses' profiling of moldings not carried around corners, their inset geometric rosettes, their sharp, sometimes curving lines of incision, and a kind of fullness and solidity in cornices that made their lithic mass more insistent than their potential for plastic depth. Incised glyphs on pilasters, short-hand for fluting, rose to concave horizontal moldings that acted as capitals.[22]

Many of these same aspects, from the successive paring of the wall to the treatment of moldings and cornices, were present in Gothic form in the Masonic Temple design. One finds an odd solidity of capping, with gables not so much undercut by crowning moldings as rising as blocky, coped walls. Naturalistic and traditional Gothic carved ornament seems

21. Bloor, "Annual Address," xi–xii.
22. Michael J. Lewis has noted characteristics on a nearly coeval row of town houses at 2102–06 Spruce Street— including X form panels similar to those within the dormers and on the front balcony of the McKean house, and a kind of vivid incision similar to that on the brackets beneath the latter—which suggest that Furness may have been responsible for their design. Lewis also points out a somewhat different front, c. 1869, on the town house of lawyer MacGregor J. Mitcheson at 1608 Locust Street, which seems to resonate with Huntian elements and may be likewise attributable to Furness in his early years.

STYLES AND MOTIVES *101*

to have been subjected to a stiffening geometry. Concomitantly, alongside elements at the McKean house declaring the presence of a modern classicism—intact classical rustication, framed panels, and balusters—there was a suggestion of Gothic imagery, as in the chamfered balcony newel and much of the incision, which portrayed the organic linear growth of plant forms more than the artifice of arrangement and conventional classical form. One might even attribute to Gothic impulses the paring of the walls, an incipient verticality in the windows, and a sense of openings growing as the walls retreated. To a degree rivalling that in Hunt's work, Furness dismissed the prevailing notion of parallel but separate classical and Gothic stylistic realms with distinct traditions and rationales for the treatment of form.

If Furness's early works merited Bloor's characterization of them as timid, it was because he tentatively attempted to straddle such a breadth of possibilities, resulting in designs that were much more static than those of his maturity. Nonetheless, these early works do show his rejection of Hunt's most florid classical indulgences. Furness had little use for Hunt's elliptical windows, shell-like crestings, upturned scrolls, or carving that stepped too far from bounding architectonic lines. He already felt a restraint on art's gratuitousness that distinguished his from Hunt's more European attitudes.

Bloor wrote in 1876 that "Hunt, more than any one else, may be considered [the] father" of "a distinctive school of American architecture" that had begun to emerge.[23] This comment invites some consideration. Hunt's early work was quite varied. Sarah B. Landau has described it as "sometimes awkwardly designed but always brimming with new ideas."[24] The new ideas encompassed both new styles and new building types—Landau enumerates studio apartments, apartment houses, large-scale commercial buildings, the *néo grec* city house, and the "Continental Picturesque" villa. These building types and styles, however, were "new" only to America, for they were well established abroad. In this respect Hunt, like Sims, was more transmitter than innovator. His efforts were broader in scope, were based on more intimate, first-hand knowledge, and were more effective in finding realization and emulation than those of his legion of predecessors fostering imported innovations in America. But even during this period of "the most significant innovations of his career," his role was chiefly that of an agent.[25]

Beyond Hunt's service as an architectural importer, though, there was indeed a real independence of mind and spirit alive in many of his early works, something that went beyond mere transfer. As he imported, he invented, adapted, reinterpreted, and recombined. He seems to have felt fewer of the obliging allegiances—less branding by partisanship and community with like-minded confreres—that would have restrained the most innovating leaders of the profession in London and Paris, fewer of the ties of polemical partisanship or monovalent affiliation. His commitment to knowledge of Europe notwithstanding, Hunt

23. Bloor, "Annual Address," xii.   25. Ibid.
24. Landau, "Hunt," 72.

foresaw an American mandate loosed from boundaries imposed abroad by national solidarity and group-identification among professionals. In the American setting, ideas and forms from Paris and London, new and old, could be examined and weighed freely and invoked at will. In addition to the challenge of European forms and standards, Hunt and his students were confronted by a national self-consciousness that told them that the shelves were stocked with wholesome ingredients, but it would be up to them to cook something American. Hunt's students, and Furness in particular, seem to have felt this desire even more strongly than the master. What seems to have been most distinctive of Hunt's school and the most plausible argument for Hunt's paternity of a distinctive American architecture was his students' awareness of historic forms and the penetrating knowledge of modern trends that they encountered in his atelier. But even more critical to Furness's case, Hunt also instilled in them a freedom to choose and manipulate that allowed for more penetrating and pregnant kinds of reinterpretation and transformation than was generally evident among the rest of the profession.

Apart from his decade of synthetic experiment, Hunt's eclecticism was mainly of a different sort. Like Sims, Hunt later preferred his borrowed strains pure. Over the course of his career he more often changed his stylistic universe to serve different building types. Notwithstanding that his commissions were often for modern building types, Hunt's behavior resembled that of other architects of the mid-century like John Notman, Richard Upjohn, and Henry Austin, who turned from an Italianate villa to a Gothic church to a Renaissance civic building with little compunction.

There was clearly an element of this approach in Furness's early work. The McKean house and the Masonic Temple project invoked a similar situational eclecticism, but continuities between these designs prefigured a distinctive constancy in Furness's oeuvre that differentiates it from Hunt's. He was carrying the two languages into one another more fully than Hunt was at the time, and certainly more than Hunt would later. In these early works and into his maturity Furness aimed toward a universal language grounded more in the dynamics of building than in the shifting associational and social dynamics of building types.

The greater constancy in Furness's work, relative to Hunt's, was founded on a more abiding notion of formal goals. His concern with expressing weight and process persisted well into the 1890s. Only rarely did the cosmopolitan eclecticism central to Hunt's later career take a commanding role in Furness's later works. In this regard he remained, like many architects, fundamentally a creature of his early maturity. Although aware of the vicissitudes of sweeping changes and redirections in the 1880s and 1890s, even paying substantial homage to them, at heart he was a man of the early 1870s. As late as 1906, in a seemingly conventional colonial revival house, the Marriott Smyth house in Ardmore (cat. 609), there were strains of form contrary to the nominal style: there was a heavy horizontality infusing inside and out with a certain ponderousness; several of the distinctive proprietary motifs he had created in the 1880s and 1890s

4.5. Richard Morris Hunt, Presbyterian Hospital

4.6. Thomas McKean house, details from the northeast corner of 20th and Walnut streets, Philadelphia

4.7. Marriott Smyth house, detail of rear corner

appeared in new forms that evolved out of a dynamic between his persistent sensibilities and contemporary stylistic currents; and here and there were explicit recollections of an older creed, tucked discretely away from the most representational faces and spaces, constrained declarations of his constancy (fig. 4.7).

Furness's Syntax

If Furness's departure from High Victorian mainstreams seems to have extended from Hunt's, it soon became his own, both by virtue of this constancy, when Hunt veered, and through his cultivation of an emerging language of distinctive forms. It is difficult to judge whether he consciously aimed to create a proprietary, self-referential vocabulary—jibed at as the "Furnessque"—or whether this was secondary to him, a result of his steadfastness in fundamental views not widely held. In any case he progressively developed not only a set of forms that were identifiable as his own, but also a cohesiveness among them that resulted from consistent kinds of formal transformation. It seems likely that he arrived at them as effective solutions to specific problems of expression that remained relatively unchanged in his eyes; subsequently he made use of them wherever similar situations recurred. Though they seem proprietary motifs, they were probably less exclusively Furness's than they seem today, and possibly were not even of his invention. Still, they seem most pointedly and persistently used by him.

One of these seemingly personalized motifs, perhaps the most famous, was in fact one of the more widely shared or emulated by his peers, from Van Brunt to Richardson. This was the compacted column that Vincent Scully has vividly evoked as "driven like brass pistons into rupturing cylinders, screeching with heat."[26] Furness & Hewitt had employed the device at the Pennsylvania Academy of the Fine Arts, most notably a pair flanking the inner portal to the main corridor of the gallery (fig. 4.8). Here their compactness was made more evident by their contrast with thinner, seemingly taller pairs of similarly treated columns at the same level, these supporting the perpendicular arcades. Both sets had polished granite shafts banded around the middle in deep black marble. The almost irresistible impression was that the shafts flanking the main corridor had been compressed and thickened by a superincumbent weight. Even the mid-shaft bands here yielded to the force, becoming more intensely molded as if collapsing into bulging horizontal pleats.

The same kind of bulbous pleating was also found above the frieze (fig. 4.9) atop the subsidiary pavilions of the Academy's facade, there made even more effective by the view of their profiled flanks. Similar brackets at the John J. Reese house, 266 South 21st Street (fig. 4.10), apparently built around 1874 by Academy stonemason William C. Struthers, suggest Furness's hand and his incorporation of such forms into a personal repertoire. In the case of both the columns and the brackets, the architect made weight sensible by alluding to its effect, showing mass abbreviating vertically and distending horizontally under its force. Gravity as the protagonist in an inexorable drama took center stage.

But in the same designs Furness countered the force of gravity with an antagonist, a counterforce that reasserted culturally established and geometrically integral forms—forms whose configurations hovered in the observer's and designer's imaginations as recognized points of departure. The black mid-shaft bands resisted the excessive spreading and the excessive abbreviation of the columns. A similar counterpoise of force and formal integrity was found in another form of bracket found beneath the compacted columns and elsewhere at the Academy (fig. 4.8). A concave form seems bent into a vulnerable shape by the force above. Meanwhile a thinner element along its face, infused with linear strength, stretches obliquely between the two extremities of the curve, as if it were a strut introduced to resist bending.

This dialogue of forms seems an unmistakable fulfillment of an approach that Henry Van Brunt wrote of in "Greek Lines," a two-part article that appeared in the summer of 1861. The article undoubtedly reflected Hunt's tutelage in 1857–58 on the subject of the *néo grec* (which Van Brunt would call "the *Romantique*"). Van Brunt wrote of "an instinctive and universal language, . . . like the gestures of pantomime," something conventional classicists would regard as "strange dispositions of unprecedented and heretical features." By such elements "the intention of the building in which they occur is at once patent to the most casual observer, and the story of its destination told with the eloquence of a poetical and monumental language."[27] A decade later Furness applied this approach beyond the classical language it was originally intended to inflect. In Furness's version of Hunt's "fusion," he inflected the Gothic as well. In fact, one local commentator wrote in 1887 that "Furness may be called a 'Free Gothic' rather than a 'Free Classic' artist."[28]

Another of the more striking aspects in Furness's work was his intent differentiation of effectively unweighted parts of walls, particularly under arches. The idea of being relieved from structural duty was made manifest both through the treatment of materials and through decorative elaboration. One early attempt to mark this distinction was seen in Fraser, Furness & Hewitt's 1868–70 Church of the Holy Apostles (cat. 13). In the wall below the facade's

26. Vincent Scully, *American Architecture and Urbanism* (New York: Praeger, 1969), 97.

27. Henry Van Brunt, "Greek Lines," Part 2, *Atlantic Monthly* 8 (July 1861): 86–87. Van Brunt, then twenty-eight years old, had an early literary inclination toward architecture that he exercised all his life, but it seems quite possible that Hunt, who knew the subject more intimately, advised him or reviewed the work. Van Brunt left for naval service in May 1861, but before that, at the time he must have written the article, he was

working in New York City under Hunt and then under Detlef Lienau. It seems certain that this notion of the *néo grec* was a strong element of Van Brunt's training under Hunt, in whose designs such effects were much more marked than in Lienau's.

28. W. N. Lockington, "Philadelphia's Architecture," *Builder and Decorator* 5, no. 2 (October 1887): 17. Lockington was referring to the Queen Anne when he wrote of the "Free Classic," but an analogous point could be taken regarding Furness and the *néo grec* in the previous decade.

rose window, uncoursed green serpentine contrasted with the general rectilinear coursing of the dark brownstone. The firm employed a herringbone pattern of brick to similar effect on the gatehouses at the Philadelphia Zoo (cat. 67).

More distinctively Furness's was his use of large-scale vegetal reliefs below arches to distinguish them as nonbearing, a means of expression that invited spirited recreations of natural form. Furness & Hewitt placed these over doorways at the Pennsylvania Academy of the Fine Arts and the Hockley house, and they appeared in much the same manner in works of Furness and Evans, as in the R. M. Lewis house (c. 1886, cat. 324A). James O'Gorman has traced these features to the influence of publications by Englishman Owen Jones and Frenchman Victor Ruprich-Robert, which Furness probably encountered in Hunt's studio. The naturalism and asymmetry of these three reliefs confirm the importance of the latter source, although in circumstances where the mass of the wall was not to be minimized Furness often turned toward flatter, more geometricized elements from nature that pointed more toward the influence of Jones. Furness used both sorts of natural form in his buildings and his sketches, and with a frequency and verve that attests to his unusual delight in this source of decorative elaboration.

Other distinctive elements—many less clear-cut in origin—appeared repeatedly in Furness's oeuvre, and were apparently integrated into his emerging syntax. Fictive roofs ostensibly substituted for frontal pediments. They often became compositional "focusers" and rhetorical accessories—as over the hearth of the University of Pennsylvania Library (cat. fig. 370k)—or enframing elements serving a hierarchical center like Palladian half-pediments—as on the facades of the Centennial (cat. 81) and Provident (cat. 86) banks. Here and elsewhere medievalizing elements, seemingly more factual structurally, took part in classical compositional schemes. If no truer in fact, they created a new, more physical imagery in place of one predicated on the continuity of tradition.

A similar transformation was evident in Furness's characteristic treatment of stone sills, a persistent part of his grammar for urban buildings. Nearly from the start of his career he exaggerated them (fig. 4.11), giving them a deep, pronounced slope and often extending them noticeably beyond the wall surface. They were sometimes doubled or even tripled in combination with similarly treated water tables, exaggerating their water-shedding function. His sills presented long, deep, oblique surfaces without vulnerable horizontal joints. Where such joints were present, a pronounced offset marked a distinct stone tier demonstratively overlapping and protecting the joint. Later in his career Furness would sometimes inflect both elements with a bottom-heavy concave profile (cat. 342, 421), but he would still exaggerate the extent and projection of the sills.

In some works of his maturity, such water-shedding stone bands became the analogues of belt courses much as small roofs became pediments, as if obeying a Puginian injunction to transform these elements in terms of physical function. In other works bands were admittedly

4.8. *Pennsylvania Academy of the Fine Arts, detail in main stairhall*

4.9. *Pennsylvania Academy of the Fine Arts, exterior detail of northeast corner*

4.10. *John J. Reese house, detail over doorway*

4.11. *Thomas Hockley house, detail*

a matter of artifice, as if the architect had drawn a strong horizontal purely as an act of compositional manipulation. In some cases a band or molding functioned both as a compositional element and as one calling out material facts, if only about itself. Courses of turned bricks or rusticated stone (cat. 65, 85A), for example, implied something beyond the surface, as if the band had a less arbitrary basis for being differentiated than mere placement according to visual criteria.

There seems to have been a purposefulness about the metamorphosis in such motifs. They departed from conventional forms, but fundamental vestiges of the referents often remained recognizable. Furness apparently felt a mandate that elements and combinations from historic work, even those he approved most strongly, must bear the visible validation of a modern transformation. Little from the past could be directly admitted into his work without the evident branding of such processes. Sometimes the premise for transformation emphasized constructive or functional logic, as in the deeply sloping sills that contrasted with the familiar, flat-topped marble sills that had long been one of the strongest plastic elements of the large, plain town houses of central Philadelphia. Even where the use and the form were not so different from convention, as in some plainer belt courses, new materials and dimensions—a substitution of brownstone for marble, or features expanded from four inches to nine—often drove home the point of differentiation.

At the Catherwood house (c.1873–74; cat. 55), the transformations are patent. Furness appears to have consciously substituted motif for motif of the neighboring fronts from perhaps a decade or two earlier (fig. 4.12). Suggestions of pediments in molded frames over the second story windows were enlivened with low pointed arches and impost blocks as incidents in a structural drama. The lintels over the third floor were given mass by their blockiness, in contrast to the placid shape outlined by thin moldings in the building to the left. The notion of springing from modillions in the cornice became a premise for a real eruption of vertical forces (fig. 4.13).

An iconoclastic spirit was evident in planning as well. In larger town houses or suburban houses whose frontal width had usually called for a center–hall plan, Furness repeatedly shifted the hall from the midpoint (cat. 32, 78, 258A), as if to center it would impose an untrue symmetry that was not merited by equivalent functions within. The shift from symmetry might be a matter of less than two feet, and was certainly more a matter of imagery than analysis of function.

Just as Furness resisted symmetry in his plans, so too did he avoid planar facades as if dissembling faces. He favored a greater rhythmic or volumetric complexity that suggested the dynamism of function and structure. Instead of a placid regular scanning, as in a typical three-register town house facade, he often paired one set of windows, to distinguish the parlor from the hall in a way that regularity would not. Similar points could be made volumetrically, as in the spatially insignificant inset at the Morton P. Henry house (c. 1874, cat. 56A, fig. 4.14), or the offsets in the facades of the Clarence H. Clark houses at 41st and Spruce streets

(c. 1877, cat. 91). Such choices ultimately reflected a preference for the seeming truth of volumetric complexity, even when this was just as unsubstantiated as a false symmetry. Furness's embrace of the factual sometimes went beyond the facts.

Furness reacted similarly against conventional usage by employing axial supports and odd colonnades, as in the entrance of the Pennsylvania Academy, or half arches, as at the National Bank of the Republic (cat. 281) and the W. B. Kempton house at 2202 Walnut Street (cat. 282). At times he syncopated runs of modillions, placing them only over implied supports. Still, amid his iconoclasm there was often a sense of a clear historic referent: the full run of modillions, the full arch, the fuller colonnade. Furness's reactions to such referents usually hinted at a subtle awareness of conventional architectural forms and they usually preserved some vestige of historical continuity.

The principal means by which Furness sought to revise such conventional forms was by wittily reinvesting them with an imagery of building and a building's reality. His imagination was spurred by related buildings, by expected styles, or by appropriate fragments from architectural history, visual elements that proposed themselves as his points of departure, as the objects to which he would apply his transforming operations.

The richest vein for Furness was past architectural form, but there were also other important layers of imagery. Furness's architecture has often been called organic, and indeed the natural world often served, if mainly in matters of decorative detail. More often than his transformations of architectural form were predicated on natural forms and processes, however, they were inspired by mechanistic ones. Industrial imagery was implicit in the piston-like columns mentioned above, and in certain instances of rotated reiteration, as on the pleated brackets at the Reese house or the drilled patterns on wooden bracket-boards. Straight lines of precisely reiterated motifs suggested the capacity of a machine more than a craftsman. Similarly, the hard-edged incision that Furness sometimes favored also implied not the variability of the sculptor's handwork, but the precision of the machine, especially where the line or pattern was rigid and uniform rather than modulated and freely curved. There was a sense of modernity in repetition that implied the machine's power to multiply, a subtle imagery embraced even in handwork.

Beyond the form of the machine and the distinctive effects of its operation, there were less literal aspects to this mechanistic, industrial analogy in Furness's designs. Among the most effective were allusions to the power of the machine. Forms seem to have engendered a kind of linear momentum within their mass—building, extending, and erupting vertically (as at the Centennial Bank), or pressing down, squeezing, and containing. This was not organic growth so much as force embodied. In their scale of action such effects seem superhuman, vestiges of great forces directing imposing weights that would be immobile without power on the scale of an engine's rather than a craftsman's capacity. Often this was a matter of weight and size, but at other times the machine's power was implied by an unnatural geometry whereby infinitely hard and rigid forms seemed to have emanated from a world less subject to the deflection and growth found in the natural world. Extruded or extended, such forms were defined and realized with impassive perfection. This magical impassivity also connoted the power of the machine.

Favored Treatments of Different Materials

In accord with Ruskinian tenets, Furness's means for transforming historic architecture, whether predicated on the facts of building or on the implication of the machine, usually tended toward different forms in different materials. Least distinctively Furness's was his response to wood, where the truth of joining and shaping that Furness felt bound to respect counted for more than mechanistic scale or classical convention. Reference to the operations of woodworking and of frame versus panel—effectively the "bone and skin" of stick style works by Upjohn and Hunt—remained fundamental (fig. 4.15), though Furness sometimes exaggerated lathed or drilled forms, endowed his stickwork with a certain muscularity, and expanded the scale of external wooden elements beyond typical handwork.

Emphasis and incident might be found in decisive chamfers and notchings, or sometimes even in a superficial grooving. Except in special situations where woodwork was more a matter of furniture than architectural trim, however, it did not partake of much linear or plastic freedom; its treatment was primarily a matter of geometrically constrained cutting, shaping, piercing, and joining, or working edges in extended or reiterative ways. In paneled doors, surrounds, stairs, and wainscoting, the different constituent elements would sometimes be distinguished as pieces, with moldings stopping abruptly at panel edges or near framing corners rather than being carried around a mitre (cat. figs. 44e, 114f). In other instances the mitre would be emphasized by the turning of multiple moldings. Rather than careful complex sequences of ogees and cymas and varied shadows, Furness would often opt for relatively simple profiles repeated four or five times or sometimes evenly spaced grooves, usually grouped between plain margins. In some instances he opposed classical sequences not with such reiterative series but with a kind of anarchy—with a set of varied moldings stacked without apparent system (cat. figs. 258Ac, 320h). Molding profiles were usually not much finer than one half an inch, smaller than those of an earlier generation that included John McArthur, Samuel Sloan, and Stephen Button, but still larger than those of the generation of Wilson Eyre and Frank Miles Day that emerged in the mid-1880s. By and large Furness treated wood as a fundamentally additive material, one in which distinct elements were applied or assembled, and pieces were usually linear or planar. Its pieced quality was rarely obscured by larger, aggregate effects or a true plasticity. (Furness entertained slightly different attitudes in his decidedly architectural furniture, where he allowed wood to take on attributes and motifs he reserved for other materials in his buildings.)

Though in Victorian times stone was often worked much as wood was—sawn and drilled by machine—Furness treated it very differently, and it was the medium for many of his most original effects. Most importantly, he handled it with a breadth and mass and resistance to superficial carving that made it seem monumental, heavy, and permanent. On occasion it was treated as a linear or planar member, but much more often stone enjoyed a three-dimensional fullness. Its ideal state was the block. It was a serious material, the one assigned the most important rhetorical roles and the most demanding structural responsibilities. It was subject to a largeness of effect, with decoration often keyed to revealing the depth of the mass. Pieces were rendered with distinctness, but even where they varied in color and treatment from neighboring ones they were knit into an effectively ashlar partnership in the plane. In some monumental works piece butted against piece in the portrayal of a wall not of bone *and* skin but of solid bone alone. As David Van Zanten has written, the effect was sometimes that of large interlocked pieces, like a Chinese apple.[29]

Classical analogues lurked persistently in Furness's stonework, more so than in any other material. Often they were invoked through the most laconic means, which gave a cultural pedigree to otherwise sheer blocks (fig. 4.16). Short vertical grooves grouped together recalled triglyphs. Single arcs as profiles were the vestigial hints of classical capitals. Rarely was there not some sort of base or cornice, or some sort of climactic cap on an axis or over a doorway on a frontal face, often an allusion to a pediment. Such gestures declaratively raised the structure from a prosaic enclosure of space to something more noble as architecture. Moldings were expanded to several inches across, and their effects were confessed to the observer in another way as well: often only one face would be modulated with curves, so that the profile showed on a flat flank. The profile would be visible as a decision of the architect, the molding would effectively be explained, its effect in shadow accounted for on the adjacent face.

Furness's treatment of brick seems to have been predicated less on historical allusion than on his vision of the nature of that material. Although bricks were often coloristically varied and turned, reflecting the High Victorian imperative to use the material and create elaboration in accord with its fundamental nature, Furness treated them more as parts of a planar mass than many of his contemporaries. Mortar was often dark, stressing the continuity of the plane, but this was not to say that the wall was inactive. Bricks could step out in corbeled ranges and erupt in gabled excrescences, while the wall could break or fold in sharp corners that seemed to emphasize this solidly planar nature, as in the Clark row (fig. 4.17) or, even more clearly for decorative reasons, at the Henry house (fig. 4.14). Furness's use of brick ultimately was less particulate than that of many of his contemporaries, as if planes of brick were the underlying referent to be expressed rather than individual bricks.

29. David Van Zanten, "The Lenox Library: What Hunt Did and Did Not Learn In France," in *The*   *Architecture of Richard Morris Hunt*, 104.

4.12. H. W. Catherwood house (right), 1927

4.13. H. W. Catherwood house, detail of upper facade

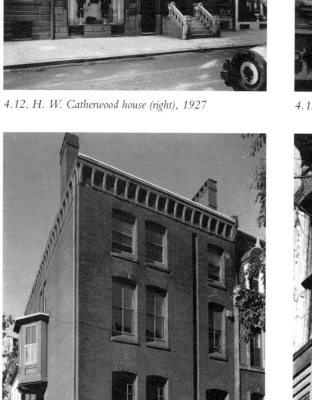

4.14. Morton P. Henry house

4.15. Emlen Physick house, exterior detail

Iron was treated in a few different ways, depending on its role and manufacture. Cast iron was perhaps the most plastic form of all for Furness. It had stone's three-dimensional capacity, but there was no need to reflect the vestige of the block and the operation of shaping or cutting into the virgin surface; the process was the model and the mold, with vestiges in seams and bolts, but Furness was not apt to emphasize these. Cast iron was easily adapted to free departures from Gothic or Classic motifs like ringed colonettes or attenuated triglyphs. Where employed in a bony role, as in newels and applied verticals, cast iron sometimes resembled the use of wood or stone in like situations, showing chamfers, stops, and incised glyphs, its differing manufacture notwithstanding. As a screening element, as in firebacks, cast iron was much different than wood; it was a continuous sheet scanned by repetitive pattern in relief, without any bone/skin differentiation. In some ways cast iron was the material least bound by the architectural past: the thin ground-story piers of the Commercial Union Assurance Company (cat. 261; fig. 4.18) are a remarkable hybrid of plant, machine, and geometry, though the memory of the classical order seems to have remained generative.

Wrought iron also played multiple roles. Furness was remarkable for his frank revelation of I-beams, repeatedly displaying their form and riveted joints unsheathed. His decisions to do so were almost certainly more aesthetic than budgetary or structural. The *néo grec* set a variety of round elements free from their conventional roles within the classical language, so that great disks, lines of small cylinders, circle-incised blocks, and rosettes found various new roles in friezes, imposts, and acroteria. Rosettes binding paired U-shaped channels to form an I-beam (cat. 261) were perhaps their happiest new home, appropriate as witty analogues to metope-scanned classical friezes. This was an allusion whose comprehensibility and ease of execution encouraged widespread use. Without concern for individualism, Furness followed the lead of others in adopting this combination, though he maintained its use past the time of its wider popularity.

Wrought iron was treated very differently at a lesser scale, most notably for urban balustrades where it became almost calligraphic (fig. 4.18, cat. figs. 324Ab, 384e). Like the inked line it was endlessly bendable. In some of these designs for wrought-iron work there was a remarkable dynamism and freedom of an unmechanical sort not often encountered in High Victorian design. Furness was equally likely to turn from free curves and concentric spirals to more rigid geometric explorations (cat. figs. 91b, 280f) or explicitly vegetal forms. At times he would juxtapose all three manners. One finds arcs bound by tangent lines, asymmetrical patterns of crossed elements, and verticals flowing into disciplined leafy forms. Furness sometimes enlisted flattened pieces frontally as if he had darkened shapes on his paper. At other times a plate of iron was a ground pierced with geometrical patterns, the void becoming the figure, a treatment Furness occasionally applied to wooden boards as well (cat. figs. 28b, 57d, 59a, 86).

4.16. *Northern Savings Fund Society, detail of facade*

4.17. *Clarence H. Clark houses, detail of corner house*

4.18. *Commercial Union Assurance Company (right), 1915*

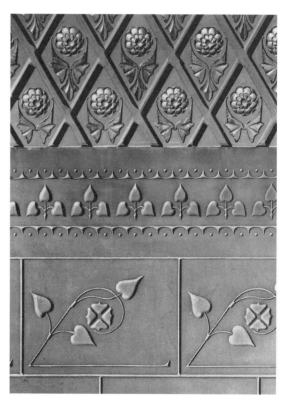

4.19. *Pennsylvania Academy of the Fine Arts, detail of wall, great entrance hall*

Most often in work at this lesser scale, a distinct sense of the mechanical prevailed. This was implied by exact reiteration, but it was also suggested by evident limits in the scope of variation that pointed to the limitations of individual machines. Examples of this were the balusters or newels whose insistent turnings, varied as they might be, inescapably implied the lathe. Architects had been employing such effects for decades (as in the insistently jig-sawed gingerbread woodwork of the previous generation), but Furness was less likely to let parts become introverted, captivated by materials or processes alone. Machined parts usually remained in touch with their roles and their referents, like classical balusters. They maintained a harmony with the greater whole; a characterizing sense of weight observed generally, for example, would also be felt in turnings or profiles.

In flat or thinly layered decorative work like stencilling or surface patterning on plaster or wood, repetition and simplification also seemed to imply machine processes. The simplification often meant distillation to a clear outline (fig. 4.19), and in many cases Furness played with figure-ground ambivalences, something he also turned to when decorating wood or stone surfaces with shallow, excised shapes. Here and elsewhere there was an implication that creative human work took place at a more commanding level of formal manipulation and choice, at whose behest the decoration of surfaces was executed almost automatically, with few signs of special craftsmanship. In this regard one might see Furness as the antithesis of William Morris and the Arts and Crafts Movement, although in their work both Furness and Morris exercised a good deal more ambivalence regarding the machine versus handicraft than a strict partisanship would suggest.

Of course many of Furness's favored treatments changed over the decades, as succeeding styles made unmistakable impacts on his buildings. But there were also indications of internal dynamics of change in his work, independent of national and international movements in taste. The two are difficult to disentangle. By the 1880s the early varicolored assemblages gave way to more unified palettes; emphasis on contrasting parts gave way to more cohesive ensembles; geometrically defined elements gave way to rusticated and more plastic ones; a sense of uncompromising internal generation of form gave way to more picturesque values. Later a new consolidation and ordering of form emerged.

All this generally coincided with ambient trends in American architecture, but a closer view shows some divergence between Furness and his contemporaries. Some pervasive national trends were reflected only minimally in his work, while certain consistencies were evident throughout his career, changing only slightly, even when they were widely unfashionable. Though his buildings grew redder in the 1880s and whiter in the 1890s, though he adopted the living hall and then a new discipline of domestic planning, though synthetic modes gave way to more literal, eclectic ones, still he maintained his central concern with the expression of weight and the self-explicating part. To a greater degree than most of his peers, he continued to employ many of these favored motifs and formal convictions from the early 1870s through the 1890s and even beyond.

Furness rarely worked alone, and at times one is tempted to attribute characteristics in certain of his works to partners and associates. Thus, for example, 1880s urban and suburban commissions connected by patronage with Allen Evans seem to most forcefully reflect the impact of the Queen Anne on composition, planning, palette, and vocabulary; the work of William M. Camac in Maine shows a surface clutter that may be more Camac's than Furness's; similar apportionments of influence might be discerned for John Fraser, George Hewitt, L. C. Baker, E. J. Dallett and others who worked with Furness. Still, the varying influences and personalities notwithstanding, the usually distinctive impress of the work that came out of Furness's varying partnerships and out of various decades attests to the continuing force of his convictions, and to the unmatched constancy with which he held to them.

An Insistence on Animation

Many of the specific motifs and tendencies in Furness's work discussed above were shared to some degree with his most prominent contemporaries, and even with those we might regard more as "garden variety" High Victorian architects. In the 1870s and 1880s in Philadelphia alone one might mention, in addition to Sims and Hewitt, such figures as the Wilson Brothers, Davis Supplee, David Gendell, Willis Hale, T. P. Chandler, Addison Hutton, Charles Balderston, and at least a handful of others. Still, something distinguished Furness's work, something visibly discernible but enigmatic in origin. It seems to have been something outside the canon of the styles to which he and his contemporaries referred, something independent of the credos those styles invoked, and something beyond even sympathetic innovation within them.

University of Pennsylvania Provost Charles Custis Harrison once described Furness as "intensely interested in his own architectural views."[30] One has the sense that the enigmatic, distinctive aspect in Furness's form-making lay in some inner directedness that had been brewing and bubbling within him for decades. Unfortunately, for a man with such decided opinions, Furness left behind few in writing.

In May 1878 Furness's sole published article, "Hints to Designers," appeared in *Lippincott's Magazine*. In what at first glance seems a relatively unsurprising paean to invoking the beauties of nature in decorative design there may lie a hint of Furness's distinguishing spark. Furness was apparently advising amateurs how to improve their skill at decorative design through drawing, but he alluded to something that went beyond this. Good design would be more effectively accomplished by imbibing the lessons of the faultless productions of the natural world than "by following blindly in the footsteps of any human being, master of his art

30. Charles Custis Harrison, "Flotsam and Jetsam," included in "Autobiography," n.p., University of Pennsylvania Archives.

although that being be." But the point was not simply replication of nature and verisimilitude. He wrote:

> There is a danger in the facility thus acquired, unless the desire is aroused, and kept alive in the mind, to preserve action in the form studied. . . . If the model be a flower, look at it well, and consider what is the present phase of its existence. Is it budding into life? is it eagerly drawing that life from Heaven's light and air? or is it drooping to decay, 'nodding to its fall'? . . . Therefore, when your first outline has a certain degree of spirit and action stop short: preserve that action; do not mind being a little out of drawing as long as you succeed in doing so. A design without action is merely a mechanical affair that might be produced by a mere machine.[31]

Furness certainly placed a high premium on "action" in design: for most of his career he seems to have valued it even more highly than the main sources for his architectural and even his ornamental designs. The need for "action" in forms outweighed the capture of a more static beauty in nature or in the man-made (i.e. through quotations from the history of design); it even led him to derogate the mechanical. Though he was writing about ornamental design, it seems that this same paramount value informed his architecture in powerful but subtle ways, for his designs often suggest some animated presence within forms. In mute matter he implied action, finding some premise for it in allusions called up by a commission or in expansion upon some key attribute. He would ultimately tap into this life to generate forms and an overall coherence. It is in this degree of animation that Furness's designs separate themselves from those of most of his Victorian peers.

Such animation may have been born in its absence, in the "Quaker style" of Philadelphia that William Henry Furness had derided in his 1870 address to the American Institute of Architects. The Philadelphia setting must have been a constant spur. Looking at the punctuated brick planes (cf. fig. 1.5 and cat. fig. 38b) repeated block after block, one can imagine Furness conjuring vital forces to animate the static, blocky marble sills that were the principal three-dimensional and coloristic incidents amid great extents of planar brick wall. One can see the endlessly regular fenestration, the nearly unmodulated cap of cornices, and the insistent equivalence and predictability of row houses engendering the willful variability of his Ashhurst (1871, cat. 30), Clark (c. 1877, cat. 91), and Evans rows (1883, cat. 280). His intent creation of irregular form did not emanate from the rural placidity of the picturesque. It was as if Furness had invested these houses with a will and a life that defied systematic regularity. In the Clark row the corner house was subject to special elaboration. The cornice was broken, the plane of the facade erupting through it (fig. 4.17). The vitality sought and the drama created might be largely gratuitous from the standpoint of physical function— here it was predicated on the visibility of the corner, the desire to punctuate it—but it was

---

31. Furness, "Hints to Designers," 614.

generative of formal exposition nonetheless. Furness seemed determined to take on the city's plain old face.

Philadelphia's more elaborated and varied buildings of the 1850s and 1860s presented him with another kind of spur. In 1869 he is reported to have said to Miller McKim that "the Buttons and Huttons & Sloans have had their day, and that real architects are now coming into request."[32] The way in which some architects were less "real" to Furness may have been a reflection of their contrast with him in terms of design, professional behavior, or training. They had certainly devoted less time to programmatic study of design outside of a setting of apprenticeship and practice, and they lacked exposure to a force like Hunt. But Furness may have been pointing mainly to their designs. Their work must have seemed to him as if stylistic detail had been applied from without, with few realities of a spatial or material nature admitted for expression. Style must have seemed to them a much less open-ended game, and architectural design a matter of chosen, fitted masks more than dynamic synthesis and departure. This kind of work was another foil for Furness's efforts.

In seeking to embody in his designs a reformatory notion, to reanimate the dead architecture of the city, Furness took the part of one who had glimpsed something better, and aimed to realize that vision. Was he still the Bostonian scion, the outsider bringing civic purpose and action, or was he now part of the native Philadelphian social fabric? He seems to have been the latter, but a specific part of that Philadelphian fabric: he was born into an active literary and artistic set somewhat apart from the stratified class structure, a set not fully coincident with the interests of old money or new. With patrons and sympathizers who shared his view or placed their trust in his vision, Furness set about to oppose a dissembling facade. He and his cohorts intended to compel the public to see and ultimately celebrate the forces and realities and potentials that confronted post-Civil War America. The vision would intently disrupt reveries of rural cottages of the 1850s and the homogenous townscape of an even more distant and wishfully imagined past. It would embrace the new industrial forces of the city and the countryside, new vying forces in social and economic life, and would find in them a new scale of urban drama. And in this would be born the architecture of independence and contemporaneity that Furness persistently sought.

An Ambivalent Heroism

In assuming the mantle of reformer Furness could expect a degree of isolation and even hostility; his might well be a career in which virtue would be its only reward. He seems to have chosen a kind of romantic heroism, both artistic and moral. He boldly addressed himself

---

32. Miller McKim to Charles McKim, 21 September 1869, cited in Leland Roth, "The Urban Architecture of McKim, Mead & White" (Ph.D. dissertation; Yale University, 1973), 103.

to the modernity of his era. In the positions he championed and in his prominence before a larger public Furness placed himself in a position much like that of his father. A famous personality and intellect in Philadelphia, minister for over a half century at the city's principal Unitarian church, William Henry Furness was a champion of moral virtue who "took the liveliest interest in the events and the books of the time in which he lived." The elder Furness was remembered for "his fidelity to the truth as he saw it" and a modesty "never disturbed by praise or blame; never fearing criticism yet never accepting mere fulsome acknowledgment."[33] His arena and medium was the realm of words, spoken publicly, meant to influence the behavior of others. The younger Furness, like other sons of ministers, can be seen as having tried to match the missives of his father, and in some ways even to surpass them. Architects, too, present their visions of virtue publicly, but in deeds rather than advice. Guidance and proscription are consummated by action. Moreover, most words and even most deeds are largely ephemeral, lost to all except momentary witness. The deeds of an architect like Frank Furness had a persistence, a monumental presence that would speak for generations.

In their vocations father and son each pursued a certain kind of unequivocating heroism. For the preacher virtuosity was not to be pridefully claimed, for rhetorical craft was not the issue. But moral virtue was, and if William Henry Furness could see it and articulate it more effectively than others, he was satisfied with being an effective instrument of larger forces. He returned his special gifts of ability to his congregation; despite accolades he never smugly displayed moral virtue as a claim to superiority. By the same token the architect, for all his pursuit of an individualized style, could also be pursuing a heroism beyond personal ambition. Though he lacked his father's equanimity, he too returned his gift to others. Despite his irresistible prominence in the streetscape, Furness seems scarcely to have talked about himself, substituting instead a gruff self-effacement.

One can infer something of the architect's aesthetic goals and vision of modernity, but, at a more personal level, his hopes and motives are difficult to reconstruct. His 1869 statement about "real architects" suggests that he started his career with a confidence in his training and in a new sophistication among Philadelphians that would bring clients. He had faith in this reward structure. His work as a "real architect" would earn its success, and he seems to have felt less need to promote his designs or his approach than did many of his comparably trained peers. By the early 1870s he had even formulated a disdain for the institutionalization of architecture in universities—it is unclear whether this was entirely because of a shallowly founded professional pretense among the new graduates, or whether he also objected to what

33. Joseph G. Rosengarten, "Obituary Notice of the Rev. Dr. William H. Furness," *Proceedings, American* *Philosophical Society, Memorial Volume 1* (Philadelphia: American Philosophical Society, 1896–1900), 10, 15.

they were taught. For whatever reason, he had begun to adopt the solitary stance of a man apart from the mainstream of his profession.

It is not clear whether his initial optimism about his prospects overlaid a dark determination to serve certain values, but Furness was already swearing as he drew in Hunt's studio and in the early 1870s, when Sullivan met him. Somehow seeds of personal disaffection were planted—perhaps through some disappointment with the profession or his clientele. Active in professional, artistic, and social affairs in the late 1860s and the 1870s, by the 1880s he withdrew. He seems to have turned inward, simply wishing to pursue the goals he had erected, embracing the virtue of keeping to his course with minimal compromise and without proselytizing. He pursued a solitary advance, showing little interest in intercourse with the growing organizational apparatus of the profession, little interest in explaining himself or keeping in step with the debate among his peers. In this he was unlike Sims, who was more deeply committed to the professional dialogue that he believed would foster a group, rather than a solitary, advance in architecture.

Furness's faith or his delight in external reward faded, and one suspects that he no longer expected that he would effectively move society or the profession to his way of thinking. But he had internalized his vision, and it would continue to guide his form-making. As his designs grew increasingly dissimilar from those of most of his fellow architects, he imposed a kind of proud exile on himself. Remarkably, he continued to find clients, clients who probably did not fully share such feelings. Ultimately, the prodigious insistence on animation that distinguished Furness's work was accompanied by this strong tinge of disaffected constancy. Together they make his self-proclamation both celebratory and, in a more subtle way, defiantly plaintive, an outsider's voice.

Michael J. Lewis

Furness and the Arc of Fame

Three times between the end of the Civil War and the beginning of the twentieth century, American architecture was swept by new and powerful stylistic currents. In 1876, in the wake of the American Centennial Exposition in Philadelphia, the forms of the English Queen Anne triumphed. Buoyed by the related movements of Eastlake taste and colonial nostalgia, the Queen Anne put an end to High Victorian moralism and structural expressionism. Less than a decade later came a second upheaval, when the heroic abstractions of H. H. Richardson's Romanesque captured America's architectural imagination. Unlike the cozy, domestic Queen Anne, Richardson's architecture was suitably monumental for commercial and public buildings, and by the middle of the 1880s its heavy rustication and oversized round arches were weighing down the walls of America's banks, courthouses, and town halls. The third stylistic revolution, like the first, was inaugurated with a world's fair. The 1893 Columbian Exposition in Chicago restored to public favor the forms and ideas of classical architecture: marble and limestone, the column and the pediment, symmetry and the axis.

These were national trends, as potent in Sacramento as in Newport. But in Philadelphia architects often bucked the trends, following their own idiosyncratic course. Until the turn of the century the city's architecture retained a vivid local color that often delighted the nation as it scandalized the profession, and that seemed endlessly eccentric and parochial. Philadelphia was not so much ignorant of national trends as she was fascinated with her own internal architectural evolution. Her architects participated prominently in the national debate, their buildings often appearing in the periodicals; nonetheless, during the large part of these turbulent decades, it seems that to Philadelphians the latest stylistic innovations in the pages of the *American Architect and Building News* were not half as exciting as the newest buildings on Chestnut, Walnut, and Broad streets. And by far the most exciting of these were the works that rose, decade by decade, with limitless invention and self-confidence, according to the designs of Frank Furness.[1]

Furness and the Architectural Profession in Philadelphia

Furness's decision to leave Richard Morris Hunt's office in 1866 to practice in Philadelphia was a shrewd piece of calculation. He had learned what he could from Hunt. Meanwhile, major commissions beckoned in Philadelphia, including several institutional buildings and a new city hall.[2] The building committees often included men with whom he had served in the Rush's Lancers at Gettysburg and Northern Virginia—or their fathers. With these ties, and his father's social connections, Furness could hope to weave a web of steady patrons.

Philadelphia's architectural ranks were in disarray at the end of the Civil War. Many of the principal figures of the 1850s were gone: John Notman and John Gries were both dead, the latter a casualty of the Civil War. Others saw brighter prospects elsewhere: Napoleon LeBrun chose New York while his German partner Gustav Runge returned to Bremen.[3] Those who remained were a motley group of former builders and carpenters such as Samuel Sloan, John McArthur, and Stephen Button. These men—Ralph Adams Cram spoke of their "stolid stupidity"—were still struggling to catch up with the Italianate forms that had displaced the Greek revival on which they had been weaned. Of the new polychrome Gothic mode, practiced so effortlessly in New York by P. B. Wight, Jacob Wrey Mould, and F. C. Withers, there were no local disciples.[4] Furness must have felt that Philadelphia was ripe for the picking.

1. See James F. O'Gorman, *The Architecture of Frank Furness* (Philadelphia: Philadelphia Museum of Art, 1973).

2. Among the major buildings built in Philadelphia between 1865 and 1875 were City Hall, the Ridgway Library, the Academy of Natural Sciences, the Pennsylvania Academy of the Fine Arts, the new campus of the University of Pennsylvania, the Masonic Temple, and the YMCA. Most of these projects were under discussion soon after the end of the war.

3. George Champlin Mason, "Professional History of the Philadelphia Chapter," *Journal of the American Institute of Architects* 6 (1918): 199. Of the nineteen architects who signed the charter for a Pennsylvania Institute of Architects in March 1861, only half remained at the close of the Civil War. The other vanished figures are presumably divided into war casualties and people who moved. Among those who left were E. T. Potter; the Civil War dead included Alfred Biles.

4. Almost alone among Philadelphia's pre-war architects, John Greis (1827–62) worked in a High Victorian mode in his Christ Church Hospital (1857). Otherwise, most of Philadelphia's polychrome architecture was the work of New York architects such as Potter (the Baptist Beth Eden Church on South Broad Street), Littell (St. James Episcopal Church on Walnut Street) and Withers (St. Michael's Episcopal Church in Germantown). Significantly, two of Philadelphia's important Victorian architects were Withers's pupils: Charles M. Burns and Thomas Richards.

Furness did not immediately plunge into a solo practice. In fact, none of Hunt's pupils did. To compete for large public buildings, the sort of commission that Hunt craved above all else, was best done in partnership and in a large office—and some time in early 1867 the firm of Fraser, Furness & Hewitt was established. The arrangement with John Fraser must have been one of convenience, the older architect lending the firm a mantle of respectability and professional responsibility. Presumably as soon as was possible, in 1871, he was discarded. There can be no doubt that Furness rejected his architectural leadership. When in the 1890s Furness recalled his education, he remarked that Fraser only taught him "the use of the instruments," his code words for describing the crude method of the builder-architect.[5] With the younger George Hewitt, a Notman pupil, the situation differed and there seems to have been a general agreement on design and method.[6]

Furness's early work was firmly based on Hunt. One of the first critical notices of Furness's work in a national publication, A. J. Bloor's 1876 address to the American Institute of Architects (A.I.A.), printed in the *American Architect and Building News*, spoke of the architect's difficulty in escaping his mentor's shadow, and suggested that he showed the "least promise" of any of Hunt's former pupils.[7] But Furness was the youngest of these and the only one struggling under an old-fashioned boss. For its first two years of its existence his firm floundered, losing nearly all of its early competitions.[8] Entries for the prestigious Masonic Temple (cat. 4) and Academy of Natural Sciences (cat. 12) competitions were each rejected in favor of James Windrim in 1868, and a third competition for the Philadelphia Saving Fund Society Bank (cat. 9) was decided in favor of Addison Hutton. Windrim and Hutton were architects of the older carpenter-builder tradition; if Furness had thought that superior education and architectural sophistication alone would guarantee his success in Philadelphia, he had been gravely mistaken.

5. See pp. 351–60 for Furness's sketch of Richard M. Hunt. Furness's contempt for training that consisted of the "use of the instruments" is reflected in his article "Hints to Designers," *Lippincott's Magazine* 21 (May 1878): 612-14.

6. Although Sullivan, writing in 1923, tried to give Furness and Hewitt distinct and opposing roles in the partnership, their working relationship appears to have been close and agreeable, and rooted in a common attitude towards design. Furness's 1871 letter accepting Allen Evans into the office clearly refers to Furness and Hewitt having a distinctive "method." Frank Furness to Mrs. Manlius Evans, 30 December 1871, Evans family papers.

7. A. J. Bloor, "Annual Address to the A.I.A.," 12 October 1876, *American Architect and Building News* 2 (24 March 1877): xi. Few of these "timid" Hunt-inspired works have been identified, although Philadelphia is still filled with buildings from the boom years immediately after the Civil War, many of which show characteristic *néo grec* incision and floral ornament of the sort that Furness had seen in Hunt's sketchbooks from 1865–66 (see Hunt Papers, A.I.A. Archives, Washington, D.C.). The McGregor Mitcheson house (1869), 1608 Locust Street, is a good example of the type. Numerous such houses remain, particularly in the area to the southwest of Rittenhouse Square.

8. It is unclear whether or not the firm entered the 1869 competition for Philadelphia City Hall, although it seems likely. Hunt himself was interested in this enormous commission and asked T. U. Walter to send a copy of the program.

The Masonic Temple competition made this clear. The symmetrical block proposed by Furness & Hewitt was a connoisseur's blend of Victorian Gothic and French Second Empire. It reprised the symmetrically grouped pavilions of Hunt's Central Park Arsenal project of 1866, while its prominent wall dormers recalled Hunt's 1865 New York Mercantile Library project, two designs which Furness must have helped prepare. But to no avail—Fraser, Furness and Hewitt were passed over for Windrim's much more poetic design, with its exotic entrance porch and pinnacled corner tower. Furness learned his lesson. Never again would he let himself be outdone—"out-picturesqued"—in a competition.

Furness's social style was as New York in spirit as his early architecture, at least at first. From Hunt he learned to deal with his colleagues in a casual and comradely manner. This was the way of Hunt's studio and of the early A.I.A., and surely had its source in the cooperative spirit of the Parisian ateliers where Hunt had studied. Immediately upon his return to Philadelphia Furness sought to establish connections with the more progressive architects in town—younger men like himself, typically in their thirties. Besides Hewitt, Henry A. Sims was part of this circle, as was Emlen Littell, who was working in both Philadelphia and New York. On 11 July 1867, Sims reported in his diary that he "went to see Furness, according to promise made to him yesterday. Spent the evening with him and his wife who is a very pretty buxom-looking woman. Littell the New York architect was also there."[9]

This modest soiree suggested the sharp reforming about to take place in Philadelphia's architectural lines. On the one side stood Furness and his friends in the Philadelphia chapter of the A.I.A., which he helped found in 1869; ranged against them were architects like Sloan and Button of the older Italianate tradition, and the younger men they had trained. Furness's circle was far more interested in the latest Victorian Gothic architecture, about which they eagerly shared ideas. Sims's diary tells of rides with Furness to see his work in Germantown, invitations to see Furness & Hewitt's designs on the drawing board, and even books being borrowed from their office.[10] For the builder-architects such easy camaraderie would have been astonishing—like borrowing tools from a competing businessman!

9. Sims diary, private collection, cited in Leslie L. Beller, "The Diary of Henry Augustus Sims" (M.A. thesis, University of Pennsylvania, 1976). Emlen Trenchard Littell (1840–91) remains an enigmatic figure in Philadelphia architecture. Although he practiced chiefly in New York, he designed some of the earliest High Victorian churches around Philadelphia, including St. Timothy's, Roxborough (begun 1862), and Christ Church, Reading (1866). He worked "three years in the office of a Philadelphia architect" (roughly 1857–60), during which time he could have known Furness. The quality of his early work suggests his training was in one of Philadelphia's best offices, perhaps that of Notman or Greis. See obituary, *New York Times* (4 April 1891).

10. Beller, "Sims." Furness visited Sims "nearly all morning" in his office on 17 April 1867, borrowed Raphael Brandon's *Open Timber Roofs of the Middle Ages* on 1 February 1868, toured Furness's Germantown work on 29 August 1868, was invited to see the Masonic Temple drawings around 1 October 1867, and so forth.

But this guildlike attitude never took—whether because of entrenched resistance from Philadelphians or Furness's own uncompromising personality remains unclear. In 1868, when Bloor wrote him asking to be put in touch with some Philadelphia architects, Furness declined with the remarkable confession that he was not on "terms of intimacy" with any Philadelphia architect.[11] The gregarious cavalryman had exchanged the fellowship of war for the solitude of business competition. With the A.I.A. the pattern seems to have been the same. After an initial burst of interest in the A.I.A.'s educational lecture series, he quickly lost interest, leaving the task of organizing to Sims and T. U. Walter. Furness was becoming less interested in raising the standards of his competitors, and more interested in besting them in the streets. By 1873 he was expelled from the A.I.A., dues two years in arrears.[12]

By the end of the 1860s, even as the cooperative atmosphere failed, the sharing of ideas and books began to pay off, as High Victorian polychromy slowly won acceptance in Philadelphia. Sims, Charles Burns, and others helped to spread the new style, but Furness's work was easily the most conspicuous. After Rodef Shalom of 1868–69 came the first of the big bank commissions, the Northern Savings Fund Society (cat. 28), the Lutheran Church of the Holy Communion (cat. 22), and the Academy of Fine Arts (cat. 27). By 1869 Frank could brag to his father's friend J. Miller McKim about his ascendancy over his builder-architect rivals, rhyming these "Buttons, and Huttons & Sloans" into Mother Goose figures of ridicule.[13]

Sims and Furness had learned the High Victorian Gothic in Canada and New York, respectively; most other Philadelphia architects would learn it from Sims and particularly from Furness. His invention, his vigor and violence of detail, and—although less often—his structural drama, were increasingly cribbed by other architects, who seemed to follow him as much as they did the periodicals. Part of the temptation to borrow was Furness's steaming imagination, the source of a score of inventive new motifs—chimneys, cornices, friezes, projecting bays. When the architect of Philadelphia's Catholic diocese, Edwin Forrest Durang, began to build Gothic churches in the early 1870s, he turned not to the obvious model of St. Patrick's Cathedral, then nearing completion in New York, but to the recent work of Furness. Unlike Renwick's monochrome continental Gothic, Durang's Gothic cluttered his churches with Furness's distinctive compressed columns and banded colonettes.[14] Other characteristic motifs showed up on buildings by David Gendell, Addison Hutton, and

11. Frank Furness to A. J. Bloor, 19 June 1868, *Letter-book*, vol. 1, A.I.A. Archives, Washington, D.C.
12. Minutes of the Local Chapter, A.I.A., Philadelphia Chapter, MS, collection of Athenaeum of Philadelphia.
13. Miller McKim to Charles McKim, 21 Sept. 1869, cited in Leland Roth, "The Urban Architecture of McKim, Mead and White," (Ph.D. dissertation; Yale University, 1973), 103.
14. These include Sacred Heart, Third and Reed streets (1873), St. Agatha's, Spring Garden (1873), and Holy Trinity, Lehigh Street (1874). Durang's own office building at 1200 Chestnut also had a strikingly Furnessic first story with squat red granite piers carrying an arcade of segmental arches.

Collins and Autenrieth. Much of the long-standing confusion about Furness's attributions reflects this cribbing. For example, the Wilson brothers' Joseph Potts house, 3905 Spruce Street (1875), was a credible Furness pastiche, down to the idiosyncratic floral ornament of impossibly squat column capitals. Even the *American Architect and Building News* took for granted that it could spot a Furness building, misattributing to him Davis Supplee's Ridge Avenue Farmer's Market of 1875 (fig. 5.1).

During the next decade Furness's hegemony over Philadelphia architecture was challenged by new stylistic fads—the Queen Anne and the Richardsonian Romanesque. But in each case Furness, and with him the city, responded to these national movements in strongly local terms, and the imported styles quickly assumed a Philadelphian character. Throughout this period, Furness kept a steady course; all that he saw or read in the journals was interpreted according to his own fierce lights. When other architects discovered Japanese architecture and design as a source of fragile and delicate form, Furness saw it through Victorian glasses: for him the essence of Japanese architecture was its vigor and power and the expressiveness of a few bold shapes, as he wrote in 1878 in *Lippincott's Magazine*. His example seems to have been important. Into the 1890s Philadelphia's domestic architecture remained heavily Victorian Gothic, much more than was the case in New York or Boston. This is not to deny that Philadelphia had its own striking Queen Anne movement, but it was largely an affair of younger men, such as R. G. Kennedy or John Ord, whose taste was formed outside Furness's sphere of influence. Those who had learned architecture in Philadelphia remained transfixed by the example of Furness.

By the end of the 1870s a number of architects were working in a more or less consistently "Furnessic" mode. Among them was the firm established by George Hewitt (1841–1916) and his younger brother William Hewitt (1847–1924), who had taken Sullivan under his wing in 1873. Whatever personal acrimony may have accompanied the dissolution of Furness & Hewitt did not prevent Hewitt and Hewitt from routinely reproducing details and facades characteristic of the old partnership into the 1890s. Typical of these was the great series of brick houses built for developer Henry Gibson around Walnut and 42nd streets after 1880. And in their downtown banks, an arena in which Furness had developed a particularly apt expression, the Hewitts remained especially tied to his example. The National Union Bank of Reading of 1888 was a compilation of several Chestnut Street banks, while their 1878 Girard Trust Bank on Chestnut Street (fig. 5.2) was actually attributed to Furness by Vincent Scully. Even after the Hewitts's architectural path diverged from Furness's and they cultivated their own language of ornament, massing, and detail, the influence of their former associate remained potent. The Travis Cochran house of 1882, still standing at 129–31 South 22nd Street, showed the Hewitts's abiding interest in abstraction and structural drama, and their disinterest in the Queen Anne and its little vignettes of prettiness. As in the best of Furness's stone and brick buildings, there was no division between the structural material and the

5.1. *Davis Supplee, Ridge Avenue Market, 1876, looking southwest*

5.3. *Willis G. Hale, Home for Incurables, 1880*

5.2. *George W. and William D. Hewitt, Girard Trust Bank, 1878*

5.4. *Willis G. Hale, Keystone National Bank, c. 1845, looking south*

decorative material; stone and brick competed for dominance across the narrow facade. As late as the turn of the century, with the house George Boldt began for his wife in the Thousand Islands and abandoned at the time of her death in 1903, Hewitt and Hewitt could still reprise a grand High Victorian composition in the Furness manner.

Most enigmatic of the Furness camp followers was Willis G. Hale (1848–1907). Much of the later abuse heaped on Furness was certainly earned by Hale. Hale's training, with Sloan and then McArthur, had followed the older office system, and his early work was in the spirit of his mentors. After running an office in Wilkes-Barre from 1873 to 1876, he returned to find Philadelphia dominated by Furness's architecture. Hale's earliest buildings—the 1879 John Hopkins Warehouse on 50 North Delaware Avenue and his United Firemen's Insurance Office of 1882—with their abrupt color contrasts, contorted imposts, and oversized blocks of stone juxtaposed against thin elongated wooden elements, were attempts to come to grips with the power of Furness's architecture. By 1880 Hale's own distinctive style was assembled, mixing baroque spatial effects with Victorian Gothic surface detail, the whole of it heavily inspired by Furness's mannerisms. His Record Building on Chestnut Street and his West Philadelphia Home for Incurables (fig. 5.3), both conceived of by that year, would have been unthinkable without Furness.

Even as he staked out his distinctly personal style, Hale continued to watch Furness closely. He particularly loved Furness's predilection for placing the heaviest and roughest stones near the top of a building, in violation of the traditional rules of masonry architecture. This motif—seen in the Provident Trust (1876–1879) and the Penn National Bank (1882–1884)— was reprised most bizarrely in Hale's Union Bank (1884) of which a fragment still survives at 715 Chestnut Street. Hale also cherished Furness's jagged asymmetry, particularly in the National Bank of the Republic (1883–1884). Hale was too confident of his own abilities to merely copy the design, as several itinerant architects of the Midwest did, but he applied the motif of the half tower to a narrow crowded front on the Hale Building, Chestnut and Juniper streets, in 1890 (fig. 5.4).[15]

Hale's later fate was exemplary for the followers of Furness. For them, style was an affair of spectacular massing, audacious surfaces, and whimsical detail. In the manufacture of these picturesque vignettes the best architects, such as Hale or Angus Wade, could match Furness crocket for crocket. But architectural form, as Furness learned it, was not an affair of surfaces but of the disposition of masses according to a rational plan. This, the legacy of his term with Hunt, was his hidden strength: Furness had learned a method of designing, not a style. If need arose, he could work in any style, as was Hunt's own talent, and for which Hunt still receives his drubbings. But Hale, Decker, and Wade, as arresting as their Victorian tantrums were, had been taught but one style. Their walls were always more clever than their plans; when they were forced to change brick and brownstone arches for marble cornices, as the tastes of the nineties demanded, the new work showed seams. Overdone and uncertain at the same time, Hale's last works were executed for one or two loyal clients from the eighties. He hung on ten years past his prime, dying a pauper in 1907, his fortune absorbed by the diabetes that overcame him at the end.[16]

The principal charge levelled against Furness's followers—and by implication Furness—was that their work was undisciplined and unacademic. To them, architectural history was a "field not for study but pillage." Was there not, the *Record* might have asked, an institution to impose academic control on local building? There was—the University of Pennsylvania—but ironically, the students of its new architecture program were among Furness's most enthusiastic followers. After graduation, Otto Wolf (1856–1916) launched his career with one of the most shameless examples of Furness pirating, the Northwestern Savings Bank at Ridge and Girard avenues (fig. 5.5), repeating the Centennial Bank on a similar angular site. In later works, Wolf translated Furness's oversized stone and brick details into brewery architecture, the most astonishing example being his massive, top-heavy Bergdoll Brewery (1889). And men such as Edward Hazelhurst (1853–1915) and Lindley Johnson (1854–1937), prominent architects in the 1890s, went from the University of Pennsylvania to Furness's office.

The legacy of these men, in short, was that Philadelphia in the 1880s continued to build in a late Victorian Gothic mode. Its characteristic elements were segmental arches, shed-roofed dormers, and rough stone belt courses alternating with planes of sheer brick wall. There is no more powerful evidence of the continuing importance of Furness's work than the city's reception of the Richardsonian Romanesque. Apart from a few churches and oversized round arches used in isolation, Philadelphia shows less Richardsonian work than any large American city. By this time Furness was in his forties, at the threshold of middle age, and no longer at the center of a band of Young Turks who represented a new and progressive movement. This banner belonged to the next generation. But Furness had not hardened into formula or repetition either. His work of the 1880s was as sure as ever, the emancipation from historical copyism more complete, the abstraction more powerful. By no means had he lost the ability to inspire younger architects. Those who passed through his office, such as Albert Kelsey and Frank Price, were clearly transformed by the experience.

Much attention was lavished in the professional press on Wilson Eyre (1858–1944), Frank Miles Day (1861–1918), Walter Cope (1860–1902), and John Stewardson (1858–1896). But to ignore one whole aspect of a city's architecture while praising another proved, in the long

15. "Architectural Aberrations, no. 9," *Architectural Record* 3 no. 2 (October–December 1893): 207–08.
16. See Carol Eaton, "Willis G. Hale" (Research paper, University of Pennsylvania, 1971); Vito J. Sgromo and

Michael J. Lewis, *Wilkes-Barre Architecture, 1860–1960* (Wilkes-Barre: Wyoming Historical and Geological Society, 1983).

5.5. *Otto Wolf, Northwestern National Bank, looking southwest*

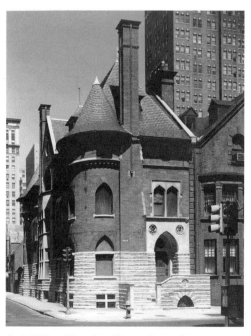

5.6. *Wilson Eyre, Jr., Clarence Moore house, 1976, looking north*

run, awkward. In 1904 the *Architectural Record* pondered how a city that produced Eyre, Day, Cope and Stewardson could have "raised to eminence a designer like Furniss [sic]," and could only conclude it presented a "psychological problem."[17] But Furness himself had helped to create Stewardson. And Stewardson's associates could not help but have been affected by Furness's example as well. This was nowhere more apparent than in the case of the University of Pennsylvania's Museum, work on which commenced in 1894 and which represented the collaboration of Eyre, Day, Cope and Stewardson. What in any other American city would invariably have been handled as a symmetrical classical volume in marble or limestone became a bold composition in Philadelphian brick, based loosely on historical precedents in Lombard, Byzantine, and even Far Eastern architecture, and melded together into a powerful and abstract unity. It was closer to the free-style "poem in brick" that Furness's brother had celebrated in the University's Library than to any other civic building of the period.

The early work of Eyre, and in particular his urban houses, bore the stamp of Furness. Among these were the 1889 Bradbury Bedell house at 22nd and Chestnut streets (1889) and the 1890 Clarence Moore house at Juniper and Locust streets (fig. 5.6). Boldly abstracted, the sheer wall surfaces and overscaled features of these houses bear little resemblance to the classicizing Queen Anne. Instead Eyre followed Furness's lead by adopting the Gothic as the style most suitable for abstraction. Big pointed arches without elaborate tracery mark these buildings, the finest of which used one or two medieval motifs in isolation on otherwise ahistorical facades. Perhaps the best example of Eyre's sensibility was the imaginative detached buttress dividing the Neill and Mauran houses on South 22nd Street (1891); around these bits of Gothic muscularity were little passages of delicate sculpture, episodes of gardens or wistful birds. It was as if Eyre were attempting to apply taste to Furness without losing the vigor and individuality. By the middle of the 1890s he finally gave in, opting for taste alone, but until then Eyre worked easily and successfully in the abstract Gothic. To that extent his buildings differed from those of Stanford White, whose work paralleled Eyre's in many respects and who, stylistically, was probably his closest counterpart.

Furness's bold shapes and scales, his abstraction of historical styles into a straightforward, ahistorical style, and his preference for brick over marble, remained lasting themes of Philadelphia architecture into the 20th century, even though the subject matter was by then more likely classical than medieval. In 1903 William Price designed a store for Jacob Reed on Chestnut Street that the older architect might well have envied. Where Furness dared to make a single Gothic arch the theme of the Provident Trust, Price inflated a Palladian motif to facade-embracing proportions. Price's brother and former partner was himself trained by Furness; through such paths did Furness's influence still reach.

17. "A New Influence in the Architecture of Phila- 1904):96.
delphia," *Architectural Record* 15, no. 2 (February

To the city's more discerning architects the impact of Furness remained apparent. Long after his style had been discredited—when Furness and Evans's clients would explicitly request that Furness *not* work on their projects—the future modernist George Howe (1886–1955) sought out the Furness office for reasons of its "probity." But if Furness still commanded respect in Philadelphia, outside the city he was forgotten, much of the responsibility for which neglect must go to the nation's architectural critics.

Furness's Philadelphia in Judgement

Once the *American Architect and Building News* was launched in 1876, the architectural profession was guided and evaluated by a steady current of critical attention. Criticism, discussion, and the regular publication of designs in the chief journals became an ever more important measure of success in late nineteenth-century America. The critics and journals recorded and confirmed the ascendance of architects who are still regarded as the principal figures of their era. For the first time, American architects like H. H. Richardson, McKim, Mead & White, and Burnham and Root could become figures of national importance and reputation. This was made possible by the national press and the appreciations by the (generally anonymous) critics of *The American Architect* and *Architectural Record*, including Montgomery Schuyler, Russell Sturgis, and Mariana van Rensselaer. Against this changing backdrop Frank Furness worked, ignored by the architectural press just as he in turn ignored them. In an age that valued the judicious and disciplining voice of the critic, Furness's work generally went unnoticed. When viewed by critics who looked to the sanction of history for their standards, his personal architecture was incomprehensible.

Furness had matured in an America without an established architectural press. Apart from the short-lived *Crayon*, a New York-based art journal that had discussed architecture according to the cooperative, guildlike tenets of the early A.I.A., there were no regular periodicals that addressed recent buildings critically. Nor was there any indication that Furness welcomed the creation of such a national press. Throughout his career he never sought more than the approval of clients, or at most of his colleagues. Nonetheless, the opening of the Centennial Exhibition in Philadelphia in 1876, coinciding with the completion of the Academy of Fine Arts, was a critical triumph for Furness. His buildings, clearly the most striking and visible in the city, must have played a large part in the impression that visitors to Philadelphia took with them. This was recognized in 1876 by the *American Architect and Building News*, which designated his work as "the most important element" in Philadelphia architecture. These first notices of Furness in the professional press were also his best. A century would pass before his stature was again as high.

As the professional press rapidly turned academic, Furness's work dropped from sight. After publishing several of his designs in 1876 and 1877, the *The American Architect* ignored his work, leaving it to unglamorous trade journals like the *Sanitary Engineer*. His work was better received in the Midwest, where taste was less delicate than in Boston and New York. As late as 1894 the Chicago-based *Inland Architect* could still publish a Furness design for a retirement home. And Furness's later work, however raw and brash in style, had other merits that could not be ignored. One of these was the sophistication of his planning. The opening of the University of Pennsylvania Library in 1890 proved a national triumph for Furness. A lengthy piece in *Harper's Weekly*, lavishly illustrated, was devoted to the new building.[18] But as far as *Architectural Record* and *American Architect* were concerned, Furness might not have existed. Surely Furness, with all his connections, could have insinuated more of his designs into print, had he wanted to. Apparently he did not. As long as his business was thriving locally, he showed little inclination to expose his work to a national audience and to have it adopted and adapted by other architects.

While the professional journals ignored Furness's work in particular, they could not ignore Philadelphia—and Philadelphia was everywhere permeated with Furness's style. To get around this problem it seems the press made a tacit decision not to mention Furness personally, but only by indirection. Generally his work was criticized by thinly veiled references or by proxy—the castigation of Furness followers. A favorite euphemism was "the architecture of Chestnut Street," a catalogue of Furness's commercial projects. This was held to be notorious, "a pathological collection, an assortment of anomalies," filled with "pretentious edifices that would be revolting to the inhabitants of Omaha, and that their authors would be ashamed to erect in Kansas City."[19]

Much of the criticism aimed by the *Architectural Record* at Willis Hale—honored repeatedly in its "Architectural Aberrations" column—applied to Furness as well. Even "Architectural Aberrations" not found in Philadelphia used the Quaker City's commercial architecture as the yardstick for comparison; the worst that could be said of the recent vulgar commercial buildings of Manhattan was that they challenged the "eminence of Chestnut Street."[20] The connection of both Manhattan commercialism and populist Midwest individualism to Philadelphia architecture was not fortuitous; commercialism and individualism were the twin pivots on which Furness's work turned. Philadelphia alone does not boast Furness's illegitimate architectural offspring; they can be found in the stubby columns and flaring brackets of 1880s commercial buildings from St. Louis to Chicago to New York.

Except for these odd spasms of abuse, Philadelphia had sunk from the architectural consciousness of the nation by the 1880s. When it resurfaced, it was peopled with artists like

18. *Harper's Weekly* (14 February 1891).
19. "Architectural Aberrations, no. 2," *Architectural Record* 1, no. 3 (January–March 1892): 261–64.

20. "Architectural Aberrations, no. 16," *Architectural Record* 7, no. 3 (July–September 1897): 219.

Eyre and Day, with their idiom of local materials and unvarying stance of tasteful picturesque. It was testimony to Furness's declining star that his role in formulating this local idiom was forgotten. Instead, he was increasingly regarded with embarrassment by his fellow architects. By the turn of the century, if he was mentioned at all, it was only as contrast to the astonishing rise of Philadelphia's younger architects. Of the national critics only Ralph Adams Cram could think of something kind to say about Furness—and even then it was couched in the fearful language of deformities and birth defects:

> Consider two buildings for example, chosen almost at random; the Library of the University of Pennsylvania and the Unitarian Meeting House in Chestnut Street. At first sight one sees only inflexible, unvarying bad taste. Well; the bad taste is there, all one could possibly claim, but besides this is something else that is more radical and demands our sympathy, or at all events our considerate recognition, and this is Personality. Bad taste is like a club-foot or a hare-lip; it is a misfortune, not a fault . . . Yet a man with a club-foot and a hare-lip may be a gentleman, and a man or a race blighted by bad taste may yet come nearer to solving the fundamental problems of artistic creation than the most consummate disciple of Walter Pater.[21]

Cram was too honest a critic to overlook the merit in Furness's work (although typically, because Furness's work was so rarely published, he persisted in misspelling his name):

> Therefore, in jeering at the Furnissic [sic] revolt, let us remember this; that its founder and its disciples tried to be something besides cheap copyists, tracing their working drawings from Vignola or Letarouilly or Welby Pugin; they tried to be live Americans, not dead archaeologists; they sought for vitality, originality, personal and ethnic expression . . . If God had given them good taste they would have succeeded beyond belief.

Cram's generous viewpoint remained the exceptional one in the ensuing decades, if the journals of the age can be taken as representative of professional opinion. The 1907 obituary for Willis Hale in the *American Architect* was more typical, a backhanded testimonial that apologized for Hale's work with the excuse that he was driven to excess by Furness's "Pre-Raphaelite" example. Furness himself died in 1912, uncelebrated.

Nor was this nadir in Furness's critical reputation—the sinking of which must have pained him during his final years—reversed with the appearance of Sullivan's *Autobiography of an Idea* in 1924. Sullivan himself had become an architectural irrelevance. His adulatory account of Furness's personality and originality received notice only in Philadelphia. Nevertheless, Sullivan's book posed a problem to later historians, particularly as he and his work were rehabilitated. When Henry-Russell Hitchcock wrote his *Architecture of H. H. Richardson and his Times* in 1936, there was a brief walk-on by Sullivan. But since the architect was only marginally involved in the book's polemical argument, Hitchcock could accept Sullivan's

21. Ralph Adams Cram, "The Work of Messrs. Frank Miles Day & Brother," *Architectural Record* 15, no. 5 (May 1904): 398–99.

statement of his debt to Furness: "the early work of Sullivan, although amazingly light and open, was of an almost incredible corruption of form, inspired by the bold vagaries of his master, Frank Furness."[22]

Twenty-five years later the situation had changed. Sullivan had been transformed into a pioneer of modernism. The connection to Furness now seemed an embarrassment. When in 1961 Hitchcock revised his Richardson monograph, he added an explanatory note that retreated from his earlier appraisal: "Although Sullivan was briefly employed by Furness it is hardly correct to call the latter his 'master'; nor, for that matter, should one say he was 'inspired,' but merely 'encouraged,' by Furness's bold stylistic innovations—if, indeed, even that is not too definite a conclusion."[23] All this, of course, flying wildly in the face of Sullivan's own testimony! Few examples of the distortion of evidence for polemical purposes are as outrageous.

In recent years, beginning in the 1960s, Furness has been rehabilitated, culminating in James O'Gorman's masterful essay in the 1973 Frank Furness exhibition catalogue. Yet still in the 1970s the temptation remained to view Furness as a "rogue architect"—an eccentric operating at the fringe rather than someone at the heart of and in tune with his society. Part of the difficulty in appraising Furness is the issue of personality and personal creativity itself. Architectural historians still under the mantle of nineteenth-century Marxist historiography, which stresses the aggregate and collective over the individual and personal, have looked at American architecture and architects according to the political, economic, and social factors acting on them. But if the same forces acted upon Furness as upon his contemporaries, the results were personal. More than a historical accident or an aberrant island of personality, Furness struck deep chords in those around him, and wrenched his city apart from the general pattern of development occurring elsewhere.

The architecture of Frank Furness was created against the backdrop of post-Civil War Philadelphia, a city whose years of national leadership were behind her. The opening of the Erie Canal in the 1830s had permanently changed the flow of wealth through America. By connecting New York to the growing American interior, the transportation watershed which drained the production of the Midwest into Chicago would channel it into New York. The hierarchy of important and influential American cities inherited from the eighteenth century was irreversibly altered, and as their economic power shifted, so did their cultural status. Philadelphia might continue to play stately Athens, but it was increasingly upstaged by New York's burgeoning Rome.

When Furness arrived, Philadelphia's architecture was no longer first-rate. Once the city had been host to the nation's leading architects—Benjamin Latrobe, John Haviland, T. U. Walter,

22. Henry-Russell Hitchcock, *The Architecture of H. H. Richardson and His Times* (1936; reprint, Cambridge, MA: M.I.T. Press, 1966), 293.
23. Ibid., 331–32.

and John Notman—men who presided over the American profession, leading the nation in stylistic innovation, architectural technology, and sophistication of design. But the architectural ideas that electrified the profession towards the end of the nineteenth century—Richardson's monumental Romanesque, the development of the tall office building, and Beaux-Arts classicism, owed little to Philadelphia. With economic and practical concerns spurring them on and perhaps with fewer cultural constraints bridling them, Chicago and New York dominated the national architectural debate. The issues they confronted—technology, the development of the large professional office, the enormous scale of twentieth-century building—were simply less pressing in traditional and small-scaled Philadelphia.

For a time Furness restored Philadelphia to architectural prominence, but by characteristically nineteenth-century means: the use of style as a vehicle of personal expression. Such a method worked best in small or medium-sized buildings, epics on twenty-five foot lots; towards the end of his career, when faced with taller and bigger buildings, Furness often stumbled. But in Philadelphia, where the scale was intimate and business conducted on a personal level, no architect found as appropriate an architectural language. Like other cities dominated for a time by one architect, Palladio's Vicenza or Schinkel's Berlin, Philadelphia was stamped with Furness's work; the force of one personality sufficed to draw artists away from conventional sources of inspiration, and set them to work trying to decipher and duplicate his achievement. Their copies and pastiches, from the eloquent to the ham-fisted, were the only consistently positive criticism Furness ever received.

Preceding page: *Color plate 1. Pennsylvania Academy of the Fine Arts (cat. 27), detail*
Above: *Color plate 2. Centennial National Bank (cat. 81), tympanum*

Color plate 3. Church of the Redeemer for Seamen and their Families and Charles Brewer School (cat. 96)

Color plate 4. William H. Rhawn house, "Knowlton" (cat. 114)

Color plate 5. William H. Rhawn house, "Knowlton" (cat. 114), stairhall

Color plate 6. Emlen Physick house (cat. 104A)

Color plate 7. Latta Crabtree cottage (cat. 320)

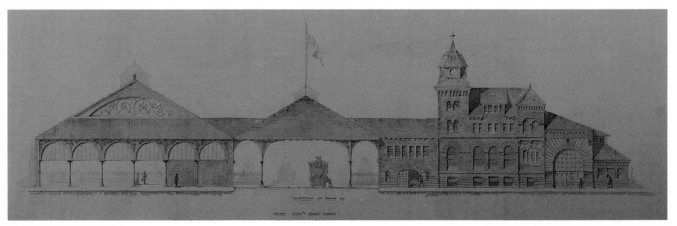

Above
Color plate 8. Green Street Station (cat. 307), Philadelphia and Reading Railroad , elevation
Opposite
Color plate 9. William Chalfont house (cat. 292A), stairhall

Color plate 10. Protestant Episcopal Church of the Evangelists (cat. 326), interior

Above
Color plate 11. Protestant Episcopal Church of the Evangelists (cat. 326), interior
Opposite
Color plate 12. Robert M. Lewis house (cat. 324A)

Color plate 13. University of Pennsylvania Library (cat. 370)

Color plate 14. Bryn Mawr Hotel (Baldwin School) (cat 389)

Catalog of Works

In the following catalog, illustrated entries are set in **bold face**. Those buildings selected for George E. Thomas and Hyman Myers, "Checklist," *The Architecture of Frank Furness*, (Philadelphia: Philadelphia Museum of Art, 1973), 200, are indicated by [1973–catalog number]; those buildings surveyed by the Historic American Buildings Survey are indicated by [HABS state initials–number]. Unless otherwise noted, all buildings are located in Pennsylvania.

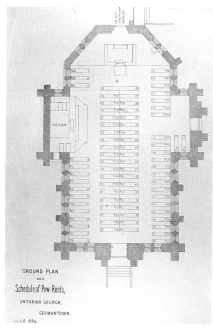

1a. *"Ground Plan and Schedule of Pew-Rents, Unitarian Church, Germantown, July 8, 1884"*

1b. *Germantown Unitarian Church, interior, after alterations to apse, c. 1910*

Frank Furness

1. Germantown Unitarian Church
Greene Street and Chelten Avenue, Philadelphia
1866–67, Demolished, FF
The central position of the Furness family in Philadelphia's Unitarian community doubtless brought Furness his first commission. The congregation was formed on 7 July 1866, and included Enoch W. Clark of the First Unitarian congregation. The church, completed in 1869, was the most English of Furness's work, deriving its detail and mass from Philadelphia's St. James the Less. The parish building was added in 1880 (J. Thomas Scharf and Thompson Westcott, *History of Philadelphia, 1609-1884* [Philadelphia: L. H. Everts, 1884], 2:1406 [hereafter *History of Philadelphia*]). The church interior was altered by Gothic woodwork in its apse in the twentieth century and was demolished after the new church was constructed at 6500 Lincoln Drive, Philadelphia in 1926. Minutes of the Board of Directors for 1866 and 1867, MS, records of the congregation.

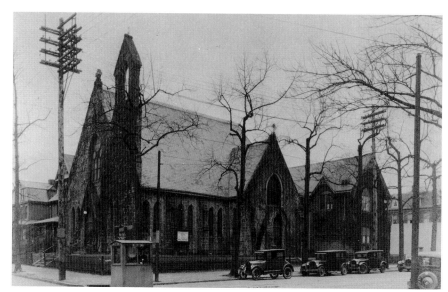

1c. *Germantown Unitarian Church, looking south, c. 1920*

Fraser and Hewitt

2. Tower for Holy Trinity Church
19th and Walnut streets, Philadelphia
1867
Greiff records the church minutes stating that a "Frazer" (sic) competed with a "Potter" (presumably Edward T.) to add a tower to John Notman's 1856 design (Constance Greiff, *John Notman, Architect, 1810-1865* [Philadelphia: The Athenaeum of Philadelphia, 1979], 215). In 1856 Fraser had unsuccessfully competed for the church commission and may have revised his original design for the tower. More likely, though, the tower was designed by Notman's former associate, George Hewitt; Hewitt records the tower as one of his commissions in *Philadelphia and Popular Philadelphians*, suggesting that he was the link between the church and Fraser. The prominent rector of the church, Phillips Brooks, later served as the client for H. H. Richardson's Trinity Church in Boston.
Philadelphia and Popular Philadelphians (Philadelphia: The North American, 1891), 223.

Fraser, Furness and Hewitt

3. Alterations to Franklin Market for Mercantile Library Company
Tenth Street below Market Street, Philadelphia
1867–69, Demolished
The Franklin Market, designed in the previous decade by John McArthur, was sold to the private Mercantile Library in 1867 and opened as a library in 1869. Scharf and Westcott described the building as "187 by 74 feet with a high arched ceiling, with ventilating windows and skylight. In the west wall is a stained-glass window, not heavy with color, as such windows usually are, but light and brilliant . . . In 1875 a gallery was added . . . The Mercantile Library is probably the most popular institution in the city." (Scharf and Westcott, *History of Philadelphia* 2:1210–13). The building was altered by Furness in 1873 (cat. 42) and again in 1877 (cat. 92); it was later demolished in the 1950s.
Forty-Fifth Annual Report of the Mercantile Library Company of Philadelphia for 1868 (Philadelphia, 1868), 7.

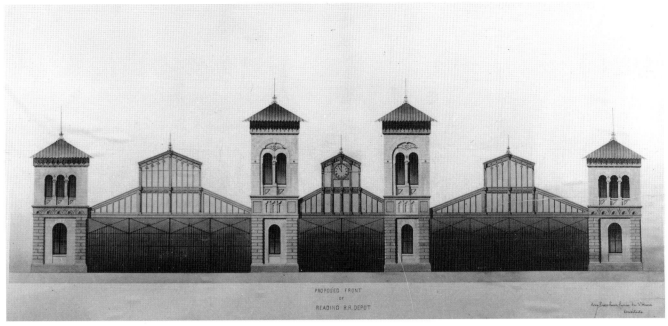

5. Philadelphia and Reading Railroad Terminal, Broad Street elevation

4. **Masonic Temple of Philadelphia, Competition**
Broad and Filbert streets, Philadelphia
1867, Unexecuted
The lot for the new Masonic Temple was proposed to the Masons in December 1866, and was acquired on 1 July 1867. Henry Sims's diary reported:

> September 16, 1867, Monday. Running about all the morning—about several things the principal one being to get a chance to compete for the new Freemason's Hall . . . I heard nothing of it till about a week ago when Furness told me he was working at a design in conjunction with Hewitt and Fraser. (Sims diary, private collection, cited in Leslie L. Beller, "The Diary of Henry Augustus Sims" [M.A. thesis, University of Pennsylvania, 1976].)

The other invited competitors included John McArthur, Collins & Autenrieth, and James Windrim, a member of the organization and the eventual winner.
John Poppeliers, "The 1867 Philadelphia Masonic Temple Competition," *Journal of the Society of Architectural Historians* 16 (December 1967): 278–85.

5. **Redesign of Philadelphia and Reading Railroad Terminal**
Broad and Callowhill streets, Philadelphia
1867, Unexecuted
The Philadelphia and Reading Railroad constructed a major terminal on Broad and Callowhill streets in 1859; its two unequal sheds were carried on monumental Italianate stone piers. Fraser, Furness and Hewitt; James Windrim; and the engineer of the railroad, C. E. Byers, each submitted a scheme for adding a third shed and updating the facade. The Fraser, Furness and Hewitt scheme introduced the incised ornament and eclectic synthesis of French and English styling that would characterize Furness's later work.
Signed elevation, collection of Athenaeum of Philadelphia; James F. O'Gorman et al., *Drawing Toward Building: Philadelphia Architectural Graphics 1732–1986* (Philadelphia: University of Pennsylvania Press, 1986), 128–29.

6. Additions to unidentified house
Germantown, Philadelphia
c. 1867
Henry Sims wrote in his diary, "Saturday, August 29, 1868. Between 1 and 2 went to Germantown with Furness to see some of his work—a Unitarian church and an addition and outbuildings to an old house."
Beller, "Sims."

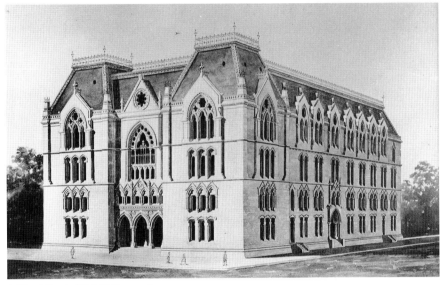

4. Masonic Temple of Philadelphia, perspective

7A. Thomas Atherton house
West River Street, Wilkes-Barre
c. 1867, Demolished save for carriage house, JF
Atherton was the director of Second National Bank (cat. 18); family records name Fraser as the architect, as reported in an interview with Mary Atherton French by Michael Lewis, 1980.

8. Fairmount Park cottages
Fairmount Park, Philadelphia
c. 1868
The cottages were probably rustic shelters and guard houses designed on the Central Park model, which Furness would have known from his study in Hunt's office. Many of these existed at various scenic locations, and were typically of rude construction, recalling structures from nineteenth-century English garden books. These were remarkable enough to be remembered in a list of Furness's works in the *American Architect and Building News* (hereafter *AABN*) in 1876. "Philadelphia Letter," *AABN* 1 (14 October 1876): 335.

9. Philadelphia Savings Fund Society Building, Competition
700 Walnut Street at Seventh Street, Philadelphia
1868, Unexecuted
The competition was lost to Sloan and Hutton; Furness, Evans and Co. later doubled the building (cat. 499).
Elizabeth Yarnall, *Addison Hutton, Quaker Architect, 1834–1916* (Philadelphia: Art Alliance, 1974), 42.

7A. Thomas Atherton house, c. 1890

8. Fairmount Park Cottage

10. Rectory for Christ Church, 1990

11A. John Rice and E. Burgess Warren double house, looking south, 1989

10. Rectory for Christ Church
Riverton, NJ
1868, JF
The records of the Protestant Episcopal Christ Church list the architect as John Fraser, who was a resident of the community until 1903 and designed the new church in 1884.

11A. John Rice and E. Burgess Warren double house
2106–08 Walnut Street, Philadelphia
c. 1868
The sandstone double was constructed between 1867 and 1869 for the builders John Rice and E. Burgess Warren and was sold in 1870 to Walter Horstmann and Samuel Clarkson. Interior finishes imply a date immediately after the Civil War, and may represent Fraser's design, while the incised floral ornament of the facade is perhaps suggestive of Furness's hand. It is also noteworthy that Horstmann's son probably commissioned a house from Furness on South 13th Street around 1883 (cat. 274A). The Hewitt, Granger and Paist list records the Horstman (sic) name, and locates a house in "W. Phila," perhaps office shorthand for the Schuylkill vicinity.
Philadelphia Deeds, 30 September 1870, 46.

12. Academy of Natural Sciences, Competition
Philadelphia
1868, Unexecuted
The competition was lost to James H. Windrim. For many years, however, the Fraser, Furness and Hewitt rendering was listed in the Academy records; it has since disappeared.
Records of the Academy of Natural Sciences.

13a. Church of the Holy Apostles, looking south, 1972

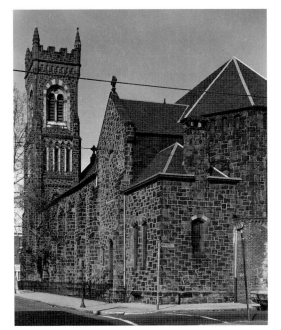

13b. Church of the Holy Apostles, looking northeast, 1980

13c. Church of the Holy Apostles, nave, c. 1918

13d. Church of the Holy Apostles, nave roof trusses, 1972

13. Church of the Holy Apostles

21st and Christian streets, Philadelphia
1868–70, Altered, GWH

Henry Sims recorded in his diary:

April 18, 1868. Saturday. Messr. Coffin, Redner and Thomas and Committee of the Ch. of the Holy Apostles called and gave me instruction about the new ch. I am to compete with Hewitt for it.

June 15, 1868. Messers. Coffin and Rednor and Rev. Mr. Cooper the rector of the Holy Apostles consulted with Hewitt and myself jointly about the position about the church on the lot. (Sims diary.)

The Protestant Episcopal congregation of the Holy Apostles was newly formed when Fraser, Furness and Hewitt were hired to design their new building. It presumably came through Hewitt's continuation of John Notman's practice, and is close in spirit to late Notman designs. According to the church history, Hewitt was in charge of the design, confirming Louis Sullivan's description of the division of responsibility in the Furness office.

The office added the Sunday School in 1873; Hewitt continued working with the client after the split of the office, adding the tower in 1890.

William Castner, *The History of the Church of the Holy Apostles, 1868–1918* (Philadelphia: n.d.), 19. [1973–1]

14. Consulting work for U.S. Government

Washington, D.C.
1868, FF

I wish to find through you from the A.I.A. what would be the proper and just charges or percentage in the following case: Subpoenaed as an expert for an investigating committee in Washington.

Two journeys from Phila to Washington.

Time occupied fourteen days. Making detailed estimates on buildings the cost of which amounted to three hundred and fifty thousand dollars.

Making two reports in writing, one to Senate and one to the House . . .

Frank Furness

Frank Furness to A. J. Bloor, 19 June 1868, *Letterbook*, vol. 1, A.I.A. Archives, Washington, D.C.

15a. Rodef Shalom Synagogue, Broad Street facade, looking east, c. 1880

15. Rodef Shalom Synagogue

Broad and Mount Vernon streets, Philadelphia
1868–69, Demolished, FF

The German Congregation Rodef Shalom followed the move of fashionable Philadelphia north along Broad Street. Their building helped establish the tradition of a brightly colored, Saracenic-styled synagogue, which continued in Henry Fernbach's Central Synagogue in New York City two years later. According to Rachel Rubin, who has researched Furness and the Jewish community, Rebecca Gratz, a prominent member of the congregation, was a longtime friend and admirer of the Reverend William Henry Furness. (Cf. David Phillipson, *The Letters of Rebecca Gratz* [Philadelphia, 1929].) Through this connection Furness later received the commissions for the Jewish Hospital (cat. 29) and for the Mount Sinai Cemetery Chapel (cat. 421). Though most of the ecclesiastical commissions are thought to have been Hewitt's work, it is likely that this building reflected Furness's hand. The property was acquired on 26 November 1868, and the cornerstone was laid the following year. Furniture designed by the office was also included.

Proceedings of the Laying of the Corner-Stone for the Synagogue . . . Rodef Shalom (Philadelphia, 1869), passim. [1973–2]

15b. Rodef Shalom Synagogue, lithograph, B. Linfoot, 1869

Above
15c. Rodef Shalom Synagogue, bimah chairs, 1972
Opposite
15d. Rodef Shalom Synagogue, interior, tabernacle, c. 1920

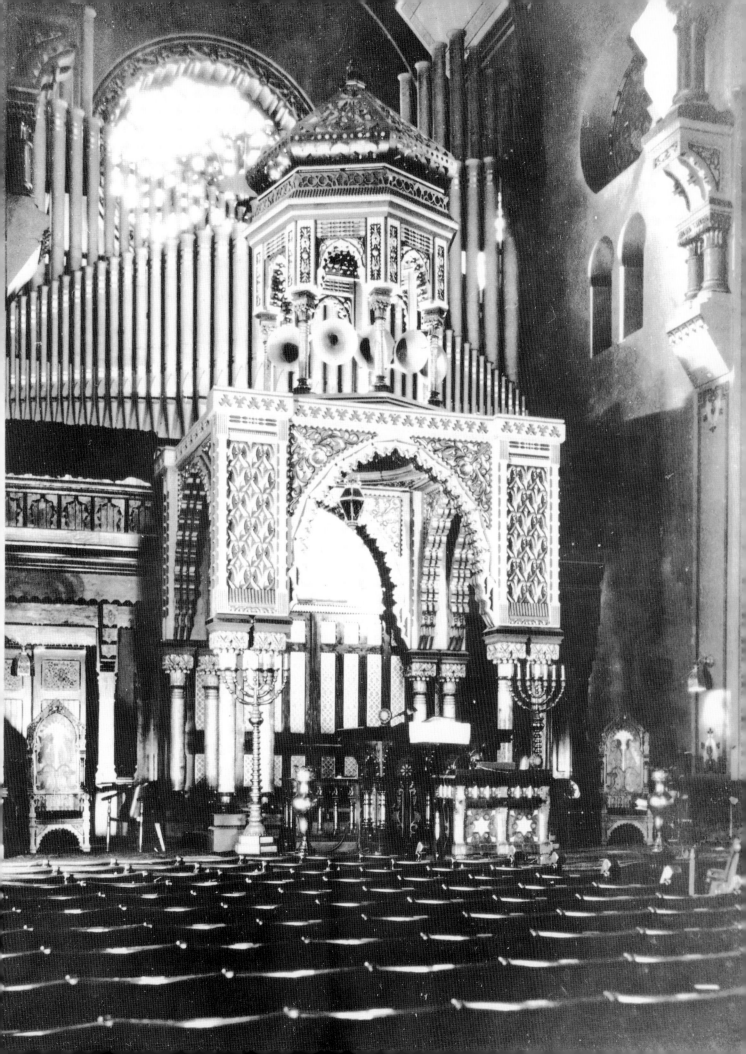

16 and 17. *Thomas McKean house (right) and H. Pratt McKean house (corner), looking northeast, c. 1890*

18a. *Second National Bank (center right), c. 1880*

18b. *Second National Bank, c. 1890, after being painted white*

19A. *Theodore Cuyler house, looking south, c. 1901*

20a. *American Institute of Architects, Athenaeum of Philadelphia, detail of door, 1990*

20b. *American Institute of Architects, Athenaeum of Philadelphia, exterior door to offices, 1990*

16. Thomas McKean house and stable

1925 Walnut Street, Philadelphia
1869, Demolished, FF
The McKean family had hired John Notman for their country house, "Fernhill," and may have come to Fraser, Furness and Hewitt through that connection. One of the more néo grec productions of the office, this certainly demonstrates Furness's hand in its design, and is so designated in a letter from Miller McKim to son Charles, then in Paris, "I saw Frank Furness while in Phila. He is one of the first architects of the city. He has recently had some fine jobs, among them a $150,000 house for Tom McKean . . . He wants you to come right to him when you return" (McKim Collection, Library of Congress). The McKean house became the home of financier Edward Stotesbury and survived until the 1920s when it was replaced by an apartment house.
James Miller McKim to Charles F. McKim, 21 September 1869 (Washington, D.C.: Library of Congress).

17. H. Pratt McKean house and stable

1923 Walnut Street, Philadelphia
1869, Demolished
According to an article entitled "Millionaires' Houses," (*Philadelphia Press*, 10 May 1885, 9) the construction of this house followed that of his father's (cat. 16). "The father selected plans for a house, and when it was done, liked it so much that he took the same plans to another builder and

had a second house built for his son along side his own." After initial resistance, McKean, Sr. ultimately paid the architects a second fee for reusing the plans. The second house was designed with doors opening through the party wall so that the entire first floor could be made into a large ball room. The H. Pratt McKean house was demolished in 1897 and replaced by two houses by Cope and Stewardson for the same family.

18. Second National Bank

Franklin and Market streets, Wilkes-Barre
1870, Altered, JF
The commission continued the relationship between Thomas Atherton, one of the bank's directors, and John Fraser, who apparently designed Atherton's Wilkes-Barre house (cat. 7A) in 1866. The date would seem to indicate that this was the work of Fraser, Furness and Hewitt, though only Fraser was mentioned in the newspaper account. The building was a modest brick and marble block with a paneled brick cornice and néo grec details. The adjoining building to the west in the same style is probably also by Fraser, Furness and Hewitt.
Identified as the work of John Fraser in an undated newspaper clipping transcribed, c. 1940, by Edward Phillips in his typescript "History of Wilkes-Barre and Luzerne County," volume titled "Miscellany," collection of Wyoming Historical and Geological Society, Wilkes-Barre; Vito J. Sgromo and Michael J. Lewis, *Wilkes-Barre*

Architecture, 1860–1960 (Wilkes-Barre: Wyoming Historical and Geological Society, 1983), 3.

19A. Additions and alterations to Theodore Cuyler house

1824–26 South Rittenhouse Square, Philadelphia
c. 1870, Demolished
Alterations nearly doubled the frontage of the house. Shortly after the house was enlarged, Cuyler was elected President of the Social Arts Club (cat. 100) for whom Furness also worked. His son, Thomas, was a brother-in-law of Allen Evans, and a frequent client of the office (cat. 284).
Charles Cohen, *Rittenhouse Square, Past and Present* (Philadelphia, 1927), 75–77.

20. Alterations to American Institute of Architects, Athenaeum of Philadelphia

East Washington Square, Philadelphia
1870, Remodeled, FF
Presumably the work undertaken on the third floor meeting rooms was little more than stenciling the ceiling, painting the walls, and modest bits of millwork, which, with the exception of a paneled door at the rear of the first floor and some millwork on the upper levels, has since been removed. The minutes reported "walls to be distempered Pompeiian red, ceiling light blue with stencilled border, Mr. Furness in charge."
Minutes of the Local Chapter, A.I.A., Philadelphia Chapter, MS, collection of Athenaeum of Philadelphia.

21Aa. I. Parker Grubb and Edward Burd Grubb monuments, 1975

21A. **I. Parker Grubb and Edward Burd Grubb monuments**
Cemetery of St. Mary's Episcopal Church
Burlington, NJ
c. 1870

The connection between Furness and Civil War General Edward Burd Grubb (for whom the office designed a house in Beverly, NJ [cat.41]), makes this commission likely. General Edward Burd Grubb presumably commissioned these monuments for his brother and father. The taller, urn-crowned monument is for I. Parker Grubb, who was killed in battle in 1864. The Easter lilies interlacing around the sword and the butterfly at the base are presumably intended as symbols of resurrection. Similar butterflies are found in the Furness sketchbooks suggesting that this is his work, although it was Hewitt who was a member of the St. Mary's congregation. The monument of Edward Burd Grubb takes the ancient shape of a cruciform sarcophagus adapted to the Huntian *néo grec* and overlaid with ornament derived from Ruprich Robert. Their rather doctrinaire character suggests an early date, around 1868.
W. Woodward, *A History of Burlington County, New Jersey* (Philadelphia: Everts & Peck, 1883), 165–66.

22. **Lutheran Church of the Holy Communion**
Broad and Arch streets, Philadelphia
1870–75, Demolished, GWH

The congregation was established as an offshoot of St. John's Lutheran Church, Sixth and Race streets, on 23 December 1870 in the office of Philadelphia mayor Daniel Fox. The cornerstone was laid on 28 November 1871 and the church building was enclosed by the fall of 1873; it was dedicated on 15 February 1875 by the Reverend Joseph D. Seiss. The church was among Fraser, Furness and Hewitt's most poly-chromatic works, with its green serpentine walls, a founda-tion of purplish Hummelstone, and trim of Caen and Franklin stone. The church was demolished in the early twentieth century, although the altar and much of the liturgical furniture were removed to the successor church. Bloor particularly favored this design of the firm in his discussion of Philadelphia architecture at the A.I.A con-ference at the Centennial.
Signed photozincographs in the archives of the successor church, the Evangelical Lutheran Church of the Holy Communion, 2100 Chestnut Street, Philadelphia.

23. Extensions to Armory, First Troop, Philadelphia City Cavalry
21st and Barker streets, Philadelphia
1870, Unexecuted
The specifications called for a serpentine front to the pre-existing single-span parade shed (cat. 47).
Specifications in the archives, First Troop, Philadelphia City Cavalry, 23rd and Ranstead streets, Philadelphia.

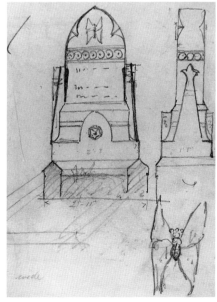

21Ab. Design for grave marker, pencil, c. 1875

22a. Lutheran Church of the Holy Communion, looking southwest, photograph with rendered spire, c. 1873

22b. Lutheran Church of the Holy Communion, nave, c. 1875

22c. Lutheran Church of the Holy Communion, organ loft, c. 1875

22d. Lutheran Church of the Holy Communion, altar and communion rail, removed to 2110 Chestnut Street, 1989

22e. Lutheran Church of the Holy Communion, pulpit,
removed to 2110 Chestnut Street, 1989

22f. Lutheran Church of the Holy Communion, baptismal font,
removed to 2110 Chestnut Street, 1989

22g. Lutheran Church of the Holy Communion, apse furniture,
removed to 2110 Chestnut Street, 1989

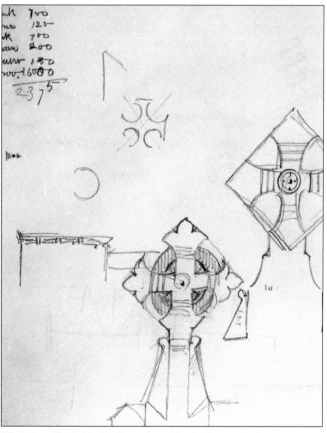

22h. Lutheran Church of the Holy Communion, pencil study of ornament for altar

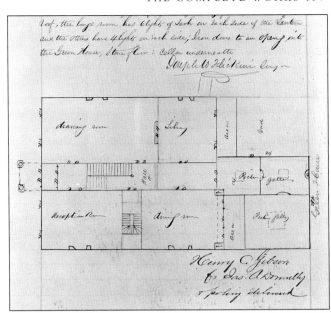

24Ab. Henry C. Gibson house, Franklin Fire Insurance Survey, 1870

24A. Henry C. Gibson house
1612 Walnut Street, Philadelphia
c. 1870, Demolished, GWH
Gibson was on the Board of the Pennsylvania Academy of the Fine Arts; a former John Notman client, Gibson seems to have stayed with Notman's successor, Hewitt, and remained with him after he and Furness parted ways. Gibson acquired the house described by the local press as "tomb-like," and set about enlivening it by the addition of the "almost Egyptian-like entrance," capped by red granite balls ("Millionaires' Houses," *Philadelphia Press*, 10 May 1885, 9). The alterations date from shortly after his purchase on 27 June 1871; they are confirmed by insurance surveys for the previous owner in 1869 and a later survey noting the added gallery as well as various other features in 1871. The interior was extensively published in *Artistic Houses*, providing the visual basis for the attribution.
Artistic Houses 2 vols. (New York: D. Appleton and Co., 1883–84), 1:149.

24Aa. Henry C. Gibson house, looking southwest, c. 1930

24Ae. Henry C. Gibson house, gallery, c. 1880

25. Consulting work for Washington, D.C. jail
1870
> Having been requested by you to state my views as to what would be a proper charge for services rendered by the Commission of Architects, in the matter of the jail in Washington City, in compliance with a letter of instruction from the Hon. Jno. Covode, Chairman of the Committee on Public Buildings and Grounds, under date of Jan. 24, 1868, I have respectfully to say that, I am of the opinion that the services required by the said letter, if fully performed, would be worth $1500. (T. U. Walter to John Fraser, 7 December 1870, T. U. Walter papers, Athenaeum of Philadelphia.)

This consulting work in Washington may have been the cue for Fraser to establish a branch office there in 1870, inadvertently giving Furness and Hewitt a chance to win the Academy of Fine Arts competition on their own. It does not appear to be the same Washington work about which Furness wrote Bloor two years earlier (cat. 14).

26. **Hospital at House of Corrections**
State Road and Holmesburg Avenue, Philadelphia
1871, Demolished, FF
The ordinances mention only Furness as the responsible architect; it was authorized by Mayor Daniel Fox. Here Furness first used the polychromatic brick band set into a schist wall that would characterize his work for the Jewish Hospital (cat. 29).
Ordinances and Joint Resolutions of Council, 1 January 1871–31 December 1871 (Philadelphia: 1872), 367. Pointed out to us by Jefferson Moak.

Opposite
24Ac. Henry C. Gibson house, screen between rooms, with Furness designed table, c. 1880
Above
24Ad. Henry C. Gibson house, stair from parlor, c. 1880

26. Hospital at House of Corrections, c. 1901

27a. *Pennsylvania Academy of the Fine Arts, looking southwest, c. 1880*

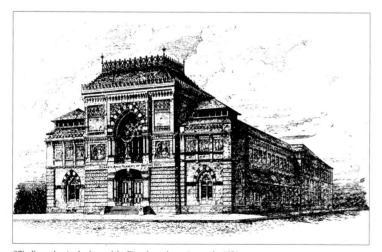

27b. *Pennsylvania Academy of the Fine Arts, photo-zincograph, 1871*

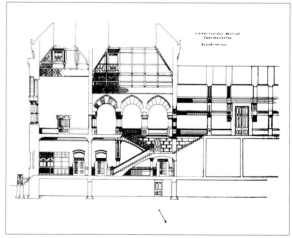

27c. *Pennsylvania Academy of the Fine Arts, longitudinal section, ink on linen, 1873*

27d. Pennsylvania Academy of the Fine Arts, main stair, 1876

27e. Pennsylvania Academy of the Fine Arts, gallery crossing, 1876

Furness & Hewitt

27. Pennsylvania Academy of the Fine Arts

Broad and Cherry streets, Philadelphia
1871–76
See color plate 1.

The competition to replace the 1846 building by Richard A. Gilpin was announced on 20 June 1871. When it closed on 1 November, entries had been submitted by Henry A. Sims, Addison Hutton, Thomas Richards, and Furness & Hewitt. Fraser had been dropped by the younger architects when he was in Washington, D.C. looking for work for the firm. His angry letter, requesting an extension to the dead-

line so that he could submit his own design, exists in the Academy Files. The cornerstone was laid in December 1872, and the building was dedicated in April 1876. The Academy also contains furniture, including a lectern and bookcases, from the designs of the office. In 1973 the building underwent an extensive restoration under the direction of Hyman Myers of Day and Zimmerman, Architects, returning its public spaces and galleries to their original brilliance.

Signed drawings and minutes of the board of directors, archives of the Pennsylvania Academy of the Fine Arts; E[verett] S[hinn], "The First American Art Academy," *Lippincott's Magazine* (February–March 1872): 143–53, 309–21. [1973–3, HABS PA–1525]

28a. Northern Savings Fund Society Building, looking south, 1976

28b. Northern Savings Fund Society Building, interior stair, 1979

28c. Northern Savings Fund Society Building, detail second floor window frame, 1979

28. **Northern Savings Fund Society Building**

Sixth and Spring Garden streets, Philadelphia
1871–72, Altered

The bank was chartered on 14 June 1871. Members of the board included Daniel Fox, former mayor of Philadelphia and a founder of the Holy Communion Lutheran Church (cat. 22). The bank was enlarged twice, first to the south by Frank Watson in 1888, (*The Philadelphia Real Estate Record and Builders' Guide* 3, no. 12 [26 March 1888] [hereafter cited as *PRER&BG*]), and later by George T. Pearson, who added the western extension (*PRER&BG* 18, no. 16 [22 April 1903]). In 1978, the building was slated for demolition and portions of the additions were demolished.
Public Ledger (18 July 1872): 4. [HABS PA–1733]

29. **Jewish Hospital**

Main building and minor structures
Broad Street and Old York Road, Philadelphia
December 1871–September 1873, Demolished
See cat. 97, 358–62, 493–94, 504, 549–50, 555, 557, 571, 592, 598, 624.

Furness & Hewitt received this commission through their work for Rodef Shalom. Their design was accepted in December 1871, the cornerstone was laid on 9 October 1872, and the building was completed in 1873. Many of the directors were members of Rodef Shalom, and several, including Meyer Sulzberger (cat. 467) and Lucien Moss (cat. 434), commissioned the firm to work on their own houses. The firm continued as architects for the hospital into the twentieth century. The polychromy was notable, as demonstrated by an 1897 drawing (cat. 494) for an alteration that denoted the original materials as the local schist in "cyclopean work" with yellow and red brick in the cornice, Hummelstone (a purplish brownstone) banding at the third floor, a belt course of soldier-course brick framed by Hummelstone courses, and, at the first story, red brick.
Ninth Annual Report of the Jewish Hospital Association of Philadelphia (Philadelphia, 1874), 48–51. [1973–4]

29a. Jewish Hospital, elevation of north facade, photo-zincograph, 1872

29b. Jewish Hospital, c. 1890

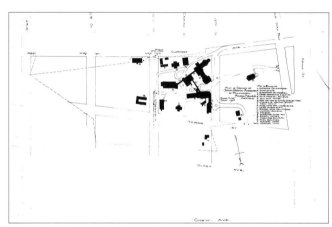

29c. Jewish Hospital, site plan, 1904

30a. *John Ashhurst row, front elevation, ink on linen*

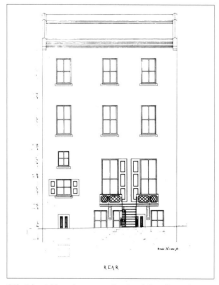

30b. *John Ashhurst house, rear elevation, ink on linen*

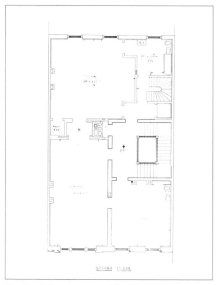

30c. *John Ashhurst house, second floor plan, ink on linen*

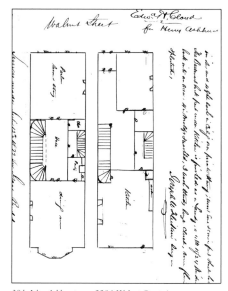

30d. *John Ashhurst row, 2206 Walnut Street, insurance survey, 1872*

30e. John Ashhurst row, looking southeast, c. 1895

30f. John Ashhurst row, 2206–08 Walnut Street, looking south, 1989

30. **John Ashhurst house and row**
2204–10 Walnut Street, Philadelphia
1871, Altered

The Ashhurst block comprised four large town houses that formed an asymmetrical composition in one of the city's most fashionable neighborhoods, across the street from Emlen Littell's St. James Protestant Episcopal Church. At the end of the century, when the approach to the Walnut Street Bridge was raised, Furness altered most of the row, although Wilson Eyre, Jr. altered 2204 (which accounts for his stamp on the surviving Furness linens). The Ashhursts were reportedly living at the address in 1872.

Drawing filed under Wilson Eyre, Jr., Historical Society of Pennsylvania.

31a. Horace Howard Furness house, dining room, c. 1875

31b. Horace Howard Furness house, bookcase

31c. Horace Howard Furness house, library, c. 1880

31d. Horace Howard Furness house, desk, detail, 1972

31e. Horace Howard Furness house, study for desk, pencil on sketchbook, c. 1876

31f. Horace Howard Furness house, desk chair, 1972

31. **Alterations to Horace Howard Furness house**
222 West Washington Square, Philadelphia
c. 1871
The Horace Howard Furness house was acquired from Evans Rogers on 1 January 1870; Horace had married Helen Kate Rogers. Photographs suggest that most of the work undertaken was furnishing and paneling, including a bookcase that survives at the University of Pennsylvania. Similarities to the work on the Roosevelt house (cat. 46) suggest a contemporary date and family documents date the house as 1871. Horace also kept a summer residence (cat. 39A).
James C. Massey, "Frank Furness in the 80s," *Charrette* 43 (October 1963): 26.

32a. Bloomfield H. Moore house, front hall, c. 1880

32b. Bloomfield H. Moore house, dining room, c. 1880

32c. Bloomfield H. Moore house, study for dining room fireplace, pencil on sketchbook, c. 1873

32d. Bloomfield H. Moore house, library, c. 1880

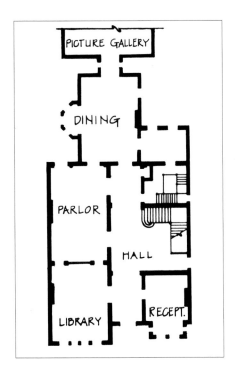

32e. Bloomfield H. Moore house, floor plan

32. **Bloomfield H. Moore house**

510 South Broad Street, Philadelphia
1872–4, Demolished, FF

The Moore family were members of the Unitarian congregation; Moore's name and numerous details for the house appear in the Furness notebooks. The house introduced young Louis Sullivan, just arrived in Philadelphia in June 1873, to the recent work of Furness & Hewitt:

> On the west side of South Broad Street, a residence, almost completed, caught his eye, like a flower by the roadside. He approached, examined it with curious care, without and within. Here was something fresh and fair to him, a human note, as though someone were talking. (Louis H. Sullivan, *The Autobiography of an Idea* [1924; reprint, New York: Dover Publications, 1956], 190–91.)

Remarkably, Albert Kelsey was able to recall the name of the owner and its location and to specify it as Sullivan's "flower" in 1924 ("Men and Things," *Philadelphia Evening Bulletin*, 18 April 1924, p. 8, col. 5), many years after Charles M. Burns had replaced its facade with a more academic French medieval design in 1900 for its new owner, F. T. S. Darley (*Philadelphia Inquirer*, 18 July 1900). It was later acquired by John G. Johnson as the home for his art collection and was demolished in the 1950s.

A Franklin Fire Insurance survey was filed on the Moore house, dated 25 July 1876, policy 47801. It is excerpted:

> A four story brick and stone dwelling house with back buildings, situated in the west side of South Broad Street, No. 510 . . . Inside dimensions: the main building is 50 ft front by 65 ft deep, two story back building 22 ft 6 in. by 31 ft deep with pantry building adjoining 16 ft by 13 ft and Picture Gallery 21 by 44 ft. Spruce joist, Carolina floor boards, the front has brownstone water table, ashlar step and platform and pressed brick and Ohio stone above; Ohio stone trimmings to doorway and windows, walnut reveal window panel, segment top, stone sills, inside shutters and outside shutters to them; sash all double hung, building plastered, gas pipes introduced throughout, building warmed by heater in cellar.

> The first story has a wide hall through the center, the south side is in 2 rooms, Library and Parlor, and the north side has a reception room and stairway; the library has a window front with four lights 34 by 56 sash in it recessed to floor and paneled below, inside walnut venetian shutters and boxes for them, moulded architraves, folding door panels 2 1/2 in thick double wide opening into hall and sliding into partition; a massive mantel piece of Walnut with pediment and enriched carvings to the fireplace; doorways between and an opening filled with one light between the parlor; the parlor is finished in walnut, paneled walnut wainscotting 3 ft 6 in. high, plank double worked folding doors opening into hall and sliding architraves; the reception room has a window front with four lights 30 by 56 and 2 lights 14 by 56, sash in each side . . . A vestibule with segmental top doorway with side lights, all walnut finish; a flight of carved rail stairs with fancy saw'd baluster, heavy ornamental walnut newel, paneled walnut wainscotting."

Below the gallery was a billiard parlor; skylights above the gallery and over the main stair lighted the interior. The top of the building was finished with a stone-bracketed cornice capped by a fourth-story slate mansard.

Artistic Houses 1:153

33a. Unidentified suburban house, perspective, ink on paper (fragment)

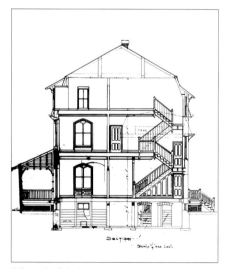

33b. Unidentified suburban house, section, ink on linen

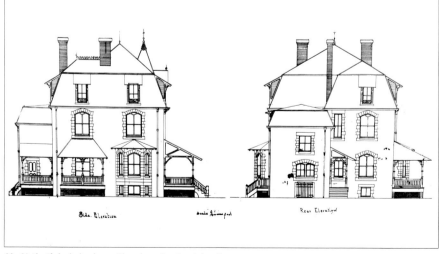

33c. Unidentified suburban house, side and rear elevations, ink on linen

34b. Fairman Rogers house, "Fairlawn," c. 1880

34c. Fairman Rogers house, "Fairlawn," parlor, c. 1876

34a. Fairman Rogers house, "Fairlawn," dining room, c. 1876

33. Unidentified suburban house

c. 1872

Nine separate sheets fully document a suburban house. Its cyclopean wall work was of the sort used at the Jewish Hospital (cat. 29), with slender porch columns ornamented with central turnings like the columns flanking the entrance to the Pennsylvania Academy of the Fine Arts (cat. 27). The plan is a four-square arrangement with a stair running across the central axis behind the parlor, screening the kitchen in the far corner. This is the most complete set of drawings known of a domestic project.

Signed drawings, collection of Athenaeum of Philadelphia.

34. Fairman Rogers house, "Fairlawn"

Newport, RI

c. 1872, Incorporated into twentieth-century Gothic house, FF

> Not far distant [from the house of Pierre Lorillard] is the home of Fairman Rogers, of Philadelphia, one of the novelties of the great mansion being broad sheets of plate-glass extending from floor to ceiling, giving a view on the one hand of the surf dashing against the rocks, and on the other of smooth lawns, winding walks and beautiful trees. (Martha Lamb, *The Homes of America* [New York: D. Appleton and Co., 1879], 204).

Fairman Rogers was a member of the Unitarian congregation, and is remembered in art circles as the subject of Thomas Eakins's *Fairman Rogers Four-in-Hand Coach.* As a director of the University of Pennsylvania, the Pennsylvania Academy of the Fine Arts, and Jefferson Hospital, and as Captain of the First City Troop, Rogers was on many boards that hired Furness.

C. W. Elliot, *The Book of American Interiors* (Boston: Osgood, 1876), pl. 113.

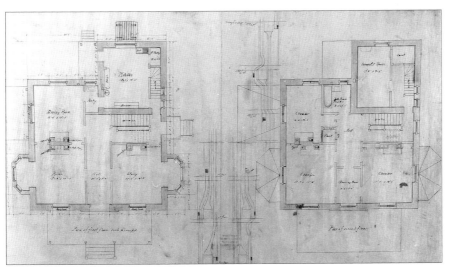

33d. Unidentified suburban house, first and second floor plans, with section of chimney flues, ink on linen

36a. Alexander J. Cassatt house, "Cheswold," c. 1880

36b. Alexander J. Cassatt house, "Cheswold," gate house looking east, c. 1890

36c. Alexander J. Cassatt house, "Cheswold," gate house, looking north, 1989

36d. Alexander J. Cassatt house, "Cheswold," c. 1890

36e. Alexander J. Cassatt house, "Cheswold," library, c. 1890

36f. Alexander J. Cassatt house, "Cheswold," music room, c. 1890

35A. Additions and alterations to Fairman Rogers house (later Alexander J. Cassatt house)
202 South 19th Street, Philadelphia
c. 1872, Demolished, FF
The Rogers house on Rittenhouse Square began as a stolid, brick, center-hall, mid-century design and then almost certainly received two alterations by Furness. (Roger's sister was married to Frank Furness's brother, Horace.) The first occurred in 1872 when the front bays were added, the entrance was moved to the side, and a large picture gallery was attached to the rear of the house. In 1888, the house was acquired by Alexander J. Cassatt and was again altered by the firm (cat. 364).
INA records. [HABS PA–1537]

36. Alexander J. Cassatt house, "Cheswold"
Cheswold Lane, Haverford
c. 1872, AE
Demolished, except for a gatehouse
Allen Evans recalled "In . . . 1871 my father sold 40 acres for $400.00 an acre to Mr. A. J. Cassatt who began building his house, calling the place Cheswold" (Evans MS, 16). Letters between the Cassatts refer to work by Evans, who became a close friend, sharing New Year's Eve celebrations for many years. The house was worked on through the 1870s and 1880s, with numerous additions (cat. 112, 644). Patricia Davis lists Evans as architect in 1880 and reports that the house was begun in 1872. (Patricia Davis, *End of the Line: Alexander J. Cassatt and the Pennsylvania Railroad* [New York: Neale Watson Academic Publications, 1978].) The house was worth $100,000 in 1890 (*Philadelphia Inquirer*, 7 October 1890, 7). After a fire in 1935, the house was demolished except for the gatehouse.

38a. Frank Furness house, smoking room, c. 1883

37. Philadelphia Warehouse Company Building

235 Dock Street, Philadelphia
1872–73, Demolished
The Philadelphia Warehouse Company was chartered on
13 April 1872. This was presumably one of the buildings in
the office when Sullivan was on staff; details of it appear on
several of his Chicago houses.
The Philadelphia Sketch-Club (Philadelphia, 1874), pl. 10.
[1973–5]

38. Alterations to Frank Furness house

711 Locust Street, Philadelphia
1873 and later, Demolished, FF
The Furness home had been owned by Evans Rogers, father
of Fairman Rogers and father-in-law of Horace Howard
Furness. It was sold to William Henry Furness, Jr. on 1 January
1870 (since William Jr. had died in 1867, it was presumably
sold to his widow), the same day that Horace acquired 222
South Washington Square from the same source. Frank was
reported as living there soon after that date. Though the
rough-hewn character of the room is unique, the fireplace
of the rear room conforms to details of Furness's work
around 1880.
The room was described at length in *Artistic Houses* as "Mr.
Frank Furness's Smoking Room":

    Mr. Frank Furness, the Philadelphia architect, recently
    conceived the scheme of building with his own hands,
    and in the simplest fashion possible, a smoking room in

*37. Philadelphia Warehouse Company Building,
engraving, 1874*

38b. Frank Furness house, exterior, 1930

*39.Aa. Horace Howard Furness summer house, "Lindenshade,"
side elevation and porch, c. 1890*

39.Ab. Horace Howard Furness summer house, "Lindenshade," prior to 1940

*39.Ac. Horace Howard Furness summer house, "Lindenshade,"
detail of closet with Shakespearean crest, 1962*

39.Ad. Horace Howard Furness summer house, "Lindenshade," rear quadrant, prior to 1940

the rear of this house . . . He has spent parts of many summers in the Rocky Mountains, whence he has returned every autumn with trophies to make a Nimrod's mouth water . . . and his idea seems to have been to house these souvenirs of the chase as inconspicuously as possible. Accordingly, he erected a one-story structure of cedar slabs, with a sloping roof of the same material, and a dado of unbarked saplings. He built a fire-place of gneiss, and a couple of tables of thick cedar plank, supported on legs of the most primitive description. What Mr. Furness has really achieved, from a chromatic point of view, can barely be surmised from our reproduction in black-and-white . . . but those who have seen the interior of his cozy little sanctum will agree that, in felicity of arrangement, both of lines and tones, it is artistic to a high degree, while its literary interest—if we may so express ourselves—is absolutely unique. (*Artistic Houses* 2:169).

39A. Horace Howard Furness summer house, "Lindenshade"

Wallingford
1873, Demolished except for 1903 library wing
"Lindenshade" was built on a tract of land owned by the Rogers family and acquired by Horace after the Civil War. Horace reported: "1 July we moved into new Lindenshade." It was painted "a lively salmon color" in the summer of 1876. "Lindenshade" began as a modest clapboarded summer cottage overlaid with a stick-style frame in the manner of Richard Morris Hunt, but enlivened by the Furness wit—chimneys rose in front of dormers and tiny windows vied with overscaled sashes in adjacent openings. The house grew with the last portion, a two story brick addition constructed in 1903 (cat. 565) to house Horace's Shakespeare library after his retirement from the Washington Square house (cat. 31). Into that library were moved many of the pieces of furniture that his brother had designed including another desk (other than that published in 1973 and now at the Philadelphia Museum of Art), bookcases, and a Karl Bitter *modello* of a sculpted tympanum for the Broad Street Station. An iron gate in characteristic Furness style survived on the railroad track side of the property until recently, though the house had long been demolished. It seems reasonable to attribute the house to brother Frank though no mention is made in the records of his having been the designer. Later alterations corroborate the attribution (cat. 565).
Lindenshade summer records, 1864–78; Horace Howard Furness Collection, University of Pennsylvania Library.

40a. St. Peter's Episcopal Church, looking west, 1980

40b. St. Peter's Episcopal Church, porte cochere looking north, 1980

40. St. Peter's Protestant Episcopal Church
6000 Wayne Avenue, Germantown
1873, GWH
St. Peter's, Germantown, was formed as a splinter of Christ Church, Germantown, and was constructed in three phases: the parish house first, the church following closely, and the rectory built at a later date, around 1880. The commission presumably reflected the Houston family patronage that Hewitt continued to enjoy. Church records confirm that this was a Hewitt project. Hewitt continued to work at the site into the 1880s and as the family architect for the Houstons until the end of the century.
Theodore Rumney and Charles Bullock, *History of St. Peter's Church, Germantown in the City of Philadelphia* (Germantown, 1873), 6.

41. General Edward Burd Grubb house
Beverly, NJ
1873, Demolished
The General Grubb house was a long, low, rambling, wood house with each portion capped by a different roof shape. Grubb was a veteran of the Civil War and held annual reunions on his front lawn looking out over the Delaware River. (See cat. 21A.)
Peerless Brick Company promotional brochure, c. 1890, collection of Library of Congress; W. Woodward, *A History of Burlington County, NJ* (Philadelphia, 1883), 165–66.

42. Alterations to Mercantile Library
Tenth Street below Market Street, Philadelphia
1873, Demolished
This commission was for the balcony that enlarged the capacity of the Library (cat. 3).
Furness sketchbooks, collection of George Wood Furness.

43. Union Banking Company Building
310 Chestnut Street, Philadelphia
1873–74, Demolished
This was the first of the Furness & Hewitt buildings upon which Sullivan worked: "Louis's first task was to retrace a set of plans complete for a Savings Institution to be erected on Chestnut Street. This he did so systematically and in so short a time that he won his spurs at once" (Sullivan, *Autobiography*, 193). A. J. Bloor described the building in his 1876 address to the A.I.A.: "a narrow front . . . where the massive treatment is modified in the upper part into a more delicate rendering" (A. J. Bloor, "Annual Address to the A.I.A.," 12 October 1876, *AABN* 2 [24 March 1877]: ix). The fact that Bloor did not mention the tenant suggests that the building was not built for the Union Banking Company, which moved in a year after it was completed, in January 1875.
Thompson Westcott, comp., *Scrapbook: Buildings, Public Places, Public Things* (Philadelphia: Historical Society of Pennsylvania, 1874–80), 2:52 (hereafter *Scrapbook*); Details of the facade can be found in the Furness sketchbooks, collection of George Wood Furness.

42. Mercantile Library, interior, 1880

43a. 310 Chestnut Street, Philadelphia, exterior looking southwest during demolition, c. 1920

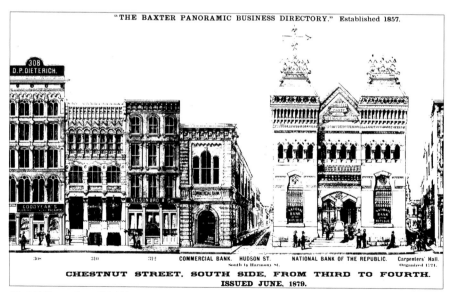

43b. 310 Chestnut Street, Philadelphia, exterior looking south, engraving, 1879

44a. *Guarantee Trust and Safe Deposit Company Building, looking southwest, 1955*

44b. *Guarantee Trust and Safe Deposit Company Building, Furness elevation study, pencil in sketchbook, c. 1873*

44. Guarantee Trust and Safe Deposit Company Building

316–320 Chestnut Street, Philadelphia
1873–75, Demolished

The Guarantee Trust and Safe Deposit Company was formed on 2 November 1872. Bloor remarked

> a new description of structures has come into vogue within the last dozen years, for the safe storage of securities, jewels, plate and other valuable effects. At the head of these both as regards size and artistic rank, whether of exterior or interior, may be placed the Guarantee Trust and Safe Deposit Company's building. (Bloor, "Annual Address," ix).

The site had been acquired by 3 February 1873, and the building was completed in 1875. Its construction, shortly after the Chicago Fire, caused its owners to ask that the building be fireproof and of brick. A newspaper article reported:

> The problem given to the architects was to design a building in brick that would not present to the eye the blank and unattractive appearance of a market house or a factory. The result has been a handsome building that attracts unusual attention from the unique appearance and bold departure from the prevailing architecture of our public buildings. (Westcott, *Scrapbook* 2:39.)

AABN 2 (22 September 1877): 308. [1973–6]

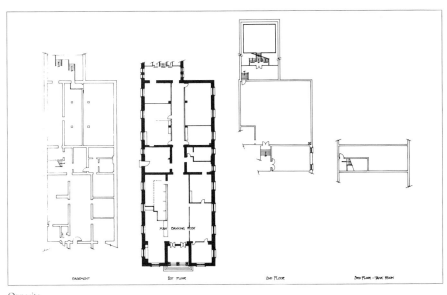

Opposite
44c. Guarantee Trust and Safe Deposit Company Building, looking south, 1875
Above
44d. Guarantee Trust and Safe Deposit Company Building, plans redrawn from originals

44e. Guarantee Trust and Safe Deposit Company Building, main banking room, teller's cage

44f. Guarantee Trust and Safe Deposit Company Building, detail of door

44g. Guarantee Trust and Safe Deposit Company Building, bracket and roof trusses of banking room

45a. *Rudolf Ellis house, looking north, 1989*

45b. *Rudolf Ellis house, library, 1883*

46a. *Theodore Roosevelt, Sr. house, library, c. 1880*

46b. *Theodore Roosevelt, Sr. house, library, c. 1880*

45. **New facade and additions to Rudolf Ellis house**
2113 Spruce Street, Philadelphia
1873
Rudolf Ellis had served with Furness in the Rush's Lancers during the Civil War. He acquired the house on 29 April 1873 from his father-in-law, William Struthers, the stone supplier for the Pennsylvania Academy of the Fine Arts (cat. 27).
Artistic Houses 1:165.

46. **Interior design for Theodore Roosevelt, Sr. house**
6 West 57th Street, New York, NY
1873, Demolished
The Roosevelt house was designed by Russell Sturgis and constructed in 1873. Furniture and paneling was ordered from Philadelphia; a letter from Theodore Roosevelt, Sr. to his wife, dated 21 September 1873, reported "Furness has dreadfully disappointed me at the last moment about his woodwork, and I fear it will not be in when you return" (Roosevelt Letters, cited in Patricia Kennedy, "Roosevelt

Furniture," MS, 8, collection of National Park Service Historic Site, Sagamore Hill, NY). The work included a library, dining room, and hall as well as furnishings for one or more bedrooms. Several pieces of the furniture survive at the Roosevelt summer house in Oyster Bay, to which they were removed after changes in taste banished them from fashionable New York. The dining room table was acquired by the High Museum in Atlanta.
Drawings in the Furness sketchbooks, collection of George Wood Furness.

46c. Theodore Roosevelt, Sr. house, dining room, c. 1880

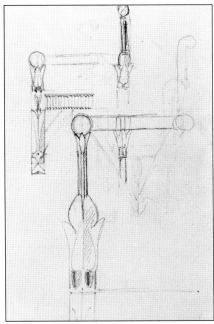

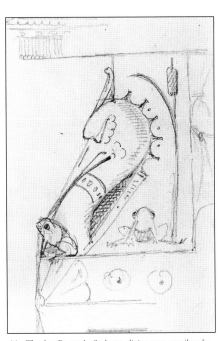

46d. Theodore Roosevelt, Sr. house, dining room, pencil study
for chairs, c. 1875

46e. Theodore Roosevelt, Sr. house, dining room, pencil study
for table base, c. 1875

Opposite
46f. Theodore Roosevelt, Sr. house, wardrobe, 1986
Above
46g. Theodore Roosevelt, Sr. house, hall, c. 1880

46h. Theodore Roosevelt, Sr. house, bedstead, 1986

47a. *Armory, First Troop, Philadelphia City Cavalry, exterior from northeast, c. 1885*

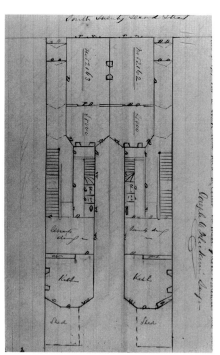

49. *Rowland Evans and Judge J. Clark Hare houses*

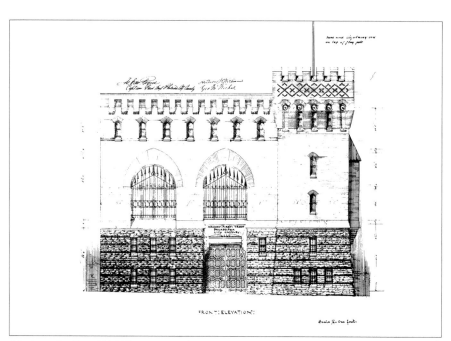

47b. *Armory, First Troop, Philadelphia City Cavalry, front elevation, ink on linen*

50. *John J. Reese house, 1989*

47. **Additions to Armory, First Troop, Philadelphia City Cavalry**
21st and Barker streets, Philadelphia
1874, Demolished
The membership of the First Troop included many of Furness's clients and in-laws: Fairman Rogers, George Harrison Frazier, Thomas Hockley, and Thomas DeWitt Cuyler, as well as a longtime member of the office, William Masters Camac. This commission added a martial fortress to the existing parade shed for which Fraser, Furness and Hewitt had received an unexecuted commission four years earlier (cat. 23). The roof of the building collapsed under the weight of a late winter storm in March 1899, leading to its replacement by the present armory. The great lintel over the portal was installed in the new armory.
AABN 1 (14 October 1876): 335; *Philadelphia Inquirer*, 6 March 1899, 10. [1973–7]

48. Alterations to Fred Brown house
2036 Delancey Street, Philadelphia
c. 1874
Brown acquired the house on 27 February 1868 from its builder, and made alterations shortly thereafter. A plan by the Furness office for a Frederick Z. Brown house—believed to be on Spruce Street—exists at the Essex Institute, Salem, Massachusetts.
Commission recorded in the Furness sketchbooks, collection of George Wood Furness.

49. **Rowland Evans and Judge J. Clark Hare houses**
118-120 South 22nd Street, Philadelphia
1874, Demolished
The property was acquired by Rowland Evans, brother of Allen, on 18 April 1874; its twin was constructed and then sold to Judge J. Clark Hare the following year.
Commission recorded in the Furness sketchbooks, collection of George Wood Furness.

50A. **John J. Reese house**
266 South 21st Street, Philadelphia
c. 1874
The incised details and exaggerated compression of the brackets link this house to other Furness designs of the early 1870s.

51a. Edmund C. Evans house, "Penrhyn-y-Coed," c. 1890

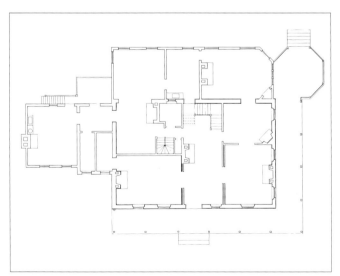

51b. Edmund C. Evans house, "Penrhyn-y-Coed," first floor after 1890

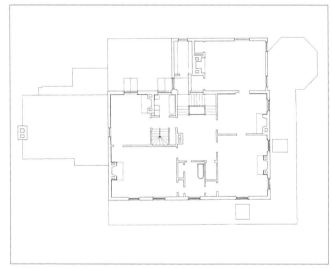

51c. Edmund C. Evans house, "Penrhyn-y-Coed," second floor after 1890

51. Edmund C. Evans house, "Penrhyn-y-Coed"
Evans' Lane, Haverford
1874, Demolished
See cat. 318, 473, 500.
The Evans family acquired more than 100 acres of land between the years 1865 and 1872. Portions were sub-sequently sold to other Furness clients including Alexander J. Cassatt (cat. 36), Clement Griscom (cat. 253), J. Randall Williams (cat. 115), and the Merion Cricket Club (cat. 252), leaving a smaller property that became the Evans family compound (cat. 116). Alterations to the house involved the construction of a kitchen wing in 1886 (cat. 318) and a new wing and dining room in 1895 (cat. 473). Allen Evans lived in the house with his father and retained possession of it into the twentieth century, after his father's death. A fire in 1898 burned the original house to the ground and Allen rebuilt the it in the colonial style (cat. 500).

Documents in possession of Allen Evans III, Bryn Mawr.

52. Charles Cushman house, "Brynhild," 1897

53Aa. Laura Barclay Wallace monument, 1990

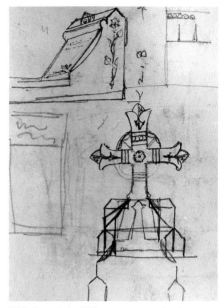

53Ab. Laura Barclay Wallace monument, pencil study

52. Charles Cushman house, "Brynhild"

Lancaster Pike, Rosemont
1874, Demolished
The house was commissioned by William Welsh, and given to his daughter Mrs. Cushman; it was occupied in June 1875. Samuel. F. Hotchkin, *Rural Pennsylvania* (Philadelphia, 1897), 182.

53A. Laura Barclay Wallace monument

St. Mary's Episcopal Church Cemetery
Burlington, NJ
1874
Identified purely by motifs, this borrows many of the forms from the Holy Communion Lutheran Church, including the lilies of the valley of the baptismal font, and the reeded, encircled cross of the altar, while the eared, pedimented form is familiar from bank doors and windows.

54. Memorial Church of the Holy Comforter

19th and Titan streets, Philadelphia
1874, GWH
The Church of the Holy Comforter was a mission of St. Peter's Episcopal Church that resulted from the generosity of Margaretta Lewis, who was soon to be Allen Evans's in-law. The parish house was erected first, followed by the church; both were built with the same green serpentine and brownstone trim used on the Lutheran Church of the Holy Communion. "T Street Church" in the Furness sketchbooks, collection of George Wood Furness; cornerstone laid on 15 June 1874; Minutes of the Vestry of St. Peter's Church.

55. H. W. Catherwood house

1708 Walnut Street, Philadelphia
c. 1873–74, Altered, GWH
The property was sold to Catherwood on 20 April 1872, and a new facade was added some time thereafter. Interior fireplaces and doors in the typical detail of the office are found on the upper stories, which were not renovated in this century. Catherwood is one of the names that shows up in a list of the works of the Hewitt firm. The Hewitt, Granger, and Paist office list is undated and catalogued by building type in alphabetical order. It includes numerous projects known to be by Furness & Hewitt. Catherwood is #842 on the list.
Commission recorded in the Furness sketchbooks, collection of George Wood Furness.

Above
54a. Memorial Church of the Holy Comforter, exterior looking southeast, 1980
Opposite
54b. Memorial Church of the Holy Comforter, nave, 1988

55. H. W. Catherwood house, looking southwest, 1927

56A. Morton P. Henry house, 1990

57a. Pennsylvania Institute for the Deaf and Dumb, detail of chimney, 1972

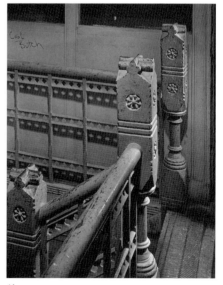

57b. Pennsylvania Institute for the Deaf and Dumb, exterior looking northeast, 1990

57c. Pennsylvania Institute for the Deaf and Dumb, exterior looking northwest, 1975

Above
57d. Pennsylvania Institute for the Deaf and Dumb, detail of stair, 1972
Opposite
58. Castle Ringstetten of the Undine Barge Club, looking northeast, c. 1878

56A. **Morton P. Henry house**
2200 St. James Street, Philadelphia
c. 1875
Among the most severe of Furness's brick city houses is this house on the site of the old Struthers Marble Yard. Several other houses on St. James Street may be by the office (cat. 83A), especially 2216.

57. **Additions to Pennsylvania Institute for the Deaf and Dumb**
Broad and Pine streets, Philadelphia

1874–75, FF
The industrial character of this addition to Haviland's classical front building is explained by its use as the location where "the manufacturing operations are principally carried on," (Scharf and Westcott, *History of Philadelphia* 2:1464). The commission was awarded in 1874 and was completed in 1875.
The Annual Report of the Board of Directors of the Pennsylvania Institution for the Deaf and Dumb for the Year 1875 (Philadelphia, 1876), 7.
[1973–8, HABS PA–1526]

Opposite
59a. St. Luke's Protestant Episcopal Church Parish House, detail of stair, 1980
Above
59b. St. Luke's Protestant Episcopal Church Parish House, exterior looking west, 1980

59c. St. Luke's Protestant Episcopal Church Parish House, entrance hall, 1980

58. Castle Ringstetten of the Undine Barge Club
Kelly Drive at Falls of Schuylkill, Philadelphia
1875
The up-river boat house of the Undine Barge Club conformed to the artistic character required by the Fairmount Park commissioners. Such small structures provided a goal and a rest facility for the oarsmen and their guests and marked the social side of the new sport of rowing.
Specifications dated 22 October 1875 at the Undine Barge Club.

59. Parish House, St. Luke's Protestant Episcopal Church
(now St. Luke and the Epiphany)
330 South 13th Street, Philadelphia
c. 1875, FF
Emlen Littell may have been responsible for bringing Furness into this project. The stair hall was constructed fronting a large column-free hall.
Commission recorded in Furness sketchbooks, collection of George Wood Furness. [HABS PA–1499]

60A. Edward A. Sibley house
235 South 18th Street, Philadelphia
c. 1875
The Sibley house was part of a plain brick row; it has since been refaced to match the neighboring Curtis Institute. Mrs. Ellen Gibson Sibley was the sister of Henry Gibson (cat. 24A). Sibley also appears in the Hewitt, Granger, and Paist office list, perhaps confirming the visual attribution.

61A. Thomas A. Scott house
1832–34 South Rittenhouse Square at 19th Street, Philadelphia
c. 1875, Demolished
Alterations were made shortly after Scott became president of the Pennsylvania Railroad in 1874; later additions are the documented work of Furness, Evans and Co. (cat. 343). Scott purchased the house from Robert Smith on 18 March 1867, mortgaged it to C. P. Mackie in 1877, and retained ownership of the house until 1901, when it was sold to Clement Newbold.

60A. Edward A Sibley house, exterior looking southeast,
c. 1935

62A. Ellwood Davis house,
east corner looking south,
c. 1885

65a. Thomas Hockley house, exterior looking northeast, 1975

63. St. Peter's Protestant Episcopal Church, exterior looking
northwest, 1989

64. Trinity Church, exterior looking north, 1990

65b. Thomas Hockley house, entrance detail, looking east, 1975

67a. Gatehouses, Philadelphia Zoological Gardens, looking southwest, c. 1880

67b. Gatehouses, Philadelphia Zoological Gardens, side gate

68. Restaurant, Philadelphia Zoological Gardens, 1876

69. Elephant House, Philadelphia Zoological Gardens, 1876

62A. Alterations to Ellwood Davis house
1318 Walnut Street, Philadelphia
c. 1875, Refaced or demolished
Alterations were made to the original house, which was probably constructed in 1833. It was sold in 1863 to Ellwood Davis, who retained the building until 1907. Details are similar to those of the Cuyler house (cat. 19A) and the Kensington National Bank (cat. 89), and presumably date from the period.

63. St. Peter's Protestant Episcopal Church
Third and Pine streets, Philadelphia
1875, FF
When Allen Evans (the future son-in-law of John T. Lewis [cat. 272], warden of St. Peter's Church) left the employ of Samuel Sloan and joined the Furness office, he brought with him the St. Peter's Church work. The original eighteenth-century design by Robert Smith was carefully respected; millwork and details followed the lines of the original. The church contains the monuments of many of the Lewis family, who remained on the east side of Philadelphia to maintain their membership in the Church.
Before the Civil War, the Church had been painted with a dark tint. A newspaper dated 10 September 1875 in volume two of the Westcott *Scrapbook* noted that the building had been repainted, the ceiling "frescoed," the windows filled with "glass of a neat pattern," the pulpit illuminated, and the stoves replaced by furnaces. Simple brick piers were added on the exterior to contain heating pipes.
Recorded in the Furness sketchbooks as "St. Peters 150 F"; Minutes of the Vestry of St. Peter's Church (14 December 1875).

64. Alterations to Trinity Church
Oxford and Disston streets, Philadelphia
1875
The Reverend Edward Buchanan was the brother of President James Buchanan and the father of Alexander J.

Cassatt's wife; his booklet, *Early History of Trinity Church, Oxford* (Philadelphia, 1885) reports that a tower and belfry were added in 1875. These are in the Flemish bond of the ancient 1711 core building, but the headers are reddish rather than black. As he did at St. Peter's (cat. 63), Furness followed the already established lines of the building; in fact, the tower is a shortened version of that at St. Peter's. The interior of the apse is ornamented with the raised plaster *sgraffito* ornament that Furness employed in the 1880s, suggesting a later alteration, perhaps at the time that a memorial window to Buchanan was installed.
Conversation, author with Allen Evans III, 1972.

65. Thomas Hockley house
235 South 21st Street, Philadelphia
1875, Altered, FF
The property was acquired on 23 April 1875 and the Hockleys were listed as residing there the following year. Hockley was a member of the First City Troop and the board of the Reliance Insurance Company. The house was described in an article entitled "Some Novel Houses":
  The unique entrance to the house of Thomas Hockley, a member of the Philadelphia bar . . . never fails to attract attention. The building is of pressed brick, super-imposed upon a seven foot basement of red Hummles-town sandstone. The lines are defined with black en-caustic brick. The roof is compound mansard with Gothic windows and large overhanging bay-window is sprung from the font at the second story. Furness and Evans [sic] were the architects. ("Some Novel Houses," *Philadelphia Press*, 5 July 1885, 12.)
The house was altered by the firm in 1894 (cat. 461).
Recorded in the Furness sketchbooks as "Hockley 300 F." [1973–9, HABS PA–1512]

66. Alterations to Women's Medical College
North College Avenue, Philadelphia
c. 1875, Demolished

Commission recorded in the Furness sketchbooks, collection of George Wood Furness.

67. Gatehouses, Philadelphia Zoological Gardens
34th Street and Girard Avenue, Philadelphia
1875–76, Altered
Fourth Annual Report of the Board of Managers of the Zoological Society of Philadelphia (Philadelphia, 1876), 9 (hereafter *Fourth Annual Report*).
[1973–11, HABS PA–1663]

68. Restaurant, Philadelphia Zoological Gardens
34th Street and Girard Avenue, Philadelphia
1875–76, Demolished, FF
  A restaurant has been built [near the Elephant House]. It is of good dimensions, containing a principal room 60 by 30 feet, with several bay windows opening into it, intended for private parties. A capacious veranda, 20 feet wide, of iron and stone, extends around it. Its total cost will be $15,000. (*Fourth Annual Report*, 9.)
Records of the Philadelphia Zoological Society; Recorded in the Furness sketchbooks as "Restaurant 50"; Drawings in the Furness sketchbooks, collection of George Wood Furness. [1973–11]

69. Elephant House, Philadelphia Zoological Gardens
34th Street and Girard Avenue, Philadelphia
1875–76, Demolished, FF
  A House for Elephants, Rhinoceros, etc. 195 feet long by 55 feet broad has been erected near the lake. It affords a single row of elevated enclosures, a broad walk and retiring room for spectators and ample accommodations for hay, etc. is of brick with granite base, with second story of wood, slate and cost, complete $38,200.(*Third Annual Report of the Board of Managers of the Zoological Society of Philadelphia* [Philadelphia, 1875], 11.)
Recorded in the sketchbooks as "Elephant 412 F"; *Fourth Annual Report*, 9. [1973–11]

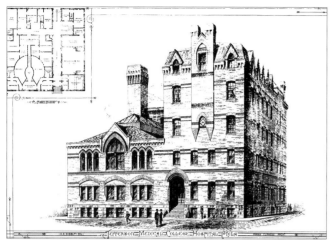

70a. Jefferson Medical College Hospital, perspective and plan, 1876

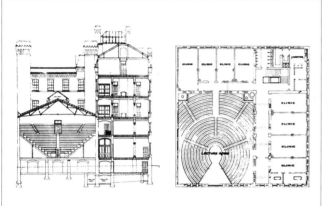

70b. Jefferson Medical College Hospital, section and plan of second story, 1876

70c. Jefferson Medical College Hospital, exterior looking north

76a. West Philadelphia Institute, looking northwest along Ludlow Street, c. 1880

76b. West Philadelphia Institute, engraved cover of Library Catalogue

77Aa. Fox barn, exterior looking northeast, 1989

77Ab. Fox barn, detail of chimney, looking southeast, 1989

77Ac. Fox barn, exterior looking northeast, 1989

70. Jefferson Medical College Hospital
Tenth and Sansom streets, Philadelphia
1875–77, Demolished
The buildings were located mid-block between Tenth and 11th streets to the rear of Napoleon LeBrun's mid-century classical temple. On 14 June 1875, the Building Committee of the Hospital asked John McArthur, Wilson and Thorn, James Windrim, Thomas W. Richards, and Furness & Hewitt to submit plans not to exceed $50,000; Windrim did not respond, but the other firms did with estimates ranging from Richards's $48,000 to Wilson's $108,000. In September Furness & Hewitt were selected; the costs were not to exceed $65,000. Bids came in at $95,000. When it was completed, a newspaper reported it as "one of Furness' happiest efforts" (Westcott, *Scrapbook* 1:46). The hospital history is discussed in Dr. Edward Teitelman, "Jefferson's Architecture, Past and Present," *Jefferson Medical College Alumni Bulletin* (Fall 1965): 12–18.
Records of Thomas Jefferson University; *AABN* 1 (9 September 1876): 292. [1973–10]

71. Alterations to Children's Hospital
207 South 22nd Street, Philadelphia

c. 1875, Demolished, FF
The hospital records alterations to their property in 1876. The *Annual Report of the Board of Commissioners of Public Charities of the State of Pennsylvania, 1876* lists an extension and mentions T. Hewson Bache as treasurer. This is presumably the Bache mentioned in the sketchbooks at the time of the split of the firm.
Commission recorded in the Furness sketchbooks, collection of George Wood Furness.

72–75. Miscellaneous unidentified projects
In addition to these known projects, there are additional names and fees listed in the Furness sketchbooks that have not been connected to specific projects. Presumably the projects listed referred to current billings at the point that the partnership split—with "F" signifying Furness and "H" signifying Hewitt—some time towards the end of 1875. Also included in the list was an entry for a piece of furniture which read: "Organ Front 50F."

72. E. Brooks 200 F

73. Kingston 183 H

74. Churchman 272 F
This project may have been for Charles Cushman (cat. 52) though there was a Churchman in the army with Furness, and C. W. Churchman later joined his office.

75. Clarence H. Clark house (?)
42nd and Spruce streets, Philadelphia
c. 1875
The sketchbook listed "Clark 75"; this probably refers to an alteration to the house of Clarence H. Clark, President of the Centennial National Bank (cat. 81). Clark also hired Furness to design a speculative row of houses on Spruce and 41st streets (cat. 91).

Frank Furness

76. West Philadelphia Institute
40th and Ludlow streets, Philadelphia
1875–76, Altered beyond recognition
The organization was chartered in 1853 and acquired the site in 1868; the building followed eight years later. In addition to a public library and chess room on the first floor, it contained a large public hall on its second story. It was constructed as a part of the campaign to provide places of learning across the city. William Welsh, a member of the Board of Directors of the City Institute, had suggested that it would be easier to raise money for six such buildings than one, resulting in the West Philadelphia Institute, the addition to the Spring Garden Institute, the City Institute, and other buildings. The West Philadelphia Institute was dedicated on 14 June 1876, with speeches by Welsh and Clarence Clark, chairman of the building committee. The newspaper reported that the building had been designed by "Frank Turner."
Westcott, *Scrapbook* 1:28, 33.

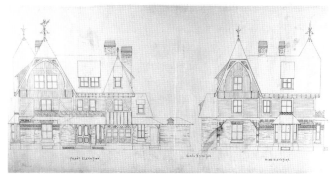

78a. Jacob Loeb house, front and side elevations (unsigned), ink on linen, 1876

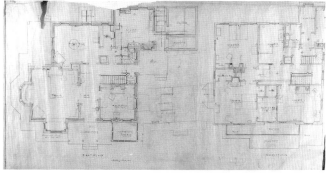

78b. Jacob Loeb house, first and second floor plans (unsigned), ink on linen, 1876

79. Institute for Feeble Minded Children, 1877

80. Brazilian Pavilion, 1876

77A. Fox barn
South of Foxburg, PA
1876
The Fox family were Philadelphians who invested heavily in timber and coal lands in western Pennsylvania. In the 1850s they built a splendid cut stone mansion overlooking the Clarion River; a generation later they built this large barn. Its assertive chimney, brick belt course, and ballooning roof are hallmarks of Furness's 1870s style. A large datestone inscribed 1876 establishes the date of the building. In the next decade, the family hired another Philadelphia architect, James P. Sims, to design a small church in the nearby town of Foxburg.

78. Jacob Loeb house
Ogontz
1876, Altered beyond recognition
The Loeb house recalls the plan of Furness & Hewitt's unidentified suburban house of 1872 (cat. 33), but with a shift across the axis of the plan, resembling the way that the Physick house (cat. 104A) shifts the plan elements of the Earl house (cat. 113). The house survives but was drastically remodelled in the 1920s by Louis Magaziner, leaving only a date plaque with the year 1876.
Drawings at the Athenaeum of Philadelphia.

79. Institute for Feeble Minded Children
Lincoln, IL
1876–77, Demolished
Frank Furness with Laing and Fehmer, Architects
Carl Fehmer (1835–?) was a German-born architect active in Boston who formed a partnership with William Ralph Emerson in the late 1870s.
AABN 2 (10 February 1877): 44; recorded in the Furness sketchbooks, collection of George Wood Furness.

80. Brazilian Pavilion
Main Building, Centennial Exhibition, Philadelphia.
1876, Demolished
The pavilion was given an architectural award and commended by judge Richard Morris Hunt: "Architectural screen and inclosure, Empire of Brazil. Report.—commended for characteristic style and suitable decoration and excellent taste."
Francis A. Walker, ed., *United States International Exhibition 1876* vol. 7, Group 27, no. 119 (Washington: Government Printing Office, 1880), 666; AABN 1 (13 May 1876): 160. [1973–12]

81. Centennial National Bank
32nd and Market streets, Philadelphia
1876, Altered
See color plate 2.
Chartered on 19 January 1876, the property was purchased on 8 April and the bank was in operation by 12 April with an office on the Centennial grounds. Bank president Clarence Clark was the son of E. W. Clark, a transplanted New Englander and an early member of the Unitarian congregation. Though Clarence joined the St. James Protestant Episcopal congregation, he regularly employed Furness in the 1870s. The interior has been much altered by a dropped ceiling, and the walls have been painted white, concealing what was described in one newspaper as an interior "of light brick of different shades, laid in ornamental designs" (Westcott, *Scrapbook* 1:43). The building was extended in the original style by Frank Miles Day in 1899.
AABN 1 (23 December 1876): 414; *PRER&BG* 14, no. 20 (17 May 1899).
[1973–13, HABS PA–1095]

81a. Centennial National Bank, exterior looking southeast, 1975

81b. Centennial National Bank, detail of west wall, 1986

81c. Centennial National Bank, study for bank

81d. Centennial National Bank, interior above dropped ceiling, 1975

82. Hotel entrance
Chestnut Street, Philadelphia
1876, Demolished
It is probable that this was an alteration to the Continental
Hotel on the 1500 block of Chestnut Street, which was
singled out for praise by Christopher Dresser when he was
in Philadelphia in 1876.
AABN 1 (14 October 1876): 334–36.

83A. 2200 block houses, St. James Street, Philadelphia
c. 1876
Though undocumented, the houses on this street are certainly in the office manner. The block includes two small
houses on the north side with large flowered plaques flanking the doors. (See cat. 56A.)
Pennsylvania Historic Sites Survey.

84A. **Ornamental stone gate**
Centennial grounds, since moved to East River Drive near
Strawberry Mansion Bridge, Philadelphia
1876
The ornamental carving of the gate is particularly close to
the work of Christopher Dresser; similar passages appear in
drawings by Sullivan of the same period. It was built as part
of the exhibit for the Connecticut Brownstone Company.
A decade after the Centennial, it was reported that the gate had
been moved to its present site (Westcott, *Scrapbook* 3:96).

85A. **Kaighn development**
2300 block, Delancey Street, north and south sides,
Philadelphia
c. 1876
The attribution is based on the similarity of the development's visual character to that of the St. James Street houses
(cat. 56A, 83A). More compelling is the evidence of elements of the office vocabulary in the mid-1870s: the vestigial acroteria of the entrances, the bands of polychromed
materials, and the pierced dormers. Of particular note here
is the dichotomy between the north side, where brownstone
predominates, and the south side, where Pennsylvania blue
marble is the principal material. Brick is used for contrast on
both sides of the block. Surely Furness was adjusting the
materials according to the effect of sunlight, with darker
colors placed where sunlight would reach them and lighter
colors on the shady side of the street.
[HABS PA–1502]

84A. *Ornamental stone gate, looking east, 1974*

85Aa. *Kaighn development, exterior looking north, 1989*

85Ab. *Kaighn development, exterior looking northeast, 1989*

86b. *Provident Life and Trust Company Building, exterior looking northeast, c.1885*

86a. *Provident Life and Trust Company Building, engraving by William M. Camac, 1876*

86c. *Provident Life and Trust Company Building, detail of iron grille over entrance, 1959*

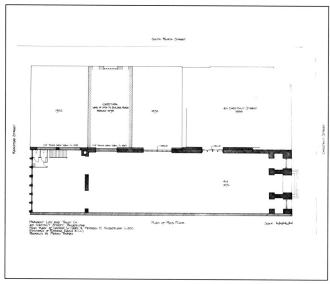

86d. Provident Life and Trust Company Building, Fourth Street facade looking west, 1979

86e. Provident Life and Trust Company Building, main floor plan, redrawn c. 1931

86f. Provident Life and Trust Company Building, main banking floor, c. 1880

86g. Provident Life and Trust Company Building, main banking room, looking south, c. 1880

86. Provident Life and Trust Company Building
409 Chestnut Street and 42 South Fourth Street, Philadelphia
1876–79, Demolished
See cat. 369, 423, 514, 553.
Competitors for this commission included George W. Hewitt (Furness's former partner), James H. Windrim, and Addison Hutton (the architect of the first Provident offices). The L-shaped building had two formal facades, the principle front on Chestnut Street and its insurance office on Fourth Street. The perspective engraving of the facade in the *Insurance Blue Book* bears a monogram of WC—perhaps the first evidence of William Camac's presence in the office. An article in the Westcott *Scrapbook* caught the general tenor of contemporary criticism:

Among the buildings put up in that 'square' of what Philadelphians call the 'fine buildings,' which one has attracted one-third the attention that this has, and entirely because of its eccentricity? . . . with the front there seems to have been a new surprise every few mornings, and there has been a constant strain on the public mind as to what might be coming. Can it really be that this is a coming American nineteenth century style which we are slow of heart to recognize? (Westcott, *Scrapbook* 2:4.)

When it was completed two years later, it was already appreciated, verifying the contention of the Reverend William Henry Furness who had argued that new forms needed time to be accepted. The Telegraph commented, "The building as a whole is impressive in its appearance, and is the most conspicuous . . . in the great bank row."
Westcott, *Scrapbook* 2:75; Minutes of the Board of Directors of the Provident Life and Trust Company MS, meeting of 7 August 1876. [1973–14, HABS PA–1058]

87. Shamokin Station, Philadelphia and Reading Railroad
Shamokin
1876, Unexecuted, FF
This is one of the first—if not the first—and later commission to Furness from the Reading Railroad. One of Frank Furness's father's closest friends, fellow New Englander Samuel Bradford, was the treasurer of the railroad from its founding. The elevation is also signed with the name W. Lorenz, engineer for the Reading Railroad. Six years later Furness was commissioned again to design the station (cat. 133).
Signed drawing, collection of Mr. and Mrs. Alfred W. Hesse, Jr., Gladwynne.

88A. Parlor addition to Horace Howard Furness summer house, "Lindenshade"
Wallingford
1877, Demolished
See cat. 31, 39A, 565.
This project is detailed by Horace in his summer log.
Lindenshade summer records, 1864–78; Horace Howard Furness Collection, University of Pennsylvania Library.

89. Kensington National Bank
Frankford and Girard avenues, Philadelphia
1877, Altered
The property was acquired by the bank on 23 January 1877; it was enlarged following the lines of the original design by Frank Watson in 1919 (*PRER&BG* 34, no. 35 [27 August 1919]). The building has since been shorn of its aggressive cornice, its entrance has been altered, and its interior has been largely covered over. The interior was skylit and surrounded by a second level gallery "of wrought iron . . . the floors are of tile supported by brick arches . . . the desks are of oiled walnut" (Westcott, *Scrapbook* 1:152).
AABN 2 (25 August 1877): 273.
[1973–15, HABS PA–1773]

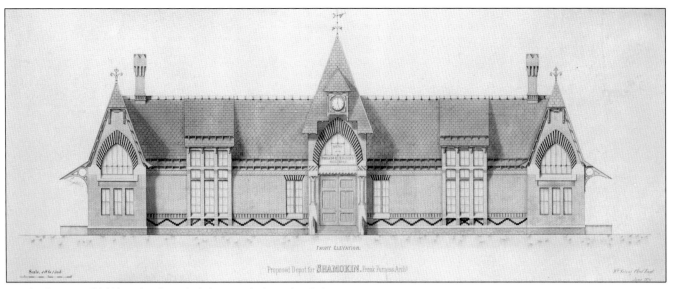

87a. Shamokin Station, Philadelphia and Reading Railroad, elevation, rendered watercolor and ink

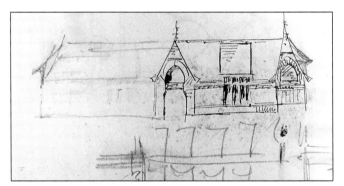

87b. Shamokin Station, ink study for front elevation

89b. Kensington National Bank, exterior looking southwest, 1986

89a. Kensington National Bank, exterior looking southwest, c. 1880

90. Maternity Ward, Women's Hospital of Philadelphia, c. 1895

91a. 4061 Spruce Street, Philadelphia, exterior detail looking northeast, 1989

91b. 4061 Spruce Street, Philadelphia, detail of iron railing, 1989

91c. 4047–61 Spruce Street, Philadelphia, exterior looking northeast, 1989

91d. 4050–66 Irving Street, Philadelphia, exterior looking southeast, 1989

90. **Maternity Ward, Women's Hospital of Philadelphia**
22nd Street and North College Avenue, Philadelphia
1877, Demolished
18th Annual Report of the Board of Managers (January 1879): 5–6.

91. **Development on 4047–61 Spruce Street and 4050–66 Irving Street, Philadelphia**
c. 1877
The client was Clarence H. Clark, President of the Centennial National Bank (cat. 81) and a major property holder in Philadelphia.
Westcott, *Scrapbook* 1:102.

92. Three-story building for Jefferson Medical College
120 South Tenth Street, Philadelphia
1877, Demolished
The shift of Professor Robert Rogers from the University of Pennsylvania to Jefferson Medical College necessitated a

new laboratory (cat. 70). It was a three-story structure containing a museum, lab, and skylit dissection room, which capped the building.
Teitelman, "Jefferson's Architecture, Past and Present," *Jefferson Medical College Alumni Bulletin* (Fall 1965): 12–18; *AABN* 2 (25 August 1877): 273.

93. Renovations to Mercantile Library
Tenth Street below Market Street, Philadelphia
1877, Demolished
After suffering fire damage, the building was renovated. The color scheme of the repaired building was an array of richly painted neutral tints. The lower portions of the wall were relieved in gold with the prevailing tint of light blue and accented by a broad band of polychromatic decoration that was "Pompeiian in character" (Westcott, *Scrapbook* 1:60). The fronts of the galleries and bookcases were edged with designs of leaves and flowers.

AABN 2 (25 August 1877): 273.

94. Lunatic Asylum, Competition
Philadelphia
1877, Unexecuted
The competition for the Lunatic Asylum was lost to the Wilson Brothers. Other competitors included Hutton and Ord, Collins and Autenrieth, and Samuel Sloan.
AABN 2 (22 September 1877): 306.

95. Stenciled decorations, St. Stephen's Protestant Episcopal Church
Tenth Street below Market Street, Philadelphia
1878
The stenciled decorations have been removed with the exception of portions surviving behind the organ case.
Minutes of St. Stephen's Church, MS, meeting of 3 July 1878.

91e. 4047 Spruce Street, Philadelphia, detail of stair newel, 1990

91f. 4047 Spruce Street, Philadelphia, living room fireplace, 1990

91g. 4047 Spruce Street, Philadelphia, detail second floor fireplace, 1990

91h. 4047 Spruce Street, Philadelphia, detail second floor fireplace, 1990

96a. Church of the Redeemer for Seamen and their Families and Charles Brewer School, exterior looking northeast, 1973

96b. Church of the Redeemer for Seamen and their Families and Charles Brewer School, exterior looking northwest, c. 1975

96c. Charles Brewer School, entrance, looking north, 1973

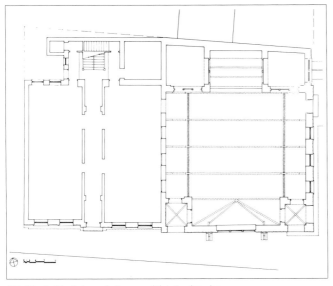

96d. Church of the Redeemer for Seamen and their Families, plan

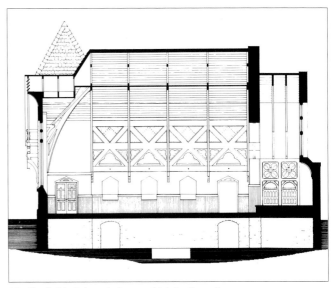

96e. Church of the Redeemer for Seamen and their Families, section

96f. Church of the Redeemer for Seamen and their Families, nave looking north, 1961

*96g. Church of the Redeemer for Seamen and their Families
and the Charles Brewer School, nave looking south, 1972*

*96h. Church of the Redeemer for Seamen and their Families,
detail of psalm plaque, 1961*

96. Church of the Redeemer for Seamen and their Families and Charles Brewer School

Front and Queen streets, Philadelphia
1878, Demolished
See color plate 3.

The Church of the Redeemer for Seamen and their Families was a double-functioning building, with a chapel at the corner and a school building on the inside of the lot. Though sharing materials, the church and the more lively school were differentiated by the school's colorful accents of brick in various patterns, as in the demonstration panels above its door. The turned posts and struts framing the large gable recall many of the domestic commissions of the period, and are typical of Evans's work. The cornerstone was laid on 15 June 1878 and the building was completed and dedicated on 9 January 1879. The complex was destroyed by arson in 1978 (Westcott, *Scrapbook* 2:78).

Records of the Board of Managers of the Churchman's Missionary Association for Seamen of the Port of Philadelphia MS, meeting of 10 September 1878; Records in possession of the Seamen's Church Institute, 1212 Locust Street, Philadelphia. [1973–16, HABS PA–1077]

97. Loeb Dispensary, Jewish Hospital, c. 1880

98a. Allen Evans and Rowland Evans joint property, "The Breezes," speculative house, c. 1890

98b. Allen Evans and Rowland Evans joint property, "The Breezes," speculative house, c. 1890

100a. Social Arts Club, engraving of facade after alterations, before 1890

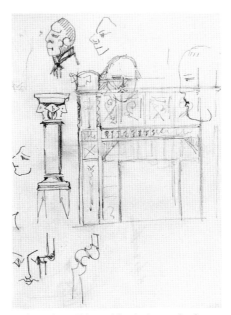

100b. Social Arts Club, second floor fireplace, pencil study

100c. Social Arts Club, dining room fireplace, 1989

100d. Social Arts Club, library furniture, 1989

100e. Social Arts Club, map case, pencil study

97. Loeb Dispensary, Jewish Hospital

Broad Street and Old York Road, Philadelphia
1878, Demolished
The dispensary continued the colorful accents of the original building of 1871 (cat. 29).
Records of Einstein Medical Center, Philadelphia.

98. Allen Evans and Rowland Evans joint property, "The Breezes"

Evans Lane, Lower Merion
1878, Altered, AE
On the exterior, only the first-story rough stonework remains; the upper level shingle was replaced with stucco and half timber in the twentieth century.
Records in collection of Allen Evans, III, Bryn Mawr.

99. Additions and alterations to Reform Club

1520 Chestnut Street, Philadelphia
c. 1878, Demolished
The Reform Club was incorporated in 1873 and established itself in an antebellum mansion originally built for Joseph Florence on Chestnut Street. In 1878 Furness was commissioned to design a two-story addition with
a flat roof and balcony [containing rooms] for the convenience of lady guests . . . [The] way of entering the restaurant is rather peculiar. From Chestnut Street they will pass through a door and go down five steps, when another door and vestibule opens into an underground passage three feet below the level of the pavement. The passage is eight feet high and runs under the restaurant floor to the back part of the building. Here it ends and a flight of winding stairs leads up to the garden back of the building . . . The passage will be paved with marble and its sides finished with marble panels. The top will be arched and have a light placed at each end. Scarcity of building space is the reason assigned for this mode of entrance. (Westcott, *Scrapbook* 1:125, 161, 164).
Furness was probably chosen by the president of the club, John Welsh, whose son was an army friend of Furness. The additions were begun in early 1878 and completed on 15 June but the building was sold shortly thereafter when many members seceded to form the rival Reform League in 1879.

100. Additions and alterations to Social Arts Club

1811 Walnut Street, Philadelphia
1878, Altered
The club was formed on Chestnut Street, and in 1878 acquired a house on Rittenhouse Square, prompting its change of name to the Rittenhouse Club, as it is currently known. Furness's work included interior modifications, furniture and fireplace design, and a new marble facade. While most of the newspaper reports on the building were complimentary, one was hostile, terming it
as cold and unsuggestive of art as a plentiful lack of art could make it. The entire front is of plain, white marble and over the door is a classic portico, which resembles nothing so much as a mausoleum, transferred from a cemetery and stuck onto the building. If it suggests anything, it is that art is dead in the neighborhood. (Westcott, *Scrapbook* 2:13.)
Furness belonged only to this one club; many of its members were his clients—including those who lived on Rittenhouse Square. In 1989 the Club sold its home of 110 years.
Records of Rittenhouse Club, MS, meetings, 1878, courtesy of J. McFadden.

Above: *101A. DeForrest Willard house, before 1901*
Opposite: *103. St. Stephen's Episcopal Church, interior of north transept looking northeast, 1990*

104Aa. Emlen Physick house, exterior looking southwest, 1974

101A. **DeForrest Willard house**
1601 Walnut Street, Philadelphia
c. 1878, Demolished
Willard was a Civil War veteran and a University of Pennsylvania Medical School graduate who worked with Horace Furness on the Sanitary Commission Fair, taught at the University of Pennsylvania, and secured the erection of the orthopedic ward at the University of Pennsylvania Hospital.

102. **Wood banner**
Whereabouts unknown
1878
This banner or shield of Native American woods was designed for Walter Lippincott for the Paris Universal Exhibit.
Westcott, *Scrapbook*.

103. **Additions and alterations to St. Stephen's Protestant Episcopal Church**
Tenth Street below Market Street, Philadelphia
1878–79
A newspaper account indicated that Furness had added a transept in the northeast corner, updated the chancel with a bronze railing and pulpit, and frescoed the walls (cat. 95) in turquoise blue and gold, with flowers, doves, and emblems of St. Stephen (Westcott, *Scrapbook* 2:25). The transept survives as do bits of the stenciling; later renovations have undone much of Furness's work.
Minutes of St. Stephen's Church, MS, 7 October 1878.

104Ab. Emlen Physick house, exterior looking southeast, 1990

104A. **Emlen Physick house**
Washington Street, Cape May, NJ
1878
See color plate 6.
The Physick house is similar to a group of suburban houses of the late 1870s. Though regularly reported in the local newspaper, its architect was never disclosed. It has been restored as the Mid-Atlantic Center for the Arts under the direction of Hyman Myers; several pieces of Furness-designed furniture have been acquired as a part of the restoration.

George E. Thomas and Carl E. Doebley, *Cape May: Queen of the Seaside Resorts* (Philadelphia: Art Alliance, 1976), 116–19.
[HABS NJ CAPMA 68]

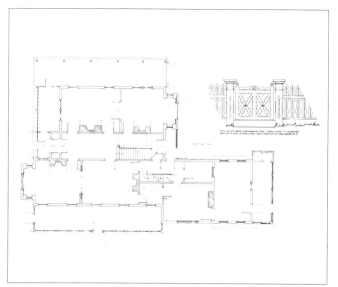

104Ac. Emlen Physick house, first floor plan

104Ad. Emlen Physick house, parlor fireplace, 1973

104Ae. Emlen Physick house, dining room fireplace, 1973

104Af. Emlen Physick house, second floor stair landing, 1973

105A. J. F. Fryer cottage, exterior looking northeast, 1973

105A. **J. F. Fryer cottage**
9–11 Perry Street, Cape May, NJ
1878–79
The Fryer cottage was built after the fire of 1878 that devastated the core of Cape May. It is similar to contemporary seaside hotels, including Bruce Price's West End Hotel in Bar Harbor, ME (*AABN* 4, [January 1879]). The stair newels recall those of the Pennsylvania Institute for the Deaf and Dumb of 1874 (cat. 57).
Attribution by William Bassett, New Jersey survey.
[HABS NJ CAPMA 67]

106a. *Library Company of Philadelphia Building, exterior looking northeast, c. 1880*

106b. *Library Company of Philadelphia Building, reading room*

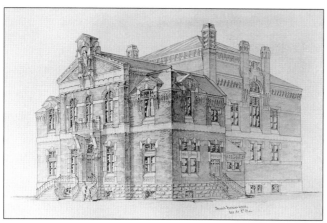

106c. *Library Company of Philadelphia Building, tinted ink perspective*

106d. *Library Company of Philadelphia Building, reading room*

106. Library Company of Philadelphia Building
Locust and Juniper streets, Philadelphia
1879–80, Demolished
The Library Company invited Addison Hutton, Theophilus Chandler, Collins and Autentrieth, James C. Sidney, and Frank Furness to submit designs on 20 January 1879. Two weeks later Furness was selected by a nearly unanimous vote for a design that was intended to recall the William Thornton Building on Fifth Street. The building was completed the following year. It was later extended by Collins and Autenrieth in 1890 and was demolished in 1940.
Public Ledger (20 February 1879): 3; O'Gorman, *Drawing Toward Building*, 145–146.
[1973–17]

107. John T. Lewis house, "Glyntaff"
Booth Road, Haverford
1879, Demolished, AE
The land was purchased on 11 March 1879 and excavation for the cellar was underway the following week. The roof was slated on 7 June, the plasterers finished on 19 July, and the family moved into the house on 17 September. Lewis's diary noted, "The new house called 'Glyntaff' after a hamlet of that name in the parish of Glamorganshire, So. Wales whence our family came to Philadelphia in 1686." (John T. Lewis, expense book, 1878–88, 19–20 [Evans files].) The simple, almost vernacular character of the design established another architectural voice of the office, one which would reappear in similar circumstances for similar clients. Others in this group include Edmund C. Evans's "Penrhyn-y-coed" (cat. 51) and J. Clark Hare's "Harford" (cat. 110). Furness also designed a house for Lewis in Philadelphia (cat. 272).

107. John T. Lewis house, "Glyntaff," c. 1900

110a. Judge J. Clark Hare house, "Harford," 1989

110b. Judge J. Clark Hare house, "Harford," detail of end gable, 1989

110c. Judge J. Clark Hare house, "Harford," stair newell, main hall, 1989

108. John Lower Welsh house, "Hillbrow"
Montgomery Avenue, Springfield
1880, Demolished
According to Emily T. C. Jernigan, who researched the family, John Lowber Welsh had joined a cavalry troop, headed by Captain William Rotch Wister, which included William West Frazier (cat. 256), and Frank Furness. Welsh was eventually captured (*Jones Wister's Reminiscences* [Philadelphia: Lippincott Co., 1920], 156).

The English looking house of John Lowber Welsh faces the end of Birch Lane on Montgomery avenue. The position is a remarkably fine one for a dwelling. Mr. Welsh is a son of the late Hon. John Welsh, who was the United States Minister to England. The mansion which he constructed is an architectural one of stone that would draw the attention of the passer-by for its

beauty. A piazza gives the privilege of a view of uncommon extent and grandeur. (Samuel F. Hotchkin, *Ancient and Modern Germantown, Mount Airy and Chestnut Hill* [Philadelphia, 1889], 443.)
AABN 7 (28 February 1880): 88.

109. Ellen Stokes house
Westview and Wissahickon avenues(?), Philadelphia
1879–80, Demolished
John Welsh (1805–86), father of John Lowber Welsh (cat. 108) was a prominent Philadelphia merchant and philanthropist and an organizer of the 1876 Centennial Exhibition. From 1877 to 1879 he was ambassador to England. The house was built for his daughter, Mrs. Ellen Stokes. Welsh signed the contract for the house on 6 November 1879. His daughter and son-in-law lived with him in his

nearby summer house until their house was completed in the middle of the following summer.
Edward Lowber Stokes, ed., *Letters of John Welsh* (Philadelphia: Harris & Partridge, 1937), 127–28, 145; *AABN* 7 (28 February 1880): 88.

110. Judge J. Clark Hare house, "Harford"
Radnor
1879–80, AE
Harford was built as a summer residence for the family of Judge J. Clark Hare (cat. 49), a nephew of John Hare Powell. According to Phyllis Maier's study of the house, family tradition states that it was the work of Allen Evans, presumably on the basis of his work on the city houses and on family interconnections.
Phyllis C. Maier, *Harford.* (Lower Merion Historical Society, n.d.); *AABN* 7 (6 March 1880): 100.

111Aa. John Welsh house, "Spring Bank," exterior detail of stair tower looking southwest, 1990

111Ab. John Welsh house, "Spring Bank," exterior looking south, 1990

111Ac. John Welsh house, "Spring Bank," stable looking northwest, 1990

113. Harrison Earl house, "Earlham," 1889

111A. Alterations and renovations to John Welsh house, "Spring Bank"
Wissahickon Avenue, Philadelphia
c. 1880
An early nineteenth-century rubble-stone farmhouse was acquired by Welsh and renovated around 1880. The entrance hall and exterior wood are characteristic of Furness's work, and the large two-story stable is typical as well.

112. Alterations to Alexander J. Cassatt house, "Cheswold"
Cheswold Lane, Haverford
1880, AE
See cat. 36.
Patricia Davis, *End of the Line: Alexander J. Cassatt and the Pennsylvania Railroad* (New York: Neale Watson Academic Publications, 1978), 80.

113. Harrison Earl house, "Earlham"
Unspecified location in Philadelphia suburbs
c. 1880
The simple cubic mass of "Earlham" relates it to the Loeb house (cat. 78), and, more directly, to the Physick house (cat. 104A).
Wells and Hope, *Philadelphia Suburban Homes*, vol. 1

(Philadelphia, c. 1889). (The only known copy is in the collection of the Historical Society of Pennsylvania.)

114. William H. Rhawn house, "Knowlton"
8001 Verree Road, Fox Chase, Philadelphia
1880
See color plates 4 and 5.
Rhawn was an officer in the Guarantee Trust and Safe Deposit Company (cat. 44) and president of the National Bank of the Republic (cat. 281). The house was completed in 1881, the date on the leaded glass in the entry. The account book for the construction of "Knowlton" has recently been given by the Rhawn family to the Athenaeum of Philadelphia and is an extraordinary document. Entitled "Account of Expenditures for Knowlton, so named for the late George Knowles, grandfather of Hattie Rhawn," it records in detail the process of building a Victorian country seat as well as providing insight into the practice of the office.
It begins, "Purchased for me by George W. Rhawn of Charles Livsey on 12 January 1880, ten acres of land $14,750." Three days later, Rhawn "visited property with Mr. Frank Furness, architect to select a site for the dwelling." Preliminary plans were received from Furness five

weeks later. Stone was quarried on the site, necessitating a visit by the owner and architect in late March. Carpenter Ezra Wright was hired as builder along with mason Joseph S. Brouse; neither appears in city directories, suggesting that they were from a village beyond the city limits. Furness visited the site in May, July, and August, and then was replaced by Allen Evans, who perhaps had been given charge of the project. In late August a check was paid to "Furness and Evans," marking Evans's new status as a partner. Evans visited the site in September and October but Furness was back in November and December. Interior finishes required less supervision and no further visits were made until the following spring. In the meantime, W. W. Smith was hired to produce mantels and furniture. He is presumably the "William W. Smith Furniture Maker, successor to Smith and Campion," whose office at 239 South Third Street was across from Furness's office. Smith was paid a total of $955 for his work. The tile for the entrance was provided by Sharpless, Watt, and Co. for $200 with a $68 charge for laying it; lamps were provided by Cornelius. Furness's net fee was $600 with an additional $100 paid for the design of the stable. The entire house with land, furniture, fees, etc. cost $32,636.16.
AABN 7 (28 February 1880): 88. [1973–18]

114a. William H. Rhawn house, "Knowlton," c. 1888

114b. William H. Rhawn house, "Knowlton," 1972

114c. William H. Rhawn house, "Knowlton," stables, 1972

114d. William H. Rhawn house, "Knowlton," transverse section

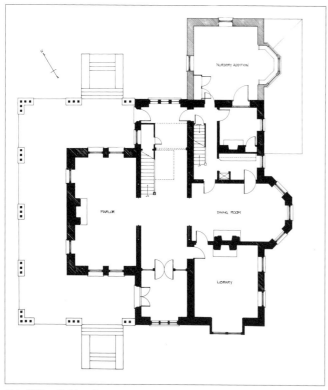

114e. William H. Rhawn house, "Knowlton," first floor plan

114f. William H. Rhawn house, "Knowlton," entrance hall, 1972

114g. William H. Rhawn house, "Knowlton," main stairhall, 1972

114h. William H. Rhawn house, "Knowlton," library, 1972

115. J. Randall Williams house, "Harleigh"
Gray's Lane, Haverford
1880, Demolished
The home of lumber merchant J. Randall Williams was built on property bought from the Evans holdings and was listed as one of the most valuable houses on the Main Line ($40,000 house, *Philadelphia Inquirer*, 7 October 1890, 7). The AABN reported that Allen Evans was in charge of the work, as he appears to have been for the other major houses in the vicinity of his home.
AABN 7 (28 February 1880): 88.

116. Rowland Evans house, "Penrhyn"
Evans' Lane, Haverford
1880, Demolished, AE
This house on the Evans property designed by Allen Evans,

is probably for his brother, Rowland Evans (cat. 49, 98); Rowland moved in on 1 May 1880. The house known as "Penrhyn-y-coed" belonged to their father, Edmund (cat. 51). Evans MS, 94; *AABN* 7 (28 February 1880): 88; Hotchkin, *Rural Pennsylvania*, 141.

117. Alexander J. Cassatt stable and coachman's house
2006 Sansom Street, Philadelphia
1880, Demolished
Alexander J. Cassatt (cat. 36) was living in the Haverford Station House at the time, making it likely that this building was actually constructed for his brother, J. Gardner Cassatt, who was living at 2045 Locust Street in 1880. A small, brick stable with a mansard loft, the building has been demolished since the 1973 Furness exhibition.
AABN 7 (28 February 1880): 88.

118. M. R. Thomas house, 1990

121. Walnut Lane Station, c. 1885

123. Conshohocken Station, c. 1885

124. Wayne Junction Station, c. 1885

121–247. New work and alterations totaling 125 executed buildings for the Philadelphia and Reading Railroad Company with additional projects ready for construction
1878–84
Letter from Frank Furness to John E. Wooten, 23 December 1884, Historical Society of Pennsylvania:

Since I have entered on my duties as Architect, the drawings have been made for some one hundred and twenty five buildings and alterations to buildings, for railroad purposes; covering a great extent of the country; the work having been carried out in most cases under my personal supervision.

Drawings have also been made for many buildings, the erection of which have not yet been authorized.

Major caches of information exist elsewhere including the Hagley Museum of Winterthur, DE and private collections. One particularly important document is a scrapbook of large-format views of the early stations taken in the mid-1880s, and presently in the collection of Theodore Xaras. On the border of each photograph are the date of completion and, in many instances, the cost of the building. (That list included catalogue entries 121–141.)
Several stations—Mount Pleasant Station (cat. 152), **Sunbury Station** (cat. 153), Lewistown Station (cat. 154), **Pottsville Station** (cat. 155), etc.—are currently the topic of a dissertation at the University of Pennsylvania by Preston Thayer, who is attempting to sort out their sequence.
In addition to the works shown here, Furness designed ninety buildings for the Reading Railroad in the early 1880s.

121. **Walnut Lane Station**
Completed 1878
Cost: $3,500

122. Norristown Station
Completed 1879
Cost: $5,500

123. **Conshohocken Station**
Completed 1881
Cost: $5,885

124. **Wayne Junction Station**
Completed 1881
Cost: $3,930

125. **Trenton Junction Station**
Completed 1881
Cost: $5,146

126. **Wernersville Station**
Completed 1881

118. **M. R. Thomas house**
310 North High Street, West Chester
1880
Perhaps this project was an alteration to this house at 310 North High Street. This 1830s, center-hall, brick house, enlarged by a gabled mansard, includes many of the details of the Reading suburban stations.
AABN 7 (6 March 1880): 100.

119A. House on Old Lancaster Pike, Devon
c. 1880, Drastically altered
This is probably a Dallett house, erected c. 1880. Its grand porch (with massive turned posts and deep knee braces at the entrance), sculptural chimneys, and awkwardly shaped

dormers are visual hallmarks of Furness's style and closely recall "Earlham" (cat. 113). The plan is the old center-hall type, with a handsome stair marked by a sculptural octagonal newel. Doors with the familiar grooved rails and stiles confirm the attribution.

120. Alterations to Philadelphia and Reading Railroad Company offices
Fourth Street and Willings Alley, Philadelphia
1880, Altered beyond recognition.
The main building was constructed in 1850 and remained the headquarters for the firm until they moved to the new terminal on Market Street.
AABN 7 (29 May 1880): 242.

127. **Manheim Station**
Completed 1881

128. **Signal towers at Wayne Junction**
Completed 1881

129. **Cordelia Station**
Completed 1881

130. Langhorne Station
Completed 1882
Cost: $2,693

131. **Douglassville Station**
Completed 1882
Cost: $5,480

132. **Logan Station**
Completed 1882
Cost: $4,956

133. **Shamokin Station**
Completed 1882
Cost: $8700
The Shamokin Station is a completely revised version of
Furness's unbuilt 1876 project (cat. 87).
James L. Holton, *The Reading Railroad: History of a Coal Age
Empire*, vol. 1 (Laury's Station, PA: Garrigues House, 1989),
235.

125a. Trenton Junction Station, c. 1885

125b. Trenton Junction Station, c. 1918

126. Wernersville Station, c. 1885

127. Manheim Station, c. 1885

134. **Petersburg Station**
Completed 1882

135. **Dispatch office at Tamaqua**
Completed 1882

136. **Wissahickon Station**
Completed 1883
Cost: $7,338

137. **Mount Airy Station**
Completed 1883
Cost: $8,139

138. **Manayunk Station**
Completed 1883
Cost: $15,790

139. **Gravers Lane Station**
Completed 1883
Cost: $8,000
[1973–19]

140. **Dispatch Office at Shamokin**
Completed 1883
Cost: $2,270

128. Signal towers, Wayne Junction, c. 1885

129. Cordelia Station, c. 1885

131. Douglassville Station, c. 1885

132. Logan Station, c. 1885

133. Shamokin Station, c. 1885

134. Petersburg Station, c. 1885

135. Dispatch office, Tamaqua, c.1885

136a. Wissahickon Station, c. 1885

136b. Wissahickon Station, c. 1885

137. Mount Airy Station, c. 1885

138a. Manayunk Station, c. 1885

138b. Manayunk Station, c. 1885

139a. Graver's Lane Station, c. 1885

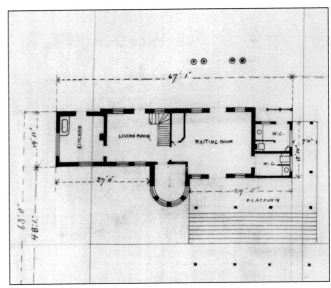

139b. Graver's Lane Station, plan, ink on linen

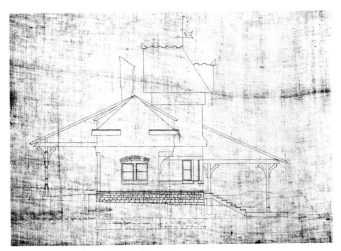

139c. Graver's Lane Station, elevation, ink on linen

140. Dispatch office, Shamokin Station, c. 1885

141. Mermaid Station, c.1885

142. Main Street Station, Norristown, c. 1885

143. Noble Station, 1989

144. Frankford Station (left), c. 1885

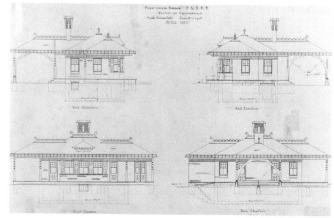

148. Collegeville Station, "Collegeville Station, Philadelphia and Reading Railroad," plan and elevations, ink on linen, 1884

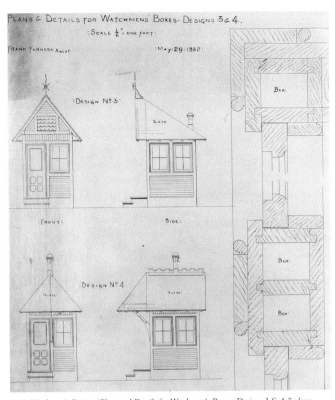

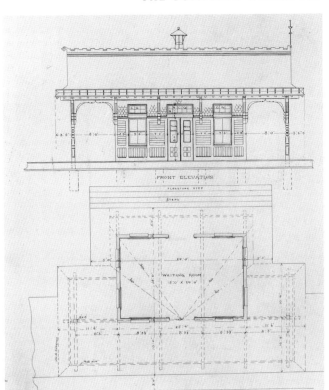

145. Watchman's Boxes, "Plans and Details for Watchman's Boxes, Designs 3 & 4," plans, elevations, and details, ink on linen, 1882

146a. Tabor Station, plan and elevations, ink on linen, c. 1883

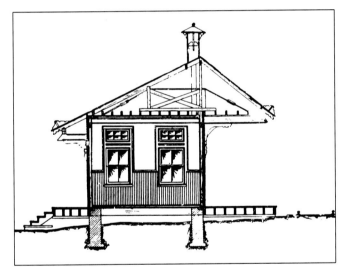

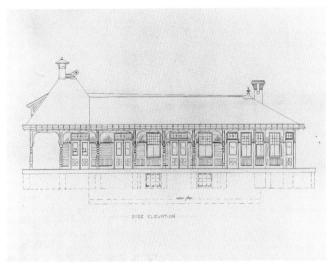

146b. Tabor Station, section, 1895

147. West Milford Junction Station, elevation, ink on paper, 1883

149. Watch Box, Ashland, c. 1918

150. Signal tower, Tabor Junction, c. 1918

151. Sedgwick Station, c. 1882

153. Sunbury Station, c. 1918

155. Pottsville Station, c. 1885

156. Lewisburg Station, 1918

157a. Wingohocking Station, interior of waiting room towards fireplace, 1931

157b. Wingohocking Station, trackside with added porch, 1931

158. Reading Station, 1930

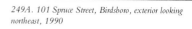

249A. *101 Spruce Street, Birdsboro, exterior looking northeast, 1990*

248A. *Levi Focht house, exterior looking northeast, 1990*

250a. *William Peddle Henszey house, "Red Leaf," c. 1888*

250b. William Peddle Henszey house, "Red Leaf," stable, 1988

250c. William Peddle Henszey house, "Red Leaf," 1920

251A. Germantown Unitarian Church, Parish House, c. 1920

252. Merion Cricket Club, c. 1880

248A. Levi Focht house
105 Spruce Street, Birdsboro
c. 1880
Focht was the builder of most of the Reading stations and track buildings and worked with Furness until the turn of the century. In the late 1880s, he began to present himself as an architect for work in the Reading vicinity; perhaps this is one of his designs. It seems more likely that Focht authored other less exuberant versions of the Furness manner in Birdsboro, such as the house diagonally across the street from his own, and the house to the east at First and Walnut.

249A. 101 Spruce Street, Birdsboro
c. 1880
The house is situated at the corner of Spruce and First streets. Its roof line recalls the Rhawn house (cat. 114) and other buildings of the period, while most of the carpentry details appear on the various stations of the Reading (cat. 121–247).

250. William Peddle Henszey house, "Red Leaf"
Lancaster Avenue, Ardmore
1881, Demolished
All but the carriage house has been demolished and replaced by an English Gothic apartment house. Hotchkin described the house:

> The main hall, extending through to the back porch, is finished in cherry, and has a paneled ceiling. On the right of this hall are the reception and drawing-rooms. The reception room is finished in mahogany, with frescoed walls and ceiling. The drawing-room is white and gold, and is a typical example of Louis XVI style. Opposite the drawing-room is the music-room, with wainscotting of oak. From the music-room you enter the dining-room, which has many novel features, and is quite beautiful. The wainscotting and beams of ceiling are of quartered oak. In the ceiling is a skylight with cathedral glass, at the end of the room a fine, large fireplace and mantel of Caen stone, handsomely carved with a semi-circular window opening through the chimney breast. (Hotchkin, *Rural Pennsylvania*, 108–09.)

Henszey was part owner of the Baldwin Locomotive Works, one of the largest industries of the city.

251A. Parish House, Germantown Unitarian Church
Greene Street and Chelten Avenue, Philadelphia
1880, Demolished
Presumably this was the work of the firm a decade after the construction of the Church (cat. 1); this would seem to be corroborated by the chimney detail which occurs on numerous houses from the late 1870s.
Scharf and Westcott, *History of Philadelphia* 2:1406.

252. Merion Cricket Club
Ardmore
1880–81
See cat. 347, 436A, 437, 458, 470, 483, 600, 613.
Allen and Rowland Evans were founding members of the Club in 1865, serving as officers into the twentieth century. In the fall of 1880 the Club acquired the property adjacent to the playing field. At the meeting of 3 December of the same year the club thanked Allen Evans for providing the designs for the new clubhouse and viewing stand, which were completed the following spring. The Club continued to commission Furness for many subsequent buildings and alterations, both in Ardmore (cat. 347) and in Haverford (cat. 436A, 437, 458, 470, 483, 600, 613).
Merion Cricket Club Board Minutes, vol. 1 (1865–84), 3 December 1880.

253a. Clement Griscom house, "Dolobran," c. 1888

253b. Clement Griscom house, "Dolobran," after restoration, exterior looking northwest, 1990

253c. Clement Griscom house, "Dolobran," stair, 1972

Furness and Evans

253. Clement Griscom house, "Dolobran"

Laurel Lane, Haverford
c. 1881, Altered

The first portion of the property was purchased from Edmund C. Evans in 1879; subsequent portions were acquired from Thomas DeWitt Cuyler and Allen Evans. Furness was Griscom's architect for all of his major projects and had a close and continuous professional relationship with "Dolobran" (cat. 460). The house was enlarged at least twice: the earliest state was largely field stone on the first story with shingle above; the east end with its stone chimneys was built after 1888; and the below-ground gallery was built probably during 1894.

Hotchkin described the extensive grounds, including a stream and lake for boating and bathing. "[N]ear the mansion is a flower garden devoted exclusively to Japanese plants. The northern portion of the estate is much rougher and splendidly adapted . . . as an American Wild Garden." Along with a stable, greenhouses, and other structures, he also reported "an attractive cottage occupied by Mr. and Mrs. Bettle. Mrs. Bettle being Mr. Griscom's daughter. [In the] portion . . . lying on either side of the brook are located buildings for the farmer, the dairy, etc." (Hotchkin, *Rural Pennsylvania*, 144–45). The house is presently being restored under the direction of James Garrison and A. Craig Morrison.

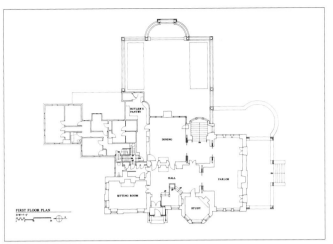

253d. Clement Griscom house, "Dolobran," first floor plan, 1989

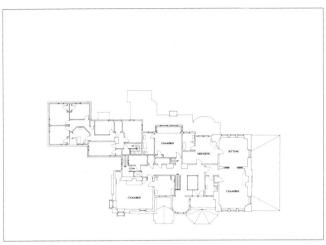

253e. Clement Griscom house, "Dolobran," second floor plan, 1989

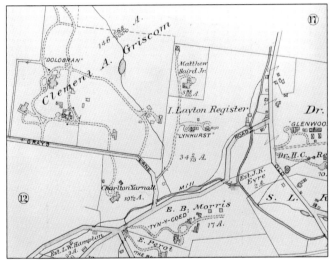

253f. Clement Griscom house, "Dolobran," site plan, 1920

253g. Clement Griscom estate, tenant farmer house, 1989

253h. Clement Griscom house, "Dolobran," first floor fireplace, 1972

254Aa. *Hoopes Brothers and Thomas Nursery, 1972*

254Ab. *Hoopes Brothers and Thomas Nursery, 1972*

255A. *Store buildings for Francis Fassitt, c. 1881*

254A. **Hoopes Brothers and Thomas Nursery**
West Chester
c. 1881, Demolished after 1973
The Hoopeses were in-laws of Dallett in Furness's office
while Thomas was presumably the real estate speculator and
auctioneer for whom the firm had previously worked.

255A. **Francis Fassitt store buildings**
1207–09 Market Street, Philadelphia
1881, Demolished
Frank Furness married Fanny Fassitt, whose brother Joseph
Fassitt was a member of Frank's architectural office. The
building for their uncle, Francis, was under construction in
June 1881, and was described as being constructed of iron
with stone infill on the upper stories.
Westcott, *Scrapbook* 5:110.

256. **William West Frazier house**
250 South 18th Street, Philadelphia
1881–82, Demolished
Frazier served with Furness in Rush's Lancers, and later was
an important client, retaining Furness to design various
family residences, churches, and institutional buildings as
well as corporate buildings (cat. 463, 475, 503, 510, 522,
541, 603). This was one of Furness's most important commissions located at the corner of Rittenhouse Square—one
of the most visible sites in the city and Philadelphia's premier
square.
AABN 9 (30 April 1881): 216.

256. *William West Frazier house, exterior looking southwest, c. 1900*

257. George B. Preston house

2135 Walnut Street, Philadelphia
1881–83, Demolished

The important corner site across from St. James Protestant Episcopal Church was acquired on 1 September 1879 by George Preston, a New Orleans-based businessman. The house on the site was demolished in the summer of 1881, and the new house was begun. The family was listed as residing in the new house in 1884.

The house attracted considerable attention in the press over the following year:

> Its striking feature is the flying bartizan or square turret which projects on the 22nd Street front and above the front door. It is three stories high and ends in a high peaked roof making a projecting gable. It is covered over its entire surface with bright red earthen tiles . . . Another peculiarity is the use of rustic stone-work for the main part, not as a foundation but as high as the second story. (Westcott, *Scrapbook* [September 1881].)

The house was further described by a nonplussed writer as:

> Gothic although modified by ideas of utility more than any of its immediate neighbors. Upon the Western elevation projects an eccentric and extremely bold combination of overhanging windows, covered with red wood shingles. Numerous irregular windows pierce the walls, and the exterior chimney is ornamented with great panels of sandstone chiselled in forms of trailing vines. (*Philadelphia Press*, 5 July 1885, 12.)

Furness designed a summer house for Preston in Cazenovia, NY in 1885 (cat. 295).

Westcott, *Scrapbook* (November 1882).

257a. George B. Preston house, exterior looking northeast, c. 1900

257b. George B. Preston house, hall, c. 1900

257c. George B. Preston house, dining room, c. 1900

257d. George B. Preston house, bedroom, c. 1900

257e. George B. Preston house, bedroom, c. 1900

257f. George B. Preston house, billiard room, c. 1900

257g. George B. Preston house, parlor, c. 1900

258A. **Aaron Fries house**
1919 Green Street, Philadelphia
c. 1883

Though no connection between Furness and Fries has been discovered, the visual character of the house and its link to contemporary work of the Furness office make this absolutely convincing. The asymmetrical composition recalls the Frazier house (cat. 256) as do the medievalizing window hoods and the sculpted band across the facade. The stair newel and door details are nearly identical to those of the Chalfont house (cat. 292) of the next year. Particularly memorable are the incised snowflake ornaments in the east gable.

In 1880, Fries was living at 2000 Green Street; he purchased 1919 Green Street, with its preexisting brick house, in 1883. Presumably this building was refaced, disguising the original symmetry of an 1850s Italianate house. The attic story was added as a part of the 1883 campaign. Fries resided here until 1907.

259A. **James D. Winsor house and stable, "Glen Hill"**
Winsor Lane, Haverford
c. 1881, Demolished

The Winsor house was of field stone crowned by a brick cornice that characterized several other early 1880s commissions. Only the stable survives.

260A. J. D. Griscom house
Montgomery Avenue and Cheswold Lane, Haverford
c. 1881, Demolished

The Griscom house shared the palette of materials of the Winsor house.

258Aa. Aaron Fries house, exterior looking north, 1990

259A. James D. Winsor house and stable, "Glen Hill," 1883

258Ab. Aaron Fries house, exterior looking northeast, 1990

258Ac. Aaron Fries house, stairhall, 1990

261a. Commercial Union Assurance Company Building, engraving, 1889

261b. Commercial Union Assurance Company Building, c. 1900

261c. Commercial Union Assurance Company Building, c. 1900

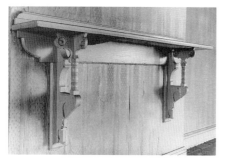

263a. Reliance Insurance Company Building, bracketed shelf, 1959

261. **Commercial Union Assurance Company Building**
330 Walnut Street, Philadelphia
1881, Demolished
The building was rented by J. H. Dingee, who commissioned a house by the firm in 1882 (cat. 271) and whose son worked for a decade or more in Furness's office. It was described as having a first floor "of iron beams and boxes, rosettes in the ceiling, and wrought iron grills. The second story is to be of Hummelstone" (Westcott, *Scrapbook* 5:96).
Carpenter and Building 3 (October 1881): 182.

262. Additions and alterations to American Fire Insurance Company Building
308–10 Walnut Street, Philadelphia
1881
Half of the American Fire Insurance Company board were Evans's in-laws and Furness associates. The building was erected as a Federal town house and was later altered for commercial use. Five years later, an attic story was added (cat. 331).
Carpenter and Building 3 (October 1881): 182. [HABS PA–1386]

263b. Reliance Insurance Company Building, 1915

264a. *Samuel Shipley house, "Windon," exterior looking northwest, 1972*

264b. *Samuel Shipley house, "Windon," exterior looking west, 1972*

264c. *Samuel Shipley house, "Windon," exterior looking southeast, 1972*

263. Reliance Insurance Company Building
429 Walnut Street, Philadelphia
1881–2, Demolished
The Reliance Insurance Company acquired the property in 1881 and held it until the 1920s. Presumably this was one of the buildings referred to by Nathaniel Burt when he wrote, "into each narrow city facade have been crowded more interrupted Egyptian columns, Venetian windows and doorways from Babylon than would seem humanly pos-

sible." (Nathaniel Burt, *The Perennial Philadelphians: The Anatomy of an American Aristocracy* [Boston: Little Brown, 1963], 360.) Westcott clipped an article in August 1881 that cited Furness and Evans as the architects, and described the plan: "The first floor will be divided into four offices; the second floor into two spacious offices and four in each wing"(Westcott, *Scrapbook* 5:129). The upper stories were used as a janitor's quarters.
[HABS PA–1465]

264. Samuel Shipley house, "Windon"
West Chester
1882
An 1857 Italianate farm house was enlarged in 1882 (date plaque on its west side) with the addition of wings in all directions. Elements of the house are familiar from other work of the period. James Massey, "Frank Furness in the 1880s," *Charrette* 43 (October 1963): 26; conversations with Mrs. E. Page Allinson, granddaughter of Samuel Shipley, July 1972. [1973–22]

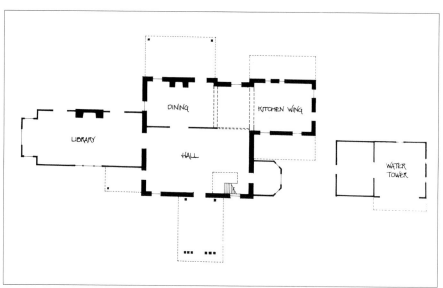

264d. Samuel Shipley house, "Windon," stair landing, 1972

264e. Samuel Shipley house, "Windon," first floor plan, 1972

264f. Samuel Shipley house, "Windon," second-floor bedroom fireplace, 1972

265. Reading Hospital
1882–86, Demolished
The Reading Hospital was begun in 1882 and was completed four years later as an asymmetrical block. In 1890, it was enlarged by an additional wing, named the "Wooten Wing" (cat. 321) after the long time director of the Reading Railroad.
The Reading Journal, 5 June 1886.

266. Boys High School
Penn Street, Reading
1882–83, Demolished
The building was commissioned in April 1882. Plans for the Boys High were submitted in the spring but not voted on until November 1882, when it was decided to use limestone rather than serpentine, at a savings of $4,000. It is part of a group of small institutional commissions that employed the scheme of a double-loaded center hall, expressed on the exterior by three parallel volumes. (See cat. 299, 429.)
Minutes of the Reading School Board (Reading, 1883), 88.

264g. Samuel Shipley house, "Windon," water tower, looking south, 1972

265a. Reading Hospital, after 1886

265b. Reading Hospital, c. 1897

266. Boys High School, c. 1897

267. Orange Street School
Orange Street, Reading
1882–83, Demolished
The school committee debated whether to build a four, eight, or twelve room school house, estimated by the architects to cost respectively $5,312, $10,100, or $14,000. Plans for the larger school were approved in May 1882. *Minutes of the Reading School Board* (Reading, 1883), 40.

268. **Penn National Bank**
Seventh and Market streets, Philadelphia
1882–84, Demolished
The Penn National Bank acquired its property on 30 September 1882. Its President, Gilles Dallett, succeeded Elijah Dallett, whose son was a draftsman in the Furness office. Similar themes appeared later on the 1885 Central National Bank in Wilmington (cat. 310). The Penn National Bank was constructed of Richmond granite, with an "iron cove" ceiling over the banking room (Westcott, *Scrapbook* 6:162). The verso of Tremaine's Architectural Photographers view of Penn National Bank (Penrose Collection, Historical Society of Pennsylvania) lists Furness and Evans as the architects.
Cf. "Men and Things," *Philadelphia Evening Bulletin,* 18 April 1924, p. 8, col. 5. [1973–21]

Above
268a. Penn National Bank, exterior looking southwest, c. 1900
Overleaf
268b. Penn National Bank, main banking room, c. 1885

269Ab. J. Dundas Lippincott house, detail of porch, 1989

272. John T. Lewis house, exterior looking northwest, 1978

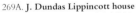

269Aa. J. Dundas Lippincott house, exterior looking east, 1989

269A. **J. Dundas Lippincott house**
507 South Broad Street, Philadelphia
1882
Lippincott is listed as a reference for Baker and Dallett, who from 1881 until 1888 were members of the Furness office. It seems likely that Baker, who had gone to Princeton with Lippincott, was the project architect.
Illustrated Philadelphia, Its Wealth and Industries (New York, 1889), 174.

270. H. W. Biddle house, "Rochsolach"
Chester Valley Road and Central Avenue, Paoli Heights
1882, Demolished
Daily Local News, 29 November 1882, cited in Ann Cook et al., "On the Trail of Frank Furness," *Pennsylvania Heritage* (Winter 1981): 27.

271. J. H. Dingee house, "Fennerton"
Central Avenue, Paoli Heights.
1882, Demolished
Dingee's son later entered the office.
Daily Local News, 29 November 1882, cited in Cook et al.,

"On the Trail of Frank Furness," 27.

272. **John T. Lewis house**
242 South 13th Street, Philadelphia
1882–83, Altered, AE
The Lewis and Beale houses (cat. 273) were erected over the winter of 1882–83 according to John T. Lewis's family expenses notebook. The contract was signed on 20 December 1882 and carpets were being installed in September 1883. Allen Evans was listed as the architect responsible for the project. Lewis was Allen Evans's father-in-law and client for other Furness projects including "Glyntaff," the Lewis summer home near Evans' Lane in Haverford (cat. 107).
John T. Lewis, family expenses notebook, 1878–88.

273. **Edward S. Beale house**
240 South 13th Street, Philadelphia
1882–83, Altered, AE
Beale was Allen Evans's brother-in-law and vice president of the John T. Lewis Paint Company; his house was built jointly with that of his father-in-law. It is slightly narrower in width and lacks the corner location, which accounts for

the lower land cost. In 1901 Beale commissioned another house; it was located in Strafford (cat. 533).
John T. Lewis, family expenses notebook, 1878–88.

274A. **Walter Horstmann, Jr. house**
236 South 13th Street, Philadelphia
c. 1882, Demolished
This house contained many of the details of the office in the early 1880s. An earlier house for Horstmann's father is attributed to the firm (cat. 11A).

275A. **J. Gardner Cassatt house**
1320 Locust Street, Philadelphia
c. 1883
J. Gardner Cassatt was the younger brother of Alexander J. Cassatt. He acquired the property on Locust Street on 28 March 1883; the house was constructed during that year, and was the Cassatts's home until 1885. The house was later altered by Joseph Huston, a former member of the office, suggesting that he may have had a hand in the original design.
PRER&BG 16, no. 1 (2 January 1901).

273. Edward S. Beale house, exterior looking southwest, 1978

274A. Walter Horstmann Jr. house, exterior looking west, 1975

276A. Dr. Caspar Wister house
1322 Locust Street, Philadelphia
c. 1883, Altered nearly beyond recognition
Dr. Caspar Wister married Frank's sister Annis Lee; they acquired the property on 28 March 1883 and the house was built over the ensuing year, apparently in concert with the J. Gardner Cassatt house (cat. 275A). The firm was called back to alter the building in 1903 when it was occupied by William Bullitt (cat. 561).

Above
275A. J. Gardner Cassatt house, exterior looking south, c. 1920
Opposite
276A. Dr. Caspar Wister house, c. 1920

LOCUST
SE JUNIPER

277a. Undine Barge Club, exterior, view from east, 1972

277b. Undine Barge Club, exterior looking southwest, 1975

277c. Undine Barge Club, detail of newel, 1972

278A. Fourth and Laurel Streets School, Reading

279A. Chestnut and Carpenter Streets School, Reading

277. Undine Barge Club
East River Drive, Philadelphia
1882–83
Furness & Hewitt had designed the Club's up-river boat house (cat. 58) a decade earlier. Pilings were driven in April 1883, the building was under roof by autumn, and completed the following spring at a cost of $14,000. Particularly noted were the "two hundred dollar carved mantel with tiles by A. B. Frost" and the walnut interior. The building was pronounced "an architectural gem" (Westcott, *Scrapbook* 6:39).
Louis Heiland, *The Undine Barge Club of Philadelphia* (Philadelphia, 1925), 40. [1973–23, HABS PA–1650]

278A. Fourth and Laurel Streets School, Reading
c. 1883, Demolished
The massive chimneys and aggressive cornices are hallmarks of Furness's Reading schools (cat. 266, 267, 279A).

279A. Chestnut and Carpenter Streets School, Reading
1883, Altered
The gable ornament of the main facade is derived directly from the Undine Barge Club (cat. 277). Given the previous work of the firm it seems likely that this building was designed around 1883, but those records are missing from the Berks County Historical Society.

280. Allen Evans house and row
237–41 South 21st Street, Philadelphia
1883, AE
The row of three houses adjacent to the Hockley house (cat. 65) was built by Allen Evans.

> Father built this house and another beside it, on the corner of 21st Street and Locust; and a third house for Mr. and Mrs. Henry Drayton. They soon sold 237 and lived in 239 only two winters, selling it in the Spring of 1886. A great distress to mother. (Evans MS, 100.)

The Drayton house was altered by the firm in 1904 (cat. 580).

280a. *Allen Evans house and row, looking southeast, 1978*

280b. *Allen Evans house, 237 South 21st Street, hall, 1978*

280c. *Allen Evans house, second floor stair landing, 1978*

280d. *Allen Evans house, fireback, second floor, 1978*

280e. *Allen Evans house, mantel, second floor, 1978*

280f. *Allen Evans house, detail of ironwork, 1978*

281a. National Bank of the Republic, exterior looking northwest, c. 1885

281b. National Bank of the Republic, main banking room before 1890

282a. William B. Kempton house, after being moved back to new building line, c. 1940

282b. William B. Kempton house, exterior looking southwest, 1889

283a. Veterinary Hospital, University of Pennsylvania, exterior looking southwest, c. 1885

283b. Veterinary Hospital, University of Pennsylvania, courtyard looking east

283c. Veterinary Hospital, University of Pennsylvania, operating amphitheater

284. Thomas DeWitt Cuyler house, during enlargement, 1908

281. **National Bank of the Republic**
313 Chestnut Street, Philadelphia
1883–84, Demolished, FF
See cat. 573.
Celebrated by Robert Venturi in *Complexity and Contradiction in Architecture* (New York: The Museum of Modern Art, 1966) as "an almost insane short story of a castle on a city street," the bank was nearly as incomprehensible to its contemporaries. A bemused writer attempted to explain its character in September 1884, remarking:

The architecture, whilst beautiful, in the eyes of many observers, is such a clear departure than anything yet seen upon the street as to strike others somewhat unpleasantly at first sight, but it has the merit of growing in favor upon acquaintance, and as it nears completion. It is of a composite style, and in deference to its well-known designer might be termed Furnessque. (Westcott, *Scrapbook* 6:161.)

A writer for the Philadelphia Press reached a similar conclusion, reporting, "It was erected by Frank Furness, and as there is no particular period or class to which it can be said to belong, local architects call it 'Furnessque'" ("Buildings of Beauty," *Philadelphia Press*, 24 May 1885, 10).
AABN 15 (26 January 1884): 48. [1973–25]

282. **William B. Kempton house**
2202 Walnut Street, Philadelphia
c. 1883, Altered beyond recognition
The Kempton house was sold at a sheriff's sale in 1896, perhaps at the time that it was condemned for standing forward of the building line; around 1896, the facade was removed and reconstructed on line with the other buildings of the street.
Harper's Weekly (12 April 1890).

283. **Veterinary Hospital, University of Pennsylvania**
3600 Pine Street, Philadelphia
1883–84, Demolished
The Veterinary Hospital was paid for by longtime board member Joshua B. Lippincott (cat. 350) and was the first veterinary hospital in the nation. It was demolished in less than a generation to make room for Cope and Stewardson's new dormitories. The campus character had yet to be determined, so the architects chose "Leiperville stone and brick with bluestone trim" (Westcott, *Scrapbook* 6:195). Its facade materials recall the Boys High School (cat. 266). It was at this point that Furness became the campus architect for the University, a position he would hold until 1894.

"1883 Receipts and Disbursements" (November 1883, 14 April 1884), University of Pennsylvania Archives general files.

284. **Thomas DeWitt Cuyler house**
Cuyler's Lane off Grays Lane, Haverford
1883–84, Demolished, AE
The Cuylers purchased the property in the spring of 1883 and the house was constructed the following summer. A letter from Cuyler to his brother-in-law, Allen Evans, congratulated him on his work and remarked on the success of the building, "I cannot consider the house completed without telling you how delighted we are with it in every respect. It far surpasses our expectations and we cannot be too grateful to our good architect for his taste and skill." The house was continually altered by the firm, ultimately transforming it from a tall, stone version of the center hall plan to a rambling medievalizing house (cat. 402, 542, 625).
Cuyler had a house in Philadelphia (cat. 476) and a cottage in Maine (cat. 638), both designed by Furness. In addition, Thomas's father, Theodore, owned a house in the city that is thought to have been altered by Furness (cat. 19A).
Thomas DeWitt Cuyler to Allen Evans, 9 July 1884, Evans MS, 99.

285a. First Unitarian Church, exterior looking north, c. 1890

285b. First Unitarian Church, exterior looking northwest, 1972

285c. Parish House, First Unitarian Church, looking northwest, c. 1950

285d. First Unitarian Church, east transept, looking northwest, 1989

285. First Unitarian Church and Parish House
Chestnut and Van Pelt streets, Philadelphia
1883–86, Altered, FF

Though Frank's father was no longer the minister, he remained an active force in the congregation making his son's selection as architect a foregone conclusion. The parish house was built first, and completed in 1884; the cornerstone of the church was laid in 1885 and the building was completed the following year. Perhaps in deference to his father's plea that church buildings serve to keep parishioners awake whether or not the sermon was stimulating, Furness devised a brilliantly polychromed interior with red ceiling and trusses both accented with raised gesso ornament picked out in gold, blue vertical walls, and a wood-grained base. The interior was unified by a great skylight down the middle of the church.

In February 1883, a newspaper reported the first scheme:

> In front of the church there will be a cloister of six arches, two of which will be occupied for doors. At one end of the cloister, there will be a circulating library. At the corner of the building there will be a tower, the lower part having a carriage porch. (Westcott, *Scrapbook* 6:62.)

When the building was completed three years later, the newspapers were complimentary:

> Its design will be readily recognized as the work of Frank Furness, the youngest son of the former pastor, whose contributions to Philadelphia architecture have been so original and important. Its general outlines are those of a Gothic rural church.

The article paid particular attention to the entrance:

> This singular structure is something between a porch and a detached tower. Although the building is not very large, the whole character of the architecture is very massive and the interior, which is reached through the porch already mentioned, presents the same effect. (Westcott, *Scrapbook* 7:133.)

PRER&BG 1, no. 6 (15 February 1886).
[1973–24, HABS PA–1508]

285e. *Parish House, First Unitarian Church, detail of west wall*

285f. *First Unitarian Church, reading desk, 1972*

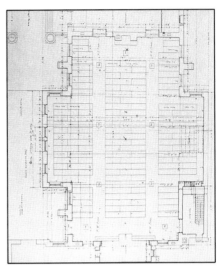

285g. *First Unitarian Church, plan*

285h. *First Unitarian Church, nave looking north, c. 1960*

285i. *Parish House, First Unitarian Church, fireplace in meeting room, 1972*

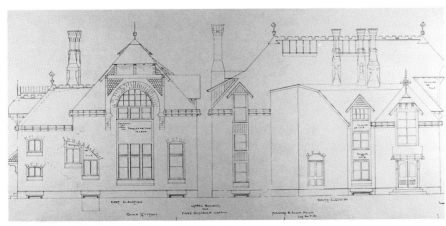

285j. *Parish House, First Unitarian Church, east and south elevations*

286A. George B. Roberts house, c. 1883

287A. 7322 Boyer Street, Philadelphia, looking southeast, 1990

288Aa. 7318 Boyer Street, Philadelphia, looking
southeast, 1990

288Ab. 7318 Boyer Street, Philadelphia, looking west, detail of chimney, 1990

**286A. Additions and alterations to George B. Roberts
house**
Bala Cynwyd
1883, ff.
Roberts was another president of the Pennsylvania Railroad,
and a close friend of the Evans family (Roberts reportedly
stayed at the Evans house when he missed his train [Evans
MS, 16]). The central porch with its turned columns and the
massive flaring brick chimneys, recalling the Griscom house
(cat. 253), are signatures of Evans's 1880s work.
HABS records; James Massey prepared the data sheet on the
house. [HABS PA-Bala-1]

287A. 7314 and 7322 Boyer Street, Philadelphia
c. 1884, 7314 Altered
Furness designed several houses near Sedgwick Station (cat.
151) on the estate of Franklin Gowen (cat. 365), President
of the Reading Railroad. Of these, the simplest in detail was
7314 Boyer Street; a gray schist base with bluestone lintels
and sills carried a shingled upper story. Turned notched, and
chamfered porch posts are similar to those on 7322, suggesting Furness's influence.
The projecting half-timber entrance bay of 7322 recalls the
first building for the Merion Cricket Club in Ardmore (cat.
252). The side gables end with curved overhangs not unlike
the houses at 3801–15 Walnut Street (cat. 378A).

288A. 7318 Boyer Street, Philadelphia
c. 1884
Though on the same estate as the preceding, this was the largest
of the three development houses. It is similar in detail to the
Gowen house (cat. 365) on Gowen Avenue and perhaps was
built at the same time.

BUILDINGS AND GROUNDS
OF THE
PENNSYLVANIA STATE AGRICULTURAL SOCIETY,
BROAD STREET AND LEHIGH AVENUE, PHILADELPHIA.

Thirty-first Annual Exhibition, September 23d to October 14th, 1885.

Manufactures, Machinery, Implements, Apparatus, Produce and Live Stock.

BIRD'S-EYE VIEW LOOKING SOUTH-WEST FROM POINT NEAR GERMANTOWN JUNCTION, PENNSYLVANIA RAILROAD, PHILADELPHIA.

REFERENCES.—**A,** Fifteenth Street; **B,** Sixteenth Street; **C** ◄————►, to Broad Street and Lehigh Avenue; **D,** Special Station Philadelphia and Reading Railroad, (Bound Brook, Germantown, and North Pennsylvania Divisions;) **E.** Connecting Railroad; **F,** Huntingdon Street.

290a. Pennsylvania State Agricultural Society Fair, buildings and grounds, 1884

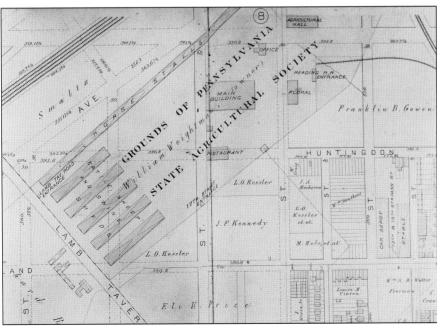

290b. Pennsylvania State Agricultural Society Fair, map, 1884

289. Ferryboat Communipaw, Philadelphia and Reading Railroad
1884, Destroyed
Designs were made to remodel the ferryboat.
Frank Furness to John E. Wooten, 23 December 1884, Historical Society of Pennsylvania.

290. Seven buildings, Pennsylvania State Agricultural Society Fair
15th and Cumberland streets, Philadelphia
1884, Demolished
The thirty acre site was recorded as follows:
    halls of glass and wood, similar to Centennial buildings; main building 300 by 150', 63' in height to roof; poultry building 150 by 150', horticultural building, 200 by 60'; restaurant 132 by 82'; bench show building 150 by 50'; tent annex 140 by 80'; kennel, 100 by 60'; department of public comfort, 60 by 40; will last two weeks.
    (*Philadelphia Inquirer*, 29 August 1884, 2.)
Completed by August of 1884, the fair persisted for several years, with diminishing success.
J. L. Smith, *Ward Atlas* (Philadelphia: J. L. Smith, 1884).

291. Passenger and parlor cars, Philadelphia and Reading Railroad
1884
Furness did seven designs for the passenger and parlor cars.
Frank Furness to John E. Wooten, 23 December 1884, Historical Society of Pennsylvania.

292Aa. William Chalfont house, exterior looking west, 1989

292Ab. William Chalfont house, exterior looking east, 1989

292Ac. William Chalfont house, parlor fireplace, 1990

292Ad. William Chalfont house, parlor fireplace, 1990

292Ae. William Chalfont house, detail of hall fireplace, 1990

292A. **William Chalfont house**
Kennett Square
c. 1884
See color plate 9.
Here was the last gasp of the 1870s center-hall suburban houses with the biggest flaring chimneys yet seen, anchored within the mass of the house by their fireplaces. Details such as the quarter lunette windows in dormers (like those of the Veterinary Hospital (cat. 283) and the massive turned newels

became stock features in the 1880s.

293. **Stephen Trump house**
1901 Priory Road, Silversides, DE
c. 1884
The pyramidal roof and bristling chimneys are hallmarks of the Furness style. A broad hall with side fireplace, terminated by a nearly freestanding stair, rises through the core of the house. Clear leaded glass in the transoms over the entrance

and in the library are also signature elements. The original shingle has been replaced with aluminum siding and the porch columns were replaced at the end of the last century when several of the fireplaces were updated in the modern colonial revival style.
Baker and Dallett were the architects in charge; they listed this project as theirs, although it was executed while they were still with Furness.
Philadelphia and Popular Philadelphians, 221.

293A. Stephen Trump house, 1990

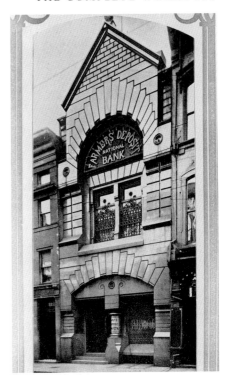

296. Farmers Deposit National Bank, c. 1890

297a. H. P. McKean house, elevation

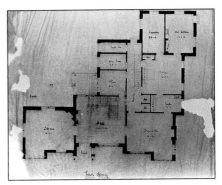

297b. H. P. McKean house, first floor plan

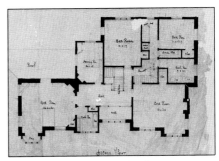

297c. H. P. McKean house, second floor plan

294. Additions to John C. Higgens house, "Fairview"
Near Route 13, near Delaware City, DE
1885
This addition was to an 1822 house for the same family. Drawings exist in the National Register Nomination and were filed circa 1985.

295. George B. Preston summer house
Cazenovia, NY
1885
Furness designed Preston's house in Philadelphia (cat. 257).
Cazenovia Republican (NY), 13 August 1885.

296. **Farmers Deposit National Bank**
66 (later 220) Fourth Avenue, Pittsburgh
c. 1885, Demolished
Maximillian Nirdlinger worked in the Furness office in the 1880s and recorded this commission in his "Memoirs," a manuscript in possession of James Van Trump of Pittsburgh.

297. **H. P. McKean house**
Germantown, Philadelphia
c. 1885, Unexecuted
The H.P. McKean of this project may be H. Pratt (cat. 17). Drawing, collection of George Wood Furness.

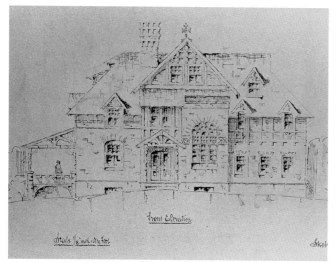

298a. Harry McCall house, front elevation, 1881

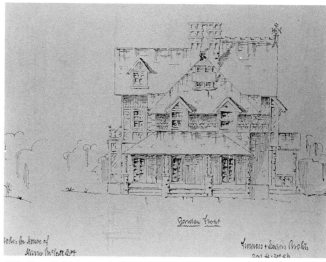

298b. Harry McCall house, garden front, 1881

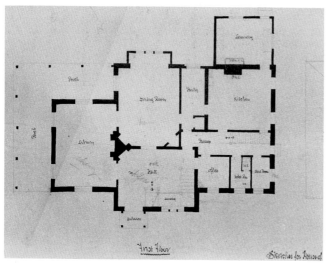

298c. Harry McCall house, first floor plan, 1881

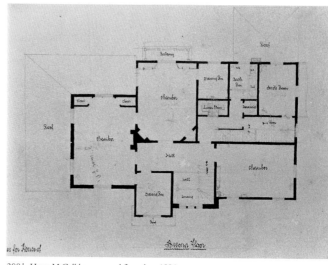

298d. Harry McCall house, second floor plan, 1881

298. Harry McCall house
Germantown, Philadelphia
c. 1885, Unexecuted
Drawing, collection of George Wood Furness.

299. Home for Consumptives, Philadelphia Protestant Episcopal City Mission
Stenton and Evergreen avenues, Chestnut Hill
1885, Altered
See cat. 409, 563, 578.
The organization was founded in 1870 in a city house. The hospital was modeled on the "world-renowned Consumptives Home, Ventnor, Isle of Wight, the 'Cottage' or 'Separate System' was adopted." In plan, a strongly marked center hall recalls the Boys High School of Reading (cat. 266).
Hotchkin, *Ancient and Modern Germantown, Mount Airy and Chestnut Hill*, 440.

299a. Home for Consumptives, Philadelphia Protestant Episcopal City Mission, c. 1890

299b. Home for Consumptives, Philadelphia Protestant Episcopal City Mission, 1989

299c. Home for Consumptives, Philadelphia Protestant Episcopal City Mission, detail of bay, 1989

302A. Carriage houses on Irving Street, Philadelphia, looking northeast, 1989

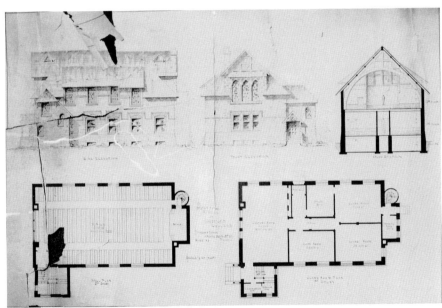

300. Haverford College, plans and elevations for a classroom building, 1885

304A. 126 South Van Pelt Street, Philadelphia, exterior looking west, 1989

300. **Classroom and auditorium building, Haverford College**
Haverford
1885, Unexecuted(?)
Signed drawing dated 25 May 1885, Haverford College Library.

301. Haverford Grammar School
Railroad Avenue, Haverford
1885, Altered, AE
The grammar school was run as a subsidiary of Haverford

College, with the intention of preparing students for admission. The Cassatts were co-organizers and specified that Allen Evans was to be in charge of the work.
Minutes of the Board of Overseers of Haverford College, MS, vol. 4 (5 June 1885).

302A. **Carriage houses on Irving Street**
1300 block, Irving Street, Philadelphia
c. 1885
The carriage houses were designed for George Wood and Samuel Shober, both of whose residences were located a

block away on Spruce Street.

303A. Additions to John T. Bailey and Company Factory
Water and Otsego streets, Philadelphia
1885, Demolished
Later documented work and stylistic similarities suggest this commission (cat. 383A, 465).

304A. **126 South Van Pelt Street, Philadelphia**
c. 1885
Pennsylvania Historic Sites Survey.

305A. *Chapel and Mortuary, University of Pennsylvania Hospital, c. 1890*

308A. *Charles Perkins house, c. 1885*

309Aa. *26 North Lime Street, Lancaster, exterior looking west, 1990*

309Ab. *26 North Lime Street, Lancaster, detail of north wall, 1990*

309Ac. *26 North Lime Street, Lancaster, detail of door and ironwork, 1990*

305A. **Chapel and Mortuary, University of Pennsylvania Hospital**
3400 block, Pine Street, Philadelphia
c. 1885, Demolished
This is one of four commissions received by Furness during the provostship of William Pepper.

306. Cottages
Lake Hopatcong, NJ
1885
Furness designed three or four cottages near the Breslin Hotel (cat. 319).
Building 3, no. 14 (October 1885): 156.

307. **Additions and alterations to Green Street Station, Philadelphia and Reading Railroad**
Ninth and Green streets, Philadelphia
c. 1885
See color plate 8.
The massing and detail suggests that this was designed at the same time that the B&O stations were being studied. By the late 1880s, the location at Ninth and Green was too far from the center of the city to effectively compete with the Pennsylvania Terminal, which had moved to Filbert and Penn Square. Instead, with New York capitalists in charge, the new terminal was planned on Market Street, with a New York designer, Francis Kimball, in charge of the appearance.
James L. Holton, *The Reading Railroad: History of a Coal Age Empire* 1:316.

310. *Central National Bank, 1980*

312Aa. A. E. Winn house, exterior looking east, 1990

312Ab. A. E. Winn house, exterior looking northeast, 1990

312Ac. A. E. Winn house, window in stairhall, (the fish is an addition to the leaded glass), 1990

312Ad. A. E. Winn house, detail of first floor stairhall, 1990

308A. Charles Perkins house
Montgomery Avenue, Bryn Mawr
c. 1885, Demolished
This is one of a group of photographs in the files of Levi Focht (cat. 248A), a Reading builder who did much of the Reading Railroad work.

309A. 26 North Lime Street, Lancaster
c. 1885, Altered
This large, robustly detailed house, includes many motifs from the mid-1880s, such as the broad brownstone band at the top of the windows. The wrought iron grill of the door is closely related to the Robert M. Lewis house (cat. 324A) front door grill; the drooping brackets of the north wall are similar to those of the Beale house (cat. 273). The interior has been modernized, but a handsome stair, with grooves

along the stringer and Japanesque rail nearly identical to that of the Evans row on South 21st Street (cat. 280), survives.

310. Central National Bank
Wilmington, DE
1885
The bank, constructed in brownstone, uses many of the motifs of the Penn National Bank (cat. 268) and the National Bank of the Republic (cat. 281). It is listed as the work of Baker and Dallett, but its date—before they were even made associates—indicates that principal responsibility belonged to Furness.
Philadelphia and Popular Philadelphians, 223.

311. First National Bank of Montrose
Montrose
1885, Drastically altered, AE

The bank was a modest two-story building with a bold brick cornice. The date of construction was emblazoned on the facade.
Peerless Brick Company promotional brochure, collection of Library of Congress.

312A. A. E. Winn house
610 Hazelhurst Avenue, Merion Station
c. 1886
This is an important design closely related in plan and details to such later works as the Crabtree (cat. 320) and Gowen (cat. 365) houses. The immense oversized drooping brackets appear on the National Bank of the Republic (cat. 281), the Beale house (cat. 273), and other 1880s designs. The parallel ranks of rooms and the clustering of four fireplaces around a great chimney are found in the Crabtree house also (cat. 320).

313A. 602 South Highland Ave, exterior looking southeast, 1990

Above
314a. James G. Blaine house, "Stanwood," from driveway
Opposite
314b. James G. Blaine house, "Stanwood," from coastal road, c. 1890

313A. 602 South Highland Avenue, Merion Station
c. 1886
Part of a group of houses erected in the mid-1880s, this shows hallmarks of the office style in the pyramidal roof and massive chimney.

Furness, Evans and Co.

314. James G. Blaine house, "Stanwood"
Bar Harbor, Mount Desert Island, ME
1885–86, Demolished, WMC
Camac summered in Bar Harbor. He was placed in charge of this project in the fall of 1885. It apparently was designed for a different site on the same property, probably one nearer the road. Mrs. James G. Blaine reported:

> We spent all our first afternoon on the lot having with us the architect, Mr. How, the builder, the stone mason and all the Blaines. We decided on the site, ran out tape measures the length of the house and L. drove in stakes for the corners . . . [The next morning] as we were ascending the hill, . . . your Father proposed to me to get out of the buckboard and look at the view, and so magnificent was the panorama, . . . that your Father without the slightest preface said, 'Camac, I shall put my house here.' So now we are to build on the heights. The plans had to be adapted to the new position, and it costs us a little more, but I am so delighted with the change and so satisfied with the whole prospect, I am very happy.

Letter, Mrs. James G. Blaine, 24 September 1885, *Letters of Mrs. James G. Blaine*, ed. Harriet Blaine Beale, (New York, 1908), 2:123–24.

The house was erected with a stone retaining wall below the house that supported a man-made terrace off the main rooms. Presumably this feature was necessitated to adapt the plans to the more alpine site. The house was one of those destroyed in the twentieth century fire that devastated Bar Harbor.
PRER&BG 1, no. 21 (31 May 1886).

315Aa. 245 South Fifth Street, Reading, exterior looking northeast, 1990

315Ab. 245 South Fifth Street, Reading, detail of bracket under bay, 1990

315A. 245 South Fifth Street, Reading
c. 1886

The asymmetrical composition, broad band course of stone across the facade, and the immense, overscaled, floral carved brackets are hallmarks of the Furness manner in the mid-1880s. Similar brackets were used on the Robert M. Lewis house of 1886 (cat. 324A).

316A. M. Harbster house,
740 Centre Avenue, Reading
c. 1886, Altered

This was one of several houses for industrialists published in *Artwork of Reading*. The Harbster house was modified with a new porch and a colonial revival interior c. 1910, leaving only the great fireplace in the stair hall. These commissions may have come through Furness's work for the Reading Railroad, or through Henry Muhlenberg, a young architect in his office who later altered the house. This suggests that he may have been the project architect when it was built. An alternate connection may have been Harbster's business partner, William Griscom, a relative of Clement A. Griscom (cat. 253).
Artwork of Reading (Chicago: W. H. Parish & Co., 1897), n.p.

317A. John Barbey house
725 Centre Avenue, Reading
c. 1886, Demolished

Barbey ran a brewery in Reading and was active in civic affairs. He built his house across the street from Harbster's (cat. 316A).
Artwork of Reading, n.p.

317A. John Barbey house, before 1897

319. Breslin Hotel, before 1890

Above
316Aa. M. Harbster house, exterior looking north, 1990
Opposite
316Ab. M. Harbster house, detail of hall fireplace, 1990

318. Additions and alterations to Edmund C. Evans house, "Penrhyn-y-coed" (later Allen Evans house)
Evans' Lane, Haverford
1886, AE
See cat. 51.
The alterations involved the addition of a kitchen wing.

Evans MS, 103.

319. Breslin Hotel
Lake Hopatcong, NJ
1886, Demolished, LCB
The Breslin was part of a typical hotel-centered resort develop-

ment intended to capitalize on a large lake near New York. The hotel was to "accommodate 300 persons; it is 312 feet long and 100 feet in width. It contains 175 rooms and will cost $70,000.00" (*PRER&BG* 1, no. 6 [15 February 1886]). It was hoped that guests would purchase lots near the hotel, creating a large resort; however few lots were sold (cat. 306).

320a. Latta Crabtree cottage, 1975

320b. Latta Crabtree cottage, 1975

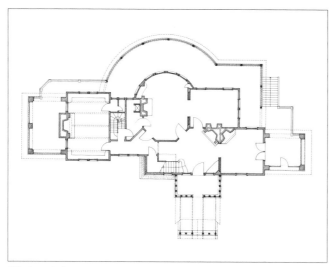

320c. Latta Crabtree cottage, first floor plan

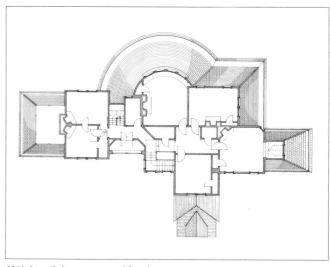

320d. Latta Crabtree cottage, second floor plan

320. Latta Crabtree cottage
Lake Hopatcong, Morris County, NJ
1886, LCB
See color plate 7.
Latta Crabtree was a well known western actress who was given this house as part of the promotion for the Breslin Hotel (cat. 319) which stood across the street. Furness may have known her from his own western excursions; she also knew Henry Van Brunt, Furness's fellow student in Hunt's office who may have referred her to his eastern atelier-mate. The dog-faced beast holding the fire screen reappeared in the Robert M. Lewis house in Philadelphia (cat. 324A), and in several sketches in the notebooks.
PRER&BG 1, no. 18 (10 May 1886).

321. Wooten Wing, Reading Hospital
Reading
1886, Demolished
See cat. 265.
This followed the original designs of the hospital which Furness had begun in 1882.
The Reading Journal, 5 June 1886.

320e. Latta Crabtree cottage, hall fireplace, detail, 1975

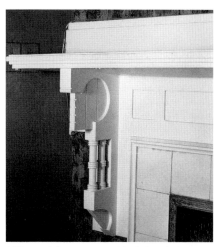

320f. Latta Crabtree cottage, second floor bedroom fireplace, 1975

320g. Latta Crabtree cottage, second floor bedroom fireplace, 1975

320h. Latta Crabtree cottage, hall and stair, 1975

320i. Latta Crabtree cottage, billiard room, 1975

320j. Latta Crabtree cottage, second floor bedroom fireplace, 1975

322. William Tiers cottage, 1886

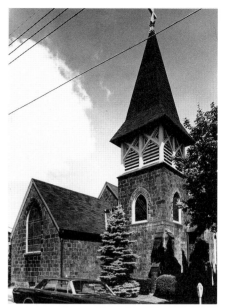

323a. St. Michael's Protestant Episcopal Church, 1978

323b. St. Michael's Protestant Episcopal Church, view towards apse, 1978

324Aa. Robert M. Lewis house, exterior looking southeast, 1989

322. **William Tiers cottage**

Bryn Mawr

1886

Tiers was a member of the Rittenhouse Club and owned the Thornbrook Avenue property in Rosemont (cat. 391A). The angled half-timber panels recalling the Watts/Sherman house are the closest Furness ever came to quoting directly from Richardson.

Sanitary Engineer (24 June 1886).

323. **Alterations and decorative painting of St. Michael's Protestant Episcopal Church**

Birdsboro

1886, FF

The church's major supporter was George Brooke; his name appears in the Furness sketchbooks in the 1870s, suggesting earlier connections with the family, perhaps for this site. It was they who donated the rectory in the early 1870s, which shares with Castle Ringstetten (cat. 58) the motif of the saw toothed wood cornice. In 1886, Furness designed the de-

corative paint scheme of blue ceiling and red walls, with gold and pewter bands overlaid with raised *graffito* plaster ornament. Furness had already used a similar paint scheme for the contemporary First Unitarian Church (cat. 285).

Daniel K. Miller, *The History of St. Michael's Protestant Episcopal Church, Birdsboro, Pennsylvania, 1851–1951* (Birdsboro, 1951), 33.

324A. **Robert M. Lewis house**

123 South 22nd Street, Philadelphia

c. 1886

See color plate 12.

Lewis purchased the property on 1 May 1886; he had been a vestryman in the family church of St. Peter's, and had been placed in charge of the Church of the Holy Comforter (cat. 54), a donation of another family member. Most of the interior motifs in this most complete city house are by now familiar from other houses, but the detail was rarely so consistently frenzied across an entire house interior in the late 1880s.

324Ad. Robert M. Lewis house, view up stair, 1989

324Ae. Robert M. Lewis house, parlor fireplace, 1989

324Af. Robert M. Lewis house, second floor fireplace, 1989

324Ag. Robert M. Lewis house, second floor overmantel, 1989

325a. Bailey, Banks and Biddle factory, exterior detail on right, c. 1900

325b. Bailey, Banks and Biddle factory, c. 1885

326a. Protestant Episcopal Church of the Evangelists, exterior looking north, 1978

326b. Protestant Episcopal Church of the Evangelists, detail of entrance, 1978

327. Four houses, Hart Lane at Frankford Avenue, 1974

329a. Rogers Commercial Block (left) and Hotel Florence (cat. 330) from village green (right), c. 1900

329b. Rogers Commercial Block, 1989

331. American Fire Insurance Company Building, exterior looking south, 1959

325. Bailey, Banks and Biddle Factory
12th and Sansom streets, Philadelphia
1886, Demolished
The site for the watch case factory was acquired the week before the designs were announced.
PRER&BG 1, no. 20 (24 May 1886).

326. Protestant Episcopal Church of the Evangelists
Seventh and Catherine streets, Philadelphia
1886, Altered, LCB
See color plates 10 and 11.
The Church of the Evangelists was founded in 1837; a brick building in the Italian style was constructed in 1856–57 which was altered and embellished by the Furness office. The building was incorporated into the Fleisher Memorial Art School in this century.
PRER&BG 1, no. 21 (31 May 1886).

327. Four houses
Hart Lane and Frankford Road, Philadelphia

1886, Partially demolished since 1973, JH
William D. Huston of Page Brothers was the developer; his son Joseph Huston was placed in charge of the project.
PRER&BG 1, no. 21 (31 May 1886).

328. H. C. Hart summer cottage
Bar Harbor, Mount Desert Island, ME
1886, WMC
According to O'Gorman, the Hart cottage "sported piazzas, a tower, stone foundation, and in the interior a large entrance hall." (James F. O'Gorman, "Frank Furness," in Earle Shettleworth, ed. *A Biographical Dictionary of Architects in Maine* 2, no. 9 [June 1985].)

329. Rogers Commercial Block
Bar Harbor, Mount Desert Island, ME
1886, WMC
The fourth-floor mansard with broad dormers was removed after a fire, leaving the building truncated and less vertical than the usual work of the office. The composition was

intensely mannered, with third-floor windows stacked directly on the peak of second-floor polygonal bays, that in turn sat on the corners of the projecting bulk windows.
O'Gorman, "Frank Furness," (1985).

330. Dunbar Brothers commercial building
Bar Harbor, Mount Desert Island, ME
1886–88, WMC
In the Dunbar block, the third- and fourth-story windows are attached in what appears to have been a two-story mansard, while the second story windows appear to hang from the eave.
O'Gorman, "Frank Furness," (1985).

331. Additions and Alterations to American Fire Insurance Company Building
308–10 Walnut Street, Philadelphia
1886
An attic story was added to the Federal town house that had previously been altered by the firm (cat. 262).
PRER&BG 1, no. 25 (28 June 1886). [HABS PA–1396]

332a. Philadelphia Terminal, Baltimore and Ohio Railroad, east elevation, c. 1930

332. Philadelphia Terminal, Baltimore and Ohio Railroad

24th and Chestnut streets, Philadelphia
1886–88, Demolished, FF

The *Builders' Guide* reported:

> Mr. Frank Furness, the architect, says that the new Baltimore and Ohio depot, to be erected at Twenty-fourth and Chestnut streets will be equally as fine as the Broad Street depot.
>
> The outward appearance of the building will be striking, The style of architecture is Flemish. The lower wall will be principally of iron, carried on iron columns and boxes, and the upper walls will be of brick, red-stone and terra cotta. The string courses, cornices and brackets will be of terra cotta, and the roof will be covered with red tile. The appearance of the building in profile will be most picturesque. (*PRER&BG* 1, no. 32 [16 August 1886].)

[1973–26, HABS PA–1220]

332b. Philadelphia Terminal, Baltimore and Ohio Railroad, exterior looking southeast, c. 1920

332c. Philadelphia Terminal, Baltimore and Ohio Railroad, north (front) elevation, del. 1968

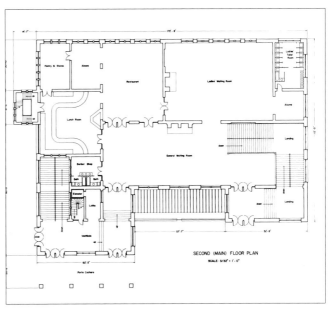

332d. Philadelphia Terminal, Baltimore and Ohio Railroad, second (main) floor plan, del. 1968

332e. Philadelphia Terminal, Baltimore and Ohio Railroad, exterior looking south, c. 1950

Opposite
332f. Philadelphia Terminal, Baltimore and Ohio Railroad, main stair, c. 1890
Above
332g. Philadelphia Terminal, Baltimore and Ohio Railroad, waiting room, c. 1930

332h. Philadelphia Terminal, Baltimore and Ohio Railroad, waiting room, c. 1930

332i. Philadelphia Terminal, Baltimore and Ohio Railroad, main concourse, c. 1930

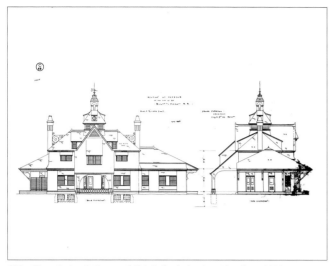

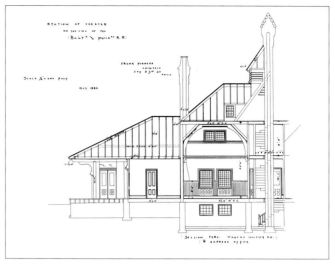

333a. Chester Station, Baltimore and Ohio Railroad, elevations, ink on linen, 1886

333b. Chester Station, Baltimore and Ohio Railroad, section, ink on linen, 1886

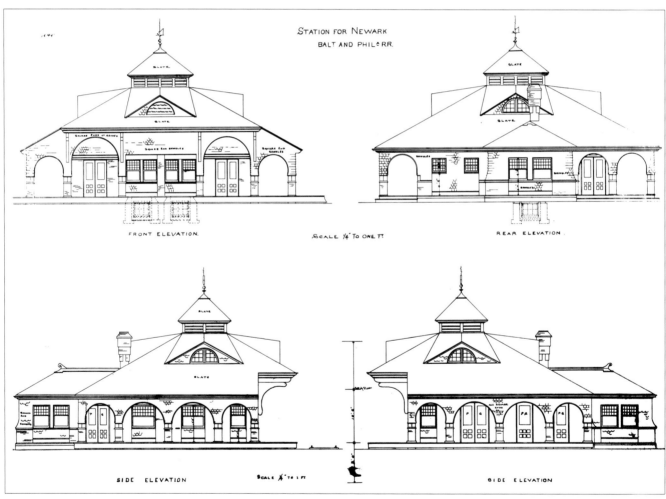

335. Newark Station, Baltimore and Ohio Railroad, elevations, ink on linen, c. 1886

333. **Chester Station, Baltimore and Ohio Railroad**
12th and Edgmont streets, Chester
1886, Demolished
Signed linens, Historical Society of Pennsylvania. [1973–27]

334. Bellaire Station, Baltimore and Ohio Railroad
Delaware and Dupont streets, Wilmington, DE
1886, Demolished
Signed linens, Historical Society of Pennsylvania.

335. **Newark Station, Baltimore and Ohio Railroad**
Newark, DE
1886, Demolished
Unsigned linens, Historical Society of Pennsylvania.

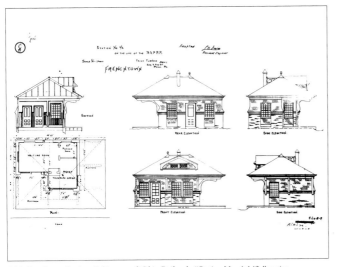

336. Frenchtown Station, Baltimore and Ohio Railroad, "Station No. 4 1/2," section, elevations, and plan, ink on linen

337a. Water Street Station, Baltimore and Ohio Railroad, 1989

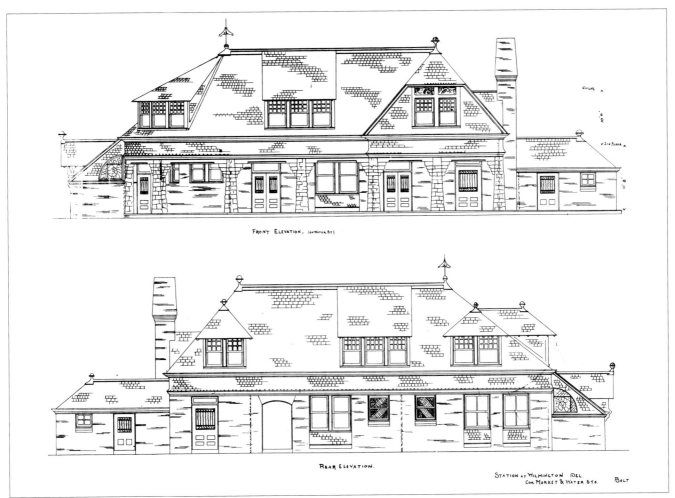

337b. Water Street Station, Baltimore and Ohio Railroad, Water Street elevation and rear elevation, detail, ink on linen, c. 1886

336. Frenchtown Station, Baltimore and Ohio Railroad
Frenchtown, MD
c.1886, Demolished
Signed, undated linens, Historical Society of Pennsylvania.

337. Water Street Station, Baltimore and Ohio Railroad
Market and Water streets, Wilmington, DE
c. 1886, Altered
The Water Street Station has been savagely altered. It has

been abandoned and is nearing collapse. The corbels on the great chimney are stepped to accommodate the slope of the roof.
Signed, undated linens, Historical Society of Pennsylvania.

338. **Wilmington Station, Baltimore and Ohio Railroad**
Dupont and Delaware avenues, Wilmington, DE
1886, Demolished
This station reversed the problem of the Philadelphia station, where the building was entered from an elevated street while the tracks were on grade. In the Wilmington Station, the main entrance was from street level, but the tracks were elevated. In one of Furness's most imaginative combinations, a baroque street level terminal was linked to the track level by a great sloping roof.
Signed, dated linens, Historical Society of Pennsylvania.

339. **Gorgas Home for Indigent Women**
East Leverington Avenue, Roxborough, Philadelphia
1886–87
Here the palette of the local rubble stone mills with brick arches above openings was adapted to an institution for the widows of the mill-hands.
PRER&BG 1, no. 37 (20 September 1886).

340. **I. Layton Register house, "Lynnhurst"**
Haverford
1886, Altered
"The house of bluish stone, with slate roof, was constructed after he purchased the farm . . . from stone on the place" (Hotchkin, *Rural Pennsylvania*, 118).

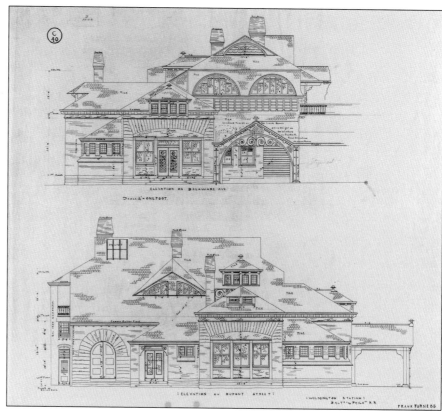

338a. Wilmington Station, Baltimore and Ohio Railroad, Delaware Avenue and Dupont Street elevations, detail, ink on linen, c. 1886

338b. Wilmington Station, Baltimore and Ohio Railroad, "B&O Depot, Wilmington, De.," c. 1892

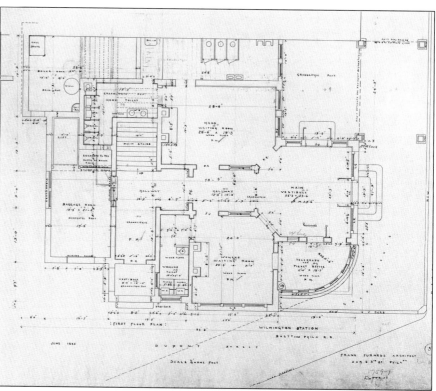

338c. Wilmington Station, Baltimore and Ohio Railroad, first floor plan, ink on linen, c. 1886

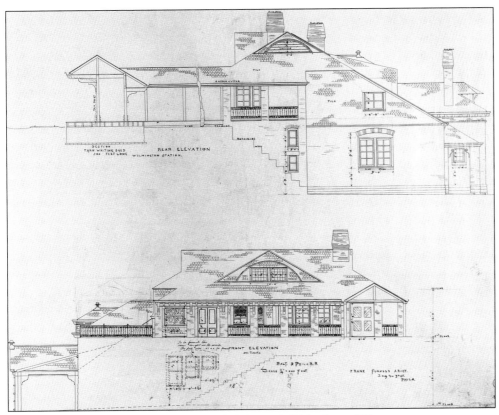

338d. Wilmington Station, Baltimore and Ohio Railroad, rear and side elevations, detail, ink on linen, c. 1886

339. Gorgas Home for Indigent Women, 1988

340. I. Layton Register house, "Lynnhurst," c. 1897

341. St. Mary's Protestant Episcopal Church

Ardmore Avenue, Ardmore

1887, AE

Rowland Evans served on the vestry, and Allen Evans was placed in charge of the Protestant Episcopal church, which is one of a group of understated ecclesiastical commissions. The firm designed an extension of one bay to the west in the early twentieth century, while minor alterations were made to the sacristies.

PRER&BG 2, no. 1 (3 January 1887); Vestry Minutes.

342. Caroline Rogers houses

124–32 South 17th Street, Philadelphia

1887, Altered, northern two demolished

Caroline Rogers was Fairman Rogers's mother; presumably it was her estate that built the four houses (one was a double house) in conjunction with the sale of Fairman Rogers's Rittenhouse Square house to Alexander J. Cassatt (cat. 364). The interior stair of the surviving pair shows yet another variation on the grooved stringer motif—here cut into vertical segments alternating with smooth wood.

PRER&BG 2, no. 3 (24 January 1887).

343. Thomas A. Scott house

1832–34 Rittenhouse Square at 19th Street, Philadelphia

1887–88, Demolished

The *Builders' Guide* reported: "Thomas A. Scott is building a fine new residence at Nineteenth and Rittenhouse Square. It will contain fifty-two rooms" (*PRER&BG* 2, no. 6 [14 February 1887]).Presumably this referred to an alteration or a major addition to an existing house in which the family had already lived for twenty years (cat. 61A). Scott was one of the presidents of the Pennsylvania Railroad for whom Furness would build; other presidents included George B. Roberts (cat. 286A), Frank Thomson (cat. 377) and Alexander J. Cassatt (cat. 364).

Harper's Weekly 34, no. 1738 (12 April 1890): 270

341a. St. Mary's Protestant Episcopal Church, exterior looking north, after 1908

341b. St. Mary's Protestant Episcopal Church, nave looking east, c. 1920

341c. St. Mary's Protestant Episcopal Church, apse, Easter Sunday, c. 1900

342a. Caroline Rogers houses, exterior looking northwest, c. 1920

342b. Caroline Rogers houses, exterior looking west, 1980

343. Thomas A. Scott house, exterior looking southeast, c. 1900

344a. 1601–43 Diamond Street, looking northwest, 1990

345a. William Winsor house, "Hedgely," stairhall, 1972

344b. 1600 block, Diamond Street, detail of cornice, 1990

345b. William Winsor house, "Hedgely," stairhall fireplace, 1972

344. 1601–43 Diamond Street, Philadelphia
1887, JH
    W. D. Huston, builder for Page Brothers, has now on hand forty-six houses for which designs in part were made by Furness, Evans and Co. Twenty-two on Diamond Street between Sixteenth and Seventeenth will have entire fronts of rock-faced trimmings with plate glass windows, etc. These houses will also have bay windows from the second story up, which will be lined with California red shingles. (*PRER&BG* 2, no. 15 [18 April 1887]).
The bays were eliminated and 1601 has been demolished.
[HABS PA–1726]

345. William Winsor house, "Hedgely"
Ardmore

1887–88, Altered
William Winsor was the father-in-law of Horace Howard Furness, Jr.; he purchased the property in 1886, retaining the firm to enlarge the existing farmhouse the following year. Signed drawings, collection of Winsor family, Ardmore.
[1973-28]

346. Dr. Henry C. Register house, "Mill Creek"
Lower Merion
1887, Demolished
    The house was described by Hotchkin: "Local stone furnished the material for the building, which is two stories high, with a red slate roof. It is of a composite style of architecture" (Hotchkin, *Rural Pennsylvania*, 118). The house was damaged by fire and was rebuilt by Edgar V. Seeler.

347. Alterations to Merion Cricket Club
Ardmore
1887, Demolished
See cat. 252.
PRER&BG 2, no. 15 (7 April 1887).

348A. Alterations to Radnor Hunt Club
Roberts and Darby-Paoli roads, Radnor
c. 1887, Demolished
Numerous relatives, in-laws, and friends of Allen Evans were on the board of the club. The scale of the fireplace threatened to devour the modest room. The andirons were a larger version of those in the Winsor house hall (cat. 345). The square windows of the dog kennels were also part of the office vocabulary.

346. Dr. Henry C. Register house, "Mill Creek," 1897

348a. Radnor Hunt Club, "The M.F.H. [Master of Fox Hounds] Radnor Hounds,"
interior, c. 1890

348b. Radnor Hunt Club, "The Radnor Hounds—The Dog Pack"
in front of the kennel, c. 1890

349. William A. Patton house, "Crestlinn"
King of Prussia and Patton roads, Radnor
1887, Demolished
Patton was the third assistant to President Frank Thomson
of the Pennsylvania Railroad; Hotchkin described the
house: "Stone and shingle are combined in . . . this pleasant
cottage" (Hotchkin, *Rural Pennsylvania*, 222).

PRER&BG 2, no. 18 (9 May 1887); *PRER&BG* 2, no. 23
(13 June 1887).

350. J. B. Lippincott memorial plaque
Whereabouts unknown
Builder and Decorator trade supplement 5, no. 1 (September,
1887): 12.

351. Hotel
Eager and Charles streets, Baltimore, MD
1887–88, Unexecuted
The hotel was one of the last of the great dreams of the
president of the Baltimore and Ohio Railroad, Robert
Garrett. The project was abandoned when he died.
PRER&BG 2, no. 41 (17 October 1887).

352. **John Livingston house**
2218 Walnut Street, Philadelphia
1887, Demolished
The *Builders' Guide* records:

> The base and trimmings will be of English red stone. The front will be of fine pressed brick . . . The house will be four stories high; the front building will be 22 x 40, the building in the rear 17.5 x 43. (*PRER&BG* 2, no. 41 [17 October 1887].)

353. **Sixth Regiment Cavalry monument**
Gettysburg
1888, FF
In tribute to Rush's Lancers, a rock-faced tapering granite shaft surrounded by eight bronze lances was built.

> Memorials like this should mark the various stations of that proud line of loyal men, and no reminder anywhere should speak for the baffled host, which was shattered here in assaulting the Union—only the peaceful fields fading out to the dim mountain passes through which the broken Confederate army had long drifted away like a phantom, and left not a vestige behind.

Address by Colonel Frederick Newhall, 14 October 1888, Colonel John Nicholson, ed., *Pennsylvania at Gettysburg, Ceremonies, Dedication of monuments* (Harrisburg, 1893), 2:820 ff.

352. John Livingston house, 1928

353. Sixth Regiment Cavalry monument, c. 1888

354. "The Villa," Department for Women, Pennsylvania Hospital for the Insane, c. 1890

356. Philadelphia Club, billiard room addition, exterior looking northwest, 1989

354. **"The Villa," Department for Women, Pennsylvania Hospital for the Insane**
48th and Market streets, Philadelphia
c. 1888, Demolished
Annual Report of the Department for the Insane of the Pennsylvania Hospital (Philadelphia, 1888), 15.

355. **Girard Life and Annuity Building**
Broad and Chestnut streets, Philadelphia
1888, Unexecuted
The building was eventually designed by Addison Hutton.
Fifty-eighth Annual Exhibition of the Pennsylvania Academy of the Fine Arts, no. 539 (Philadelphia, 1888).

356. **Additions and alterations to Philadelphia Club**
13th and Walnut streets, Philadelphia
1888

T. P. Chandler was a member, but the weight of membership of Furness's clients, including three Cassatts, Cuyler, Ellis, Griscom, and Welsh, may have given Furness the edge.
(*Builder, Decorator and Woodworker* 7, no. 3 (November 1888).

357. **St. John the Divine Cathedral, Competition**
New York, NY
1888, Unexecuted
The competition was lost to Heins and LaFarge.

358. **Home for Aged and Infirm Israelites, Jewish Hospital**
Broad Street and Old York Road, Philadelphia
1888, Demolished
See cat. 29.

The building was described as being of "Moorish" design in 1915, presumably linking it and its architect to the Rodef Shalom Synagogue (cat. 15).
PRER&BG 3, no. 2 (16 January 1888).

359. **Addition to old building, Jewish Hospital**
Broad Street and Old York Road, Philadelphia
1888, Demolished
See cat. 29.
PRER&BG 3, no. 2 (16 January 1888).

360. **Boiler House, Jewish Hospital**
Broad Street and Old York Road, Philadelphia
1888
See cat. 29.
Twenty-fourth Annual Report of the Jewish Hospital Association (Philadelphia, 1889), 68.

358. Home for Aged and Infirm Israelites, Jewish Hospital, c. 1965

361. Jewish Hospital, laundry and dormitory, c. 1910

361. **Laundry building, Jewish Hospital**
Broad Street and Old York Road, Philadelphia
1888, Demolished
See cat. 29.
Twenty-fourth Annual Report of the Jewish Hospital Association
(Philadelphia, 1889), 68.

362. **Kitchen and dormitory, Jewish Hospital**
Broad Street and Old York Road, Philadelphia
1888, Demolished
See cat. 29.
Twenty-fourth Annual Report of the Jewish Hospital Association
(Philadelphia, 1889), 68.

363. **Additions to Haverford Grammar School**
Railroad Avenue, Haverford
1888, Altered, AE
See cat. 301.
Minutes of Board of Overseers of Haverford College, MS
vol. 4 (1883–91), 2 March 1888, 226.

362. Jewish Hospital, kitchen building, c. 1910

363. Haverford Grammar School, 1988

364a. *Alexander J. Cassatt house, exterior looking southwest, 1969*

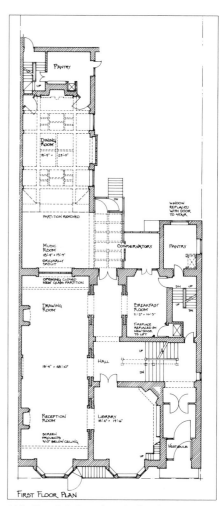

364b. *Alexander J. Cassatt house, first floor plan, 1975*

364. Additions and alterations to Alexander J. Cassatt house

(formerly Fairman Rogers house)
202 South 19th Street, Philadelphia
1888, Demolished, AE

The preexisting house was owned previously by Fairman Rogers (cat. 35A). Fifteen years after their country house had been built (cat. 36), the Cassatts bought the house in the city and commissioned Furness to design additions and alterations to it. In 1888 the office changed the stairwell, modernized the old gallery of the 1871 addition, and added an immense skylit gallery on the west side of the house. Exterior alterations were made at the same time, with a new sculptured lintel above the entrance and a large copper-clad mansard. A letter from Cassatt to Evans thanked him for his efforts, and reported that a sofa loaned from the Evans house fit perfectly under the stairs, as Evans had predicted (Evans MS).

Signed blueprints last seen in the Episcopal Church papers, Historical Society of Pennsylvania. [HABS PA–1537]

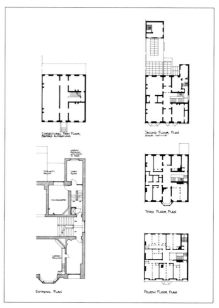

364c. *Alexander J. Cassatt house, conjectural plan c. 1860; upper stories as altered, 1975*

364d. Alexander J. Cassatt house, gallery fireplace, 1969

364e. Alexander J. Cassatt house, gallery window, 1969

364f. Alexander J. Cassatt house, parlor plasterwork, 1969

364g. Alexander J. Cassatt house, entrance hall, 1969

365a. Franklin Gowen house, 1990

365b. Franklin Gowen house, exterior view from garden side, 1989

Above
366a. Edward Brooke house, exterior looking west, 1990
Opposite
366b. Edward Brooke house, hall, south door, 1990

365. **Franklin Gowen houses**
Mount Airy, Philadelphia
1888
Sharing elements from the Haverford Grammar School (cat. 301) and the early building for the Merion Cricket Club (cat. 252), these two houses reflect the continuing office vernacular of the 1880s. Furness designed at least four houses for Gowen, three already noted on Boyer Street (cats. 287A and 288A) and another on Gowen Avenue, depicted here. Presumably the *Builders' Guide* referred to two of the four.
PRER&BG 3, no. 26 (2 July 1888).

366. **Edward Brooke house**
300 block, Washington Avenue, Birdsboro
c. 1888, Altered
Standing on a commanding site that overlooks the entire Schuylkill Valley and the Brooke Iron mills below, this is the most spectacular of the 1880s houses. Here sculptural mass, rugged materials, and a mountain site found an ap-propriate expression. The interior is organized around an L-shaped stairhall which connects to each of the major first floor rooms, a parlor and dining room in the north wing, a round library in the corner and a ladies' parlor on the long south wing. All the major rooms are finished in dark oak except for the ladies' parlor. Detailing parodies Queen Anne with a mixture of overscaled Gothic and colonial motifs, recalling the contemporary Richard D. Wood (cat. 368A) and Robert M. Lewis houses (cat. 324A).
Signed drawings in hands of present owner.

366c. Edward Brooke house, hall, 1990

366d. Edward Brooke house, hall fireplace, 1990

366e. Edward Brooke house, front parlor fireplace, 1990

366f. Edward Brooke house, front parlor, detail of fireplace, 1990

366g. Edward Brooke house, ladies' parlor, 1990

367a. Pittsburgh Terminal, Baltimore and Ohio Railroad, c.1890

367b. Pittsburgh Terminal, Baltimore and Ohio Railroad, c. 1910

367c. Pittsburgh Terminal, Baltimore and Ohio Railroad, after alterations, c. 1920

367. Pittsburgh Terminal, Baltimore and Ohio Railroad
Pittsburgh
1888, Demolished
The domestically scaled balconies flanking the central chimney were sufficiently unusual to cause their removal within a decade of the building's completion.
James Van Trump, "Pittsburgh Railroad Station," *Charrette* 28 (January 1956): 21–30; *PRER&BG* 3, no. 30 (30 July 1888).

Opposite
368Aa. Richard D. Wood house, dining room fireplace, 1989
Above
368Ab. Richard D. Wood house, dining room cabinet, 1989

368Ac. Richard D. Wood house, detail of console, entrance hall, 1989

369b. Provident Life and Trust Company Building, president's office

368A. **Richard D. Wood house**
1920 Spruce Street, Philadelphia
c. 1888
Family connections make this a likely attribution, while the shingled, roofed fireplace, derived from Richard Norman Shaw, had become a commonplace of the office in the 1880s.

369. **Provident Life and Trust Company Building**
401 Chestnut Street at Fourth Street, Philadelphia
1888–89, Demolished
See cat. 423, 514, 553.
Other competitors for this project included George C. Mason, William Ralph Emerson (Boston), and George T. Pearson. The new building was ten stories tall, ornamented in bands of brick and stone across its surface, and crowned by a three-story-high red tile roof. It was intended to harmonize with the original building (cat. 86) in the motifs of its lower stories. Minutes of the Board of Directors of the Provident Life and Trust Co., MS, 13 February 1888.

369a. Provident Life and Trust Company Building, exterior looking northwest, c. 1900

370a. *University of Pennsylvania Library, "Design of the Library of the University of Pennsylvania," 1888*

370b. *University of Pennsylvania Library, exterior looking southeast, c. 1895*

370c. *University of Pennsylvania Library, exterior looking southwest, c. 1890*

370. **University of Pennsylvania Library**
34th Street and Woodland Avenue, Philadelphia
1888–90, Altered, FF
See color plate 13.
In 1888 the University of Pennsylvania determined to commission the finest collegiate library in the world. It organized a committee headed by Horace Howard Furness; and advised by Justin Winsor, head librarian at Harvard University, and Melvil Dewey, the originator of the Dewey decimal system and the leading library theoretician of his day; shortly they added Frank Furness as architectural advisor. The library was initially proposed for a site at 36th and Spruce streets, but that location was given to the Wistar Institute. The plan developed between Furness, Winsor, and Dewey was a librarian's dream, with a large skylit reading room joined to a self-sustaining iron and glass bookstack whose south wall could be moved south, permitting stack extension as required by the growth of the collection. After his consultation, Dewey wrote Provost Pepper:

The plans I sketched with Mr. Furness late that evening

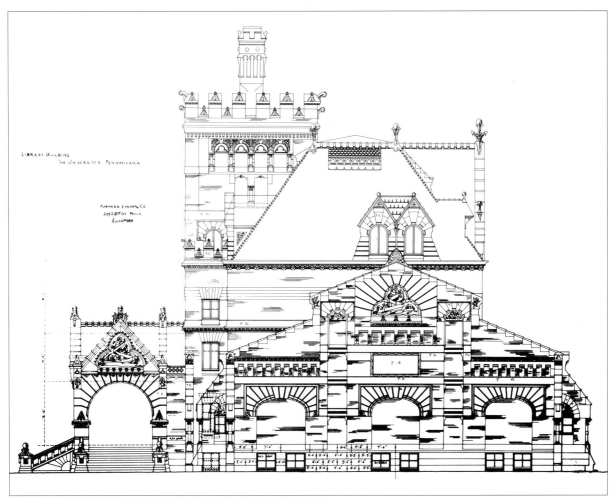

370d. University of Pennsylvania Library, south elevation, 1888

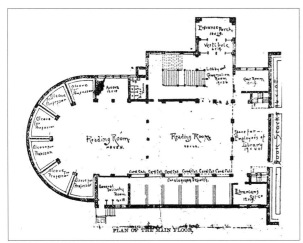

370e. University of Pennsylvania Library, preliminary plan of main floor, c. 1887

seem better than any college library has yet adopted. I should like to see your building by odds the best model for similar institutions to follow & it will be a great pleasure if I can be of any service in that direction." (Melvil Dewey, letter to Provost Pepper, 20 April 1888.)

The building was constructed during 1889 and 1890 and dedicated in February, 1891. The firm made numerous additions to the building, including the Tower Book Collection bridge in the reading room (1895), the Duhring Wing stack extension (1916), and the Lea Reading room and periodicals room (1924).

PRER&BG 3, no. 28 (16 July 1888).

[1973–29, HABS PA–1644]

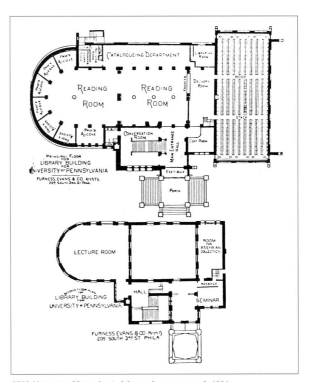

370f. University of Pennsylvania Library, plan as constructed, 1891

370g. University of Pennsylvania Library, stair hall, c. 1895

370h. University of Pennsylvania Library, glass and steel book stack, looking south, c. 1900

370i. University of Pennsylvania Library, detail of doors between "Conversation Room" and library, 1987

Above
370j. University of Pennsylvania Library, second floor auditorium during use as University Museum, c. 1895
Opposite
370k. University of Pennsylvania Library, main reading room looking north, 1895

Opposite
370l. University of Pennsylvania Library, "Rotunda Reading Room," 1891
Above
371a. Frank Furness summer cottage, "Idlewild," exterior looking southwest, 1990

371b. Frank Furness summer cottage, "Idlewild," 1972

374. George Fox house, c. 1888

376. Frederick Fox house, c. 1888

371. Frank Furness summer cottage, "Idlewild"
Idlewild, near Media
c. 1888, FF
This small house was based on the plan of the University of Pennsylvania Library (cat. 370); the rotunda reading room became the living room while the seminar rooms were recalled by the porch.
Conversations with George Wood Furness.

372A. Alterations to 1023 Market Street, Philadelphia
c. 1888, Demolished
The similarity of this building to 1025 Market Street (cat. 457), designed by Furness, Evans and Co. in 1894, suggests that this was an office work, while the chamfered lintels were an office convention during that decade.

373A. Firehouse
313 Branch Street, Philadelphia
c. 1888, Demolished

374. George Fox house
Old York Road, Ashbourne
c. 1880, Demolished
The radically different character of the Fox houses suggests that they were constructed at different times, with this perhaps in the early 1880s and the Frederick Fox house (cat. 376) perhaps in the late 1880s. Lacking newspaper information, they are left together with the Caleb Fox house (cat. 375). Baker and Dallett list Fox stables among their commissions, which were perhaps also works dating form their years in the office, and hint that they may have served as

project architects for one or both of these commissions.
Samuel F. Hotchkin, *Old York Road* (Philadelphia, 1892) 153.

375. Caleb Fox house
Old York Road, Ashbourne
Before 1888, Demolished
See cat. 374.
Hotchkin, *Old York Road*, 153.

376. Frederick Fox house
Old York Road, Ashbourne
c. 1888, Demolished
See cat. 374.
Hotchkin, *Old York Road*, 153.

Opposite
377. Frank Thomson house, "Corkerhill," c. 1897
Above
378Aa. 3801–15 Walnut Street, Philadelphia, looking north, c. 1965

378Ab. 3809 Walnut Street, Philadelphia, detail of porch, c. 1965

378Ac. 3809 Walnut Street, Philadelphia, dining room fireplace, 1990

378Ad. 3809 Walnut Street, Philadelphia, stairhall, 1990

378Ae. 100–108 South 38th Street, Philadelphia, 1970

377. **Frank Thomson house, "Corkerhill"**
Union Avenue, Lower Merion
1889, Demolished
See cat. 418, 459.

Frank Thomson was yet another president of the Pennsylvania Railroad for whom Furness designed a house. Perhaps Furness was also involved with the original house, erected c. 1875. This house replaced the burned building. Hotchkin described the second house:

> It is a stone house and there is a conservatory near it. The light-coloured woodwork and pretty porch and pleasant hall are noteworthy features. 'The Cabin' is a

shingled rustic building for recreation. (Hotchkin, *Rural Pennsylvania*, 38.)
PRER&BG 4, no. 6 (13 February 1889).

378A. **3801–15 Walnut Street and 100–08 South 38th Street, Philadelphia**
1889, JH

Four double houses fronting Walnut Street and a porch-fronted row on 38th Street were built over the summer of 1889. The outer pair of doubles were faced with rough coursed brownstone; one survives, covered with a 1960s bronze grill. The row was demolished in the late 1960s for the widening of 38th Street.

Interior details are directly derived from the contemporary projects of the office. The turned stair newels are consistent in detail with contemporary houses, while the squared Ionic console ornamenting the fireplace bracket of 3809 is identical to a similar form on the University of Pennsylvania Library (cat. 370). Presumably these were an economical developer's project—but one that still received attention to the salient details. William D. Huston, father of Joseph Huston (cat. 327) of Furness's office, was a member of the Page office.
PRER&BG 4, no. 9 (6 March 1889).

379a. St. Michael and All the Angels Church, detail of entrance, 1988

379b. St. Michael and All the Angels Church, exterior looking southwest, 1988

Above
384a. Williamson Free School of Mechanical Trades, main building, 1891
Opposite
384b. Williamson Free School of Mechanical Trades, main building, 1972

379. St. Michael and All the Angels Church
42nd and Wallace streets, Philadelphia
1889, WMC
This was a Protestant Episcopal mission church in the black community of Philadelphia.
PRER&BG 4, no. 16 (24 April 1889).

380. Alterations to 202 South Ninth Street, Philadelphia
1889
Permit listed, *PRER&BG* 4, no. 19 (8 May 1889).

381. Charles Chauncey house
Summit and Righter's Mill Road, Elm Station (now Narberth)
1889, Demolished
According to the *Builders' Guide*, this was a stone and shingle house.

PRER&BG 4, no. 23 (12 June 1889).

382. New building, Racquet Club
923 Walnut Street, Philadelphia
1889, Demolished
Furness added a one story racquet court addition to the rear of the property, which is believed to have been the first of such courts in the country. The building remained the clubhouse until 1912, when Horace Trumbauer's building on 17th Street was completed. The size and contractor are recorded in permit #3626, 22 October 1889; 34' x 160' x one story (33' high). An addition was made in 1900 (cat. 531). *PRER&BG* 4, no. 30 (21 July 1889).

383A. Additions to John T. Bailey and Company Factory
Water and Otsego streets, Philadelphia

1889
This is similar to the 1895 additions (cat. 465) and was, like the original 1885 building (cat. 303A), probably by the office. Building permit #2628, 26 September 1889, Allen B. Rorke contractor.

384. Williamson Free School of Mechanical Trades
Middletown Road, Elwyn
1889–90, Altered
Other competitors for the commission included the Wilson Brothers, Cope and Stewardson, G. W. and W. D. Hewitt, and Thomas Lonsdale. Williamson was a notable philanthropist who had helped fund the project for the University of Pennsylvania Library (cat. 370).
O'Gorman et al., *Drawing Toward Building*, 159–162; *Philadelphia Inquirer*, 24 August 1889, 3. [1973-30]

384c. Williamson Free School of Mechanical Trades, dormitories, 1891

384d. Williamson Free School of Mechanical Trades, dormitory, 1972

384e. Williamson Free School of Mechanical Trades, stairhall, 1972

384f. Williamson Free School of Mechanical Trades, detail of fireplace, 1972

385. R. Winder Johnson house, exterior looking northeast, 1989

386A. William West Frazier, Jr. and George Harrison Frazier double house, exterior looking southeast, 1989

387A. 1707 Sansom Street, exterior looking north, 1989

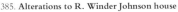

385. **Alterations to R. Winder Johnson house**
Northeast corner of 22nd and Spruce streets, Philadelphia
1889
The Johnson family acquired the "three story brick house with brownstone front," at the corner of 22nd and Spruce streets in the 1870s. R. Winder Johnson, who had been recorded as living at 2109 Spruce, retained Furness to remove the brownstone and to reface it in a modern design. *PRER&BG* 4, no. 34 (28 August 1889).

386A. **William West Frazier, Jr. and George Harrison Frazier double house**

2132–34 Spruce Street, Philadelphia
c. 1889
These were two of the children of Furness's long-time friend, William West Frazier (cat. 256). The property was acquired 17 April 1889 and was held by the Frazier family into the 1920s. Detailing is related to the University of Pennsylvania Library of the same year (cat. 370).

387A. **1707 Sansom Street, Philadelphia**
c. 1889
The narrow facade is a quick tour through the motifs of Victorian Philadelphia as selected by Furness: an exposed

iron lintel at the first floor, overscaled corbeled brick cornice at the top, and an oddly shaped dormer as a crown.

388. **Four two-story houses**
West Side of Manayunk Avenue, south of Kalas Street, Philadelphia
1889, WMC
The *Builders' Guide* recorded a permit indicating that this was presumably a property of the father of William M. Camac, who was a member of St. Timothy's Episcopal congregation at the top of the hill, and had investments in the area. *PRER&BG* 4, no. 45 (13 November 1889).

389a. Bryn Mawr Hotel, exterior looking northeast, 1975

389b. Bryn Mawr Hotel, exterior looking northwest, 1990

389c. Bryn Mawr Hotel, lobby fireplace, 1972

389d. Bryn Mawr Hotel, detail of stair, 1972

389. **Bryn Mawr Hotel**
(now the Baldwin School)
Bryn Mawr
1890
See color plate 14.
Railroads had long built great hotels as magnets along their rail lines; in the early 1870s, the Pennsylvania Railroad had built such a hotel at Bryn Mawr from the designs of the Wilson Brothers. This building burned in 1889, resulting in a competition for its replacement, including the Wilson Brothers and Addison Hutton; it was won by Furness, Evans and Co. who proposed a much larger building of the rough local stone and brick that was a familiar part of their suburban designs. Within a year or two it was apparent that changing times had made the suburban resort hotel obsolete, leading to its lease by the Misses Baldwin for their school. It was later sold to the school and remains its centerpiece.
Philadelphia Inquirer, 26 January 1890, 7. [1973–31]

391a. William Tiers development house, 1990

391b. William Tiers development house, stair hall, 1989

392a. 1219–21 Locust Street, Philadelphia (center double house), 1916

392b. 1221 Locust Street, Philadelphia, second floor mantel, 1980

393. George Gerhard house, St. Joseph's College, 1990

394. 1203–05 (right) and 1207–09 (left) Locust Street, Philadelphia, double houses, 1917

390. Additions to John Welsh house
1034 Spruce Street, Philadelphia
c. 1890, Demolished
Though owned by John Welsh (cat. 109, 111A), the building for a long time was the city residence of Samuel Shipley, who presumably altered it to suit his taste and later purchased it 31 May 1890 (cat. 264). According to the *Philadelphia Inquirer* on 27 September 1886, the house was converted into a fashionable boarding house by the Welsh estate in 1886.
The work on the house was recalled by the Samuel Shipley's granddaughter, Mrs. E. Page Allinson, in 1972.

391A. William Tiers development house
322 Thornbrook Road, Rosemont
c. 1890, Altered
Tiers had commissioned an earlier building (cat. 322). The turned and notched stair and the rugged massing are hallmarks of the Furness office. The interior was altered toward more traditional detail in the early twentieth century.

392. Additions and alterations to 1219–21 Locust Street, Philadelphia
1890, Altered
Building Permit #1878, 28 May 1890; A. B. Rorke contractor; *Builder, Decorator and Woodworker* 14, no. 5 (July 1890).

393. Alterations to George Gerhard house
Ardmore
1890
See cat. 581, 631.
"The new part will be in unison with the present building" wrote the *Builders' Guide*. The visual evidence suggests an earlier house, probably by the office, from the early 1870s.
PRER&BG 5, no. 22 (4 June 1890).

394. Additions and alterations to houses at 12th and Locust streets, Philadelphia
1890, Altered
Builder, Decorator and Woodworker 14, no. 5 (July 1890).

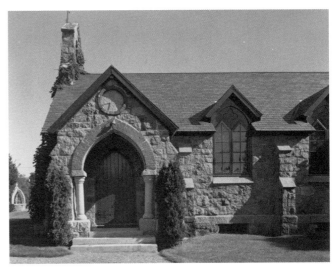

Opposite
396. New Castle Public Library, 1975
Above
397A. Hannah Kay Furness house, 1990

398a. Church of Our Father, 1989

395. Sailors' home
Swanson and Catherine streets, Philadelphia
1890
According to Building Permit #2610, dated 6 July 1890, William R. Dougherty was selected as contractor for a 32' by 72' by three-story building. The *Builders' Guide* reported that it was paid for by a group of Episcopal churchmen headed by William West Frazier. The building was sold at a sheriff's sale in 1907.
PRER&BG 5, no. 27 (9 July 1890).

396. **New Castle Public Library**
New Castle, DE
1890, WMC
The interior was lighted by the giant glass slates of the top of the roof, which in turn lighted a basement through a glass floor recalling, in miniature, elements of the University of Pennsylvania Library (cat. 370).
PRER&BG 5, no. 29 (23 July 1890).

397A. **Hannah Kay Furness house**
York Harbor, ME
c. 1890, Altered
According to Maine historian Kevin Murphy, this property was acquired in 1890 by Hannah Kay Furness, widow of Frank's brother William, Jr. (York County Register of Deeds, Alfred, ME, Book 439, p. 33). She owned it until her death in 1897, at which time it passed to her brother Alfred Kay in trust for her daughter who had predeceased her in the same year. The original house was modest, shingled on its surfaces, with a gambrel roof punctuated by shed dormers recalling the rear wings of many Furness-designed houses of the period. After its sale in December 1902, the house was considerably enlarged by local builder E. B. Blaisdell (S. Carlisle, York Historic Landmarks Architectural Survey, 1980). In 1902, the last summer of ownership by the Furness family, the house had a famous summer tenant, Mark Twain, who rented it to be near his longtime friend, William Dean Howells, who was in Kittery. It was there that Twain's wife was taken gravely ill, causing morbid associations for Twain in his later recollections of the house. (Kenneth Eble, *Old Clemens and W.D.H.* [Baton Rouge: LSU Press, 1985], 3, 113.) Twain had long known the Furness family through various visits with Horace. (For Twain's acquaintance with the Furnesses see James M. Gibson, *The Philadelphia Shakespeare Story: Horace Howard Furness and the New Variorum Shakespeare* [New York: AMS Press, 1990], 115.) Ironically, the event of Mary Kay Warner's death in childbirth shortly before her mother's death foreshadowed the near death of Twain's daughter when his wife was dying. (Henry Nash Smith and William M. Gibson, *Mark Twain-Howells Letters: The Correspondence of Samuel L. Clemens and William Dean Howells, 1872–1910* [Cambridge, MA: Belknap Press of Harvard University, 1960], 758, 808–809.) That Twain knew the Furness family through Horace is apparent from his com-

ment on the ownership of the York Harbor house as by a Cambridge branch of the "Shakespearian Furnesses of Philadelphia."

398. **Church of Our Father**
Hull's Cove, Mount Desert Island, ME
1890–91, WMC
This Protestant Episcopal Church is a reprise of the Germantown Unitarian Church (cat. 1); its basic form reappeared in later churches, such as the Church of Our Saviour (cat. 422).
O'Gorman, "Frank Furness," (1985).

399. James G. Blaine house
Washington, D.C.
1890, Unexecuted, WMC
A letter from Mrs. James G. Blaine to her son dated 30 January [1890] reported that
    Camac is here. He arrived yesterday afternoon armed with a roll of plans for the new house. Of course he will be disappointed to find that scheme abandoned and the old Seward house determined on, as it is, but he has addressed himself to the new issues with smiling cordiality and unaffected sweetness. (Beale, *Letters*, 240.)
Furness also designed a house for Blaine in Bar Harbor, Maine (cat. 314).

400. Alterations to James G. Blaine house
Lafayette Square, Washington, D.C.
1890
After the scheme for the new house was abandoned, the Blaines decided to lease, with an option to buy, William H. Seward's 1830s house. After serving as a government office the building required steel girders to reinforce its second story. Presumably their insertion was part of the work of the office. Mrs. Blaine wrote in a letter to her son, "I cannot bear the idea of a furnished house, nor do I want the trouble and delay of building. Willie Camac will be put in charge of all improvements, or rather he will be given the opportunity of doing it." (Blaine, *Letters*, 237). The commission was reported the following summer in Philadelphia.
Philadelphia Inquirer, 27 August 1890, 7.

401. **Interior alterations to James G. Blaine house**
2000 Massachusetts Avenue, NW, Washington, D.C.
1890–91, Altered
The Blaine house was designed by Furness's former partner John Fraser. It features a great cast iron porte cochere, whose ornament appears on Furness's Guarantee Trust (cat. 44) and the Provident Bank (cat. 86). Terra-cotta ornament with sunflowers and other period motifs suggest that Fraser directly copied the Furness manner. That those features were in place when Furness's firm altered the house is confirmed by engravings of the house made prior to the date when Furness is known to have worked on the building, and thus presumably were the work of Fraser. The house

398b. Church of Our Father, nave, 1989

401. James G. Blaine house, 1974

was built at the peak of Blaine's national importance, but was later rented out. When it was damaged by fire, the always affable Camac was called back to make the repairs. The *Builders' Guide* reported: "Recently burnt, the plans comprehend an entire new interior and much of the exterior as well . . . It will be rebuilt on a grand scale." (*PRER&BG* 6, no. 2 [14 January 1891].)

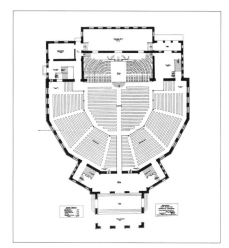

403a. Alumni Auditorium, University of Pennsylvania, plan, 1890

403b. Alumni Auditorium, University of Pennsylvania, "Sketch Showing Position of Alumni Auditorium . . . ," engraving, 1890

403c. Alumni Auditorium, University of Pennsylvania, "Sketch of Alumni Auditorium, University of Pennsylvania," engraving, 1890

402. Additions to Thomas DeWitt Cuyler house
Cuylers' Lane off Grays Lane, Haverford
1890, Demolished, AE
Wings were added to the modest center-hall house of 1883 (cat. 284).
Philadelphia Inquirer, 7 October 1890, 7.

403. **Alumni Auditorium, University of Pennsylvania**
34th and Walnut streets, Philadelphia
1890, Unexecuted
The Alumni Auditorium was to be the last component of the main campus of the University. It was to be constructed of red brick and red terra-cotta, but with a great cast frieze. Had it been built, it would have provided the long-needed large auditorium for the University's outreach to the community.
Philadelphia Inquirer, 27 October 1890, 6.

404. **Charles C. Harrison house, "Happy Creek Farm"**
Devon
c. 1890, Demolished
See cat. 645.
The farm buildings of the estate are still extant and stylistically suggest an earlier date. The Harrison country seat is part of the later group of sprawling stone houses that contrast with the earlier, more vertical Victorian look.
Hotchkin, *Rural Pennsylvania,* 289.

405. Protestant Episcopal Chapel of the Holy Spirit
11th and Snyder streets, Philadelphia
1890, Demolished
The building was first reported in the *Builders' Guide* of 3 December 1890 and its progress was noted several times.
PRER&BG 5, no. 48 (3 December 1890); *Builder, Decorator and Woodworker* 16, no. 4 (June 1891).

406. Walter Rogers Furness cottage
(later Jekyll Island Infirmary)
Jekyll Island, GA
1891
Walter Rogers Furness, son of Horace, was in charge of the project. The overhanging shingled volume of the second story is carried on slender, turned porch posts.
William B. McCash, *The Jekyll Island Club* (Athens, GA: University of Georgia Press, 1979), 61.

407. Percy C. Madeira house
Ogontz, Philadelphia
1891, Demolished
See cat. 605, 632.
The house was described as being stone; it was to be three stories with a slate roof.
Philadelphia Inquirer, 14 January 1891, 7.

404. *Charles C. Harrison house, "Happy Creek Farm," c. 1897*

412. *Recitation Hall, Delaware State College, c. 1900*

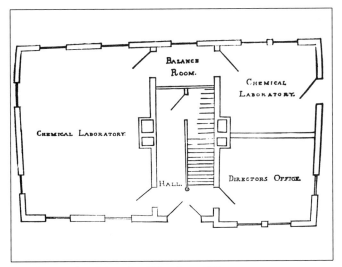

414a. *Oratory Building, Delaware State College, plan, c. 1900*

414b. *Oratory Building, Delaware State College, 1976*

408. Reconstruction of 1820 Delancey Street, Philadelphia
1891
Philadelphia Inquirer, 11 March 1891, 7.

409. Cottages for Home for Consumptives, Protestant Episcopal City Mission
Stenton and Evergreen avenues, Chestnut Hill, Philadelphia
1891–92
The various cottages of the complex begun in 1885 (cat. 299) were erected as funds became available.
Philadelphia Inquirer, 12 March 1891, 7.

410. Alterations to 1821 Delancey Street, Philadelphia
1891
PRER&BG 6, no. 11 (18 March 1891).

411. "The Villa," Department for Women, Pennsylvania Hospital for the Insane
48th and Market streets, Philadelphia
1891, Demolished
See cat. 354.
The building was to be built "three stories high, of brick" (*PRER&BG* 6, no. 17 [29 April 1891]).

412. **Recitation Hall, Delaware State College**
(now University of Delaware)
Newark, DE
1891, Drastically altered
The original limestone imposts, belt courses, and stone voussoirs in the gable were removed to convert the building into a colonial revival design by Howell L. Shay after World War II.
Philadelphia Inquirer, 8 July 1891, 7.

413. Proposal for Water Works to Philadelphia
Norristown
1891
This was a plan of an aqueduct for the Schuylkill Navigation Company.
Signed drawings, collection of Franklin Institute.

414. **Oratory Building, Delaware State College**
(now University of Delaware)
Newark, DE
1891, Altered
PRER&BG 6, no. 28 (15 July 1891).

415. Alterations to Ferryboat Chicago, Pennsylvania Railroad
1891

In the 1890s, the Pennsylvania Railroad added a second deck to many of its ferries; Furness redesigned the interiors at this time.
Linens dated July 1891, private collection.

416. Clubhouse
Lansdowne
1891
Philadelphia Inquirer, 21 July 1891, 7.

417. H. Allen house
1524 North Seventh Street, Philadelphia
1891, Demolished since 1973
The *Builders' Guide* recorded: "three stories of brick and stone" (*PRER&BG* 6, no. 30 [27 July 1891]).

418. Frank Thomson stable
Union Avenue, Lower Merion
1891, Demolished
See cat. 377.
After the fire, the *Builders' Guide* reported the new stable to be a stone and half timber two-and-one-half-story structure with slate roof (*PRER&BG* 6, no. 39 [30 September 1891]).
Philadelphia Inquirer, 1 October 1891, 7.

Opposite
419. 1804 Rittenhouse Square, Philadelphia, exterior looking southeast, 1989
Above
421a. Mortuary Chapel, Mount Sinai Cemetery, exterior looking northeast, 1972

421b. Mortuary Chapel, Mount Sinai Cemetery, interior, 1972

422a. Church of Our Saviour, exterior looking northwest, 1989

422b. Church of Our Saviour, nave, 1989

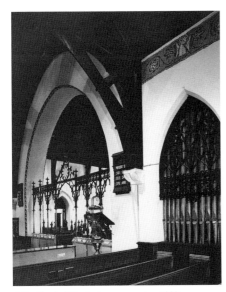

422c. Church of Our Saviour, nave crossing, 1989

419. **1804 Rittenhouse Square, Philadelphia**
1891–92, GWC
Sixty-second Annual Exhibition, Pennsylvania Academy of the Fine Arts, no. 488 (Philadelphia, 1892).

420. First National Bank of Darby
Darby
1892, GWC
Sixty-second Annual Exhibition, Pennsylvania Academy of the Fine Arts, no. 489 (Philadelphia, 1892).

421. **Mortuary Chapel, Mount Sinai Cemetery**
Bridge and Cottage streets, Frankford, Philadelphia
1891–92
This was another of the commissions that came from the Rodef Shalom (cat. 15) work of a generation earlier. Like the Home for Aged and Infirm Israelites (cat. 358), it picked up the Moorish themes from the original synagogue commission. The functional tile interior and open truss roof have been covered since 1973. A brick caretaker's cottage on the site is probably also the work of the firm.
Philadelphia Inquirer, 27 February 1892, 7. [1973-32]

422. **Church of Our Saviour**
Jenkintown
1892
See cats. 440, 489, 591, 610.
Vestry minutes report a continuing series of commissions to Furness, Evans and Co, beginning in 1890 (18 December 1890; 7 October 1891); on 28 December 1892 Furness, Evans and Co. were hired to prepare plans for a new Parish House (cat. 440). The accounting warden of the church was William West Frazier.
PRER&BG 7, no. 2 (13 January 1892).

423. Additions to Provident Life and Trust Company Building
401 Chestnut Street at South Fourth Street, Philadelphia
1892, Demolished
The *Builders' Guide* wrote of the additions to the Provident Life and Trust Company Building:
> The new structure will be in keeping with the architecture of the present structure on the corner [cat. 369], and will be of buff and enamelled brick, with dark granite trimmings, slate roof, copper cornice, sand finished walls. (*PRER&BG* 7, no. 9 [2 March 1892].)

424a. *Lippincott, Johnson and Company store (right), looking north, c. 1880*

424b. *Lippincott, Johnson and Company store, exterior looking northeast, c. 1906*

425. *Lippincott, Johnson and Company Building, exterior looking northeast, c. 1910*

426. *Chapel, Christ Church, exterior looking northeast, c. 1930*

424. **Lippincott, Johnson and Company Store**
629 Market Street, Philadelphia
1892, Demolished
The office undertook the "rebuilding of 629 Market Street, recently destroyed by fire. The structure will be about six stories high" (*PRER&BG* 7, no. 10 [9 March 1892]). The building appears to have been an earlier design by the office.

425. **Lippincott, Johnson and Company Building**
1025 Walnut Street, Philadelphia
1892, Demolished
The laconic statement of the *Builders' Guide* read: "The structure will be of buff brick, stone trimmings, iron columns and beams" (*PRER&BG* 7, no. 10 [9 March 1892]). In fact, this was one of the remarkable Furness assaults on the conventions of classicism. The story-high voussoirs screening the attic are particularly memorable on this five-story building.

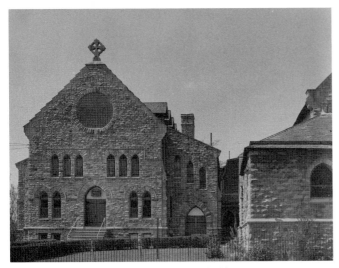

428a. Chapel and Parish House, Protestant Episcopal Church of the Atonement, exterior looking west, 1988

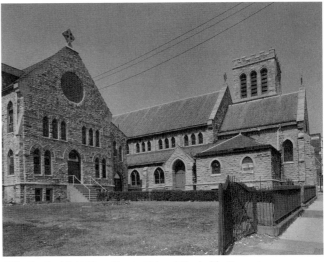

428b. Chapel and Parish House, Protestant Episcopal Church of the Atonement, exterior looking northwest, 1988

429. Bryn Mawr Hospital, 1989

426. **Additions and alterations to Christ Church Chapel**
1915–23 Pine Street, Philadelphia
1892, Altered
A small brick entrance porch was added in the open side yard of the church.
Philadelphia Inquirer, 21 May 1892, 7.

427. Mercantile Club, Competition
1200 block, North Broad Street, Philadelphia
1892, Unexecuted
The competition, lost to Baker and Dallett, included Hazelhurst and Huckel, William Decker, Wilson Brothers, and Frank Miles Day.
PRER&BG 7, no. 21 (25 May 1892).

428. **Chapel and Parish House, Protestant Episcopal Church of the Atonement**
47th Street and Kingsessing Avenue, Philadelphia
1892
The church property was partially paid for by William West Frazier (cat. 256), a trustee of the church that for a time was used by the Episcopal Seminary as their chapel.
Philadelphia Inquirer, 30 June 1892, 7.

429. **Bryn Mawr Hospital**
Bryn Mawr
1892
See cats. 539, 639, 648.
The board included many Furness clients: T. Wistar Brown, Rudolf Ellis, J. Randall Williams, and George Gerhard. The women's board was equally connected to Furness and included Mrs. Alexander J. Cassatt, Mrs. Ellis, Mrs. James Winsor, and Mrs. J. R. Williams, (*PRER&BG* 7, no. 35 [August, 1892]). The building was largely paid for by Mrs. Clement Griscom. Based on the center-hall scheme of the hospital in Chestnut Hill (cat. 299), the design was less aggressively original. The porch (recalling that of St. Mary's Protestant Episcopal Church in Ardmore [cat. 341]) is a later addition by the firm.
PRER&BG 7, no. 22 (1 June 1892).

430a. Broad Street Station, Pennsylvania Railroad, perspective of additions

430. Additions to Broad Street Station, Pennsylvania Railroad

Broad and Market streets, Philadelphia
1892–93, Demolished
The *Builders' Guide* records:

> It will have an imposing front and all the rooms will be
> opened so that at all times the best light attainable can
> be had. It will be eight stories without counting the
> ground floor and second story, or in all a ten-story
> building which will cost anywhere between $1,250,000
> to $1,500,000. The building will partake of the same
> style of architecture as the present one, the style being
> called the modern Gothic. (*PRER&BG* 7, no. 30 [27
> July 1892].)

[1973–33, HABS PA–1527]

Above
430b. Broad Street Station, Pennsylvania Railroad, perspective of additions, looking northwest
Opposite
430c. Broad Street Station, Pennsylvania Railroad, exterior looking northwest, c. 1915

430d. *Broad Street Station, Pennsylvania Railroad, ground plan of train floor*

430e. *Broad Street Station, Pennsylvania Railroad, exterior looking northwest, c. 1895*

430f. *Broad Street Station, Pennsylvania Railroad, exterior looking northeast, c. 1895*

430g. *Broad Street Station, Pennsylvania Railroad, trainshed, looking east, c. 1905*

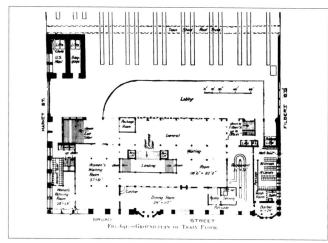

430h. *Broad Street Station, Pennsylvania Railroad, waiting room, c. 1930*

430i. *Broad Street Station, Pennsylvania Railroad, waiting room, c. 1930*

430j. Broad Street Station, Pennsylvania Railroad, main waiting room, c. 1930

431. 626 Alaska Street (now Kater Street), Philadelphia
1892
The building was described as a four-story "tenement for [the] 'lower classes'" with three-room suites; Sinclair B. Lewis was the architect in charge.
PRER&BG 7, no. 36 (7 September 1892).

432. Reconstruction of 1222–24 Locust Street, Philadelphia
1892
Furness drew up "plans for rebuilding Nos. 1222–24 Locust Street . . . The new houses will be of a very handsome design . . . They are to be practically five stories high, fronts of stone" (*PRER&BG* 7, no. 41 [12 October 1892]).

433. Jersey City Ferry Terminal, Pennsylvania Railroad
Jersey City, NJ
1892
In 1909 the Philadelphia based Stephens Terra Cotta Com-

pany published selections of their work in *American Art Marble*, and included several works by Furness, Evans and Co., notably the cast ornament of Broad Street Station (cat. 430), the interior detail of the Red Star Line steamships (cat. 444), and what was described as "a unique railroad station and ferry-house, the largest ever built on pilings." The main lobby was 600 feet long and was flanked by restaurants and waiting rooms; a published photograph shows a classicizing interior with a skylit ceiling.
American Art Marble (Philadelphia, 1909), 53–57.

434. Alterations to building for Lucien Moss estate
267 South 21st Street, Philadelphia
1892, Altered
"The material to be used will be Conshohocken stone and brick, chiefly, roof to be red slate on portions" (*PRER&BG* 7, no. 44 [2 November 1892]). The building has since been refaced with modern red brick. An interior stair retains the

conventional grooved Furness pattern.

435A. 269 South 21st Street, Philadelphia
c. 1892, Altered
Typical office details on the interior suggest that this building was also the work of the office. The facade has been replaced in this century.

436A. Training quarters and locker room, Merion Cricket Club

Montgomery Avenue, Haverford
1892, Demolished
See cat. 252, 437.
A simple shingle-style locker room was constructed on the new Cricket Club property in 1892. Its stylistic similarity to the new clubhouse (cat. 437) suggests that it too was the work of Allen Evans.
Evans Scrapbooks.

437. **Additions and alterations to Merion Cricket Club**
Montgomery Avenue, Haverford
1892, Destroyed by fire, AE
See cat. 252.
In 1892, the Merion Cricket Club took a 999 year lease on the property on Montgomery Avenue; it contained two houses on the Montgomery Avenue side of the tract. One of these was moved towards the other and then Evans designed a shingle-style, porch-fronted infill that linked the two houses, and joined the entire structure under a gambrel-roofed third story that made the building appear to be a new structure. However, the rough stone work of the lower walls and the segmental-headed windows are hallmarks of the 1870s and betray the hybrid origins of the building. It was destroyed by fire in 1896 and rebuilt, leading to the present building (cat. 483).
Rowland Evans, Paul Casey, and Charles Wister, *The Merion Cricket Club, 1865–1965* (Philadelphia, 1965); *Philadelphia Inquirer*, 24 November 1892, 2.

438. Elevated street railroad proposal
Market Street, Philadelphia
1892, Unexecuted
Philadelphia Inquirer, 8 December 1892, 1.

439. Letter concerning Harrisburg Competition
1893
The letter was a request to make the competition for the Harrisburg public buildings an open one.
Signed by Frank Furness, Samuel Huckel, A. J. Boyden, James H. Windrim, T. P. Chandler, George C. Mason, Allen Evans, Wilson Eyre, Jr., Frank Miles Day, and Joseph Wilson (*Philadelphia Inquirer*, 8 February 1893).

440. Parish House, Church of Our Saviour
Jenkintown
1893, Altered
See cat. 422.
PRER&BG 8, no. 15 (12 April 1893).

441. Boiler House stack, Girard College
Girard Avenue, Philadelphia
1893, Demolished
PRER&BG 8, no. 34 (23 August 1893).

442A. J. P. Evans and Company laboratory
217–19 North Tenth Street, Philadelphia
1893, Demolished

443. "Old Parsonage" Retirement Home
Baltimore, MD
1894, Altered
Inland Architect 23, no. 5 (June 1894).

444. **Interior designs of Red Star Line steamships St. Louis and St. Paul**
1894–95, FF
"The dome contains two allegorical panels broken by a seated figure of Neptune . . . The walls of the saloon are broken into alcoves which are filled with fish, fowl and flesh panels." In other rooms, the decorations were intended to describe "the Bacchic origin of wine and the Indian origin of tobacco." The work was "executed under the immediate direction of Mr. Furness" for Clement Griscom. The St. Louis sailed for the first time in June 1895, and the St. Paul followed shortly thereafter.
Scientific American 72, no. 54 (15 June 1895): 376.

436A. Merion Cricket Club, training quarters, c. 1892

437. Merion Cricket Club, c. 1892

444. St. Louis steamship, lounge, 1894

454a. *George W. Childs house, exterior*

454b. *George W. Childs house, dining room, c. 1900*

454c. *George W. Childs house, stairhall, c. 1900*

445. Thomas Riley [Reilly] stable
Maloney Street, west of 20th Street, Philadelphia
1894
The *Builders' Guide* said of the stable: "the structure will be of brick and stone." (*PRER&BG* 9, no. 4 [24 January 1894]).

446. Colonial-style house
Main and Carpenter streets, Germantown, Philadelphia
1894
The Furness office has "made plans for a new residence to stand upon the site of the old Carpenter mansion . . . It will be in the Colonial style and brick and stone construction" (*PRER&BG* 9, no. 6 [7 February 1894]).

447. Alterations to Broad Street Station, Pennsylvania Railroad
Broad and Filbert streets, Philadelphia
1894, Demolished
Additional stories were added in the attic zone of the original section of the old Wilson Brothers design. Previous work had been done on the station by the Furness office in 1892–93 (cat. 430).
PRER&BG 9, no. 8 (21 February 1894).

448. Additions to Nixon house
842 North Broad Street, Philadelphia
1894, Demolished

Philadelphia Inquirer, 8 March 1894, 12.

449. Alterations to 2210 Walnut Street, Philadelphia
1894, Demolished
This work to a house from the previous generation was necessitated by the construction of the Walnut Street Bridge, which raised the street level.
PRER&BG 9, no. 17 (25 April 1894).

450. Alterations to 2212–14 Walnut Street, Philadelphia
1894, Demolished
This work was also necessitated by the Walnut Street Bridge construction.
Signed permit #1619, 5 May 1894 for 2214–16; Thomas Little contractor; *PRER&BG* 9, no. 17 (25 April 1894).

451. 2216 Walnut Street, Philadelphia
1894, Demolished
This project was a remodel of earlier work after new bridge raised street level.
Thomas Little contractor; permit #1210, 25 April 1894.

452. Good Samaritan Hospital
Broad and Ontario streets, Philadelphia
1894, Unexecuted (?), JH
A drawing of the hospital
    shows an elevation of four stories, of Moorish architec-

ture, [that] . . . will be of stone, brick, and iron construction. In the centre of [the] structure will rise an immense dome, under which will be located a handsome aquarium and a pleasant resting place for inmates and visitors. This will also contain flowers and other ornamentation. (*PRER&BG* 9, no. 23 [6 June 1894]).

453. C. Kennedy house
2203 Walnut Street, Philadelphia
1894, Demolished, JH
The house has a "stone front, ornamental in design" (*PRER&BG* 9, no. 23 [6 June 1894]).

454. George W. Childs house
K Street near 16th Street, NW, Washington, D.C.
1894, Demolished, AE
The *Builders' Guide* wrote:
    The structure is practically a double front, three stories and a basement. The front will be of light colored brick with terra cotta trimmings, very ornamental in design and finish." (*PRER&BG* 9, no. 23 [6 June 1894].)
Several motifs recalled earlier commissions; the carved stone lintel over the entrance recalled the houses for R. Winder Johnson (cat. 385) and Alexander J. Cassatt (cat. 364) while the gabled chimneys had appeared on the Thomas A. Scott house (cat. 343). They were new to Washington, however.

457a. 1025 Market Street (center), Philadelphia, c. 1910

457b. 1025 Market Street, Philadelphia, looking north, 1973

460. Clement Griscom house, "Dolobran," before 1897

463. Franklin Building, exterior looking southeast, c. 1900

455. Barclay Warburton stable
2058 Sansom Street, Philadelphia
1894, LFM
Permit #2328, 26 June 1894; Thomas Little contractor,
$3,000; *Philadelphia Inquirer*, 27 June 1894, 9.

456. Alterations to Thomas Biddle house
122 South 22nd Street, Philadelphia
1894
A copper front bay was added to the house.
Signed permit #2327, 26 July 1894.

457. 1025 Market Street, Philadelphia
1894, Demolished
PRER&BG 9, no. 35 (29 August 1894).

458. Steel-frame pavilion for Merion Cricket Club

Montgomery Avenue, Haverford
1894, Demolished
See cat. 347.
The pavilion was designed " . . . to seat 5000 persons."
(*PRER&BG* 9, no. 35 [29 August 1894].)

459. Temporary building for Frank Thomson
Lower Merion
1894, Demolished
This temporary building was of great size.
    It will be 45 x 250 feet, three stories high, and built of
    staff, the same material used in construction of the White
    City, at Chicago, Ill. and will be fashioned after those
    structures in some degree. It will be painted white
    throughout. (*PRER&BG* 9, no. 35 [29 August 1894].)
Furness had designed other buildings–house (cat. 377) and
stable (cat. 418) for Thomson on his Lower Merion estate.

460. **Alterations to Clement Griscom house, "Dolobran"**
Laurel Lane, Haverford
1894
Presumably it was at this time that the shingled east end of
the house (cat. 253) was replaced by stone, and the large
sunken rear gallery was added under the lawn so as not to
obstruct views from the house.
PRER&BG 9, no. 35 (29 August 1894).

461. Additions and alterations to Thomas Hockley house
235 South 21st Street, Philadelphia
1894
Originally designed by Furness in 1875 for Thomas Hockley
(cat. 65), the house was altered for Mrs. Albiona Whartenby,
the daughter of John Wanamaker. The interior was modernized, leaving the exterior essentially as it was first constructed.
PRER&BG 9, no. 38 (19 September 1894).

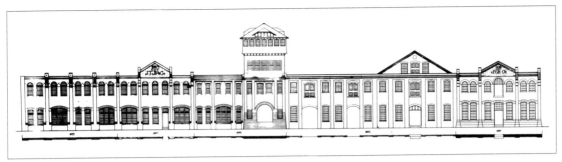

465a. *John T. Bailey and Company Factory, reconstructed elevation*

465b. *John T. Bailey and Company Factory, before 1901*

462. Six-story building for Armstrong Wilkens and Company
Fourth Street and Appletree Alley, Philadelphia
1894, Demolished
The Builders' Guide reported: "The structure will be 40 by 80 feet, of light or buff colored brick, stone trimmings" (*PRER&BG* 9, no. 49 [5 December 1894]).

463. **Franklin Building**
125 South 12th Street at Lawson Street, Philadelphia
1894–95, Demolished
See cat. 532, 575, 594.
The Franklin Building housed the offices of the Franklin Sugar Company, which was the business of the Frazier and Harrison families. The Atlas figures on the front were carved by Karl Bitter, who had also worked on the Broad Street Station (cat. 430). The *Builders' Guide* described it as being "of white terra cotta with inside structural iron or steel" (*PRER&BG* 10, no. 1 [2 January 1895]).
Building permit #860, 19 March 1895; signed permit for W. W. Frazier, Jacob Myers contractor: "Materials of floor beams Furness patent floor"; *Philadelphia Inquirer*, 3 January 1895, 8. [1973–35]

464. Additional wings to Pennsylvania Hospital
Eighth and Pine streets, Philadelphia
1895, Probably unexecuted
See cat. 383A.
Original drawing, collection of the Pennsylvania Hospital, Philadelphia.

465. **Addition to John T. Bailey and Company Factory**
Water and Otsego streets, Philadelphia
1895, Demolished
See cat. 303A, 383A.
PRER&BG 10, no. 8 (20 February 1895). [1973–36]

466. Alterations to 34 South Third Street, Philadelphia
1895, Demolished
This is listed as the work of "M. M. Camac, 1215 Filbert Street"; presumably it is W. M. Camac, who reported

himself a member of Furness's office for twenty years (Charles J. Cohen, *Faires Classical Institute* [Philadelphia]). The work described included the addition of a story with modern utilities (*PRER&BG* 10, no. 10 [6 March 1895]).

467. Additions to Judge Meyer Sulzberger house
1305 Girard Avenue, Philadelphia
1895, Demolished
The house was built originally for the Meehan family; it was sold to Judge Sulzberger in 1892. The alterations were described as "quite extensive including a library and other detail work" (*PRER&BG* 10, no. 16 [17 April 1895]).

468. **Dr. Horace Jayne house**
320 South 19th Street, Philadelphia
1895
Dr. Jayne was an in-law of Furness. His house was arranged with his medical offices on the south below his library, and the family sitting rooms on the north. The house is one of the more remarkable compositions, recalling the conventions of the colonial revival. The facade is divided down the middle by a jog in the facade with its door just off the midpoint, hinting at the reversals of the norm within. The stair passes behind the fireplace and reappears using the mantel as a stair-landing between the split flues of the fireplace. The mantel was originally visually interrupted by a large mirror in the center, contrasting with the real void above the fireplace. Above, the balcony is hung by wrought iron straps, recalling the top run of stairs of the University of Pennsylvania Library (cat. 370). The whole is lighted by a colorless, leaded-glass skylight.
PRER&BG 10, no. 21 (22 May 1895); *Philadelphia Inquirer*, 16 May 1895, 5. [1973–37]

469. Five-story building for New York Biscuit Company
South side of Evelina Street, east of Third Street, Philadelphia
1895, Demolished
The New York Biscuit Company was recorded as a "five story brick and stone construction" (*PRER&BG* 10, no. 45 [6 November 1895]).

470. Reconstruction of Merion Cricket Club
Montgomery Avenue, Haverford
1895
See cat. 252.
With the destruction by fire of the new Merion Cricket Club (cat. 437), Furness, Evans and Co. were asked to design a new building along the western side of the Club property. It recalls, but parodies, the already established conventions of the colonial revival cricket club that had been established by McKim, Mead & White at Germantown, and by George T. Pearson at Philadelphia. Instead of white stone and wood trim Furness worked the red brick, red terra-cotta, red tile, and red wood trim of the late 1880s, on a porch-fronted building. Numerous later additions by the firm continue to use red brick and terra-cotta. While this building was under construction, it too burned, and was replaced with the present structure (cat. 483).
Philadelphia Inquirer, 2 November 1895, 8. [1973–34]

471. M. J. Earl offices
925 Penn Street, Reading
c. 1895, Demolished
Furness designed a copper-bayed commercial building in downtown Reading for a paper company.
Illustrated handbill courtesy of Allen Evans, III, Bryn Mawr.

472. Fancy doll house for Alexander J. Cassatt
Haverford
c. 1895, Presumed destroyed
Newspaper clipping, Evans Scrapbooks.

473. Additions and alterations to Edmund C. Evans house, "Penrhyn-y-coed"
(later Allen Evans house)
Evans' Lane, Haverford
1895
The alterations gave the Evans house (cat. 51) a new dining room and wing.
Evans MS.

468a. *Horace Jayne house, exterior looking west, 1972*

468b. *Horace Jayne house, stairhall, c. 1895*

468c. *Horace Jayne house, stairhall, 1978*

468d. *Horace Jayne house, skylight above hall, 1978*

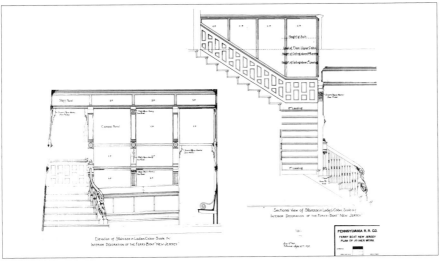

475. *Interior designs for the Ferryboat New Jersey, signed ink on linen*

477. *Public Baths and Wash House, c. 1900*

483a. *Merion Cricket Club, rebuilding, 1972*

483b. *Merion Cricket Club, porte-cochère, 1972*

474. Interior designs for Ferryboats New Jersey and Princeton, Pennsylvania Railroad
1895, Destroyed
These designs are discussed in *Drawing Toward Building*. They were part of a series of notable industrial designs that Furness undertook, beginning with the railroad cars for the Philadelphia and Reading Railroad, and including steamship interiors and the ferryboats. In each of these drawings, Furness merged medievalizing paneling with his personal distortion of classical elements in the "staff" plaster of the Chicago Fair.
O'Gorman et al., *Drawing Toward Building*, 172; Linens dated 19 August 1895, private collection.

475. William West Frazier cottage
North East Harbor, Mount Desert Island, ME
1895, WMC
The flaring piers recall the Brooke house in Birdsboro (cat. 366), while the rustic design continued to be characteristic of the office. Frazier's house in Philadelphia was also a Furness design (cat. 256).
O'Gorman, "Frank Furness," (1985).

476. Additions and alterations to Thomas DeWitt Cuyler house
1830 Delancey Street, Philadelphia
1896
Cuyler leased the house; the work was described as alterations and a four-story addition of brick and stone. Furness also designed a house for Cuyler in Haverford in 1883–84 (cat. 284).
PRER&BG 11, no. 4 (22 January 1896).

477. Public Baths and Wash House
Gaskill and Berlin streets, Philadelphia
1896, Demolished, LFM
"The objective of the Public Bath Association was to afford to the poor, facilities for bathing and to promote health and cleanliness in a neighborhood characterized by a dense immigrant population"(*PRER&BG* 11, no. 4 [22 January 1896]). Barclay Warburton was the Chairman of the Finance Committee, and previously had used Louis F. Marie for his stable. The building cost $22,619.80

478. J. Withens store and warehouse
Fourth Street and Appletree Alley, Philadelphia
1896, Demolished
Philadelphia Inquirer, 9 February 1896, 9.

479A. Dr. Horace Jayne summer house, "Sub Rosa"
Turner Road, Wallingford
c. 1896, Demolished
The summer house for the Jayne family (cat. 468) conforms to the understated character of the Furness country houses from the 1870s until the end of his practice.
[HABS PA-Walf 3–1]

480. Alterations to Holy Trinity Episcopal Mission
(also called Prince of Peace Episcopal Mission of Holy Trinity Church)
22nd and Morris streets, Philadelphia
1896, Demolished
The alterations to the Holy Trinity Mission, also referred to as the Prince of Peace Episcopal Mission (cat. 521, 528, 604,

606), were "of stone with terra-cotta trimmings and or-namentation and . . . a tiled roof" (*PRER&BG* 11, no. 31 [29 July 1896]).

481. Alterations to M. J. Hoy house
1823 Delancey Street, Philadelphia
1896
"A stone and brick addition of four stories . . . [was] erected" (*PRER&BG* 11, no. 31 [29 July 1896]) for Miss M. J. Hoy.

482. Alterations to Rosemont Hospital of the Good Shepherd
Rosemont
1896, Unexecuted (?)
Plans called for an addition of 62' by 84' of brick and iron, general remodeling, and lighting of the old building. According to vestry minutes, only the renovation work was undertaken, but the *Builders' Guide* records a contract issued for the addition.
PRER&BG 11, no. 34 (19 August 1896); *PRER&BG* 11, no. 31 (29 July 1896); Vestry minutes of the Church of the Good Shepherd, Rosemont.

483. Reconstruction of Merion Cricket Club
Montgomery Avenue, Haverford
1896–97
See cats. 252, 437.
"The almost completed new Merion Cricket Clubhouse [cat. 470] was again destroyed by fire on the 23rd last" (*PRER&BG* 11, no. 40 [30 September 1896]). The designs of the previous campaign were followed in the rebuilding.

484. Hotel Windsor, view from boardwalk, c. 1900

488a. All Hallows Episcopal Church, detail of chancel, 1989

488b. All Hallows Episcopal Church, exterior looking northwest, 1989

488c. All Hallows Episcopal Church, nave towards apse, 1989

484. Additions and alterations to Hotel Windsor
Illinois Avenue and the Boardwalk, Atlantic City, NJ
1896–97, Demolished
The alterations were recorded: "remodeling of present hotel and addition of . . . five stories high with basement. It will be built of frame with a shingle roof. $20,000" (*PRER&BG* 11, no. 52 [23 December 1896]). Earlier work had been undertaken by William Decker who was probably responsible for its Moorish character. Hotels depended on visual style to establish identity and the Windsor was a success. A decade later it was overwhelmed by William L. Price's reinforced concrete masterpiece, the Traymore, located across Illinois Avenue.

485. Additions to 400 Arch Street, Philadelphia
1896–97, Demolished
Philadelphia Inquirer, 30 December 1896, 11.

486. Baker Building
Lansdowne
1896, Demolished
Morgan Bunting was the architect in charge of this project.
Hotchkin, *Rural Pennsylvania*, 408–10.

487. "Aunt Ogden" [Hoffman?] summer house
Mount Desert, ME
c. 1896
Evans MS.

488. All Hallows Episcopal Church
Wyncote
1896
The church followed the lines of St. Mary's Episcopal Church, Ardmore (cat. 341); it was built as a mission of the Church of Our Saviour in Jenkintown (cat. 422).
PRER&BG 11, no. 14 (1 April 1896).

489. Additions to Church of Our Saviour
Jenkintown
1897
The work encompassed the "entire alteration of interior [cat. 422] and small addition" (*PRER&BG* 12, no. 2 [13 January 1897]).
Philadelphia Inquirer, 15 January 1897, 11.

490. G. R. Griscom house
Haverford
1897, Demolished
The house was recorded as being "stone and frame with a shingle roof; three stories high; 33 feet on the front, depth of 50 feet. $10,000. 00" (*PRER&BG* 12, no. 3 [20 January 1897]).

491. R. E. Griscom house
Saelter Lane, Haverford
1897, Demolished or altered
The house was stone with a shingle roof 20 feet wide and

90 feet deep, three stories, "built after the Colonial style of architecture,"(*PRER&BG* 12, no. 4 [27 January 1897]) and estimated to cost $10,000. It was altered in 1905 (cat. 595).

492. Interior designs for Ferryboat New Brunswick, Pennsylvania Railroad
1897, Destroyed
Linens dated 1897, private collection.

493. Lucien Moss Home for Incurables, Jewish Hospital
Broad Street and Old York Road, Philadelphia
1897, Demolished
See cat. 29.
This was a continuation of the work of the early 1870s (cat. 29).
Philadelphia Inquirer, 5 March 1897.

494. Alterations to Jewish Hospital
Broad Street and Old York Road, Philadelphia
1897
See cat. 29.
Signed and dated linens, Athenaeum of Philadelphia.

495. Parish House, St. Nathaniel's Episcopal Church
600 East Allegheny Avenue and E Street, Philadelphia
1897, Altered
See cat. 562.
Philadelphia Inquirer, 17 July 1897, 11.

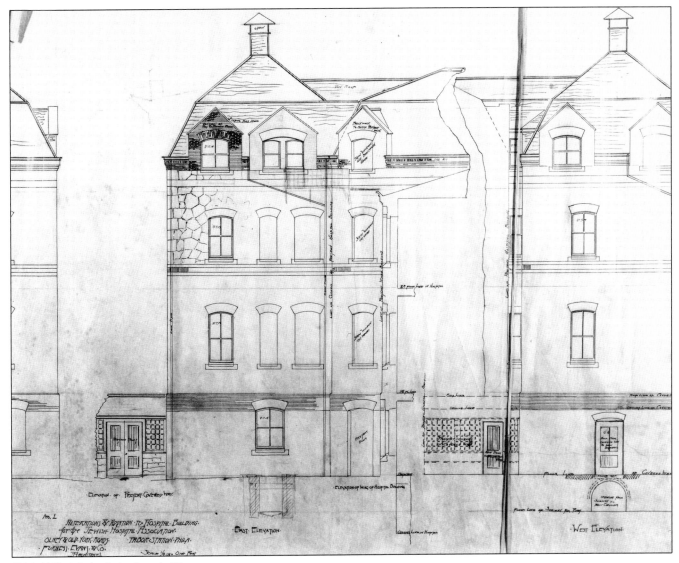

494. Jewish Hospital, plans for alterations and addition

493. Lucien Moss Home for Incurables, Jewish Hospital, c. 1910

496. **Pennsylvania State Capitol, Competition**
Harrisburg
1897, Unexecuted

The competition for the replacement for the fire-damaged state capitol building was organized by the University of Pennsylvania's professor of architecture, Warren Powers Laird, and at its outset deemed "a model competition" with strict requirements and a clear program. Ultimately, it was a fiasco that ended with one of the competitors, Frank Furness, claiming correctly that the project could not be built for the price. The governor and Laird withdrew from the commission and no winner was selected; modifications were requested, and the chosen design of an out-of-state architect (Henry Ives Cobb) could not be erected at the low budget. The Furness design continued the office practice of separating and expressing functions, celebrating the Senate and House chambers in great curved volumes.

After the competition, Furness sent his drawings to William Ware, his classmate at Hunt's atelier and by then the dean of the Beaux-Arts architecture school at Columbia. Ware, in a letter thanking him remarked: "They show how much can be done, even in unfamiliar fields, by a practiced hand. But they also show, as I wrote to Horace, how impossible it is really to hit the spirit of one style when all one's experience is in another" (James F. O'Gorman, *The Architecture of Frank Furness* [Philadelphia: Philadelphia Museum of Art, 1973].) *PRER&BG* 12, no. 37 (15 September 1897); ink on paper drawings, Avery Archives, Columbia University; Open letter to Philadelphia Chapter of the A.I.A., September 1897.

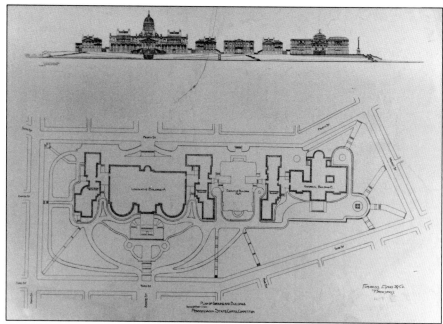

496a. Pennsylvania State Capitol, site plan and elevation, ink on paper, 1897

496b. Pennsylvania State Capitol, plans of legislative building, longitudinal section and rear elevation, ink on paper, 1897

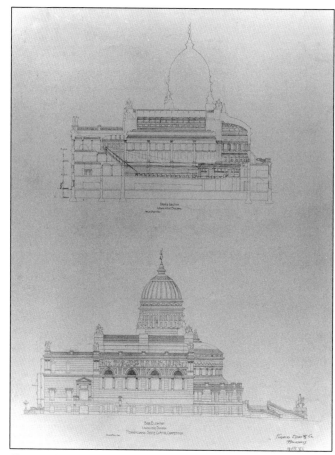

496c. Pennsylvania State Capitol, plans of legislative building, cross-section and side elevation, ink on paper, 1897

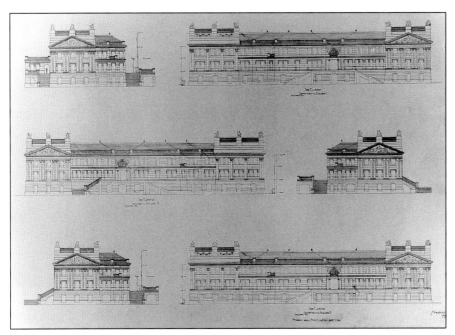

497. F. L. Dubasque house
South Orange, NJ
1897
The house was described as being of frame and stone.
PRER&BG 12, no. 39 (29 September 1897).

498. Morrisville Station, Pennsylvania Railroad
Morrisville, PA
1897, Demolished
The construction of the station was recorded as: "iron frame,
face brick and tile roof, 22 by 52 feet" (*PRER&BG* 12, no. 47
[24 November 1897]).

496d. Pennsylvania State Capitol, elevations of departmental buildings, ink on paper, 1897

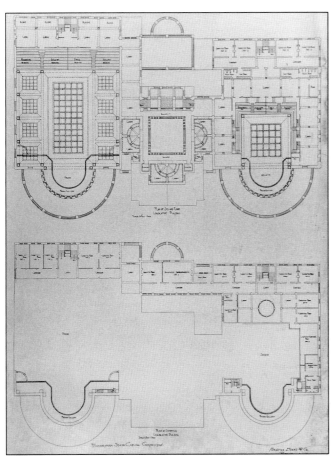

496e. Pennsylvania State Capitol, plans of legislative building, ink on paper, 1897

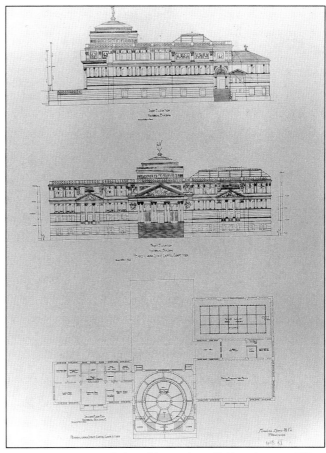

496f. Pennsylvania State Capitol, plans and elevations, historical building, ink on paper, 1897

499a. *Philadelphia Savings Fund Society Building, exterior looking southeast, 1972*

499b. *Philadelphia Savings Fund Society Building, main banking room, 1972*

499c. *Philadelphia Savings Fund Society Building, detail of capital, 1972*

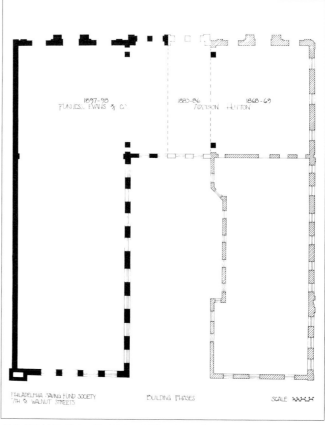

499d. *Philadelphia Savings Fund Society Building, phasing plan, 1972*

499. **Additions and alterations to Philadelphia Savings Fund Society Building**
700 Walnut Street at Seventh Street, Philadelphia
1897–98
This began a series of alterations to earlier banks by other architects in the style of the original (cat. 9). Here the exuberant scale of the great room that spans the old and new work proved the ongoing vitality of the Furness conception of a banking space.
James Willcox, *A History of the Philadelphia Savings Fund Society, 1816–1916* (Philadelphia, 1916), 79. [1973–38, HABS PA–1461]

500. **Allen Evans house, "Penrhyn-y-coed"**
(reconstruction of Edmund C. Evans house)
Evans' Lane, Haverford
1898, Altered, AE
The plain, gambrel-roofed house of the 1870s (cat. 51) was replaced after fire damage by an equally simple colonial revival house, with details similar to those of the alterations to the George B. Roberts (cat. 286A) house of the same period.
Philadelphia Inquirer, 21 January 1898, 14.

501. **J. Gardner Cassatt stable**
Foxcroft Lane, Berwyn

1898, Altered
The *Builders' Guide* reported that this was "erected upon the old lines and material of brick, stone and frame," suggesting that the firm had designed an earlier stable for Cassatt. Furness had designed a house in the city for Cassatt in 1886 (cat. 275A).
PRER&BG 13, no. 11 (16 March 1898).

502. **West End Trust Company Building**
1404 South Penn Square at Broad Street, Philadelphia
1898, Demolished
See cat. 536, 560.

500. Allen Evans house, "Penrhyn-y-coed," exterior looking north, c. 1920

502. West End Trust Company Building, exterior looking southwest, c. 1895

503. Harrison Day Nursery, exterior looking north, 1988

507. Alexander J. Cassatt stable, "Chesterbrook Farm," exterior looking northwest, 1989

The building was to be "very ornate in character, twelve or fourteen stories high, the first two of granite and remainder of hard red brick or terra cotta" (*PRER&BG* 13, no. 13 [30 March 1898]). In the end it was constructed of pink granite for the base, yellow brick and terra-cotta for the main shaft, and capped by a red tile roof with copper trim. [1973–39]

503. Harrison Day Nursery
19th and Ellsworth streets, Philadelphia
1898
The building was erected with the support of William West Frazier (cat. 256) and the Harrison family, and was part of the Settlement House movement.
Philadelphia Inquirer, 20 April 1898.

504. Consumptives Ward and Sun Parlor, Jewish Hospital
Broad Street and Old York Road, Philadelphia
1898, Demolished
See cat. 29.

Philadelphia Inquirer, 4 May 1898.

505. Alterations to Philadelphia Contributionship
212 South Fourth Street, Philadelphia
1898
Thomas U. Walter's brick, residential-scale office had previously been altered by Collins and Autenrieth. All changes were restricted to the interior and have since been removed.
PRER&BG 13, no. 26 (29 June 1898).

506. Axel Petre house
Johnston Street, Germantown, Philadelphia

1898
Of "cut stone, brick, frame and rough cast work," this is the first Gothic Revival house design by the office.
PRER&BG 13, no. 28 (13 July 1898).

507. Alexander J. Cassatt stable, "Chesterbrook Farm"
Berwyn
1898
The immense barn "of stone, brick and frame" still stands with minor modifications befitting its new role as a day care center in the midst of a suburban development.
PRER&BG 13, no. 29 (20 July 1898).

508. Episcopal Academy, exterior looking east, c. 1915

509a. John Frederick Lewis house, exterior looking northeast, 1990

509b. John Frederick Lewis house, main hall, 1990

510. Clubhouse for William West Frazier, exterior looking west, 1989

508. Additions to Episcopal Academy
Southwest corner of Locust and Juniper streets, Philadelphia
1899, Demolished
A new top floor was added to John Notman's mid-nineteenth century building in the original style; shortly thereafter the school moved out to City Avenue in Overbrook.
Philadelphia Inquirer, 27 May 1899, 12.

509. John Frederick Lewis house
Zermaft
1899
Though shorn of its front porch, the Lewis house and its great stone stable still overlook a broad valley. The flaring chimneys, now in stone, and the broadly handled colonial revival detail mark one of the first instances of the use of the style by the office. The interior hall is similar in detail to the contemporary Edward Sayres house (cat. 526). The house was enlarged with a spectacular two story library in 1911, and has since been restored as the headquarters of the Roy F. Weston Company.

Philadelphia Inquirer, 27 May 1899, 12.

510. Clubhouse for William West Frazier
Glenwood Avenue and Old York Road, Jenkintown
1899
The building for William West Frazier (cat. 256) was of "brick with red terra cotta trimmings." It was to contain shops on the first floor, with a library and reading room to the rear; a billiard room and game room on the second floor; and a gymnasium and guest rooms on the third floor. The red terra-cotta has since been painted white.
Philadelphia Inquirer, 14 June 1899, 10.

511. Additions to Warden estate
19th Street and Allegheny Avenue, Philadelphia
1899, Demolished
The "brick and cut stone" additions were made to an immense factory belonging to a partner of the Standard Oil Company.
PRER&BG 14, no. 39 (27 September 1899).

512. Alterations to Dr. Horace Jayne house
320 South 19th Street, Philadelphia
1899
See cat. 468.
Philadelphia Inquirer, 4 October 1899, 15.

513. Three-story house
States Avenue near Pacific Avenue, Atlantic City, NJ
1899, Demolished
J. Thornly Dingee made plans for this house which was a "three story dwelling, to measure 40 x 80 feet" (*PRER&BG* 14, no. 44 [1 November 1899]). Furness had designed a house for the Dingee family in the previous decade [cat. 271].

514. Alterations to Provident Life and Trust Company Building
401 Chestnut Street at Fourth Street, Philadelphia
1899, Demolished
This project was entirely interior work in the ten-story building (cat. 369).
PRER&BG 14, no. 50 (13 December 1899).

516a. Avenue of Fame, looking north, 1899

516b. Avenue of Fame, detail, 1899

518a. Church of the Atonement, exterior looking northwest, 1988

518b. Church of the Atonement, detail of entrance, looking north, 1988

515. Additions to Samuel Bettle house
Haverford
1899, Demolished
"Cut stone, shingle, iron" were the materials listed by the *Builders' Guide*. Bettle was Clement Griscom's son-in-law, and lived in a house on the Griscom property (cat. 253). His was one of the names recalled by Maximillian Nirdlinger in his manuscript.
PRER&BG 14, no. 50 (13 December 1899).

516. **Temporary decorative ornament for Avenue of**

Fame for Grand Army of the Republic Encampment
Broad Street, Philadelphia
1899, Demolished
Giant "staff" columns with massive plinths supported figures of soldiers and sailors sculpted by J. J. Boyle.
Albert Kelsey, ed., *Architectural Annual 1900* (Philadelphia, 1900), 234–36.

517. Bank
Cumberland, MD
c. 1899

This was published in an 1899 newspaper and described as "by the architect of the National Bank of the Republic [cat. 281]."
Evans Scrapbooks; Architectural Archives, University of Pennsylvania.

518. **Protestant Episcopal Church of the Atonement**
47th Street and Kingsessing Avenue, Philadelphia
1900
The chapel and parish house were built earlier (cat. 428).
Philadelphia Inquirer, 3 January 1900, 10.

519. John C. Bullitt house, exterior looking east, 1990

521. Parochial building, Prince of Peace Episcopal Chapel of Holy Trintiy Church, c. 1910

524. Henry R. Hatfield cottage, "Thingvilla," c. 1910

525. Eighth Ward Settlement House, exterior looking southwest, c. 1900

519. John C. Bullitt house, stable, and gardener's cottage
Cobblestone Drive, Paoli
1900
Levi Focht (cat. 248A), the builder of the Reading Railroad stations, was in charge of construction. The flaring shingled skirt over the first-floor rough stone base, the vertical proportions, and the great square chimneys emerge as the Furness accommodation to the shingle style, but the warm red-brown of the round river stone, the sculptural massing of the building and the expressive fenestration link it to the ongoing office manner. The bedroom over the porte cochere recalls the Shipley country house (cat. 264) of a generation earlier. Across the street, a stable with gardener's residence also survives with some modifications.
Bullitt's son, William, also commissioned Furness (cat. 561).
Philadelphia Inquirer, 24 January 1900, 5.

520. Alterations to 1424–26 Chestnut Street, Philadelphia
1900, Demolished
The transformation of a mansion into offices was undertaken by Furness for the Commercial Trust Company. He later designed their new offices located at 15th and Market streets (cat. 535).

PRER&BG 15, no. 4 (24 January 1900).

521. Parochial building, Prince of Peace Episcopal Mission of Holy Trintiy Church
22nd and Morris streets, Philadelphia
1900, Demolished
Two story; faced brick and terra-cotta trimmings; parlors, offices, and reading room on the first floor and auditorium on the second for the Protestant Episcopal congregation of Prince of Peace Mission (cat. 480).
PRER&BG 15, no. 13 (28 March 1900).

522. Alterations to 1123 Walnut Street, Philadelphia
1900
Another of the William West Frazier (cat. 256) holdings; this was a Federal town house converted into shops based on plans made in 1889.
PRER&BG 15, no. 14 (4 April 1900).

523. Reconstruction of 627 Market Street for Brierly estate
Philadelphia
1900, Demolished
See illus. 424a.

Philadelphia Inquirer, 18 April 1900, 11.

524. Henry R. Hatfield cottage, "Thingvilla"
Kebo Road, Bar Harbor, Mount Desert Island, ME
1900–01, Demolished
Compared to contemporary cottages, "none [is] more odd and picturesque." Stone chimneys were "built of the common field stone in their natural shapes," as were the foundations. "The entrance porch, balconies, verandas are supported by cedar posts from which the knots stand out prominently and the builders received careful instructions that no bark should be removed." The entrance hall was "finished up to a height of about three feet with natural cedar posts—with the bark left on, set closely together." Fireplaces were roughly fashioned.
O'Gorman, "Frank Furness," (1985).

525. Eighth Ward Settlement House
Hutchinson and Locust streets, Philadelphia
1900, Demolished since 1973
Described as being "of brick with fine copper bays in front," it had an expressive exterior with its central stair clearly noted.
PRER&BG 15, no. 19 (9 May 1900).

526a. Edward Sayres house, "The Boulders," exterior, 1989

526b. Edward Sayres house, "The Boulders," hall, c. 1905

526c. Edward Sayres house, "The Boulders," dining rooms, c. 1905

526. Alterations and renovations to Edward Sayres house, "The Boulders"

Black Rock Road, Gladwynne
c. 1900

An abandoned, structureless, late Federal country house with mid-century additions was converted into a modern country house by the addition of a new kitchen wing. The house has since been altered towards a more conventional colonial revival by Walter Duhram. His drawings and the Furness blueprints are in the Athenaeum of Philadelphia. Sayres was an officer of the Merion Cricket Club (cat. 252, 483).

Mabel T. Priestman, *Artistic Homes* (Chicago, 1910), 65–72.

527. One-story addition to Second Presbyterian Church
21st and Walnut streets, Philadelphia
1900

Furness later added the spire to the bell tower (cat. 529), completing the facade.

Philadelphia Inquirer, 6 July 1900.

528. Alterations to Prince of Peace Episcopal Mission of
Holy Trinity Church
22nd and Morris streets, Philadelphia
1900, Demolished
See cat. 480.
Philadelphia Inquirer, 6 July 1900, 7.

529. **Bell tower, Second Presbyterian Church**
21st and Walnut streets, Philadelphia
1900
Henry Sims's original design called for a tall spire; a generation after Sims's death, Furness completed the facade.
Philadelphia Inquirer, 25 July 1900, 5.

530. **John T. Lewis and Bros. Company mill and
warehouse**
Cumberland and Aramingo streets, Philadelphia
1900
Along with the three-story mill building and one-story
warehouse, additional buildings at the site are possibly also
by the firm; these include a two-story building with a plaque
inscribed "John T. Lewis, 1879." This building was later
enlarged from two to three stories, perhaps when a three-
story building was constructed adjacent to it.
Philadelphia Inquirer, 1 September 1900, 13.

*529. Bell tower, Second Presbyterian Church, exterior looking
southwest, 1976*

*530. John T. Lewis and Bros. Company mill, exterior looking
northeast, 1990*

533. Edward S. Beale house, 1989

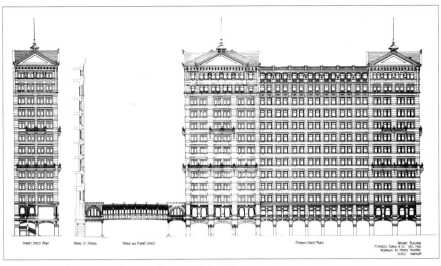

535a. Arcade Building, elevation redrawn from blueprint original, 1973

535b. Arcade Building, exterior looking west, 1903

535c. Arcade Building, detail of west facade, looking southeast, 1963

535d. Arcade Building, with later Furness, Evans and Co. additions, c. 1915

531. Additions to Racquet Club
923 Walnut Street, Philadelphia
1900, Demolished
See cat. 382.
"A squash ball court [was added] . . . on the third floor, [made] of iron [and measuring] 22 x 32 feet" (*PRER&BG* 15, no. 49 [5 December 1900]).

532. Additions and alterations to Franklin Building
125 South 12th Street at Lawson Street, Philadelphia
1900, Demolished
Alterations were made to the interior of the building (cat. 463) based on an 1894 design. The *Builders' Guide* recorded 127 South 12th Street as the address.
PRER&BG 15, no. 51 (19 December 1900).

533. **Edward S. Beale house**
Deepdale Road, Strafford
1901
Beale was Allen Evans's brother-in-law and had commissioned an earlier house (cat. 273).
Ann Cook et al., "On the Trail of Frank Furness," *Pennsylvania Heritage* (Winter 1981): 27 ff.; *PRER&BG* 16, no. 4 (23 January 1901); *PRER&BG* 16, no. 6 (6 February 1901); *Philadelphia Inquirer*, 28 March 1901, 15.

534. Alterations to 1719 Walnut Street, Philadelphia
1901
"[C]onsiderable alteration and a four story rear addition" was done for Dr. F. X. Dercum.
PRER&BG 16, no. 12 (20 March 1901).

535. **Arcade Building and pedestrian bridge**
15th and Market streets, Philadelphia
1901, Demolished
See cat. 576.
The Arcade Building was constructed above the sidewalk along 15th Street, connecting two properties, owned by the Commercial Trust financiers, at each end of the block. A bridge across Market Street to Broad Street Station permitted commuters to cross the busy street and exit past the banking offices of the Commercial Trust. Like other major works of the period, it was entirely red.
PRER&BG 16, no. 12 (20 March 1901). [1973–40, HABS PA–1493]

535e. Arcade Building, elevator enclosure, 1962

535f. Arcade Building, stair, 1962

537a. Bryn Mawr College, "College Inn," 1979

537b. Bryn Mawr College, "College Inn," rear wing, 1979

538. Lansdowne Station, Pennsylvania Railroad, looking north

539. Bryn Mawr Hospital, 1989

536. Extension to West End Trust Company Building
1404 South Penn Square at Broad Street, Philadelphia
1901, Demolished
See cat. 502.
Philadelphia Inquirer, 28 March 1901, 15.

537. **Additions to Bryn Mawr College, "College Inn"**
Bryn Mawr
1901, Demolished since 1979
This commission probably referred to the College Inn, a small, gray, stone, two-and-a-half-story Victorian house that was "wrapped" with a shingled addition across the top and at each end.
PRER&BG 16, no. 14 (3 April 1901).

538. **Lansdowne Station, Pennsylvania Railroad**
Lansdowne
1901, Demolished
Philadelphia Inquirer, 5 April 1901, 9.

539. **Additions to Bryn Mawr Hospital**
Bryn Mawr
1901
The three-story stone addition at the north end of the building [cat. 429] cost $27,000 and followed the original design. It was at this time that the canopy was added to the old entrance. (*PRER&BG* 16, no. 21 [22 May 1901].)

540. Ferryboat Baltimore, Pennsylvania Railroad
1901, Demolished
Linens dated May 1901, private collection.

541. Alterations to 133 South 18th Street, Philadelphia
1901, Demolished
Alterations to this house were for William West Frazier for whom Furness had designed another house at 250 South 18th Street in 1881-82 (cat. 256).
PRER&BG 16, no. 29 (17 July 1901).

542. Alterations to Thomas DeWitt Cuyler house
Cuyler's Lane off Grays Lane, Haverford
1901, Demolished
This was one of a series of alterations that turned a Victorian house (cat. 284) into a Gothic one (cat. 625).
Philadelphia Inquirer, 27 August 1901, 7.

543. **Pennsylvania Railroad offices**
Filbert Street, west of 15th Street, Philadelphia
1901, Demolished
PRER&BG 16, no. 37 (11 September 1901).

544. **32nd Street Station, Pennsylvania Railroad**
32nd and Market streets, Philadelphia
1901, Demolished
The project called for a "two story granite structure with terra cotta and copper trimmings, measuring 112 by 78 feet" (*PRER&BG* 16, no. 42 [16 October 1901]). Its irregularly shaped waiting room and concourse filled the awkward site between Market Street and the railroad tracks. Light was provided by a clerestory, recalling the apse end of the University of Pennsylvania Library (cat. 370). The front was set back from the street to provide a drop-off zone and parking for cabs.

543. Pennsylvania Railroad offices, c. 1900

544a. 32nd Street Station, Pennsylvania Railroad, looking east, c. 1924

544b. 32nd Street Station, Pennsylvania Railroad, looking north, c. 1931

549. Guggenheim Wing, Jewish Hospital, c. 1905

551. Haverford Grammar School, exterior looking southeast, 1990

552. William Sellers house, exterior looking north, 1901.

545. H. G. Lloyd stable
Bryn Mawr
1901–02, Altered
The stable consisted of a one-story stuccoed garage of indeterminate style.
Philadelphia Inquirer, 2 November 1901, 15.

546. C. W. Middleton stable
Between Grant Avenue and Stevenson Road, Torresdale, Philadelphia
1901–02, Demolished
Philadelphia Inquirer, 4 November 1901, 14.

547. Dr. McNichol double house
222–224 North 19th Street, Philadelphia
1902, Demolished
Philadelphia Inquirer, 4 January 1902, 6.

548. Y.M.C.A., Pennsylvania Railroad Branch
Pitcairn
1902, Demolished
Philadelphia Inquirer, 1 February 1902, 11.

549. Guggenheim Wing, Jewish Hospital
Broad Street and Old York Road, Philadelphia
1902, Demolished
See cat. 29.
The building contained separate rooms for well-to-do patients, marking the shift in medicine from home to hospital care. The three elements of the facade—the patients wing,

the circulation, and the solarium—are clearly differentiated.
Philadelphia Inquirer, 25 February 1902, 6.

550. Loeb Operating Ward, Jewish Hospital
Broad Street and Old York Road, Philadelphia
1902, Demolished
See cat. 29.
Philadelphia Inquirer, 29 March 1902, 7.

551. Haverford Grammar School
Lancaster Avenue, Haverford
1902
Haverford College's need for the original school building (cat. 301, 363, 559) led to the construction of a new school on a nearby site, "three stories, of brick and stone." It was originally to have been designed by Cope and Stewardson, but, perhaps because of Cope's death, the building was turned over to Furness's office.
Philadelphia Inquirer, 16 April 1902, 6.

552. Additions and alterations to William Sellers house
1819 Vine Street, Philadelphia
1902, Demolished
Details on the facade of the "new back building," particularly the dormers, suggest that Furness had previously altered the building in the 1880s. Sellers was a trustee of the University of Pennsylvania and a prominent industrialist whose business served the Baldwin Locomotive Company.
Philadelphia Inquirer, 16 May 1902, 7.

555. Eisner Home for Nurses, c. 1910

558. Edgewood Station, Pennsylvania Railroad, 1988

553. Additions to Provident Life and Trust Company Building
401 Chestnut Street at South Fourth Street, Philadelphia
1902, Demolished
A four story addition was made to the 1889 tower (cat. 369) on Fourth Street.
Philadelphia Inquirer, 4 June 1902, 7.

554. Exterior alterations and improvements to Western Savings Fund Society Building
Tenth and Walnut streets, Philadelphia
1902, Demolished
Furness later doubled the facade along the original lines of James Windrim's work of the 1880s (cat. 636).
Philadelphia Inquirer, 25 June 1902, 7. [HABS PA–1703]

555. Eisner Home for Nurses, Jewish Hospital
Broad Street and Old York Road, Philadelphia
1902, Demolished
See cat. 29.
Three layers of stone, shingle, and mansard are given late Victorian flavor.
Philadelphia Inquirer, 14 July 1902, 13.

556. Additions and alterations to Southwark Foundry
Fifth Street and Washington Avenue, Philadelphia
1902
PRER&BG 18, no. 31 (5 August 1903).

557. Alterations to Home for Aged and Infirm Israelites, Jewish Hospital
Broad Street and Old York Road, Philadelphia
1902, Demolished
See cat. 29, 358.
Philadelphia Inquirer, 3 September 1902, 11.

558. Edgewood Station, Pennsylvania Railroad
Edgewood
1902–03
The functional massing, the overhanging canopies carried on hoop-filled iron struts, and the long, low train canopy recall the Reading designs of a generation before. The building is now an antique shop.
Philadelphia Inquirer, 16 September 1902, 7.

559. Alterations to Haverford Grammar School
Railroad Avenue, Haverford
1902–03, Altered
See cat. 301.
Alterations were made to the Grammar School buildings, converting them into a dormitory for Haverford College.
Minutes of Haverford Board of Overseers, MS, vol. 6 (1900–1909), 112, 122, 126.

560. Additions to West End Trust Company Building
1404 South Penn Square at Broad Street, Philadelphia
1903, Demolished
See cat. 502, 536.
The additions were projected to be the "same height as the original building and [to] conform in the same style of

architecture . . . 20 x 59 feet" (*PRER&BG* 18, no. 6 [11 February 1903]).

561. Additions and alterations to William Bullitt house
1322 Locust Street, Philadelphia
1903, Altered beyond recognition in the 1920s
This was previously the house of Dr. Caspar Wister (cat. 276A) and his wife, Annis Lee Wister who was Frank's sister.
Philadelphia Inquirer, 17 February 1903, 7.

562. Parish House, St. Nathaniel's Protestant Episcopal Church
600 East Allegheny Avenue, Philadelphia
1903, Altered beyond recognition
See cat. 495.
Philadelphia Inquirer, 31 March 1903, 7.

563. Buildings for Home for Consumptives, Protestant Episcopal City Mission
Stenton and Evergreen avenues, Chestnut Hill, Philadelphia
1903
See cat. 299.
Philadelphia Inquirer, 27 March 1903, 4.

564. Bellewood Station, Pennsylvania Railroad
Bellewood
1903, Demolished c. 1980.
Philadelphia Inquirer, 9 April 1903, 4.

565. Library addition for Horace H. Furness summer house, "Lindenshade"
Wallingford
1903
This piece is all that survives of "Lindenshade" (cat. 39A, 88A).
Philadelphia Inquirer, 23 April 1903, 6.

566. Alterations to Walter Rogers Furness house
222 West Washington Square, Philadelphia
1903, Demolished
This had been Horace Furness's house (cat. 31), and was altered for his son Walter when Horace moved permanently to "Lindenshade" (cat. 39A, 88A, 565).
Philadelphia Inquirer, 22 May 1903, 16.

567. Port Allegheny Station, Pennsylvania Railroad
Port Allegheny
1903, Demolished
Philadelphia Inquirer, 16 June 1903, 15.

568. Alterations for McLentock-Marshall Construction Company offices
Pottstown
1903
Philadelphia Inquirer, 15 July 1903, 15.

569. Norristown Station, Pennsylvania Railroad
Norristown
1903, Demolished

560. West End Trust Company Building, exterior looking southwest, c. 1910

Philadelphia Inquirer, 15 July 1903, 15.

570. Three-story restaurant
Juniper and Sansom streets, Philadelphia
1903, Demolished
Philadelphia Inquirer, 5 September 1903, 9.

571. Isolating Ward, Jewish Hospital
Broad Street and Old York Road, Philadelphia
1903, Demolished
See cat. 29.
Philadelphia Inquirer, 19 September 1903, 15.

572. H. H. Smith house
Cape May, NJ
1903
The house was to be "three stories of frame with stone foundations, 38 x 50 feet" (*Philadelphia Inquirer*, 30 November 1903, 6).

573. Alterations to 313 Chestnut Street, Philadelphia
1904, Demolished
Though the building was no longer occupied by the National Bank of the Republic (cat. 281), Furness made extensive alterations to it.
PRER&BG 19, no. 10 (9 March 1904).

574. Alterations to W. D. Weaver house
249–51 West Harvey Street, Germantown, Philadelphia
1904
Alterations were made to a bay window and porch of the house.
Building Permit 1904 #2057; *Philadelphia Inquirer*, 24 March 1904, 11.

565a. *Horace Howard Furness summer house, "Lindenshade," library after 1903*

565b. *Horace Howard Furness summer house, "Lindenshade," library interior, 1962*

582. *Commons Building, Lehigh University*

589. *East Liberty Station, Pennsylvania Railroad, c. 1910*

575. Alterations to Franklin Building
125 South 12th Street at Lawson Street, Philadelphia
1904, Demolished
See cat. 463.
Philadelphia Inquirer, 25 April 1904, 6.

576. Additions to Arcade Building
15th and Market streets, Philadelphia
1904, Demolished
The properties screened from the street by the Arcade Building (cat. 535) were gradually acquired and incorporated into the building.
Philadelphia Inquirer, 21 May 1904, 6.

577. Philadelphia Orphans Asylum, Competition
Near Wallingford
1904, Unexecuted
The architects Delano and Aldrich of New York won the competition, which included Cope and Stewardson, as well as Field and Medary.
PRER&BG 19, no. 23 (8 June 1904).

578. Additions to Home for Consumptives, Philadelphia Protestant Episcopal City Mission
Stenton and Evergreen avenues, Chestnut Hill, Philadelphia
1904
See cat. 299.
PRER&BG 19, no. 24 (15 June 1904).

579. Joseph Rittenhouse building
55th and Vine streets, Philadelphia
1904, Demolished or unexecuted
The *Builders' Guide* reports: "three stories, brick and stone" (*PRER&BG* 19, no. 24 [15 June 1904]).

580. Alterations to H. E. Drayton house
2049 Locust Street (also 241 South 21st Street), Philadelphia
1904
This was part of the Evans row (cat. 280) on South 21st Street.
PRER&BG 19, no. 28 (13 July 1904).

581. George Gerhard house
58th Street and Overbrook Avenue, Philadelphia
1904
The house was "three stories, brick and stone, [and] Colonial in design" (*PRER&BG* 19, no. 32 [10 August 1904]).

582. **Commons Building, Lehigh University**
Bethlehem
1904
Blueprints on file at the Athenaeum of Philadelphia; *Philadelphia Inquirer*, 15 August 1904, 9.

583. Two houses for J. Ogden Hoffman
Lancaster Avenue near County Line Road, Villanova
1904
The two stucco houses are similar to other works by the office in the early twentieth century; by detail the earlier was c. 1885 and the later around 1904. An adjacent cottage, now used for Villanova University's infirmary, also looks like an earlier work by the office c. 1880. These are next to the F. L. Paul house, which was recalled by Allen Evans III as a work of the office.
Philadelphia Inquirer, 19 August 1904, 12.

584. Infirmary for orphanage
66th Street and Lansdowne Avenue, Philadelphia
1904, Demolished
Philadelphia Inquirer, 6 September 1904, 9.

585. Pavilion for Church Home
58th Street and Baltimore Avenue, Philadelphia
1904, Demolished
This was a low, schist building with only minimal detail.
Philadelphia Inquirer, 15 September 1904, 7.

586. Alterations to William Henry Furness, Jr. house
2034 Delancey Street, Philadelphia
1904
The alterations for Horace's son, William Henry, included rebuilt fireplaces and an office.
Philadelphia Building Permit #2786 (5 November 1904).

587. Standard Ice Manufacturing Plant
24th and Lombard streets, Philadelphia
1904–05, Demolished
Philadelphia Inquirer, 11 December 1904, 11.

588. French Street Station, Pennsylvania Railroad
Wilmington, DE
1905
The complex consists of three red brick, red terra-cotta buildings with red tile roofs—a main station, which is raised to reach the elevated track level; a canopy; and a separate freight office. It is scarcely a hundred feet from the Water Street Station of the Baltimore and Ohio Railroad of twenty years earlier (cat. 337).
PRER&BG 20, no. 1 (4 January 1905).

589. **East Liberty Station, Pennsylvania Railroad**
1905, Demolished
The station was projected to be constructed of "Pompeiian brick and Indiana limestone, [to measure] 89 x 167 feet, and [to] cost $100,000" (*PRER&BG* 20, no. 3 [18 January 1905]).

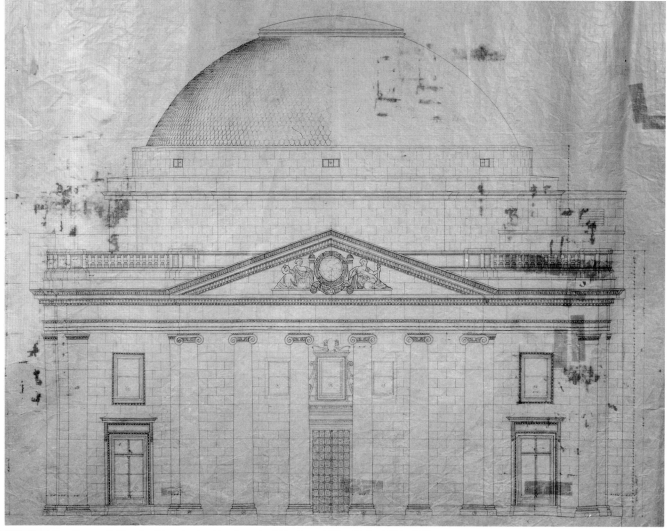

590a. Girard Trust Company Building, Broad Street elevation, ink on linen, signed Allen Evans, McKim, Mead and White, 1905

590. **Girard Trust Company Building**
Broad and Chestnut streets, Philadelphia
1905–07
Furness was the designer of the preliminary scheme, but detailing was handled by Allen Evans with McKim, Mead & White according to the request of the bank. In the previous year, Effingham B. Morris indicated that Furness had not been asked to compete because the bank did not wish to have a building along "his well-known lines." When Cope and Stewardson dismissed the banker's idea of a low temple, stating that it was historically inappropriate to build a temple without a podium, the banker turned to Allen Evans, who brought the question to Furness. Furness sketched out the plan shown here, and it was approved by Morris, subject to the requirement that the detail be handled by Evans with the assistance of McKim, Mead & White. The skylit main banking rooms of all of the earlier banks was again explored, demonstrating that Furness's method could transcend style.
George E. Thomas, "Masterpieces of Finance, the Banks of Frank Furness," brochure for Mellon Bank exhibit in conjunction with *Drawing Toward Building*, 1986; *Philadelphia Inquirer*, 7 March 1905, 15. [HABS PA–1510]

591. Alterations to Church of Our Saviour
Jenkintown
1905
See cat. 422.
Philadelphia Inquirer, 21 March 1905, 15.

592. Two-story laundry building, Jewish Hospital
Broad Street and Old York Road, Philadelphia
1905, Demolished
See cat. 29, 361.
Philadelphia Inquirer, 21 March 1905, 15.

593. Parish House, St. Luke's Protestant Episcopal Church
B Street east of Huntington Avenue, Kensington, Philadelphia
1905
The Parish House was described as having "two stories and [a] basement, [of] brick and stone" (*Philadelphia Inquirer*, 17 April 1905, 5).

594. Alterations to Franklin Building
125 South 12th Street at Lawson Street, Philadelphia
1905, Demolished
See cat. 463.
Philadelphia Inquirer, 25 April 1905, 16.

595. R. E. Griscom house
Saelter Lane, Haverford
1905, Demolished
This was a remodel to an earlier design (cat. 491).
Philadelphia Inquirer, 6 May 1905, 15.

596. 218–230 Lombard Street, Philadelphia
1905, Demolished
The building was remodeled for the Jewish Sheltering Home.
Philadelphia Inquirer, 8 June 1905, 11.

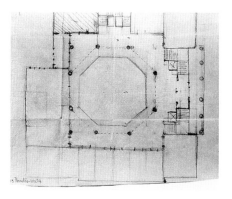

590b. Girard Trust Company Building, preliminary plan, pencil on paper, 1904

590c. Girard Trust Company Building, exterior looking northwest, c. 1907

590d. Girard Trust Company Building, main banking room, c. 1950

590e. Girard Trust Company Building, dome interior, 1986

605. Percy C. Madeira garage, c. 1960

609. Marriott Smyth house, 1988

615a. Drown Memorial Hall, Lehigh University

615b. Drown Memorial Hall, Lehigh University

597. Messiah Universalist Home
York Road and Ruscomb Street, Philadelphia
1905, Demolished
Philadelphia Inquirer, 14 June 1905, 9.

598. Hydro-therapeutic apparatus, Guggenheim Wing, Jewish Hospital
Broad Street and Old York Road, Philadelphia
1905, Demolished
See cat. 29, 549.
Philadelphia Inquirer, 15 June 1905, 9.

599. Alterations to Samuel Shipley house, "Town's End"
West Chester
1905
The original property was acquired from the Townsend family with the name a *double entendre* on its owners and its location at the end of the town. Shipley's other house, "Windon," of 1882 was also in West Chester (cat. 264). Conversations with Mrs. E. Page Allinson, daughter of Samuel Shipley, July 1972.

600. Additions to Merion Cricket Club
Montgomery Avenue, Haverford

1905
See cat. 252, 437, 483.
PRER&BG 20, no. 20 (16 May 1905).

601. Additions to Union League, Competition
Philadelphia
1905, Unexecuted
The competition for the additions to the Union League was lost to Joseph Huston. Other competitors included Horace Trumbauer (the eventual winner after Huston was jailed because of the Harrisburg Capitol scandal), Price and McLanahan, Cope and Stewardson, and Edgar Seeler.
PRER&BG 20, no. 30 (16 July 1905).

602. Chapel
Willow Grove
1905, Demolished
A small temporary wood chapel was constructed in the expectation that it would be replaced by a stone church; it survived until after World War II when it was finally replaced.
Philadelphia Inquirer, 1 August 1905, 12.

603. Additions and alterations to William West Frazier house
Northeast corner of 18th and Moravian streets, Philadelphia

1905, Demolished
See cat. 256.
Philadelphia Inquirer, 2 September 1905, 5.

604. Additions to Prince of Peace Episcopal Mission of Holy Trinity Church
22nd and Morris streets, Philadelphia
1905, Demolished
See cat. 480.
Philadelphia Inquirer, 22 December 1905, 13.

605. **Percy C. Madeira garage and stable**
Ogontz, Philadelphia
1906, Altered, LFM
Furness had designed the house in 1891 (cat. 407).
Philadelphia Inquirer, 2 February 1906, 6.

606. Prince of Peace Chapel of Holy Trinity Episcopal Mission
22nd and Morris streets, Philadelphia
1906, Demolished
See cat. 480.
The chapel was to be of "stone with [a] slate roof, 64 x 120 feet" and later was altered to brick.
PRER&BG 21, no. 6 (7 February 1906).

618. *Jayne Building, south entrance, 1957*

625. *Thomas DeWitt Cuyler house, during renovations, 1908*

607. J. Ogden Hoffman house
Villanova
1906
See cat. 583.
Hoffman was the brother-in-law of Allen Evans; he owned several properties including those adjacent to Villanova University, and another on Haverford Avenue.
Philadelphia Inquirer, 6 February 1906, 5.

608. Latrobe Iron Coupler Works
Location unknown
1906
PRER&BG 21, no. 6 (7 February 1906).

609. **Marriott Smyth house**
Cherry Lane, Ardmore
1906
Philadelphia Inquirer, 14 February 1906, 7.

610. Alterations to Church of Our Saviour
Jenkintown
1906
See cat. 422.
Philadelphia Inquirer, 22 February 1906, 11.

611. Wistar Morris stable
Green Hill Farm, Overbrook
1906
Philadelphia Inquirer, 16 March 1906, 11.

612. Alterations to Parish House, St. Andrew's Protestant Episcopal Church
Eighth and Spruce streets, Philadelphia
1906
Philadelphia Inquirer, 3 May 1906, 15.

613. Additions and alterations to Merion Cricket Club
Montgomery Avenue, Haverford
1906
See cat. 252, 437, 483.
The *Builders' Guide* records a "two-and-a-half-story addition and general interior remodelling" (*PRER&BG* 21, no. 20 [16 May 1906]).

614. Alterations to 1118 Spruce Street, Philadelphia
1906
Alterations were made for William Mall [Maule].
Philadelphia Inquirer, 13 June 1906, 11.

615. **Drown Memorial Hall, Lehigh University**
Bethlehem
1906
The description furnished by the newspaper read: "three stories of stone, 125 x 60 feet with an auditorium seating 500" (*Philadelphia Inquirer*, 3 August 1906, 6).

616. Thomas Leaming house
Wayne
1906
The *Builders' Guide* records a house of "two and a half stories, 40 x 70 feet with a wing 25 x 45 feet, of stone," built in the colonial style (*PRER&BG* 21, no. 39 [September 1906]).

617. Firehouse
Merion
1907
The *Builders' Guide* reported the firehouse to be "three stories high, of brick" (*PRER&BG* 22, no. 5 [10 January 1907]).

618. **Alterations to Jayne Building**
242 Chestnut Street, Philadelphia
1907, Demolished
Furness added a side entrance to William Johnston and Thomas U. Walter's landmark early skyscraper for Dr. David Jayne, father of Dr. Horace Jayne (cat. 468).
Philadelphia Inquirer, 2 March 1907, 6. [HABS PA–188]

619. Girard Trust Company buildings
1413–17 Chestnut Street, Philadelphia
1907, Demolished
See cat. 590.
These were to be "three stories high, [with] marble fronts, 20 x 100" (*Philadelphia Inquirer*, 5 March 1907, 14).

620. 1403 Chestnut Street, Philadelphia
1907, Demolished
Philadelphia Evening Bulletin, 25 March 1907.

621. Mikveh Israel Synagogue gymnasium
Broad and Jefferson streets, Philadelphia
1907, Demolished
Philadelphia Inquirer, 28 June 1907, 9.

622. Alterations to 105–07 South Third Street, Philadelphia,
1907
Alterations to the building were done for Dr. David Jayne.
Philadelphia Inquirer, 27 July 1907, 7.

623. Additions and alterations to Marriott Smyth house
Cherry Lane, Ardmore
1907
Work was done to the entrance and grounds of an earlier Furness design (cat. 609).
PRER&BG 22, no. 42 (16 October 1907).

624. Sterilizing Room, Jewish Hospital
Broad Street and Old York Road, Philadelphia
1907, Demolished
See cat. 29.
PRER&BG 22, no. 43 (23 October 1907).

625. **Alterations to Thomas DeWitt Cuyler house**
Cuyler's Lane off Grays Lane, Haverford
1908, Demolished
Extensive alterations were made and a wing added to the house originally designed by Furness (cat. 284). "This is the work being undertaken in the accompanying photograph" (*PRER&BG* 23, no. 2 [8 January 1908]).

626. J. Ogden Hoffman cottage
Bass Rocks, North East Harbor, Mount Desert Island, ME
c. 1908, AE
Hoffman also owned property in Villanova (cat. 583, 607).
Evans MS.

627. **Additions and alterations to Philadelphia National Bank**
421 Chestnut Street, Philadelphia
1908
Signed drawings, collection of Athenaeum of Philadelphia.

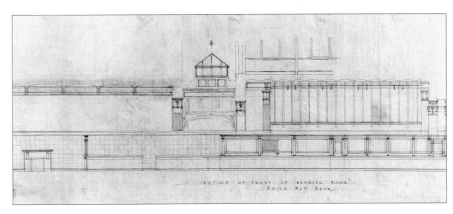

627. *Philadelphia National Bank, section of front of banking room, ink on linen*

630a. Wilmington Station, Pennsylvania Railroad, view along French Street, 1974

630b. Wilmington Station, Pennsylvania Railroad, track elevation, 1974

630c. Wilmington Station, Pennsylvania Railroad, 1974

633. Samuel Curwen house, 1990

628. W. F. Stewart concrete garage
Haverford
1908
PRER&BG 23, no. 8 (19 February 1908).

629. Additions and alterations to E. B. Cassatt house
Berwyn
1908

"General alterations, with the erection of a two and a half story stone wing, 48 x 24 feet," were made to the house (*PRER&BG* 23, no. 9 [26 February 1908]).

630. **Wilmington Station, Pennsylvania Railroad**
Wilmington, DE
1908
This is the last building that shows the characteristic Furness

hallmarks of striking proportion, strong color, and clear separation and articulation of function. (See cat. 588.)
Philadelphia Inquirer, 27 June 1908, 11.

631. George Gerhard house
58th Street and Overbrook Avenue, Overbrook, Philadelphia
1908
See cat. 581. *PRER&BG* 23, no. 31 (19 July 1908).

634. *Morris Building, Girard Trust Company, exterior looking northwest, 1986*

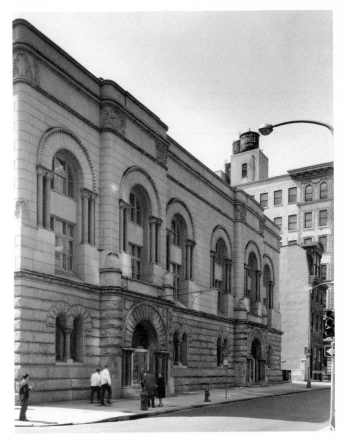

636. *Western Savings Fund Society Building, exterior looking southwest, 1963*

632. Additions to Percy C. Madeira house
Ogontz, Philadelphia
1908, Demolished
See cat. 407.
Philadelphia Inquirer, 4 November 1908, 12.

633. **Additions and alterations to Samuel Curwen house**
Spring Mill Road, below Montgomery Avenue, Bryn Mawr
1909
The house appears to be an earlier Furness design, c. 1895.
PRER&BG 24, no. 11 (17 March 1909).

634. **Morris Building, Girard Trust Company**
1413–23 Chestnut Street, Philadelphia
1909–10, AE
This "eighteen-story office building for [the] Girard Trust Co., [costing] $1,000,000," (*PRER&BG* 24, no. 15 [14 April 1909]) was adjacent to the main office (cat. 590).

635. Mason Smith house
Staten Island, NY
1909
This house was for Allen Evans's son-in-law
Evans MS, 164.

636. **Additions and alterations to Western Savings Fund Society Building**
Tenth and Walnut streets, Philadelphia
1909
Like the 1902 work (cat. 554), this was described as "conforming to the architecture of the present building" (*PRER&BG* 24, no. 21 [26 May 1909]).

637. Coxe Building, Lehigh University
Bethlehem
1910
See cat. 582.

Evans family records; dedication booklet.

638. Thomas DeWitt Cuyler cottage
North East Harbor, Mount Desert Island, ME
1910
Cuyler's house in Haverford (cat. 284) and in Philadelphia (cat. 476) were also Furness designs.
Evans MS.

639. Additions to Bryn Mawr Hospital
Bryn Mawr
1910, Demolished
A pair of two-story wings were added to the rear of the original building (cat. 429).
PRER&BG 25, no. 1 (3 January 1910).

640. V. S. Pownell house
Swarthmore
1910
The Pownell property was adjacent to land owned by George W. Casey of the office.
PRER&BG 25, no. 2 (10 January 1910).

641. Additions to Philadelphia Suburban Gas and Electric Company Building
700 Locust Street, Philadelphia
1910
The offices were constructed on the site of the Horace Howard Furness house (cat. 31A).
Drawings, collection of Athenaeum of Philadelphia.

642. **T. Zurbrugg house**
Riverside, NJ
1910
This immense, brick house looks out over the Delaware River; a balcony attached to the front portico provides the best view.
PRER&BG 25, no. 24 (15 June 1910).

643. Arcade store building
Ardmore
1910
PRER&BG 25, no. 24 (15 June 1910).

644. Alterations to Alexander J. Cassatt house, "Cheswold"
Cheswold Lane, Haverford
1910, Demolished
This was yet another alteration to "Cheswold" (cat. 36).
PRER&BG 25, no. 27 (6 July 1910).

645. Additions to Charles C. Harrison house, "Happy Creek Farm"
Devon
1910, Demolished
The additions were made to an earlier house (cat. 404).
PRER&BG 25, no. 28 (13 July 1910).

646. Odd Fellows Orphanage
20th Street and Ogontz Avenue, Philadelphia
1911, Demolished
PRER&BG 26, no. 14 (5 April 1911).

647. M. A. Metz Factory
Sixth and Spring Garden streets, Philadelphia
1911, Demolished
PRER&BG 26, no. 11 (15 March 1911).

648. Additions to Bryn Mawr Hospital
Bryn Mawr
1911
Furness had done previous work for the hospital (cat. 429, 539, 639).
PRER&BG 26, no. 36 (6 September 1911).

649. Additions and alterations to Ardmore Grammar School
Ardmore
PRER&BG 27, no. 14 (3 May 1912).

642a. T. Zurbrugg house, rear facade, c. 1911

642b. T. Zurbrugg house, carriage house, exterior looking northwest, 1990

642d. T. Zurbrugg house, music room, 1990

642c. T. Zurbrugg house, exterior looking southeast, 1990

Hints that other Furness projects exist abound. The late Dennis Steadman, in a letter to James O'Gorman, noted that he had discovered six commissions in Reading; we have subsequently found a cluster of schools and houses there, but have no way of determining if those were the ones to which Steadman referred. Certainly other towns on the Reading and Pennsylvania lines would be likely candidates for finding additional projects.

The search for Furness commissions makes clear several principles. They tend to fall in clusters, suggesting that his clients were friends, or friends of friends. They tend to be in the vicinity of Episcopal churches. They tend to be within commuting distance of Philadelphia. Based on the pace of commissions during the period when documentation is better, it is our guess that a hundred or more projects, mostly suburban houses, remain to be found. We leave that task—as well as filling out the 125 plus designs for the Reading Railroad—to another generation. We are confident that Furness's work will never again require the rediscovery entailed by the destruction of his records and the antagonism towards late nineteenth-century design of a generation ago.

642e. T. Zurbrugg house, library, 1990

Frank Furness

Hints to Designers

There can be no doubt that at the present day people in general, and women in particular, think a great deal more of ornamentation as applied to their homes and employed in their various occupations than they did twenty years ago. Then the cold polished white marble-topped table with shiny varnished legs and its weight of daguerreotypes in morocco cases was regarded as the suitable thing for the centre of the drawing-room, while black horsehair furniture was ranged close around its walls as if in gloomy awe of the marble tomb holding the caskets for the ghastly forms of departed relatives and friends. The ladies of the family, seated on black slippery sofas or chairs, worked diligently at filling in with some delicate gray shade of German wool or with white beads the groundwork of various patterns of cherries, moss-rosebuds, grapes, etc., destined to be worn as slippers at some future day by husband, lover or favorite divine. Now we have changed all this, and we aim chiefly to make our rooms comfortable, not only for the body by multiplying in them luxurious arm-chairs and lounges, but also for the mind by filling them with pretty objects, artistically arranged, ministering to the "delight of the eye." The German worsted slipper pattern is supplanted by screen, curtain or cushion embroidered in silks or crewels. With regards to the designs and the coloring of this kind of women's work or pastime, as also to the art of making designs for ornamentation to be applied either to wall, curtain or screen, the writer would humbly offer a few hints to the student in this charming branch of household art.

To begin at the beginning. In the acquirement of the indispensable knowledge of drawing and facility with the pencil let the first work be that which is thought the most

Frank Furness, "Hints to Designers," *Lippincott's Magazine* 21 (May 1878): 612–14.

difficult of all kinds of drawing—the copying directly from life or Nature. Intelligent students
are often cramped and hand-bound by a course of practice in what is termed "learning the
use of the instruments." The unfortunate is made to rule straight lines with a square and
describe curves with a compass until both mind and hand are so cramped that a lifetime
hardly suffices to obliterate the miserable traces of habits engendered and confirmed in a
few lessons.

Start with nothing but paper and pencil and a free hand: have no fear—the paper is not
poison to the touch, nor are lead-pencils highly combustible and liable to explode and
destroy the holder. Coarse brown paper is best for a first attempt, as pure white paper or
Bristol board is very terrifying to the beginner. Take as a model some simple leaf or
flower—plant-form is the clearest of all the numerous volumes that kind Nature offers to
the student of ornamentation—and banish from your mind any idea that what you are
about to attempt is, in your case, impossible of accomplishment. Be sure, instead, that
gracious Nature will unfold all her treasures to the earnest student. Remember that the
drawing you wish to make is for your own instruction, and not to elicit praise or applause
from admiring friends. Place your model in any position you may fancy, and then try to
draw the outline of petal and leaf in a firm, clean line. Having once put pencil to paper,
continue firmly to the first turn or stopping-place: complete the figure without erasure or
use of rubber. There! it is funny, perhaps but withal there is some likeness to the model,
some one fraction of a line that is nearly right. Start again, making that part still more nearly
what it should be, and trying to improve the rest. Go on; repeat the attempt forty, fifty, a
hundred times—there is no royal road to learning in this world—and at last you will begin
to get a fair outline of the flower, and its form will be so impressed upon your mind that
you will have learned one of the myriad notes that Nature uses in her wondrous harmonies.
This acquisition of forms, and the capacity to reproduce them in outline, are the keynotes
of all skill in designing ornament.

As soon as the slightest facility with the pencil is thus obtained it will be well to open any
book on ornamentation, study closely with the eye any one pattern it may contain, and then,
closing the book, try to draw this pattern from memory. This is to cultivate the memory of
the eye: the more retentive it becomes, the larger store of material will the student accumulate
for future use. Books on ornamentation containing various patterns are useful only for this
purpose—as a means of cultivating the memory of the eye—unless, indeed, you consult them
in order to see how other minds have conquered the problem you are trying to solve. In all
cases the student must go for knowledge to the fountain-head, Nature. If the author of the
best book upon ornamentation gives original designs, he went to Nature for them: go and
look for yourself, trust nobody's eyes but your own. As well might a surgeon hope to perform
successfully a difficult operation while all knowledge of his art was derived from anatomical
plates, and he had never dissected the real body (Nature's volume for him), as would the

student of ornamentation attempt to produce an original design without having drawn and investigated the forms perpetually offered to his glance by Nature.

After the hand has been thoroughly practised and the memory well stored with a variety of forms, it will be found that the power to reproduce these forms, binding them into patterns to suit certain spaces and places, has also been acquired—involuntarily, as it were, almost without the consciousness of the student. And now there is danger in the facility thus acquired unless the desire is aroused, and kept alive in the mind, to preserve action in the form studied. This is too often lost sight of in a wish to produce a clean, pretty drawing. Outlines are touched up and redrawn until every particle of life and spirit is lost, and a stiff, unmeaning mass of carefully-drawn lines is the result. If the model be a flower, look at it well, and consider what is the present phase of its existence. Is it budding into life? is it eagerly drawing that life from Heaven's light and air? or is it drooping to decay, "nodding to its fall"? All this and much more is clearly portrayed in its outlines to the observing eye.

It is action that so fascinates us in the designs of the Japanese. Look at their cheapest fans. On this there will be a flower beaten by the wind, shown in fewer lines than it takes words to express the thought. On that a bird flying—oh yes, unmistakably flying to catch some insect or fish far down in an opposite corner. Therefore, when your first outline has a certain degree of spirit and action stop short: preserve that action; do not mind being a little out of drawing as long as you succeed in doing so. A design without action is merely a mechanical affair that might be produced by a mere machine.

And the study of color must be pursued in the same manner. Cultivate your memory by the closest and most untiring observation. The color of your flower-model is perfect in its combinations. Nature never makes a mistake in taste (so called). Fix it in you mind: that combination may be used without fear; it is right, and you have absolute authority for using it. Remember also that in all ornamentation it is better to use only clearly-defined colors, not attempting the more delicate and subtle effects of shade and shadow, just as sharp outline is better in order to portray action than are timidly-blended lines and curves.

In thus recommending a flower for the first study the writer would by no means confine the student to plant form and coloring for suggestions of form and color in designing. There is nothing in Nature—plant, bird, beast or fish—that cannot be brought into play as either the main feature or an accessory in a design. A *motif* or principle of design either for form or color can be found in the whole or a part of any one thing that exists or has been created. The mineral, vegetable and animal kingdoms all afford inexhaustible fields for study in designing.

All I have tried to say of the study of form applies also to that of color. The eye and the memory must be trained in the same way. Be sure that the designer who goes directly to Nature for his outlines and combinations of color will arrive at results infinitely more satisfactory than those achieved by following blindly in the footsteps of any human being, master of his art although that being be. Learn that Nature in any one flower—gorgeous poppy, cool white calla or unobtrusive daisy—presents every hour of the day a different combination of color for the instruction of those who seek it earnestly at her all-bounteous hands.

Frank Furness

A Few Personal Reminiscences of His Old Teacher by One of His Old Pupils

I was a boy of sixteen, when I first saw Mr. Hunt. It was at my father's house, there on a friendly visit to my father and brother, on his way from Washington to New York. He was, I believe, at that time in a government office at Washington under Mr. Walters [sic], the Government Architect, or, possibly, had just left this office, and was on his way to establish himself in the practice of architecture in New York. My brother, who was an Artist, had met Mr. Hunt in Paris when they were both studying there. This first meting with my future Master is deeply and vividly impressed on my mind. I was then in my pupilage with an architect [John Frazier] of some repute, and fairly successful from whom I hoped to "learn the use of the instruments," as the phrase was.

When during this visit, and in talking to my brother, Mr. Hunt spoke of his profession, there at once fell upon me a fascinated admiration, which is destined to end only with my life. Never shall I forget the enthusiastic alacrity with which, in describing some object—I think [it] was a weathercock, on a European cathedral—he seized a piece of paper, and with a pencil from his pocket, made one of those wonderful "cobweb" sketches as he called them—not one useless stroke, every line had its meaning and due emphasis, and dashed off with such unerring foreknowledge! I had never imagined that there could be such drawing!

Frank Furness, edited typescript for Memorial to Richard Morris Hunt, (1895), 28pp., collection of George Wood Furness. The text exists as a typescript, presumably from dictation, with pencilled modifications in Furness's handwriting. The piece is printed here according to Furness's editing.

His face, too, and his manner took me captive. He had not then the lines of deep thought, that his face wore in later life, but his whole being seemed compact of joyous, living energy, every nerve on the stretch to convey his meaning most vividly.

I remember that after he had gone, my brother in a response to my expressions of admiration, with one that "when he was in Paris, young Hunt had the reputation of being far and away the brightest man at that time in the School of the Fine Arts."

Not long after this, in 1855, my brother, Horace, received such enthusiastic accounts of Mr. Hunt as a teacher of Architecture from two of his Harvard Classmates, Charles Gambrill and Henry Van Brunt, who had just entered Mr. Hunt's newly opened Studio, that my Father decided to ask Mr. Hunt to receive me also as a pupil. Before I moved, however, to New York, Gambrill and Van Brunt had been in the meanwhile joined by Edmund Quincy and George Post. Not long after my arrival we had a most welcome addition in William Robert Ware, whose refinement, culture and kindness of heart endeared him to all of us; he was afterwards so widely known as the Professor of Architecture in Columbia College. Such were Mr. Hunt's first pupils. The first building completed by Mr. Hunt in New York was, I think, the Studio Building on Tenth Street. Before it was finished he had rooms in the University Building, Washington Square. By the time I reached New York, the school had been moved to the Studio Building, completed only the week before, here we had a large room; its walls were covered with casts that Mr. Hunt had selected and collected with the greatest care. A long table, at which three people could work, one at each end and one in the centre, stood before the long front window. There were also two large drawing boards, standing on trestles, for each student; and a blackboard, albeit made of canvas, stretched on a hinged frame. Behind this blackboard our crockery, knives, forks and spoons, teacups and saucers, with other table equipments were kept. It was arranged that we, the students, were to have the entire use of the studio.

Four of us had sleeping rooms in the building. We took our breakfasts in the studio, the provender being purchased for us by Mrs. Winter, the janitress, one of us paying and keeping accounts for the mess. Be it here noted a sigh for the good old times that our breakfast bills never exceeded $1.30 a week for each of us.

One word as to the casts—who that witnessed it can forget Mr. Hunt's face, nor his tragic attitude of distress when he discovered, one morning that some overzealous cleanser in the Building had sedulously dusted every one of their casts, whereon the precious dust had been gently gathering for more than a year. The look of downright agony with which in turn he gazed at the clean white casts—only the day before he had been admiring them for their beautiful coloring of dust—is indescribable; as is also, it must be added, his language to the cleanser.

On my first morning at the Studio, after I had waited a short time, Mr. Hunt came in. He nodded cordially to the other fellows, and, shaking hand with me, said he was very glad to see me there among them all. He then said to me, what I found afterwards he said to all newcomers; and his words proved to be, for me, to the end a great incentive to unflagging zeal. They ran somewhat thus:

Now, look here, don't you see, I am not going to be any kind of a bear-leader, schoolmaster, or taskmaster to you in any way. You come here to get out of me everything I know about architecture, and for what you pay me, I am willing to give you all I know. If you choose to loaf and throw away the opportunity of getting all that you might out of me, why, that is your lookout, it isn't mine. You will never, by word, look, or action, on my part, know that I do not think you are doing exactly right. In short, I am here to teach you, if you want to be taught. I am not here to force you in the smallest degree to learn.

This is as nearly as I can remember what every man heard who entered Mr. Hunt's Studio.

The first thing he required of us as pupils, was to learn thoroughly the Orders of Architecture, so thoroughly that if he gave us merely a moulding taken from any one of the different Orders, we could construct therefrom the entire order.

He was most decided in his belief that everyone should be thoroughly trained in the orders; he used to say: "No matter if you never practice classical architecture, you acquire a certain idea or instinct of proportion that will never leave you, and this is essential to good designing in any of the different schools."

In addition to the study of the Orders, we were given each month a problem, which we first sketched and then worked up during the month. If the work as not finished in a month, he gave us a new problem; what he declared however to be most important was to "Draw, draw, draw! Sketch, sketch, sketch! if you can't draw anything else, draw your boots; it doesn't matter, it will ultimately give you a certain control of your pencil so that you can the more rapidly express on paper your thoughts in designing. The greater facility you have in expressing those thoughts, the freer and better your designs will be."

The first careful drawing in Indian ink was indeed a truly frightful ordeal. Mr. Hunt had such perfect mastery over both his pencil and his brush, that it seemed to him impossible that everybody else should not have the same facility. The consequence was that the pupil had heart-rending, a terrible time; it generally ended by Mr. Hunt's snatching the brush from the pupil's hand, saying: "There, you clumsy idiot, don't you see it is perfectly easy to do? Why don't you do it?"

The neophyte's experience over his first drawing was so familiar that when my turn came, all of my fellow students stopped work, and listened with enjoyment, vividly mindful of their own experiences during the same ordeal.

However I had my opportunity not long after, of witnessing the effect of the Indian ink ordeal on a newcomer. He was a simple-hearted fellow from somewhere down East—I should imagine from one of the fishing town on the New England coast. He held in his hand a brush full of Indian ink, and was attempting to lay the tint evenly over a large surface of paper. Mr. Hunt was standing over him, watching every trembling stroke of the brush, which in an unlucky moment over-ran the line where the wash of Indian ink ought to have stopped. "There you go! There you go!" shouted Mr. Hunt, "floppety, flop!" The pupil looked up at him in a piteous way, saying: "What do you mean by 'floppety, flop'? Do you take me for a codfish in the bottom of a boat?" "Right you are," was the grim reply.

I had been in the Studio but a few days when Ware joined us. I think Mr. Hunt's initiation speech was rather thrown away upon Ware, a more studious, hardworking man I have never met.

As I look back upon this time in my life, it was indeed delightful; the daily visit in the morning that Mr. Hunt always paid us was the bright spot in the day.

The whip used by Mr. Hunt to keep us well up to the collar was a critical bludgeon, with now and then, between the blows, a very small dose of praise, of course infinitely prized for its rarity; the bitter medicine was always administered first; then came the jam, to bring oblivion of the fearful dose.

I well remember his going up to Ware's board—and my dear friend Ware can amply afford to have the scene recalled—not long after the latter's arrival; the monthly problem had been, as I remember it, "a public fountain to be erected in the central park of a town." The faithful Ware had worked at his design for most (if not all) of the previous night. mr. Hunt looked at the drawing and ejaculated: "Heavens! we have the wash tubs, where are the washerwomen?" and then: "Well, I don't know but that the wash tubs might be fixed up, if so and so and so were done, to make it look something like a fountain."

Ware was a little crestfallen, but when his master began to show him how it should be done, he became intensely interested, and by the end of the month succeeded in his design beyond expectation.

Mr. Hunt constantly sent us to the street with our sketch books; telling us it was a great deal too fine a day to stay indoors, and that we had better sketch outside. One of his most empathetic instructions to us was: "Never work at a thing when you are in the least tired of it. Put it aside: do something else, and then st some other time, when you begin to remember with a little curiosity what you have done, take it up and go to work at it again."

We all indeed worked very hard, and we also played very hard. I shall never forget one morning when we had unanimously decided that architecture was clearly out of place and a bore, and that a fine oyster stew, to be cooked in a large tin pan belonging to our cupboard, was the thing that demanded our most earnest attention and study.

We sent Mrs. Winter to the Jefferson Market for oysters and milk; butter we had, and bread we had, and a good fire to toast the bread by. Our gas stove was started; the oysters were beautifully cooking and the bread toasting, each fellow dropping his own particular piece of well-buttered toast into the pan and trying to keep track of it, when, in the midst of a lively dispute between Post and myself as to the ownership of a certain lovely piece of toast, the door opened and in walked Mr. Hunt!

A dead silence fell crushingly upon the partakers of the feast. Mr. Hunt, however, said "Hullo! that smells mighty good. Here, give us a piece of toast, let's have a shy at that stew." Of all charming mornings that ever were spent, this was the most charming. Mr. Hunt launched into stories of student life in Paris and the Strange incidents in his life at the School of Fine Arts. After a couple of hours, he got up and looked at his watch, with "Hullo! we have no time for architecture this morning. Goodbye. I shall probably see you tomorrow."

Treating us in this way broke down all barriers and made us all, master and pupils alike, feel that we were eagerly pursuing one sole object; he, wherein having thoroughly explored all paths and roads, and knew them well, was our trusted guide and leader.

For all his familiar manner with us students and his remarkable power of making the most biting and cutting criticisms of our work, never did he lose an atom of dignity, nor was he ever addressed by any of us in a way that could be construed, in the faintest degree, as disrespectful. He was, of course, indeed so far above us all in genius, in capacity for work, and in knowledge, that I cannot imagine any young man who could fail to be rather awestricken in his presence. He never did anything by halves. He was the hardest worker I have ever known, and when he played, it was just as energetically, and as earnestly. I look back to a certain evening when we had quite a spree in the sHunttudio of Hayes, the animal painter. It was a large room, with, among many other things, a grand piano. The walls were hung with the skins of the birds and beasts that Hayes had from time to time admirably represented on canvas. On the night in question there were gathered there twenty or thirty of the painters living in the Studio Building, together with Mr. Hunt's students. Mr. Hunt, of course, was one of the party.

After a deal of singing and story telling, someone at the piano struck up "the Lancers." There were of course no girls to dance with. However, all chose partners, and we vigorously danced the entire set of Lancers, Mr. Hunt going through the grand chain in his furiously energetic manner, with a long clay pipe—a "Churchwarden"—crosswise in his mouth. The dexterity with which he got through the dizzy mazes of the dance without breaking the pipe was and always will be a matter of great wonder. It is pleasant to recall these scenes; they reveal more distinctly the companion and friend Mr. Hunt was to us all. He never praised us to our faces, but when other people, outsiders, asked him how his students were getting on, I have heard that he was loud in praise of each and all of us, saying that we were a very determined, hard-working set of fellows.

Once upon a time, as he entered the Studio for his morning visit, I happened to be at the blackboard engaged in drawing a rough caricature of Quincy. My back was turned to the door, and unconscious of Mr. Hunt's presence, went on with the drawing, although dimly aware that my drawing did not seem to be meeting with as loud applause as when I first began. All of a sudden I was horrorstruck at the sound of Mr. Hunt's voice exclaiming: "Great Heavens! Furness, if you can only caricature a plan as well as you can Quincy, and get as much ink on paper as you have on your coat, you will be a Michael Angelo [sic]." I dropped the chalk and tried in some way to sneak to my drawing board, but it was not to be. Mr. Hunt kept me at the blackboard making attempts at caricaturing the whole party, including himself. I could not help feeling a little flattered that he seemed very much amused. After I had exhausted the caricatures of my fellow students and my master, the inspection of our real work by Mr. Hunt went on as usual; but, there after, I was frequently ordered to the blackboard to finish off the hour of daily instruction by showing, as it appears to me, how badly a man can draw and yet produce some slight resemblance to the individual whose face and figure he is attempting to render ridiculous.

The last summer that I was with Mr. Hunt, he was in ill health and was going to take a three months holiday. Accordingly he transferred Quincy and myself to his brother William, the painter, who had a studio in Newport. Of course I passed a delightful two months there, well knowing that I had a great opportunity, and trying, as best I might, to avail myself of it. The third and last month which I was to have stayed with Mr. Hunt's brother was, however, passed in New York, as the draughtsman who had been left in charge of his down-town office was suddenly taken ill and, as Mr. Hunt was then in Newport, he came to his brother's studio and asked me to return to New York and "keep shop" for him, as he expressed it, until the Fall, when he was to return. Of course, I did as he requested.

The next winter I remained with him at his business office, and in the following spring the war broke out, and I went to Virginia, serving in the army for the next four years.

A young stripling with an almost boundless admiration for another man several years his senior, naturally strives to be in every respect as much as possible like the object of his enthusiasm, and I now freely acknowledge that I tried to acquire Mr. Hunt's forcible manner of expressing himself. This was the only accomplishment I acquired during my "apprenticeship" in Mr. Hunt's studio which proved of energetic efficacy in the army— especially to a cavalry officer, and, above all, proverbially, to a dragoon.

On one occasion after my return to New York, when the responsibilities of the business were more or less committed to my charge, I was in the outer office, and Mr. Hunt was in his private room, shut off by sliding doors from where I was. Some contractor or other had vexed me by what I considered was his stupidity, whereupon, to use a slang expression, I "cut loose at him" for about one steady minute. The sliding doors were quickly pushed aside, and Mr. Hunt's face with a comical expression appeared in the opening: "Good heavens! Furness," he cried, " the pupil has surpassed the master in one respect at any rate!"

I have thus attempted to set forth merely a few of those traits of Mr. Hunt's power wherewith he impressed his pupils in those early days. To set forth the severe criticisms, cruel only to be kind, the learned disquisitions, drawn from an inexhaustible store, and the pungent wit of the Great Master— they may all need an ampler page than this. They are become, however, a part of my professional life, and I am confident that the same was true of every one of that earnest youthful band, as long as they were breathers of this world. Not a day now passes in the exercise of my profession, that I do not vehemently, yearn lo! these fifty years, for the criticism or approval of such a commanding genius, as Richard Hunt, who was at once, so wise, so generous, so genuine, so kind, and so true.

Louis H. Sullivan

Reminiscences of Frank Furness

So he said a warm good-bye to Boston, to Wakefield (to his dear South Reading of the past), to all his friends, and made straightway for Philadelphia where he was to find his uncle and his grandpa. On the way he stopped over in New York City for a few days. Richard M. Hunt was the architectural lion there, and the dean of the profession. Louis called upon him in his den, told him his plans and was patted on the back and encouraged as an enterprising youngster. He listened to the mighty man's tale of his life in Paris with Lefuel, and was then turned over to an assistant named Stratton, a recent arrival from the Ecole to whom he repeated the tale of his projects.

Friend Stratton was most amiable in greeting, and gave Louis much time, receiving him in the fraternal spirit of an older student toward a younger. he sketched the life in Paris and the School—and in closing asked Louis to keep in touch with him and be sure to call on him on the way abroad. Thus Louis, proud and inflated, went on his joyous way to face the world. He arrived in Philadelphia in due time, as they say. He had noticed in New York a sharper form of speech, an increase of energetic action over that he had left behind, and also a rougher and more arrogant type of life. Stratton had mentioned that Louis, on his arrival in Philadelphia, should look up the firm of Furness & Hewitt, architects, and try to find a place with them. But this was not Louis's way of doing. Once settled down in the large quiet village, he began to roam the streets, looking quizzically at buildings as he wandered. On the west side of South Broad street a residence [Bloomfield H. Moore house, cat. 32], almost

Louis H. Sullivan, *The Autobiography of an Idea* (1924; reprint, New York: Dover, 1956), 190–196.

completed, caught his eye like a flower by the roadside. He approached, examined it with curious care, without and within. Here was something fresh and fair to him, a human note, as though someone were talking. He inquired as to the architect and was told: Furness & Hewitt. Now, he saw plainly enough that this was not the work of two men but of one, for he had an instinctive sense of physiognomy, and all buildings thus made their direct appeal to him, pleasant or unpleasant.

He made up his mind that next day he would enter the employ of said Furness & Hewitt, they to have no voice in the matter, for his mind was made up. So next day he presented himself to Frank Furness and informed him he had come to enter his employ. Frank Furness was a curious character. He affected the English in fashion. He wore loud plaids, and a scowl, and from his face depended fan-like a marvelous red beard, beautiful in tone with each separate hair delicately crinkled from beginning to end. Moreover, his face was snarled and homely as an English bulldog's. Louis's eyes were riveted, in infatuation, to this beard, as he listened to a string of oaths yards long. For it seems that after he had delivered his initial fiat, Furness looked at him half blankly, half enraged, as at another kind of dog that had slipped in through the door. His first question had been as to Louis's experience, to which Louis replied, modestly enough, that he had just come from the Massachusetts Institute of Technology in Boston. This answer was the detonator that set off the mine which blew up in fragments all the schools in the land and scattered the professors headless and limbless to the four quarters of earth and hell. Louis, he said, was a fool. He said Louis was an idiot to have wasted his time in a place where one was filled with sawdust, like a doll, and became a prig, a snob, and an ass.

As the smoke blew away he said: "Of course you don't know anything and are full of damnable conceit."

Louis agreed to the ignorance; demurred as to conceit; and added that he belonged to that rare class who were capable of learning, and desired to learn. This answer mollified the dog-man, and he seemed intrigued that Louis stared at him so pertinaciously. At last he asked Louis what in hell had brought him there, anyway? This was the opening for which Louis had sagaciously been waiting through the storm. He told Frank Furness all about his unaided discovery of the dwelling on Broad street, how he had followed, so to speak from the nugget to the solid vein; that here he was and here he would remain; he had made up his mind as to that, and he looked Frank Furness in the eye. Then he sang a song of praise like a youthful bard of old to his liege lord, steering clear of too gross adulation, placing all on a high plane of accomplishment. It was here, Louis said, one could really learn. Frank Furness admitted as true a part of what Louis had said, waving the rest away as one pleasantly overpraised, and said: Only the Greeks knew how to build.

"Of course, you don't want any pay," he said. To which Louis replied that ten dollars a week would be a necessary honorarium.

"All right," said he of the glorious beard, with something scraggy on his face, that might have been a smile. "Come tomorrow morning for a trial, but I prophesy you won't outlast a week." So Louis came. At the end of that week Furness said, "You may stay another week," and at the end of that week Furness said, "You may stay as long as you like." Oh what a joy! Louis's first task was to retrace a set of plans complete for a Savings Institution [Guarantee Trust and Safe Deposit Company, cat. 44] to be erected on Chestnut street. This he did so systematically and in so short a time that he won his spurs at once. In doing this work he was but carrying out the impulsion of Moses Woolson's training in accuracy and speed; and Moses Woolson followed him thereafter everywhere.

The other members of the firm was [sic] George Hewitt, a slender, moustached person, pale and reserved, who seldom relaxed from pose. It was he who did the Victorian Gothic in its pantalettes, when a church building or something of that sort was on the boards. With precision, as though he held his elements by pincers, he worked out these decorous sublimities of inanity, as per the English current magazines and other English sources. He was a clean draftsman, and believed implicitly that all that was good was English. Louis regarded him with admiration as a draftsman, and with mild contempt as a man who kept his nose in books. Frank Furness "made buildings out of his head." That suited Louis better. And Furness as a freehand draftsman was extraordinary. He had Louis hypnotized, especially when he drew and swore at the same time.

But George Hewitt had a younger brother named John, and John was foreman of the shop. He was a husky, smooth-faced fellow under thirty. Every feature in his clean cut, rather elongated face, bespoke intelligence and kindness, in fact a big heart. He had taken a fancy to Louis from the start. He was the "practical man" and Louis ran to him for advice whenever he found himself in a tight place. John was patience itself and made everything clear with dainty sketches and explanatory notes. These drawings were beautiful and Louis frankly told him so. He begged John to teach him "touch" and how to make such sketches, and especially how to "indicate" so crisply. This John did. In fact, it was not long before he had made of Louis a draftsman of the upper Crust, and Louis's heart went out to lovable John in sheer gratitude.

In looking back upon that time Louis Sullivan gives thanks that it was his great good fortune to have made his entry into the practical world in an office where standards were so high—where talent was so manifestly taken for granted, and the atmosphere the free and easy one of a true work shop savoring of the guild where craftsmanship was paramount and personal. And again he goes back to the day of Moses Woolson and his discipline. We may say in truth that Moses Woolson put him there. For without that elastic alertness and courage, that grimness Moses Woolson imparted, it is sure that Louis would not have broken through the barrier of contempt in that first interview.

Louis worked very hard day and night. At first he had lived with his grandpa and uncle in West Philadelphia. But soon he decided to move into town to be nearer the office and to be freer to study into the small hours. His relaxation on Sundays was Fairmont Park and a walk up the rough road of the Wissahickon valley, a narrow beauteous wilderness such as Louis had never seen, and with which he was completely charmed. He loved the solitude through which the Wissahickon purled its way. The companionship of the wild was soothing to him. The isolation gave him confort and surcease. Thus passed a hot summer.

The offices of Furness & Hewitt occupied the entire top floor of a new, brick, four-story building at the northeast corner of Third street and Chestnut.

One day in September, it was very warm, all windows were open for air, the force was wearily at work. As they worked, there came through the open windows a murmur, barely noticed at first; then this murmur became a roar, with wild shouting. Then, all to the windows. Louis saw, far below, not pavement and sidewalks, but a solid black mass of frantic men, crowded, jammed from wall to wall. The offices of Jay Cooke & Co. were but a short distance south on Third street. Word came up that Jay Cooke & Co. had just closed its doors. Louis saw it all, as he could see down both Chestnut street and Third. Chestnut westward from Third also was a solid mass. The run on the banks had begun. The devastating panic of 1873 was on, in its mad career. Louis was shocked, appalled at the sight. He was too young, too inexperienced, to understand what it really meant, even when told it was a panic in finance, that credit had crumbled to dust, that men were ruined, and insane with despair; that this panic would spread like wildfire over the land leaving ruin in its wake everywhere. And still he could not understand what had brought it about.

The office held steady for a while; there was work on hand which had progressed so far that it must be completed.

One day in November Frank Furness said: "Sullivan, I'm sorry, the jig is up. There'll be no more building. The office now is running dry. You've done well, mighty well. I like you. I wish you might stay. But as you were the last to come it is only just you should be first to go." With that he slipped a bill into Louis's hand, and wished him farewell and better days.

Men and Things

Yesterday, in the story of Louis Henri Sullivan, reference was made to the association of that eminent Chicagoan with Frank Furness of this city. Mr. Albert Kelsey, who knew them both, says Furness deserves all the encomiums of his genius and his personality which Sullivan has given, in his autobiography, to this old Philadelphia employer of his. Kelsey goes further by saying that Furness, along with Stanford White, Sullivan and Frank Lloyd Wright, deserves to rank as "one of the four strongest figures in American architecture." Yet in his day there was no man of his calling subjected to more scathing criticism, by the classicists and conformists of his craft, than Furness, whose originality and eccentricities of design brought down upon him the thunders of the fundamentalists. In his life-time it became a sort of fad among critics to scoff at his works. That, for the most part, they belong to no other man than he, that they are not of any "school" of architecture, and that they are, in some cases, flatly contradictory of the canons of the craft, is true. But the personality which was stamped upon them was the reflection of the mind of a man of marked independence of thought who, as Sullivan says, "created buildings out of his head."

The son of the well-known Unitarian clergyman, William Henry Furness, who was as scholarly as he was devout and who was looked up to in his day as one of the most lovable characters of old Philadelphia, Frank Furness was an original genius of dominating personality. As a youth he had fought in the Civil War, where, as an officer in Rush's Lancers, he won the Congressional Medal of Honor for feats of exceptional bravery. Fearless in every inch of his make-up, he strode across the field of battle with a box of

"Men and Things," *Philadelphia Evening Bulletin*, 18 April 1924, p. 8, col. 5.

ammunition on his shoulder when word came that an outpost was without ammunition; in another engagement, observing a Confederate soldier lying wounded and bleeding to death, he crossed the field under fire, applied a tourniquet, supplied the soldier with a canteen of water and then returned to his own troop, while the Confederates, admiring his gallantry, withheld their fire.

Before he opened his own office in this city he worked with Richard M. Hunt in New York, where, under the tutelage of the dean of the profession, he found a congenial exemplar in another picturesque personality. When he returned to Philadelphia and began the practice of his profession, with George W. Hewitt, as a partner, it was not long before the architects of this city realized that an aggressive force had entered their ranks. Determined America should create an art of its own making and opposed to the copying of European styles whether of ancient or medieval design, he struck out boldly along independent lines and soon directed attention to his works, such as the Academy of the Fine Arts, which was one of the first of his larger efforts. Of course, he provoked the criticism of those who preferred to follow trodden ways but, as a pioneer in thought and treatment, he did much, as an artist, to pave the way for the rapid advance of architectural achievement.

"No one who ever knew Furness," says Kelsey, "could ever forget him. He was one of the most picturesque personalities I have ever known. It is easy to understand how Sullivan, who was such a kindred spirit, was impressed by his early association with him. Masterful, domineering, fearless and aggressive, he was a real red-blooded artist. Never for a moment would he brook interference with his plans and neither client nor critic would be spared if he saw fit to speak his mind plainly on any subject. With pungent wit and a caustic tongue he challenged and invited criticism. To see him go down the street, with his shoulders squared, head erect, and with a free, swinging soldierly stride, and a devil-may-care attitude was to realize that 'here was a man' who neither gave nor asked for quarter. Some of his works, of course, are open to criticism. Eccentricities of design and treatment abound in them, but Frank Furness was too good an architect not to know what he was doing and I sometimes think that some of the oddities he introduced were merely the rebellion of a freedom-loving soul that refused to be bound by rules.

"In all that he did, however, there was the impress of a masterful mind. Take the Graver's Lane station [cat. 139], for instance, on the road to Chestnut Hill. The whole sweep of the structure there, relatively unimportant as it is, is masterful. In the design of the Zoological Gardens and buildings [cat. 67–69] he showed he could deal with a large acreage in a big way. The bank building at Seventh and Market streets [Penn National Bank, cat. 268], which he designed, is admirable. He was always trying to do something original—sometimes it was freakish, as in the case of the Academy of the Fine Arts [cat. 27], where he supported the keystone of an arch with columns—as in his use of semi-arches in the design of the Guarantee Trust and Safe Deposit Company's building [cat. 44] at Fourth and Chestnut streets. Of course, the University of Pennsylvania's Library [cat. 370], which he designed, is absolutely ridiculous and without rhyme or reason. But he was never afraid of doing new things and he showed Philadelphia some points as, for instance, when in the design of the lower end of Broad street station on Market street [cat. 430], he erected a seven-story office building across Fifteenth street, or when, later on, in the design of the Commercial Trust Building he introduced the arcaded sidewalk [cat. 535] under a tall office building. That he never hesitated a minute in striking out boldly along lines of his own making, was to his credit and in most of his works here and elsewhere—for he did much for the Pennsylvania Railroad at other points—he displayed masterly directness in achieving the objects he had in mind. What he did was entirely of his own making and, although it was sometimes hastily and roughly done, as when he would sit down beside a pile of lumber on a building job and sketch out, on wrapping paper, a new design for the workmen, it was always serviceable and to the point."

In the course of his career Furness executed a number of other structures in this city, such as the building of the Provident Life and Trust Company [cat. 86], the Jewish Hospital [cat. 29], the Rodelph Shalom synagogue [cat. 15], at Broad and Mt. Vernon streets, the Unitarian Church [cat. 285], at Twenty-second and Chestnut streets, and the West Philadelphia station of the Pennsylvania Railroad [cat. 544]. In these, as in other structures designed by him, among them the former Bloomfield Moore mansion [cat. 32] of South Broad street that caught Sullivan's eye there is an individuality of treatment and design that is inescapably noticeable. "You can tell the works of Furness anywhere," remarked one of his former associates yesterday, "even in such minor details of design as the decoration of the cabins of the 'Pennsy' ferries between Jersey City and New York [cat. 433]."

The individuality of Furness stood out in everything that he did. As another of his contemporaries and fellow-artists has phrased it, "he was the Whistler of his craft." It was a characteristic that in his dress he always wore the loudest and biggest plaids that he could find. Even in the way he wore his hat, with a rakish tilt over the eye, he was different from the ordinary run of men. In many ways he was the exact antithesis of his equally distinguished brother, Horace Howard Furness, the great Shakespearean scholar, a quiet, mild-mannered, scholarly man, who lived in and for his books and studies. Frank Furness liked to enjoy life to the full and to mingle in friendly camaraderie with his fellows.

Never having attended any school of architecture he was severe in his strictures on those who thought architects could be turned out by a teaching machine. He is reputed to have told a mother, who had asked him to what school she should send her son, "Send him to none. All schools are bad. They destroy the power of creative thought. Put him in an architect's office and let him work out his own salvation. Give him a chance to upset the rules."

In his own office he was a severe and strict disciplinarian but as ready in kindly counsel and friendly aid as he was quick to wrath and explosive anger over any exhibition of indifference or stupidity. Of those who worked with, or under him, Sullivan was acclaimed the most distinguished. His earlier partner, Geroge W. Hewitt, who had studied under the great John Notman, whose skill in design is shown by many notable ecclesiastical structures in this city, left him to go into business with his brother and left his mark in such buildings as the Bellevue-Stratford, the Bourse and the Bullitt offices, and in churches like St. Martins-in-the-Fields, the Holy Apostles and the tower of Holy Trinity.

The greater part of Furness' work after that separation was done in partnership with Allen S. Evans, the once noted cricketer, who is now an elderly resident of the Main Line.

Family Trees:
Frank Furness and Clients

The following charts show the connections between Frank Furness's family and those of his clients.

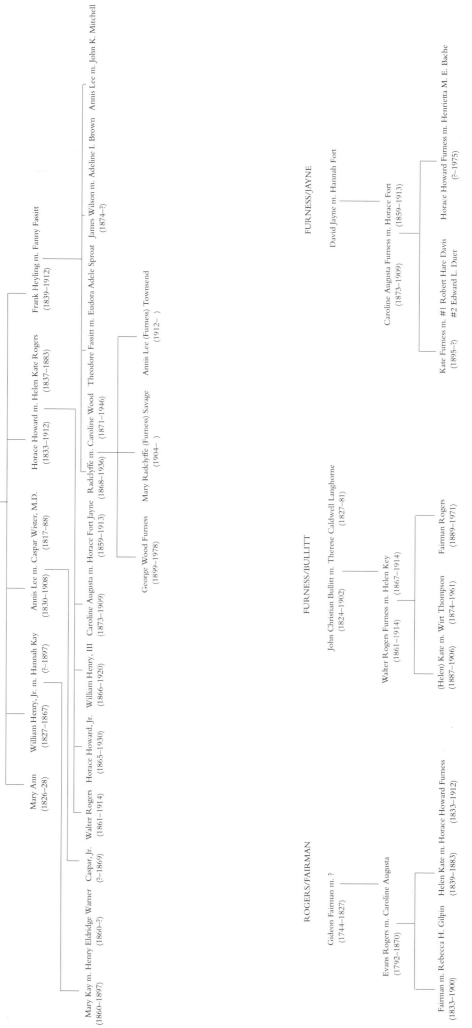

FURNESS

William Henry Furness m. Annis Pulling Jenks
(1802–96)   (?–1885)

Mary Ann   William Henry, Jr. m. Hannah Kay   Annis Lee m. Caspar Wister, M.D.   Horace Howard m. Helen Kate Rogers   Frank Heyling m. Fanny Fassitt
(1826–28)   (1827–1867)   (?–1897)   (1830–1908)   (1817–88)   (1833–1912)   (1837–1883)   (1839–1912)

Mary Kay m. Henry Eldridge Warner   Caspar, Jr.   Walter Rogers   Horace Howard, Jr.   William Henry, III   Caroline Augusta m. Horace Fort Jayne   Radclyffe m. Caroline Wood   Theodore Fassitt m. Eudora Adele Sproat   James Wilson m. Adeline I. Brown   Annis Lee m. John K. Mitchell
(1860–?)   (?–1869)   (1861–1914)   (1865–1930)   (1866–1920)   (1873–1909)   (1859–1913)   (1868–1936)   (1871–1946)   (?–1946)   (1874–?)

                                                                                                           George Wood Furness   Mary Radclyffe (Furness) Savage   Annis Lee (Furness) Townsend
                                                                                                           (1899–1978)   (1904–)   (1912–)

FURNESS/JAYNE

                                                              David Jayne m. Hannah Fort

                                                     Caroline Augusta Furness m. Horace Fort
                                                     (1873–1909)   (1859–1913)

                                         Kate Furness m. #1 Robert Hare Davis   Horace Howard Furness m. Henrietta M. E. Bache
                                         (1895–?)   #2 Edward L. Duer   (?–1975)

FURNESS/BULLITT

                                         John Christian Bullitt m. Therese Caldwell Langhorne
                                         (1824–1902)   (1827–81)

                                              Walter Rogers Furness m. Helen Key
                                              (1861–1914)   (1867–1914)

                                    (Helen) Kate m. Wirt Thompson   Fairman Rogers
                                    (1887–1906)   (1874–1961)   (1889–1971)

ROGERS/FAIRMAN

Gideon Fairman m. ?
(1744–1827)

Evans Rogers m. Caroline Augusta
(1792–1870)

Fairman m. Rebecca H. Gilpin   Helen Kate m. Horace Howard Furness
(1833–1900)   (1839–1883)   (1833–1912)

FURNESS/FASSITT

EVANS

LEWIS

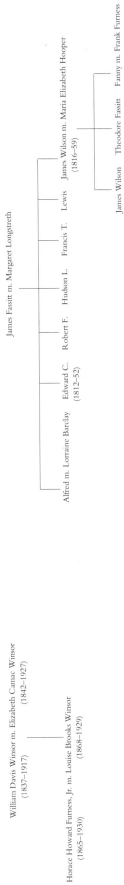

William Davis Winsor m. Elizabeth Camac Winsor
(1837–1917)   (1842–1927)

Horace Howard Furness, Jr. m. Louise Brooks Winsor
(1865–1930)   (1868–1929)

James Fassitt m. Margaret Longstreth

Alfred m. Lorraine Barclay   Edward C.   Robert F.   Hudson L.   Francis T.   Lewis   James Wilson m. Maria Elizabeth Hooper
                             (1812–52)   (1816–59)

James Wilson   Theodore Fassitt   Fanny m. Frank Furness
                                              (1839–1912)

Edmund Cadwalder m. Mary L. Allen   Rowland
        (1812–81)   (?–1861)

Manlius

Rowland m. Mary B. Montgomery   Mary   John Lewis   Mary Allen m. M. Mason Smith   Allen m. Rebecca C. Lewis
     (1847–?)   (1844–1925)

Edmund C.   Elizabeth B. Binney m. Algernon Roberts   Rowland m. Elizabeth Downs   Allen m. Elizabeth Holloway

John Thompson m. Maria Litchfield Scott
              (1823–1905)

Mary Emlen   Rebecca Chalkley m. Allen Evans   Maria Litchfield m. Edward F. Beale   Helen Scott m. J. Ogden Hoffman   Frances Lewis m. T. DeWitt Cuyler   Sophy Dallas   Amy m. S. Pemberton Hutchinson
(1852–1854)   (1854–1927)   (1856–1928)   (1858–1929)   (1860–?)   (1862–1882)   (1863–?)

Bibliography of Recent Publications

Most of our sources are listed in the essays and checklist; the following is intended to cover the major publications on Furness since the 1973 catalogue. Because of the overlap between Furness, Hunt, and Sullivan, important studies since 1973 are noted here as well.

Bibliographies

Doumato, Lamia. "Frank Furness, 1839–1912." Monticello, IL: Vance Bibliographies, 1980.

Orlowski, Mark B. "Frank Furness and the Heroic Ideal." Ph.D. diss., University of Michigan, 1986, 472–492.

Furniture

Ames, Kenneth. "Sitting in (Neo Grec) Style." *Nineteenth Century* 2 (1976): 51–58.

Hanks, David. "Reform in Philadelphia, Frank Furness, Daniel Pabst and 'Modern Gothic' Furniture." *Art News* 74 no. 8 (October, 1975): 52.

———. "Desk" and "Side Chair." In *Three Centuries of American Art*, edited by Darrell Sewell, 401–402. Philadelphia: The Philadelphia Museum of Art, 1976.

———. *In Quest for Unity: American Art Between World's Fairs, 1876–1893*. Detroit: The Detroit Institute of Fine Arts, 1983, 263–264.

Hanks, David and Donald C. Peirce. *The Virginia Carroll Crawford Collection of American Decorative Arts*. Atlanta: The High Museum of Art, 1983, 78–79.

Hanks, David and Page Talbott. "Daniel Pabst—Philadelphia Cabinetmaker." *Philadelphia Museum of Art Bulletin* 73 no. 316 (April 1977): 4–24.

Johnson, Diane C. *American Art Nouveau*. New York: H. Abrams, 1979, 73, 148, pl.77.

Kaplan, Wendy. "The Furniture of Frank Furness." *Antiques* 131 no. 5 (May 1987): 1088–1095.

[Metropolitan Museum of Art]. *In Pursuit of Beauty*. New York: Rizzoli, 1986, 146–147; 429–431.

Page, Marian. *Furniture Designed by Architects*. New York: Whitney Library of Design, 1980, 70–79.

Restoration

Berman, Avis. "Two Masterworks by Frank Furness: Pennsylvania Academy of the Fine Arts, Philadelphia, 1871 and the Furness Building, the first library at the University of Pennsylvania." *Architectural Digest* 46 no. 10 (October 1989): 314–322.

Freeman, Allen. "Restoring the Remaining Railroad Extravaganzas, Three of the Thirteen being Redone by SOM in the Northeast Corridor." *Architecture: the A.I.A. Journal* 77 no. 6 (June 1988): 90–93.

Mehlman, Robert. "House into Office: a Frank Furness Landmark Converted for a Law Firm." *Interior Design* 56 no. 5 (May 1985): 268–273.

Morton, David. "Pennsylvania Academy of the Fine Arts Restoration, Furness Unfettered." *Progressive Architecture* 57 no. 11 (November 1976): 50–53.

Myers, Hyman. "The Three Buildings of the Pennsylvania Academy." *Antiques* 121 no. 3 (March 1982): 679–689.

Scully, Vincent. "Emlen Physick House, Cape May, NJ." *Architectural Digest* 46 (March 1989): 34 ff.

Thomas, George E. "Furness Building." In *Masterplan for the Restoration and Adaptive Reuse of the Furness Building* 3. Unpublished study by Venturi, Rauch and Scott Brown, 1986.

General

Alexander, Edwin P. *Down at the Depot, American Railroad Stations from 1831–1920*. New York: C. N. Potter, 1970.

Baker, Paul. *Richard Morris Hunt.* Cambridge, MIT Press, 1980.

Boyle, Richard. *In this Academy: the Pennsylvania Academy of the Fine Arts 1805–1976.* Washington, D.C.: Museum Press, 1976.

Drexler, Arthur, ed. *The Architecture of the Ecole des Beaux-Arts.* New York: Museum of Modern Art, 1977.

Gebhard, David and Deborah Nevins. *200 Years of American Architectural Drawing.* New York: Whitney Library of Design, 1977, 130–133.

Jervis, Simon. "Furness, Frank." *Penguin Dictionary of Design and Designers.* London: A. P. Lane, 1984, 192.

Lewis, Edward. *Reading's Victorian Stations.* Strasburg, PA, 1976.

Massey, James C. *Frank H. Furness and his Centennial Sensation, the Pennsylvania Academy of the Fine Arts.* Philadelphia: Pennsylvania Academy of the Fine Arts, 1976.

Marcus, George and David Van Zanten. "Second Empire Architecture in Philadelphia." *Philadelphia Museum of Art Bulletin* 74 no. 322 (September 1978): passim.

Menocal, Narciso. *Architecture as Nature, the Transcendentalist Idea of Louis Sullivan.* Madison: University of Wisconsin Press, 1981.

Morrison, Andrew Craig. "Frank Furness." *MacMillan Encyclopedia of Architecture* 2. New York, 1982, 127–130.

Mumford, Mark. "Form Follows Nature: the Origins of American Organic Architecture." *Journal of Architectural Education* 42 no. 3 (Spring 1989): 26–37.

O'Gorman, James F. "Furness, Evans and Co." *Biographical Dictionary of Architects in Maine* 2. 1985, passim.

O'Gorman, James F., George E. Thomas, and Hyman Myers. *The Architecture of Frank Furness.* Philadelphia: Philadelphia Museum of Art, 1973. 2d ed. 1987, with addenda to "Checklist" by George E. Thomas, Hyman Myers, and Jeffrey A. Cohen.

Reiff, D. D. "Viollet-le-Duc and American Nineteenth Century Architecture." *Journal of Architectural Education* 42 (Fall 1988): 35–39.

Robinson, Cervin. "Furness in '73." *Architecture Plus* 1 (August 1973): 26–33.

Sprague, Paul. *The Drawings of Louis Henry Sullivan.* Princeton: Princeton University Press, 1979, 4–5.

Stein, Susan, ed. *The Architecture of Richard Morris Hunt.* Chicago: University of Chicago Press, 1986.

Stillman, Damie, ed. *Architecture and Ornament in Late 19th Century America.* Newark: University of Delaware Press, 21–28.

Tatman, Sandra L. and Roger W. Moss. *Biographical Dictionary of Philadelphia Architects, 1700–1930.* Boston: G. K. Hall, 1985, 287–296.

Teitelman, Edward and Richard Longstreth. *Architecture in Philadelphia: A Guide.* Cambridge: MIT Press, 1974.

Thomas, George E. "Frank Furness," "George W. Hewitt," and "The Pennsylvania Academy of the Fine Arts." In *Three Centuries of American Art*, edited by Darrell Sewell. Philadelphia: The Philadelphia Museum of Art, 1976, 388–390.

———. "Pecksniffs and Perspectives: The Changing Role of the Drawing in the Architectural Profession after the Civil War," "Design for the Philadelphia and Reading Railroad, Broad Street Depot," "Furness and Hewitt," "The Pennsylvania Academy of the Fine Arts," "Ornament for Students' Doorway at the Pennsylvania Academy of the Fine Arts," and "The Ferryboat 'New Jersey'." In James F. O'Gorman et al.: *Drawing Towards Building, Philadelphia Architectural Graphics 1732–1986*, 117–125. Philadelphia: University of Pennsylvania Press, 1986.

———. "Architectural Patronage and Social Stratification in Philadelphia Between 1840 and 1920." In *The Divided Metropolis*, edited by William Cutler and Howard Gillette, 85–123. Westport, CT: Greenwood Press, 1980.

Thomas, George E. and Carl E. Doebley. *Cape May: Queen of the Seaside Resorts.* Philadelphia: Art Alliance Press, 1976.

Twombley, Robert. *Louis Sullivan, his Life and Work.* New York: Viking, 1982, 38–45.

VanTrump, James. "Pittsburgh Railroad Stations Past and Present." In *Life and Architecture in Pittsburgh*. Pittsburgh: Pittsburgh History and Landmarks Foundation, 1983. Originally published in *Charette* 37 no. 12 (December 1957): 20–22; 38 no. 1 (January 1958): 23–26; 38 no. 2 (February 1958): 25–28.

de Wit, Wim, ed. *Louis Sullivan, the Function of Ornament.* New York: W. W. Norton, 1986.

Webster, Richard. *Philadelphia Preserved: Catalogue of the Historic American Building Survey.* Philadelphia: Temple University Press, 1976.

Weigley, Russell, ed. *Philadelphia: A Three Hundred Year History.* New York: W. W. Norton, 1982.

Weingarden, Lauren. "Naturalized Nationalism: a Ruskinian Discourse on the Search for an American Style." *Winterthur Portfolio* 24 no. 1 (Spring 1989): 43–68.

Credits

Photographs are listed by illustration number with the catalogue number first.

Unless otherwise noted photographs were taken by George E. Thomas.

American Architect and Building News: vol. 1 (9 September 1876), 70a, b; vol. 2 (10 February 1877), 79.

The Architectural Annual, 1900 (Philadelphia, 1900): 516a, b.

Architectural Archives of the University of Pennsylvania: 139b, c; 145; 146; 148; 149; 151; 370a.

Artistic Houses (New York, 1883): 24c, d, e; 32a, b, d; 38a; 45b.

Artwork of Reading, (Chicago, 1897): 265b; 317A.

Athenaeum of Philadelphia: 4–5; 5; 33a, b, c, d; 78a, b; 494; 627.

Atwater Kent Museum: 106a.

Avery Library of Columbia University: 496a–f.

Penelope Hartshorne Bacheler for Independence National Historic Park: 44e, f, g.

Bar Harbor Historical Society: 314a, b; 329a.

Baxter Panoramic Business Directory (Philadelphia, 1879): 43b; 86e.

Walter Berg, *Buildings and Structures of American Railroads* (1895): 139; 430d.

Dr. James Calhoun: 259A.

William Castner, *History of the Church of the Holy Apostles* (Philadelphia, n.d.): 13d.

Miriam Caskey: 286A.

Leon Clemmer: 605.

Jeffrey A. Cohen, photographer: 4–7.

Emily T. Cooperman, photographer, 366b, e, g.

Clio Group, Inc.: 468b.

Einstein Medical Center: 29a, b, c; 97; 361; 362; 493; 549; 555.

George Eisenman of James L. Dillon and Co.: 44a; 282a; 285c, h.

C. W. Elliot, *The Book of American Interiors*, (Boston, 1876): 34c.

Family of Allen Evans, III: 2–4; 51a; 98a, b; 107; 284; 341a, b, c; 430a; 500; 521; 625; 642b, c.

First City Troop of Philadelphia: 47a, b.

First Unitarian Church of Philadelphia: 285e, i.

Free Library of Philadelphia: 24Ac, d, e; 32a, b, d; 37; 38a; 44c; 45b; 76b; Frank H. Taylor (ca. 1900), 268a; 369a; 543.

George Wood Furness: 1–8; 1–9; 1–10; 2–3; 3–1; 3–2; 3–3; 3–5; 21Ab; 22h; 31e; 32e; 44b; 46d, g; 53b; 81c; 87b; 100b, e; 369a; 590b.

Haverford College Library: 300.

HHF [Horace Howard Furness] *Fairman Rogers* (Philadelphia, 1903), 2–2.

James Garrison: 4–3; 253d, e.

Helga Studios, Montclair, New Jersey: 46f, h.

Mr. and Mrs. Alfred Hesse: 87a.

Historic American Buildings Survey, Library of Congress: 4; 104Ac; 332a, c, d, f, g, h, i; 565a; Robert Harris, 28b, c; 31c; 39Aa, b, d; Ned Goode, 39Ac; 565b; Jack Boucher, 86c; 96f, h;104Ac; 535e, f, 636; Cervin Robinson, 263a; 331; George Eisenman, 364a, d, e, f, g; 535c; Theo B. Dillon, 618.

Index of Works

In this index of works, and the following index by location, illustrated entries are set in **bold face**. Catalog entries are denoted by "c.," color plates by "pl.," text illustrations by "f.," and text pages by "p."

Index by Location